Tyulkova – Conversations with Nikolai Kapustin

Yana A. Tyulkova

CONVERSATIONS WITH
NIKOLAI KAPUSTIN

Bibliografische Information der Deutschen Nationalbibliothek
Die Deutsche Nationalbibliothek verzeichnet diese Publikation in der Deutschen Nationalbibliografie; detaillierte bibliografische Daten sind im Internet unter http://dnb.d-nb.de abrufbar.

978-3-95983-590-9 (Hardcover)
978-3-95983-591-6 (Paperback)
978-3-95983-592-3 (e-Book)

© 2019 Schott Music GmbH & Co. KG, Mainz

www.schott-buch.com

Alle Rechte vorbehalten. Nachdruck in jeder Form sowie die Wiedergabe durch Fernsehen, Rundfunk, Film, Bild- und Tonträger oder Benutzung für Vorträge, auch auszugsweise, nur mit Genehmigung des Verlags.

Pictures are used by the permission of Nikolai Kapustin, Peter Andersson, Leonid Peleshev, and Pavel Korbut. Also included the pictures from Yana Tyulkova archive.

Umschlagmotiv: Nikolai Kapustin, © Leonid Peleshev

For my dearest teacher Dr. James Miltenberger

Sometimes, looking back at the decades of my life, I wish I could rewrite my past and make it perfect like the music I compose ... but no, our life is like jazz improvisation, it should always be spontaneous, always in the moment, and always free.

Content

Acknowledgement 10

About the Author 11

Introduction 13

Prologue 15

Chapter One: Childhood and First Steps in Music (1937-1952)   17

    The Beginning of World War II 21

    Early Interest in Music 24

    Piotr Ivanovich Vinnichenko 27

    The End of World War II and Beginning of Study at School 29

    Lubov' Borisovna Frantsuzova 37

    First Steps in Composition – Piano Sonata (1950) 40

    Entering Exams at the Moscow Musical College 43

Chapter Two: Study in Moscow Musical College (1952-1956)   49

    Avrelian Grigorievich Rubbakh 52

    Connection to the Family and Teachers Frantsuzova and Vinnichenko 60

    Recitals at the Musical College 64

    Teachers and Courses at the Musical College 70

    Self-Education 74

    Composition 77

    New Friends of Nikolai Kapustin 81

    Life at the Mikhalkov House 84

    Acquaintance with Jazz 89

    Music in Mikhalkov's House 91

    The Visit of Kapustin's Parents to Moscow 97

    Final Exams of the Musical College and Entering the Moscow Conservatory 98

Chapter Three: Study at the Moscow Conservatory (1956-1961)   103

Alexander Goldenweiser 104

Study in the Class of Goldenweiser 107

Concerts of Goldenweiser's Students..117

Kapustin's Piano Repertoire and Interest in Atonal Music..122

Courses at the Conservatory..130

Accompanying...136

Kapustin's Injury of the Right Hand 139

Master-Classes and Concerts at the Moscow Conservatory 142

Student Life at the Moscow Conservatory and Kapustin's Friends 145

Composing Music at the Conservatory 152

The Festival of Youth and Students (Moscow, July 1957) 157

Jazz Quintet Experience...160

Last Exams at the Moscow Conservatory 163

A Serious Conversation..165

Postlude: Goldenweiser..166

Chapter Four: Years of Work with the Oleg Lundstrem Big Band (1961-1972)   169

History of the Oleg Lundstrem Big Band – The Beginning..170

Nikolai Kapustin Joins the Big Band..174

Kapustin and His Duties in the Big Band..177

The Musicians of the Lundstrem Big Band...185

On the Road with the Lundstrem Big Band: Repertoire and Performances 191

Other Musical Projects of Nikolai Kapustin 201

Jazz Environment of USSR in the 1960s-1970s 206

Compositions of 1961-1972 (Ops. 2-13) 215

Nikolai Kapustin: Connection to His Family and Old Friends....................................218

Alla..220

Oleg Lundstrem – Postlude...230

Chapter Five: Years of Work with the Boris Karamyshev »Blue Screen« Orchestra (1972-1977) and the Russian State Symphony Orchestra of Cinematography (1977-1984)   231

Boris Karamyshev and His »Blue Screen« Orchestra 232

Nikolai Kapustin – Transitional Period 235

Kapustin Joins the Karamyshev Orchestra 236

Kapustin's Duty in the Karamyshev Orchestra/ A New Life in a New Band 239

Karamyshev Orchestra: Instrumentation and Repertoire 243

Karamyshev Orchestra: Recordings on Radio and Television, Touring 246

New Acquaintances of Nikolai Kapustin: Varlamov, Lyadova, and Silantiev 251

Disintegration of the Karamyshev Orchestra 266

Russian State Symphony Orchestra of Cinematography/Audition for
the Open Position of Pianist 268

Work at the Russian State Symphony Orchestra
of Cinematography (1977-1984) 272

Growing Family of Nikolai Kapustin/Accident in the Summer of 1979 277

1980: Performance of the Piano Concerto No. 2/ Acceptance to
the Union of Moscow Composers 283

First Publishers 286

Russian Jazz Scene in the 1970s-1980s / Music of Nikolai Kapustin 289

Compositions of 1972-1984 (Ops. 14-39) 293

A New Turn of Life: Decision to Resign from Orchestra of Cinematography 303

Chapter Six: Freelancing Composer (1984-1999)   305

Life in the Soviet Union in the 1980s-1990s 306

Musical Life of Nikolai Kapustin in the 1980s-1990s/Recording of
the Vinyl Records and Compact Discs 311

New and Old Friends of Nikolai Kapustin: Nikolai Petrov,
Alexander Zagorinsky, and Hideaki Takaoki 322

Beginning of Interest around the Figure of Kapustin/Back to the Life of
Performing Artist 334

Life Complications: Worries about Alla 342

First Tour in Germany/ Collaboration with Alexander Korneev 344

A Second Trip to Germany 354

Compositions of 1984-1999 (Ops. 40-99) 358

Ruza 368

Chapter Seven: Years of Increasing Popularity (2000-2018)   371

Kapustin's Trip to London (May 2000) 373

Continuation of Recording CDs 383

Concerts of the Music of Nikolai Kapustin in Russia after 2000 390

Burst of Popularity: Publishers and Performers of the Music of
Kapustin after 2000 403

The 80th Birthday of Nikolai Kapustin 414

Presentations and the Beginning of Research on the Music of
Nikolai Kapustin 419

Compositions of 2000-2017 (Ops. 100-161) 421

Family Sorrow: Loss of Fira Grigorievna Kapustina 428

Kapustin's Flow of Life 430

Epilogue: How I met Nikolai Kapustin 434

Appendix A: Nikolai Kapustin – Chronology 436

Appendix B: Nikolai Kapustin – Discography 447

Appendix C: Nikolai Kapustin – Dedications 450

Appendix D: Catalogue of Works by Genre 451

Appendix E: Letters about Kapustin 457

Appendix F: Personalities 463

Appendix G: Miscellaneous 475

Bibliography 477

Acknowledgement

First, I would like to thank Nikolai Kapustin and his wife Alla Kapustina for their invaluable help for this book: our weekly Sunday skype conversations during the last four years and your warm acceptance of my visits to Moscow and Ruza. Thank you for allowing me into your lives!

This project would never have started without my teacher Dr. James Miltenberger, who introduced the music of Nikolai Kapustin to me. Thank you Doc for your creative ideas, revisions, and always wise suggestions.

It is hard to overestimate the support of my family. I would like to thank my parents Natalie Tyulkova and Anatoly Tyulkov, my brother Kirill Tyulkov, and my husband Curtis Johnson for their belief in my ability and unlimited source of help and inspiration. Curtis, thank you for correcting all my drafts a million times and being patient with the editing process. Kirill, thank you for the graphic design and all the work that you have done with the pictures. It looked like those seven chapters would never be done, but we did it!

I would like to thank also all the amazing people who were willing to correspond with me. My sincere thanks to Mark-André Hamelin, Steven Osborne, Ludmil Angelov, Oxana Yablonskaya, Carlo Levi Minzi, Vito Reibaldi, Masahiro Kawakami, Alexei Zoubov, Alexander Zagorinsky, Wim de Haan, Natsuko Samejima, Leonid Peleshev, Pavel Korbut and Cyril Moshkov.

Finally, I would like to thank Dr. Jonathan Mann, who opened the door to the world of Nikolai Kapustin to me. Thank you Jonathan! You never know how powerful a short letter can be.

About the Author

Dr. Yana Tyulkova is a Russian born classical/jazz pianist and jazz singer-songwriter.

She received her Master's Degree in Piano Performance from the Nizhny Novgorod State Conservatory (Russia) and the Doctoral Degree from West Virginia University (USA), where she studied classical and jazz piano under Dr. James Miltenberger.

As a performer, Dr. Tyulkova attended numerous educational programs and music festivals all over the world, including study at the Berklee College of Music (Boston, USA), participating in Berklee Summer Performance Program (Perugia, Italy, 2005), International Summer Jazz Academy (Krakow, Poland, 2007), International Jazz Summer Workshop (Prague, Czech Republic, 2009) and others. She became the winner of »Nizhny Novgorod State Competition of Young Composers« (1994), Russian Piano Competition (Novomoskovsk, 1995), »Nizhny Novgorod State Pop-Rock-Blues Competition« (1997), International Jazz Vocal Competition »Jazz Voices« (Klaipeda, Lithuania, 2006), and International Jazz Vocal Competition »Finsterwalde Singer« (Finsterwalde, Germany, 2006). As a classical pianist she won the Young Artist Competition and in March 2012 performed with West Virginia University Symphony Orchestra. She has performed in masterclasses with such legendary classical pianists as Leon Fleisher and Ann Shein.

In 2013 Dr. Tyulkova began research on the music of Nikolai Kapustin. In 2015 she wrote the dissertation called »Classical and Jazz Influenced in the Music of Nikolai Kapustin: Piano Sonata No. 3, Op. 55«. In June 2014 Dr. Tyulkova presented the music of Nikolai Kapustin at the International Festival and Competition »The Intersection of Jazz and Classical Music« in Morgantown, WV (USA). In March 2017 she participated in the Music Teacher National Conference (MTNA) as a part of the presentation »The Intersection of Classical and Jazz: Introduction to the Music of Nikolai Kapustin« in Baltimore, MD (USA).

In February 2015 Nikolai Kapustin composed the piece called »Curiosity« (Op.157) and dedicated it to Yana Tyulkova. She premiered this piece in June 2015 at the Festival »The Intersection of Classical and Jazz« at West Virginia University.

In July 2015 Yana Tyulkova participated in a European Tour with »James Miltenberger Jazz Quintet« as a jazz singer and classical pianist. The series of concerts took place in Belgium, the Netherlands, and Germany.

Dr. Tyulkova is currently teaching piano at California University of Pennsylvania.

Dr. Tyulkova is a member of »Who's Who in Russia« (Ralph Hubner Edition, 2008), Vladimir Feiertag's »Encyclopedia of World Jazz Music« (St. Petersburg, Russia, 2008), and is now the official biographer of Nikolai Kapustin.

Introduction

Nikolai Grigorievich Kapustin is a contemporary Russian-Ukrainian composer and classical/jazz pianist. During the last twenty years his music began to receive large-scale popularity through recordings, presentations, competitions, festivals, as well as Kapustin's recordings of his own music. Kapustin is widely known in the USA, Japan, China, South Korea, United Kingdom, Germany, Italy, and Spain. Surprisingly, the Russian audience is not very familiar with the music of Kapustin.

His music fuses the idea of perfectly structured classical form with the complexity of harmonic language and rhythmic identity of jazz. Kapustin developed a highly unique and distinct style that is recognizable, fresh, and fun to play and to listen to. To this day Kapustin has written 161 opuses that includes solo piano music, chamber, and orchestral music.

My goal is to encourage a greater appreciation to the music of Nikolai Kapustin and continue developing the international recognition of this outstanding modern-day composer.

My first acquaintance with the music of Nikolai Kapustin was in 2011 when I began to study at West Virginia University (Morgantown, USA) as a doctoral student in piano performance. My teacher Dr. James Miltenberger introduced me to the music of Kapustin, and also suggested I play one of Kapustin's piano sonatas. That's how this story began.

The research project that I completed in May 2015 is called »Classical and Jazz Influences in the Music of Nikolai Kapustin: Piano Sonata No. 3, Op. 55«. The information gathered through the interviews with Nikolai Kapustin became an essential part of the research.

Our meetings with Nikolai Kapustin and his wife Alla Kapustina led to the idea of writing his autobiography. I truly believe that it is important to get acquainted with Kapustin not only through his music but also through his words.

This book »Conversations with Nikolai Kapustin« consists of seven chapters representing Kapustin's memories in different periods of his life, starting from years living in the Ukraine to becoming one of the most significant composers of our time. The book also includes Kapustin's recollections on musical life in Russia during 1950s -1970s, as well as his vision of his own works. The material that was used in the book consists of the home archive of Kapustin gratefully given to me by the composer. It includes letters to his parents and his wife, family pictures, program notes and posters from the concerts, the composer's handwritten scores of his early unpublished works, as well as my correspondence with Kapustin's close friends and their insight on Kapustin's personality.

During the years that I have known Kapustin's family, we have developed close relationships and become very good friends. It is hard to believe that in the spring of 2013 I didn't even think about the opportunity to meet one of the best composers of our time – Nikolai Grigorievich Kapustin.

Prologue

In the morning of June 18, 2015 I woke up surprisingly early for me, just right after seven. The reason for this sudden awakening was the sound of the fireplace, a real one. The sound of burning wood was filling out the whole house, and its' smell, so remarkably familiar to me, brought back memories from my childhood. I was a guest... I was a guest in the house of one of the most promising composers of our time – Nikolai Grigorievich Kapustin.

Every summer Nikolai Grigorievich and his wife Alla Semionovna spend their time in their summer convent, which is around sixty miles west of Moscow in the small city of Ruza. There is something unusual about this place... maybe because of the majestic old spruce, maple, and birch trees that surround the house and make the special effect on everyone who attempts to visit this place, I don't know. Maybe because for more than fifty years this place was the summer retreat for all major Russian composers who used to come here... all in the past.

His way of saying things – this is something you want to hear to have a complete understanding of what kind of person he is. He talks very slowly, like trying to put the best possible meaning in each and every word. His speech is full of life-long rests, just like in the music. He has a special intonation in his voice, the mode of which changes depending on the direction of our conversation. Every time he is really interested in something his eyes become incredibly big and bright, as if the center of our universe. He likes to talk about music, linguistics, and physics.

It was early in the morning...

Ruza, June 18, 2015

Chapter One:
Childhood and First Steps in Music (1937-1952)

Biographical Information
Kapustin, Nikolai Girshevich (Grigorievich)
Date of birth: November 22, 1937
Place of birth: Ukraine, Donetsk Region, Gorlovka, Nikitovskii district

Historical Information
The Nikitovskii district, or simply »Nikitovka« (»Mykytivka« in Ukrainian), is a small city which is situated in the southern part of Gorlovka. The history of this place goes back to the middle of the eighteenth century, when in 1776 it was named by one of its inhabitants, Nikita Deviatilov. At the beginning of the nineteenth century, as a result of the rapid growth of the coal industry, Nikitovka became a significant city in the Donetsk region becoming a part of the Kursko-Harkovsko-Azovskaya railway line. In 1869 Nikitovka became the main railway station in the city Gorlovka.[1]

This short historic overview allows us to understand that Nikolai Kapustin was not born in just some small city, but in the place that at the beginning of the twentieth century had an important impact on the development of both countries – Ukraine and Russia.

While Nikitovka was considered a part of Gorlovka for more than two hundred years, Nikolai Kapustin prefers to see his birthplace independently.

NK^2 : *I was born in Nikitovka, not in Gorlovka.*

From the Russian perspective the population of Nikitovka is relatively small. For the all-union population census on January 17, 1939 Nikitovka reached the number of 14, 047 people,[3] and for the last Soviet Union population census on January 19, 1989 the number reached up to 78,762.[4] This could lead us to the conclusion that in the past the citizens of Nikitovka probably knew each other very well, or were even distant relatives of each other.

Kapustin's mother Klavdia Nikolayevna Kapustina-Kozmina (1910-1993) had Russian ancestry. She worked for a period of time as a typist in the

---

[1] History of Gorlovka. Accessed February 8, 2018. http://gorlovca.ru/index/istorija_gorlovki/0-8.
[2] NK – abbreviation for Nikolai Kapustin.
[3] All-Union Population Census, January 17, 1939, page 190. Accessed February 8, 2018. http://istmat.info/files/uploads/46314/rgae_7971.16.54_naselenie_po_perepisi_1939.pdf.
[4] All-Union Population Census, January 19, 1989 (Demoscop Weekly, ISSN 1726-2887). Accessed February 8, 2018. http://www.demoscope.ru/weekly/ssp/sng89_reg2.php.

department of the People's Commissariat of Internal Affairs (NKVD) in Glorlovka.[5] She loved music and could play the piano. Klavdia Kapustina would be the person to introduce the small Nikolai to the world of music and his first and only favorite instrument – pianino.[6]

Klavdia Kapustina (front) and Sonia Kapustina (back), the sister of Grigory Kapustin

His father Grigory Efimovich Kapustin (1901-1983) had Belarusian ancestry[7] and was a butcher by profession. Grigory Kapustin worked as a senior manager at the meat factory.

Nikolai Kapustin had a very special relationship with his parents. He loved them deeply. Even now, deceased more than twenty years, when talking about

---

[5] From the middle 1950s this organization was known as the Committee of State Security (KGB).
[6] Piano is known in Russia as the pianino.
[7] Belarus is a landlocked country that borders Russia to the northeast, Ukraine to the south, Poland to the west, and Lithuania and Latvia to the northwest.

them Kapustin has intonations of warmth and tenderness in his voice. They will be forever his mama and papa.

NK: They lived in Nikitovka through their entire lifes.

Young Nikolai was named in honor of his grandfather – Nikolai Timofeyevich Kozmin, who was a musician. Nikolai Kozmin served in the military through his whole life as a member of the military band.

NK: My mother told me that he died in the trenches during the Civil War.[8]

As with most Russian and Ukrainian children, young Nikolai grew up in the hands of his grandmother – Pilageya Stepanovna Kozmina (1869-1972). Nikolai Kapustin says with proudness in his voice,

NK: My grandmother lived for 103 years, and her daughter, my aunt, Alexandra Nikolayevna Kozmina, exactly 100 years.
YT[9]*: What did you do with your grandmother when you were young? What kind of activities did you share together?*
NK: It is hard to tell because I don't remember that much. One thing I do remember – I was sitting on her knees all the time. (And then, after a long pause, Nikolai Kapustin continues) She was absolutely an uneducated person. That was my upbringing.

At that pre-World War II period, music was a big part of Russian and Ukrainian life but, because Nikolai was living in a small city, the most entertaining things for him were his mother's tales. The tales are an important part of a child's growth through the centuries in Russian and Ukrainian cultures as they teach you about the good and bad, the basic rules of our life. The most distinctive feature of the tale is that good always triumphs over evil. Young Nikolai loved to listen to his mother's tales. Even now he is still fascinated by them.

YT: What is your attitude now towards the tales?
NK: Very positive.

It is difficult for us to remember something from our childhood when we were around three or four years old, but there is one fact from his life that Kapustin remembers clearly – the beginning of World War II. In the summer of 1941 young Nikolai, his mother, grandmother, and sister Fira, were evacuated to the Kyrgyz Republic (Kyrgyzstan).[10] Nikolai was just three years old!

---

[8] Civil War in Russia (1917-1922).

[9] YT – abbreviation for Yana Tyulkova.

[10] Kyrgyz Republic (Kyrgyzstan) is part of the Central Asian territory, which borders China on the east, Tajikistan on the south, Uzbekistan on the west, and Kazakhstan on the north.

The Beginning of World War II

Historical Information

At the beginning of WWII, in the summer of 1941, Ukraine was occupied by fascist Germany. It took until October 20, 1943 for the Soviet troops to organize four Ukrainian fronts to fight in the war. General casualties in the Ukraine reached the number of 14 million people. From January 1941 to January 1945 the population of the Ukraine decreased from 40.9 million to 27 million people. In addition, financial losses to the Soviet Union consisted of 40% of all countries involved in World War II, where over 40% of the Soviet Union losses belonged to the Ukraine.[11]

Nikolai's family was evacuated to the city of Tokmok, which is situated in the northern part of the Kyrgyz Republic near the city of Bishkek.

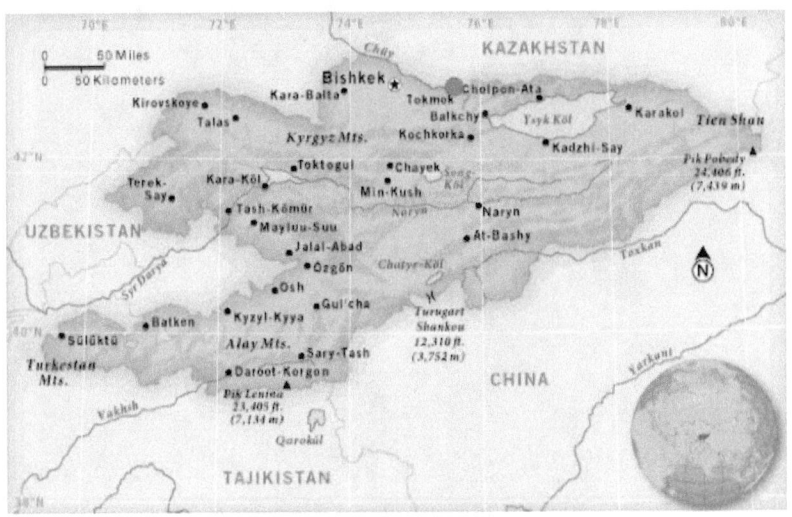

Tokmok, Kyrgyzstan Republic

At the beginning of the evacuation Nakolai's father stayed with the family in Tokmok but then was ordered to go to the West Kazakhstan territory. He was to become a part of the reserve military forces. The only possible way of communication with his family was through letters. Unfortunately, the existence of

---

[11] BBC Ukraine: WWII for the Ukraine – Rethinking. Anastasia Zanuda, May 6, 2015. Accessed November 8, 2017. http://www.bbc.com/ukrainian/ukraine_in_russian/2015/05/150506_ru_s_ukraine_ww2.

these letters is highly questionable by now as they might have been lost through time. Nikolai Kapustin remembers that those letters were an essential part of their existence during that period of time.

As with many other people at that time, Kapustin's family tried to keep track of the hostilities through the national radio. Today it is hard to believe that the radio and letters from the front were the only opportunities to stay informed about your relatives.

Being far away from the hostilities of war, Kapustin's family still had to go through struggles, starvation and poverty. They tried hard to maintain the basic flow of a normal life.

YT: *What are your memories of the war time?*
NK: *We lived in the evacuation two years, 1941 through 1943. Somehow we scratched along.*

Nikolai (on the left) and his cousin Vladimir (on the right), ca. 1943-1944

Kapustin's family occupied a private house in Tokmok where they lived on the first floor. As a part of its property this house had a large garden. A lot of different bushes and trees, such as cherry and apple, grew in that garden.

NK: *Our apples were large and very tasty. This garden helped us a lot.*

The family used to make pickled tomatoes and cabbage to avoid poverty. In addition, Nikolai's mother Klavdia Kapustina and his grandmother Pilageya Kozmina used to sell their apples on the market.

One interesting episode happened in the summer of 1942, when Nikolai was around four and a half years old.

AK[12] (joining the conversation): They (Nikolai's mother and grandmother) went somewhere and left you at home.
NK: They went to the market and locked me at home. I became very upset about it. There were apples in the bags that were prepared for the market. I took a bite of each apple so they wouldn't leave me by myself anymore.
YT: What happened when they got back?
NK: I didn't want to open the door to punish them.
AK: You can see what kind of boy he was – young but already willing to get what he wanted.

Indeed, this episode, when Nikolai prepared the penalty for his »slow-witted« family, demonstrates that even at this early age Nikolai had a clear understanding of what he wants in his life and what he does not.

---

[12] AK – abbreviation for Alla Kapustina, the wife of Nikolai Kapustin.

Early Interest in Music

Nikolai's sister Fira, who was six years older than Nikolai, studied violin at that time. She had a private teacher in Tokmok.

NK: We did not want to interrupt her violin lessons.

»We« in this context obviously means »Nikolai's mother«. It is fascinating that even in the evacuation Klavdia Kapustina wanted to continue the musical education of her daughter. We cannot talk about Nikolai's musical study yet because he was too young at that point.

Nikolai and his sister Fira, Nikitovka, ca.1948-1949

Although, being a young boy, Nikolai had some advantages over Fira. Nikolai Kapustin shared with me another funny episode from his childhood memory.

NK: Fira used to practice her homework in our beautiful garden, and I was asked to help her in this process.
YT: What did you do?
NK (smiling): My task was to swat flies away from the »practicing« Fira.
YT: That's so funny! What an interesting job you had!
NK: It was fun and helpful at the same time.
YT: Did you try to play violin?
NK: Yes, I tried but it didn't work out. I had a complete aversion to it.

However, the music eventually began to become a part of his life.

YT: Do you remember any musical experiences from that time?
NK: For some reason I remember one of the Kyrgyz folk melodies.

Nikolai Kapustin came up to the grand piano and played a two-voiced melody.[13] This melody, in lively character, sounded quite complicated to my ear. It was in D Mixolydian mode with a left hand ostinato pattern. It sounded very Eastern, almost Asian.

YT: What mode is it? (I couldn't identify it from the first listening)
NK: That's the thing, this is not an easy melody; tricky business.
YT: How did you remember it? You were just four or five years old.
NK: I have no idea (laughing). I remembered and that's it.

The fact that a four or five-year-old boy remembered a two-voiced melody and carried it through his whole life tells us that Nikolai naturally had unique musical abilities. It is important to note that during the evacuation Nikolai didn't have a piano, so he just held this melody in his head.

NK: It was my idée fixe.[14] It haunted me.

In 1943, when the Ukraine was freed from fascist German forces, Nikolai's family returned to their motherland Nikitovka. They discovered a horrible consequence of the reality of the war – their house was destroyed by German forces. During the next two years the family had to live in the home of their neighbors.

Despite the fact that the war was a part of all Ukrainian people's lives, something positive still occurred in young Nikolai's life. One of the most significant moments happened when Nikolai was around six-seven years old. A musical instrument appeared in his life to stay forever. The name of this instrument was piano.

NK: My mother managed to get the piano. Our neighbors suggested to us. And really, it turned out to be our piano.

Here, we need to clarify his meaning of the phrase about the piano being their instrument. During the time of 1941-1942, when Nikitovka was occupied by fascists, their house was destroyed but their piano was spared. It was taken away to the place where fascists lived and used to play on as their entertainment. After Nikitovka was returned to the Ukrainian control, the piano was transferred to the local Ukrainian administration. When Kapustin's family returned from the

---

[13] Interview with the author, July 9, 2014, Ruza, Russia.
[14] Idée fixe is an idea or desire that dominates the mind; an obsession.

evacuation their neighbors suggested they try to get their instrument back, since they were the actual owners. After all these manipulations the piano was successfully returned home.

> NK: And then everything began. It was impossible to tear me away from the piano.

Klavdia Kapustina, watching the enormous interest of her child in playing the piano, set up a meeting with a tuner to fix the piano. Musicians can tell what difference it makes to play on the tuned instrument instead of the unturned one. It made an even bigger effect on the young boy who was attempting to take his first steps in music.

> NK (with the intonations of victory and proudness in his voice): And then I learned six Clementi Sonatinas.
> YT: By yourself? Being six years old?
> NK: I consulted with Fira on which line which note is situated. Fira knew the notes.
> YT: In other words, you learned to play piano on your own?
> NK: Basically, yes. By the way, my mother also knew the notes. I asked them both. I bothered them enormously and at the end they got tired of me.

Nikolai Kapustin was a child prodigy. He learned to play piano on his own, beginning his musical journey with Muzio Clementi *Six Sonatinas*, Op. 36. This sounds truly amazing for the young boy who had no understanding of music theory and just began to study music on his own. The thing he did have was his deep desire to play the piano, which moved him tremendously.

The fact that Nikolai learned all six pieces without an actual preparation in understanding of the notes on the staff makes us assume that Nikolai's first practice on the piano was by ear, an equivalent of the Suzuki method nowadays. In reality Kapustin made a different choice.

> NK: I learned to read the notes. My mother and Fira taught me where the notes are situated on the staff. Somehow gradually I learned it. I've always sought being self-educated.
> YT: And then your mother found your first piano teacher?
> NK: No, he appeared on his own.

Piotr Ivanovich Vinnichenko

Nikolai's love for the piano, which would become an essential part of his life, led to his acquaintance with Piotr Ivanovich Vinnichenko. Nikolai's relationship with this man would last through their entire lives.

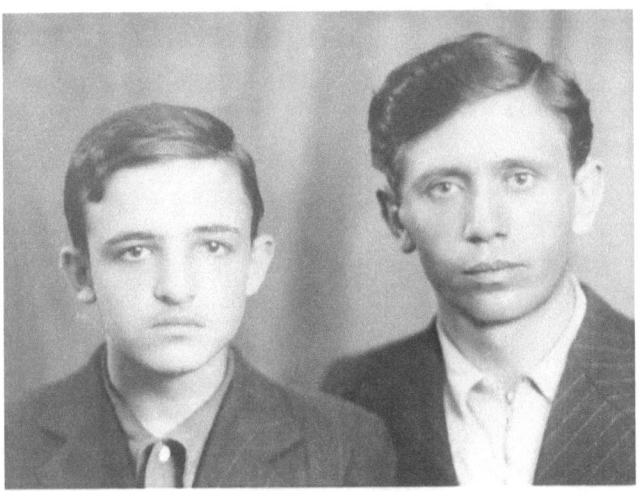

Nikolai Kapustin and Piotr Vinnichenko, Nikitovka, 1952

Piotr Ivanovich Vinnichenko was a violin teacher who could also play piano. Through his life he lived in the different cities situated in the surrounding areas of Nikitovka. He used to travel to the houses of his students to give private violin lessons. One of his students was Fira Kapustina. Fira used to take lessons from Piotr Vinnichenko even before the beginning of the war. In 1943, when Kapustin's family returned to Nikitovka from the evacuation, Piotr Vinnichenko came back from the war.

NK: He was wounded, that's why he came back home before the end of the war.

Piotr Vinnichenko's return became a good reason to renew the lessons with Fira. That's how Piotr Vinnichenko appeared in the house of Nikolai Kapustin. He was the person who gave young Nikolai the piano scores of the Clementi *Sonatinas*, Op. 36.

NK: He noticed what was happening with me and decided that it was time to get me involved.

Probably, the fact that from that point Nikolai had his own piano teacher helped him not only in the study of piano but also supported him in his desire to play this instrument. Vinnichenko cared not only for Nikolai and Fira's progress but he also cared for their instruments.

> YT: *Did you play on that same piano until the time when you moved to Moscow?*
> NK: *No, the instruments changed twice after that. After the war my teacher Piotr Vinnichenko suggested we buy a better one. That was a very beautiful instrument but played very poorly. This instrument had very bad repetitions so later on we bought another one. That was a Ukrainian piano »Chernigov.« I played on that instrument until the time I moved to Moscow and later, during my visits to Nikitovka.*

In other words, Nikolai had three different instruments just during the period of nine years, from 1943 until 1952. This fact demonstrates that Nikolai's parents wanted to give whatever possible to their children in order to help them achieve their goals, especially if it was about the music.

The End of World War II and Beginning of Study at School

In September of 1944, Nikolai was almost seven years old, the age when children begin to attend school. Unfortunately, that did not happen with Nikolai Kapustin.

NK: I was so frail that they refused to take me in the first grade.

Nikolai was asked to wait one more year and begin school in September of 1945. Indeed, the years of starvation reflected on the health and growth of the young boy. In addition, the conditions of life at that time were probably still very poor since the war would not be over for almost a year.

In May 1945 a long-expected event happened in the world that put an end to suffering and loss. It was the end of World War II.

Historical Information

On May 8, 1945 in Berlin at 22:43 European time (00:43 Moscow time) the »Act of Unconditional Surrender« of Germany was signed. From the German side this act was signed by Generalfeldmarschall Wilhelm Keitel, from the Russian side by Marschall Georgy Zhukov, and from the Supreme Headquarters Allied Expeditionary Forces side by Air Chief Marshall Sir Arthur Tedder. The day of May 9th 1945 was announced in Russia as the Victory Day for the Soviet Union against fascist Germany.[15]

The big celebration happened in the family of Nikolai Kapustin in the summer of 1945 when Grigory Efimovich Kapustin came back home from the war. Words cannot express how much Nikolai's family was happy and relieved about his return. Grigory Kapustin was not only the beloved father and husband; he was also the main provider of financial support for the family.

YT: Did you know the date when your father was supposed to return? Did he inform you somehow or did it happen suddenly?
NK: My mother told us about it. They wrote the letters to each other.
YT: Do you remember when your father came back home? What was your impression?

---

[15] Surrender of Germany. Accessed February 8, 2018.
http://geroiros.narod.ru/wwsoldat/OPER/ARTICLES/041-kapitul.htm; Russian Archive: World War II, Vol. 15 (4-5). The Battle for Berlin, M., 1995. Accessed February 8, 2018.
http://militera.lib.ru/docs/da/berlin_45/12.html.

NK: For me he was a completely foreign man. I was three years old when he left for the war. I did not remember anything.
YT: So, because you were so young you just forgot him?
NK: Yes.
YT: Then how did your mother reintroduce your father to you?
NK: She said – »Kolia (a term of endearment for Nikolai), this is your father.«

At that moment Nikolai was almost eight years old. This is the age when children begin to understand life. That brought additional tension into this awkward family situation. Indeed, the story of Nikolai Kapustin's life has real drama in it!

YT: How long did it take for you to get used to this foreign man actually being your father?
NK: I got accustomed to it very quickly.

One of the most memorable episodes from that time for young Nikolai was the fact that his father brought home a huge bag of dried apricots.

YT: Was it tasty?
NK (laughing): It was considered to be a sweet present for us. He said it was from Iran.[16]

From the moment when Grigory Kapustin came back from the war he immediately began to restore the normal flow of life. The first thing he did was to begin to reconstruct their house.

YT: Was the house completely destroyed by the fascists?
NK: Absolutely.
YT: Did your father have any friends to help rebuild the house?
NK: Yes, he had one friend who was working with him.
YT: What company for building the whole house! Probably, this assistant was very knowledgeable.
NK: Yes, he was.

The new house was built during a short period of time and was situated on the exact place as the old one.

---

[16] Kazakhstan territory borders with Turkmenistan and Turkmenistan territory borders with Iran.

Family of Nikolai Kapustin: Klavdia Kapustina (first from the right), Grigory Kapustin (second from the right), Fira Kapustina (center in the back), Mikhail Kapustin, brother of Grigory Kapustin (second from the left), Mikhail's wife (center in the front), Mikhail's son Vladimir Kapustin (first from the left), Nikitovka, ca. 1948

On September 1st 1945, Nikolai Kapustin entered the doors of Elementary School No. 30 as a pupil for the first time.

Historical Information

School No. 30 is one of fifty-eight schools that are located in Gorlovka today. Despite the tragic events that had happened in Gorlovka during 2014, School No. 30 is still functioning well.[17]

Unfortunately, today's pupils of this school have no understanding that seventy two years ago one of them was Nikolai Kapustin, one of the best-known present day Ukrainian-Russian composers.

The first grade of September 1945 was very special in the history of the school and in the history of the country. It was the first generation of young children who began their education right after the end of the WWII. There are no doubts that there was something unique about this new generation of youth, the new growth of life at that post-war period.

---

[17] Ukraine Crisis: Pro-Russian Attack in Ukraine's Horlivka, BBC News. Accessed February 8, 2018. http://www.bbc.com/news/world-europe-27018199.

YT: My first question is – how far was the school situated from your home?
NK: Not that far, within walking distance. I think something like five-ten minutes by walk.
YT: Did you used to go to the school by yourself?
NK: At the beginning I used to go there with my mother and Fira, because Fira also studied at the same school as me for a while, but later of course by myself.
YT: Do you remember how many students were in your class?
NK: These first post-war classes were large; the war was over and everybody wanted to go to study. I think there were about thirty or thirty-five pupils in our class.
YT: That's a lot. In comparison to now we usually have no more than twenty to twenty-five pupils in a class.
NK: And they all needed to be taught.
YT: Do you remember your first day at school?
NK: I don't remember it very clearly; and for some reason the first few years too. I don't know, in comparison with other pupils I could read easily by then. It was not very interesting for me at the beginning.

The truth is that the young Nikolai was an independent boy who liked to study by himself. Of course, his sister Fira and his mother Klavdia Kapustina were always around him, being ready to help, but it is obvious that the desire to study was generated from the young heart.

NK: I had good teachers in the school; it was enough.

During these first years of the post-war time the military topic was in the air surrounding Nikolai's life. The whole generation of young people who were raised during this period was dreaming about having a military profession and looking like a military man. Even the children's games were dedicated to war. This trend lasted very long, up to the 1980s, when children were still playing scouts and guerrillas, »shooting« and chasing around their courtyards.

Partially because of the economic difficulties and limitations of this period, Nikolai was wearing the military coat that was re-sized for a young boy.

NK: There was nothing else to wear. Also I loved to wear a tunic, like all military people did.

Nikolai was one of a few boys in school who was wearing the tunic, since it takes a lot of work to remake it to the child's size. He was very proud about himself and the way he looked. It is important that during the war time the tunic was worn only by the people who belonged to the command staff. The tunic was made out of half-woolen material which was very comfortable and pleasant to wear. Indeed, Nikolai's mother always wanted her children to be special and different from other pupils. She managed this goal very well.

In the late 1940s the young generation of pupils was going to school with their own inkwells. These inkwells were filled up by pupils' parents at home and not in the school.

NK: Each student had a schoolbag plus the inkwell. The goal was to carefully transport the schoolbag with the inkwell to the school.

The risk of spilled ink was always a part of this journey. It is easy to imagine what kind of problems it may cause for the student. The spilled ink could ruin not only the whole day in school but also may be the reason for serious punishment from your parents.

NK: Although, writing with the quill was helpful for the development of your hand-writing.

This is true, the development of handwriting also affected Kapustin's writing of the handwritten scores. Looking at these scores, you can't stop thinking about how long it took for him to write so precise and accurate. All Kapustin's original scores are written by hand by the composer himself.

As with many of us, talking about our first years of study in school, we would definitely remember our first teacher. Nikolai Kapustin also has something to say about it.

NK: I remember her face very clearly but I don't remember her name. She was a very good teacher, and later in 1952 when we went to Moscow with Piotr Vinnichenko, she helped us. She gave us the address of her relatives, so we would have a place to stay overnights.

Luckily Nikolai studied with this teacher for a few years, when she was teaching all the subjects.[18] At this post-war period School No. 30 experienced a lack of the teachers. That's why she was asked to teach all the subjects for the pupils of the 4th grade and older. Nikolai and his teacher became good friends and kept warm relationships over the years.

NK (with a smile): Of course she loved me.

---

[18] According to the rules of education in the Soviet Union, starting from the 4th grade pupils supposed to study different subjects with individual teachers.

Nikolai Kapustin (third row, third from the left), School No. 30, 4th grade, Nikitovka, Ukraine, ca. 1947

In a standard way, Nikolai studied in the school seven years, during 1945 through 1952.

YT: What kind of memories do you have from the years of study in the school?
NK: Only the good memories. I kept receiving certificates of achievements one after another. It was interesting to study in the school.

Beginning from the 5th grade Nikolai started to learn a foreign language. The most common language that pupils used to study in the school, even now, is English. That's why Nikolai tried to learn English by himself for some period before that. Surprisingly, in School No. 30 the foreign language turned out to be French.

NK: All my English language preparations ended up as useless material, but I was also delighted to study French.

French language was the language of nineteenth-century Russian aristocracy, the language of the high society. All well-educated people in Russia at that time spoke French. The French language would become something serious for Kapustin too. Later it would help Kapustin in his reading of the literature on physics, linguistics and music.

NK: Through my whole life I was engaged in self-education. It is a special pleasure for me.

Another of Kapustin's passions that continued throughout his life was physics. He was a very talented pupil in this area of science.

NK: My physics teacher got upset when he found out that I was going to pursue music in my life. He thought I had serious potential in physics.
YT: Do you remember the first physics book that impressed you?
NK: Of course I remember that. It was the bestseller written by Stephen Hawking »A Brief History of Time«.[19]
YT: Was the book translated into Russian?
NK: No, I read it in English.

Nikolai Kapustin (fourth row, fourth from the left), physics teacher (third row, fourth from the left), biology teacher (third row, fifth from the left), Ukrainian language teacher (third row, sixth from the left), School No. 30, 7th grade, Nikitovka, Ukraine, May 1952

---

[19] This book was written in 1988 and by 2001 translated into thirty-five languages.

This is a Student Qualification document on the student of the 7th grade, Nikolai Kapustin:

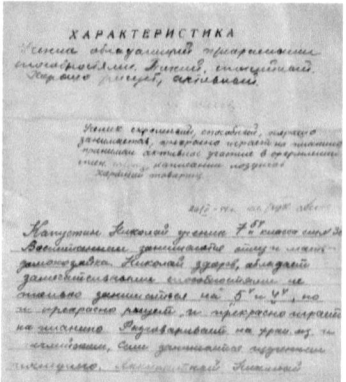 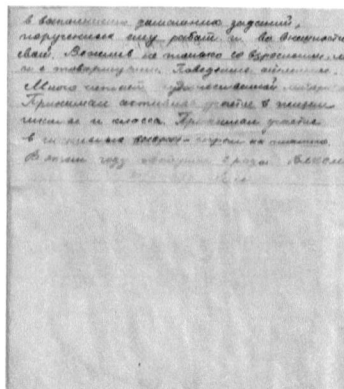

Student Qualification of Nikolai Kapustin, May 20, 1952

This pupil possesses creative abilities, is quiet, drawing very well, and active.
This student is a modest, gifted student, and plays the piano wonderfully. Nikolai had an active role in writing slogans on the wallpaper. Everybody wants to be his friend.
His upbringing came from his mother who is a house keeper. He is healthy, has great abilities not only to study with A's and B's, but also drawing wonderfully and playing piano. He is studying French and English languages, the last one he studies on his own. Nikolai is organized in the fulfilment of his studies, the work that he is doing, and in his appearance. He is polite not only with the adults but also with his friends. His behaviour is perfect. He reads a lot; he actively participated in the life of the school and his class. He participated in the evening school concerts playing piano. This year he became a part of the VLKSM [Komsomol].[20]

---

[20] Komsomol was the youth division of the Communist Part of the Soviet Union. It was founded in 1918 and dissolved in 1991.

Lubov' Borisovna Frantsuzova

Coming back to Kapustin's musical education in the late 1940s, our conversation returns to Piotr Ivanovich Vinnichenko.

YT: Can I ask you a strange question?
NK: Go ahead.
YT: Why did you and Fira choose private lessons with Piotr Vinnichenko rather than study in a music school?
NK: There was no music school in Nikitovka. If you wanted to go to a music school, you would have to go to the city of Artemovsk, which is twenty-five kilometers[21] away from Nikitovka, to have lessons.
YT: So to study with the private teacher was the only option for you.
NK: Yes, and I got very lucky on this matter having the best teacher I could ever imagine for myself.

That's why during the years of 1943 to 1949 Nikolai studied piano with Piotr Ivanovich Vinnichenko. At some point, watching the enormous growth of his young student, Vinnichenko realized that Nikolai needed a serious piano teacher. Since Vinnichenko's major instrument was violin, he probably felt not as strong in the piano area.

NK: Unfortunately, the violinist would not be able to teach a pianist.

Thus, in 1949, Piotr Vinnichenko found a new piano teacher for Nikolai. This teacher was the virtuoso pianist Lubov' Borisovna Frantsuzova.

YT: Usually it is hard for the young child to change the teacher. In a way, the child gets attached to the teacher. How did you survive this change?
NK: Easy.

Lubov' Frantsuzova graduated from the Saint-Petersburg Conservatory. She studied with the well-known pianist, composer, musical educator, and writer Samuel Maykapar. Maykapar's teaching achievements and talents were in the area of working with young children. He composed a wide range of the repertoire for young pianists. Lubov' Frantsuzova inherited Maykapar's interest in working with children.

Nikolai used to travel on the bus to Artemovsk every Sunday in order to have lessons with Lubov' Frantsuzova.

---

[21] The distance of twenty-five kilometers is equal to approximately fifteen and a half miles.

YT: You were just twelve years old at that time. I would be afraid to go alone to another city.

NK: I was not afraid. It was safe to travel at that time; there were no bullies. Nothing could hurt you.

Interestingly enough, his older sister Fira, watching Nikolai's passion for playing piano, decided to switch from violin to piano. She also started piano lessons with Lubov' Frantsuzova.

YT: What was your relationship with Lubov' Frantsuzova? Was she a demanding teacher?

NK: She was a very kind person. I still have the gift she presented for my birthday, Chopin's Twenty-Four Preludes, Op. 28.

Nikolai went through a wide variety of educational repertoire studying with Lubov' Frantsuzova. Among the pieces that he learned with her were Beethoven *Pathetique Sonata*, Op. 13, Grieg *Poetic Tone Pictures*, Op. 3, Mendelssohn *Rondo Capriccioso in E minor*, Op. 14, and many other works.

YT: Did you take those lessons at the musical college?
NK: No, I went to her home.
YT: What kind of atmosphere was at her house?
NK: There was a comfortable and beautiful atmosphere in her house. Her husband was a violinist and they both taught at the Artemovsk Musical College. I remember her piano had a very special sound, although, it was an upright piano not a grand piano.

For many years Lubov' Frantsuzova was a piano professor in Artemovsk Musical College. Her former students used to visit and play music for her. As in the past, this is still considered to be a serious gesture of respect and reverence to the teacher. Nikolai Kapustin used to listen to those performances quite often, gaining more understanding of playing piano and the importance of his teacher in the musical society of city Artemovsk.

YT: How long were your lessons with Lubov' Frantsuzova?
NK: Around one hour.

In just three years, 1949 through 1952, Lubov' Frantsuzova was able to prepare Nikolai Kapustin for the entering exam to the Moscow Musical College.

YT: What was the main direction in her work with you? Did she work on the development of technique, expression, or the sound concept?
NK: Generally, she worked on the sound.
YT: Yes, you can develop the good technique, but the sound is a serious thing.

NK: *I have a different opinion in this question. I think the technique is a serious thing. I hear how some pianists play my pieces. Their technique is not good enough.*
YT: *Yes, your music is very demanding technically. The parameters are set very high.*
NK: *Maybe. This is because I gave serious attention to the technique myself. I learned Liszt's Reminiscences de Don Juan. When I heard that Scriabin hurt his hand playing this piece, I decided to try it on my own.*
YT: *How was your hand after working on Don Juan?*
NK: *It was alright.*

Nikolai Kapustin, Nikitovka, ca. 1952

YT: *I keep looking at this picture of you in Nikitovka, sitting in front of your house. The first thing you notice is big hands with the long fingers of a young man.*
NK: *This was a photo trick. It may happen when the photographer is too close to you with some angle on the camera.*
YT: *You wanted to be a great pianist.*
NK: *Yes, that was my dream at that time.*
YT: *And in reality your hands are absolutely normal.*
NK: *Absolutely.*

First Steps in Composition – Piano Sonata (1950)

Starting from this period, late 1940s, Nikolai Kapustin began to compose his own music.

YT: Did Lubov' Frantsuzova know that you were composing the music?
NK: Sure she did. She tried to prohibit my composing.
YT: Why?
NK: Because it was a distraction. It took me away from the main thing – practicing piano.

The result of these debates with Frantsuzova had the complete opposite effect. Being just twelve-thirteen years old, and without any study in composition, Nikolai composed his first piece *Piano Sonata*. However, knowing the character of Nikolai Kapustin and his desire to reach the goals that he sets for himself, this doesn't sound surprising at all.

NK: I was ready for this; I didn't need a teacher. Do you think I asked someone about the sonata form?
YT: Did you?
NK: No, I learned it by myself. I read about it.

Nikolai Kapustin began his acquaintance with music as a self-taught pianist at the age of six. Now, being twelve years old, he became a self-taught composer. Simply reading about the sonata form was enough for Nikolai Kapustin to compose his own sonata. Does this sound impressive or it is just something that normal children do on a regular basis?

The *Sonata* was written in the traditional classical style and consisted of three movements (fast/slow/fast). The score of this sonata is preserved in Kapustin's home archive. The manuscript is written by his teacher Piotr Ivanovich Vinnichenko.

YT: I noticed one interesting detail – this Piano Sonata was composed in 1950 but the manuscript is dated by May-June 1952. Why is it that way?
NK: It's because right before my enrollment to the Moscow Musical College my teacher Piotr Vinnichenko decided to prepare a present for me – to write this sonata in a professional way so I would have something to show to people in Moscow.
YT: So, it was a present from Vinnichenko.
NK: Yes. I had my own manuscript but Vinnichenko decided to do a new version of it and he finished the work right before our trip to Moscow.
YT: I also noticed that your handwriting looks very similar to the hand of Vinnichenko.

NK *(smiling): I was his student. He knew that this sonata would represent me as a composer in Moscow, that's why he decided to do everything he could for me.*

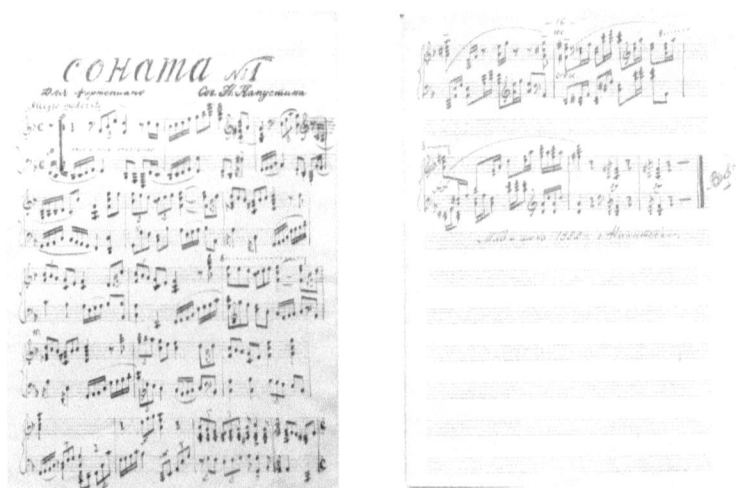

First and last pages of the Piano Sonata, May-June 1952, Nikitovka

YT: *I played a couple of pages of this sonata. It is clear that the music is based on triadic harmonies and it has a very traditional Russian rooted sound.*
NK: *Of course. In Nikitovka I didn't know about jazz.*
YT: *So, you were not interested in jazz at the beginning.*
NK: *I started to listen to jazz music only when I studied at the Musical College and that's how I got involved in jazz.*
YT: *It is interesting that Vinnichenko put the number in the score – Piano Sonata No. 1.*
NK: *Yes, he believed that I would continue writing piano music.*
YT: *And he was right.*
NK: *Unfortunately, it turned out that my other piano sonata would become my Piano Sonata No. 1, which is my Op. 39.*
YT: *Did anyone perform this sonata?*
NK: *Except myself, nobody of course.*

Having a different piano teacher, Nikolai did not stop his relationship with Piotr Vinnichenko. Piotr Vinnichenko used to visit Kapustin's family from time to time and became a family friend. Developing a good relationship with Kapustin's parents is why they let Nikolai go to Moscow with Piotr Vinnichenko.

Now, listening to Nikolai Kapustin speaking about Piotr Vinnichenko, it is impossible to miss the attitude of respect and complete adoration by Nikolai of his teacher, an attitude that was preserved through the years. After listening to these stories, one may think that at the time when Nikolai was around ten years old Vinnichenko was around middle fortes-early fifties. It was a big surprise for me when Kapustin said:

NK: He was just eight years older than me.
YT: Really? So in a way you were the same age as Piotr Vinnichenko?
NK: I am telling you – eight years older.

Entering Exams at the Moscow Musical College

The idea to study in the Moscow Musical College jointly appeared after the conversations of Poitr Vinnichenko and Nikolai about Moscow.

NK: He was a literate, well-educated musician, not just a violinist. He was a composer as well. Piotr Vinnichenko noticed that I have the talent, same as his but on a larger scale. He was the one who brought me to Moscow.
YT: Had he ever been in Moscow before, maybe worked or studied there?
NK: No. He was just curious if something like this may happen in reality. As you know, we lived deep in the village.

In August of 1952 Nikolai went to audition for the Moscow Musical College, he was just fourteen years old. A few observations arise from this fact in Nikolai's life. First, it takes great courage from a person to make that kind of the decision at such an early age. This person should have very strong belief in his abilities. Second, living through his whole life with his parents, it was probably very hard to leave them.

YT: Why did your parents allow you to go by yourself to study in Moscow? You were so young.
NK: I am wondering myself about that too. They were afraid to let me go to the creek alone. I have no idea how they decided to let me to go to Moscow. Maybe they thought that nothing bad can happen with me there.

Piotr Vinnichenko and Nikolai Kapustin arrived to Moscow a few days early before the beginning of the auditions. They settled in the house of Nikolai's teacher from the elementary school whose relatives lived in Moscow. Fortunately, the relatives of this teacher had a piano at their house and Nikolai used to practice every day on this instrument preparing himself for the final audition, the most important day in his life.

NK: First, we needed to know if I had a chance to be selected to study in the Musical College.
YT: How did you find out about it?
NK: Piotr Vinnichenko accidently met Alexander Nikolaev in the hallway of the college and asked him to listen to my audition. I played Bach's Prelude and Fugue in B flat major (Book I) and something else.
YT: Did Piotr Vinnichenko know who Alexander Nikolaev was?
NK: Of course he did. His famous teaching book was known everywhere.

Biographical Information

Nikolaev, Alexander Alexandrovich (1903 - 1980) was a famous musicologist, pianist, and teacher. During the 1930s through 1970s Nikolaev was a Professor at the Moscow Musical College and the Moscow Conservatory. Nikolaev wrote a large number of essays on different topics. Among them were teaching methods of playing piano, questions about the aesthetics of Russian musical performance, performance and teaching principles of Goldenweiser and Neuhaus, piano music of Shostakovich, and much more. He was the editor of one of the most famous teaching books »The Russian School of Piano Playing« (1950).[22]

YT: How did you perform on your pre-audition for Nikolaev?
NK: It was a good performance, not great though. I thought that I am not going to make it. Nikolaev said that I should not worry about it and that I would undoubtedly be selected.
YT: How did you feel about Nikolaev's comments?
NK: He strengthened my will to win.

The day of the audition came to pass for Nikolai Kapustin and he was ready for it. For some reason Piotr Vinnichenko was not able to attend the entering exam and Nikolai went to perform by himself.

YT: It sounds scary that your teacher was not there on the day of your entering exams.
NK: I was not scared about being by myself. I mostly was worried about my upcoming performance.

One of the difficulties that pianists were faced with during the entering exam is that it was not allowed to try the instrument before the actual performance. The enrollee had to adjust himself immediately to the sound of the grand piano. In addition, the stress was increased by the committee members of five-six professors, who were judging to determine the level of the enrollees. As one would expect, the level of competition in Moscow Musical College was extremely high.[23]

YT: How many pianists were competing for one spot?
NK: Something like eight people for one spot. Some of the performers were trying to enter the college multiple times, and didn't make it this time either.

---

[22] Alexander Nikolaev. Accessed November 9, 2017.
https://dic.academic.ru/dic.nsf/enc_biography/91502/Николаев.
[23] It should be noted that up to the 1990s education in Russia was completely free. This was one of the reasons why the level of competition in some educational institutions was set very high.

An important factor of the successful performance on the audition of that type is the program itself, the level of difficulty of your program. The pianist should present himself in his best shape, showing all possible facets of his talent. The pieces should not be too difficult or too easy, they must simply be the best fit for the performer. Also, the pianist should remember that the idea of taking well-known pieces has its' pluses and minuses. Performing a well-known piece gives more responsibility to the pianist. On one hand, original interpretations may gain additional benefits to the pianist, but on the other hand it is a risk to perform the piece where every note is perfectly familiar to each member of the committee. Nikolai Kapustin never tried to find easy ways in his life, and, as it would be expected, he chose to play very famous compositions.

YT: Do you remember the pieces that you played for the entering exam?
NK: I played Mendelssohn's Rondo Capriccioso in E minor, Op. 14, the famous Rachmaninov's Prelude in C sharp minor, Op. 3 No. 2, J. S. Bach's Prelude and Fugue in B flat major from the WTC (Book I), and something else.

This program looks very extensive and difficult for the pianist of fourteen years old. However, this is understandable because the level of requirements in Moscow musical institutions was always higher than in any other cities.

The atmosphere of the entering exams in different colleges feels different. In some places enrollees communicate with each other, ask questions, but in some other places the surroundings feel tense and stressful.

YT: Did you have a chance to listen to any other enrollees?
NK: Of course I did. I wasn't impressed by any of the performers, in the same way I wasn't impressed by my own playing either. Yes, before Rubbakh I didn't play well.

The second part of the entering exam was solfeggio. For some pianists, this part of the exam is more difficult than the performance.

NK: From the solfeggio I was freed immediately.
YT: How did that happen?
NK: My ear was developed at a very high level.
YT: How did they determine this?
NK: By means of dictation.

Nikolai Kapustin wrote a few dictations surprisingly quickly and without any mistakes.²⁴ After that the entering committee made a decision that Nikolai should skip the rest of the entering exam.

YT: Who prepared you for the solfeggio exam? Was it Lubov' Frantsuzova?
NK: No, Piotr Vinnichenko helped me at the beginning and then I continued to prepare by myself. I have perfect pitch, so that was not a problem for me.

Perfect pitch is something that not many of us may have. Unfortunately, it is impossible to achieve perfect pitch through ear training; a person should be born with perfect pitch.²⁵ From the outside this ability looks similar to magic. It is hard to believe that a person can hear any note or sound and identify its' relationship to pitch. However, people who have perfect pitch also have things to struggle with.

YT: Because of your perfect pitch, have you experienced any problems?
NK: Yes, one big problem I have had since childhood is that our instrument was tuned lower, so I was used to hearing different tuning. I still have this from my past, plus the tuning system changes through the years. I have to adjust my hearing.

Nikolai Kapustin was accepted to the Moscow Musical College. Even more impressive, he was selected to join the class of the famous teacher Avrelian Grigorievich Rubbakh. Nikolai Kapustin could not dream for anything more. It was a moment of big victory and complete happiness.

YT: Had you ever heard about Rubbakh before?
NK: Yes, I knew Rubbakh earlier, from the time when I lived in the Ukraine. In addition to teaching he was also a famous editor.²⁶
YT: Do you remember if anyone from Artemovsk tried to enter Moscow Musical College before you?
NK: I don't think so.
YT: How did you find out that you were accepted to the class of Avrelian Rubbakh?
NK: After the entering exam Piotr Vinnichenko talked to him and asked if he will be willing to take me in his class. Rubbakh agreed with pleasure, especially when he found out about my interest in composition.
YT: Why do you think Rubbakh selected you for his class?

---

[24] One of the dictations was the theme from Prokofiev's oratorio On Guard for Peace.
[25] It is possible to develop a high degree of relative pitch.
[26] Avrelian Rubbakh was the editor of the Moscow music journal Muzgiz.

NK: *I think he understood that there is something he could work on. I had a horrible sound; he taught me how to touch the piano. Actually, there was an emotional and memorable story behind my entrance exams to the Musical College.*
YT: *Could you tell me about it?*
NK: *The fact is I was not accepted to the piano performance major to begin with.*
YT: *Then where were you accepted?*
NK: *I was accepted as the theoretical-compositional major.*
YT: *What do you mean?*
NK: *I still remember that day of my life. They put the lists with the names of accepted students on the wall inside of the college and everybody was crowding around that lists to see if their names were there, and me too. I looked through the list of names of accepted students in the piano performance major a couple of times and didn't find mine. I could not understand what just happened... So, it took me a while to realize what the problem was. I was totally in shock, ruined, and completely crushed. I set aside and burst into tears, I was a child... The amount of my disappointment was enormous; it's hard to tell in words what I felt at that moment. Then I remember somebody came up to me and said: »Don't cry, you are accepted as a student of theoretical-compositional major.« I looked into the list of accepted students as a theoretical-compositional major and indeed found my name in there.*
YT: *Unreal! How did that happen?*
NK: *I have no idea. The members of the committee decided to put me into the compositional major without my will, but I didn't want it. I didn't want anyone teaching me how to compose music, and I was right! See, I was a farseeing boy even then.*
YT: *You wanted to be a student of piano performance major.*
NK: *Of course, that was my goal. They had no right to do that; they did it without my permission. Did I ask them to do that?*
YT: *Did you pass the portion of the exam that theoretical-compositional students do during your entrance exam?*
NK: *Of course not. I passed only what was required for the piano majors.*
YT: *What happened next?*
NK: *I called to my mother and she came to Moscow almost immediately to help me to solve this difficult situation. My mother and Rubbakh were able to talk to some important people from the college and transfer me to the piano performance major. In spite of the fact that Rubbakh appreciated my ability to compose the music, he still agreed to help me to be a piano major student. I respected that a lot from him! Rubbakh and my mother were the two people who made that change and made my dream come true.*
YT: *What a happy ending! It's hard to predict what would have happened now if you were a compositional major student in the musical college.*

NK: There were a few examples in music history when composers didn't graduate as a composer, for example Nikolai Medtner, which did not prevent him from becoming a preeminent composer of the twentieth century. He graduated only as a piano performance major, but Rachmaninov and Scriabin graduated in both piano performance and composition.

YT: Did you go home with your mother Klavdia Nikolayevna?

NK: No, the entering exams were right before the fall semester began, so I stayed in Moscow. By the way, she also came to our dormitory during that visit. She was in shock at how poor the conditions of life were there, but it was ok with me. For me, the main thing was that I was accepted to the Moscow Musical College, that's the first thing, and the second, I was accepted as a piano student in the class of Avrelian Rubbakh. That was the main part!

The fact is that Kapustin came to Moscow to study at the Musical College and brought his first composition – Piano Sonata. He performed this piece on a few occasions, and Rubbakh heard the conversations about the young composer. Probably, being an experienced teacher, Rubbakh noticed Kapustin's passion for composing, and that could be one of the reasons why Rubbakh selected Kapustin in his class. From the moment Nikolai Kapustin saw his name on the list of the accepted students the new life immediately started for him – a life that would lead him to significant success, admiration, and esteem!

Composing music would become Kapustin's passion through his entire life. Now, for more than sixty-five years, he has composed a large variety of different types of music, gaining popularity in the entire world. Did he assume that resonance of popularity when he began composing in 1949? Surely not, but at the very least he knew at such a young age that he had found something that would guide him through his life.

Chapter Two: Study in Moscow Musical College (1952-1956)

There are two distinguished schools of piano performance in Russia that were fully established by the first part of the twentieth century. These are the Moscow and Saint Petersburg schools of playing. It is interesting that these two conservatories were originally founded by two brothers – Anton and Nikolai Rubinstein. In 1862 Anton Rubinstein became a founder and the first director of the Saint Petersburg Conservatory[27] and four years later, in 1866, his younger brother Nikolai became a co-founder and the first director of the Moscow Conservatory.[28]

YT: What is the difference between these two schools of piano performance?
NK: The main difference lies in sound itself.
YT: Do you mean in the performer's touch?
NK: Yes. The Moscow sound, for example the sound of Rachmaninov, is full, real, and almost physically tangible.

One of the major representatives of the Saint Petersburg school of playing was Teodor Leschetizky.[29] It was noted that the playing of Leschetizky was distinguished by a soft, cantabile tone, »singing« legato touch, careful and elegant execution of detail, perfect phrasing, and flexible agogic.[30] Leschetizky's method is still considered to be one of the most influential approaches of teaching piano.[31]

---

[27] In 1944 the Saint Petersburg Conservatory (also known as Leningrad Conservatory) was named for Nikolai Rimsky-Korsakov, where Rimsky-Korsakov taught composition. Some of the remarkable professors of Saint Petersburg Conservatory were Teodor Leschetizky (pupil of Karl Czerny, teacher of Ignacy Paderewski, Anna Esipova, and Arthur Schnabel), Anna Esipova (pupil and later wife of Teodor Leschetizky, teacher of Prokofiev), Leonid Nikolaev (teacher of Dmitry Shostakovich, Vladimir Sofronitsky, and Maria Yudina), and Pavel Serebryakov. Accessed November 8, 2017. http://www.conservatory.ru/.

[28] In 1940 the Moscow Conservatory was named for Piotr Ilyich Tchaikovsky, where Tchaikovsky was a professor of theory and harmony (1866-1878). Some of the remarkable professors of the Moscow Conservatory were Nikolai Zverev (teacher of Sergei Rachmaninov and Alexander Scriabin), Alexander Ziloti (pupil of Franz Liszt, teacher of Konstantin Igumnov, Alexander Goldenweiser, and Sergei Rachmaninov, who was his cousin), Felix Blumenfeld (pupil of Nikolai Rimsky-Korsakov, teacher of Vladimir Horowitz, Alexander Tsfasman, Avrelian Rubbakh, Simon Barere, and Maria Yudina), Konstantin Igumnov (pupil of Nikolai Zverev, Sergei Taneyev, and Anton Arensky, teacher of Lev Oborin, Maria Grinberg, and Rosa Tamarkina), Alexander Goldenweiser (pupil of Sergei Taneyev and Vasily Safonov, teacher of Dmitry Kabalevsky, Tatiana Nikolaeva, Nikolai Petrov, and Nikolai Kapustin), and Heinrich Neuhaus (nephew of Felix Blumenfeld, teacher of Sviatoslav Richter and Emil Gilels). Accessed November 9, 2017. http://www.mosconsv.ru/ru/book.aspx?id=131310&page=131311.

[29] Theodor Leschetizky. Accessed November 9, 2017. https://www.britannica.com/biography/Theodor-Leschetizky.

[30] Theodor Leschetizky. Accessed February 12, 2018. http://w.histrf.ru/articles/article/show/lieshietitskii_leszetycki_leschetizky_tieodor_teodor_theodor_fiodor_osipovich.

[31] Annette Hullah, »Theodor Leschetizky«. Accessed November 9, 2017.

Kapustin remembered an interesting episode from the history of the Moscow school of piano:

> NK: *Once Rachmaninov played a concert dedicated to his friend Alexander Scriabin, right after Scriabin's death. Everybody was outraged about this performance because it didn't sound like Scriabin at all. (After a long pause he continued) Rachmaninov was far from impressionism.*
> YT: *Which school of playing did Scriabin belong to?*
> NK: *They were both from Moscow, but for some reason Scriabin's sound was quite different. It was a light sound with the element of floating in it.*

This episode demonstrates that even within one school of playing there were some differences in the approach to sound. On the other hand, it may be that Scriabin was an exceptional composer and pianist and everything he did was different from what we would expect.

---

https://www.gutenberg.org/files/43915/43915-h/43915-h.htm.

Avrelian Grigorievich Rubbakh

One of the major influences for Kapustin in his development as a classical pianist was his teacher, Avrelian Rubbakh.[32]

Avrelian Grigorievich Rubbakh (1895-1975) was a gifted pianist, talented teacher, composer, arranger, and editor. He was a student of Felix Blumenfeld, who was also a teacher of Vladimir Horovitz and Simon Barere. It is interesting to note that Felix Blumenfeld was born in the Ukraine and during different periods of his life taught in Moscow, Kiev, and Saint Petersburg Conservatories.[33] These facts of Blumenfeld's life demonstrate that he had a wide range of different influences that affected his musical style. Therefore, Blumenfeld represented a synthesis of both Saint Petersburg and Moscow piano performance schools. That explains why in one of our conversations Kapustin said:

NK: Rubbakh represents a Russian school of playing.[34]

In other words, Rubbakh inherited the essence of Blumenfeld's musical nature, which was obviously transmitted to his own students.

Rubbakh was a teacher with a variety of different interests which were all connected to the teaching process. In the 1950s Rubbakh was teaching at the Central Music School[35] (CMS) and at the same time at the Moscow Musical College, where both institutions existed under the Moscow Conservatory.[36] He was also the editor of the *Muzgiz* (State Music Publishing House) in Moscow. One of Rubbakh's milestone works as editor was the *Anthology of Pedagogic Repertoire for Music Schools: Pieces of Foreign Composers* for students in fifth and sixth grades of music school.[37] The major advantage of this anthology was the fact that it was published with pedagogical suggestions for teachers.[38]

---

[32] Unfortunately, the amount of sources on Rubbakh is limited because not enough information was preserved.

[33] Felix Blumenfeld graduated from Saint Petersburg Conservatory in 1885, where in addition to the piano he studied composition under Nikolai Rimsky-Korsakov. Blumenfeld taught piano in Saint Petersburg Conservatory (1885-1905 and 1911-1918), Lysenko Music and Drama Institute (1918-1920), Kiev Conservatory (1920-1922), and until the end of his life in Moscow Conservatory (1922-1931). Accessed November 9, 2017. http://www.krugosvet.ru/enc/kultura_i_obrazovanie/muzyka/BLUMENFELD_FELIKS_MIHALOVICH.html.

[34] Interview with the author, June 17, 2015, Ruza, Russia.

[35] Central Music School. Accessed November 9, 2017. https://cmsmoscow.ru/.

[36] Moscow Musical College. Accessed November 9, 2017. http://www.amumgk.ru/.

[37] *Anthology of Pedagogic Repertoire: Fifth Grade* (Moscow: Muzyka, 1962, 1965, 1968), *Anthology of Pedagogic Repertoire: Sixth Grade* (Moscow: Muzyka, 1962, 1965, 1967, 1969).

[38] Russian State Library, Avrelian Rubbakh: *Collection of Pieces for the Beginners: From the Music Book of Leopold Mozart* (Moscow: Muzgiz, 1933, 1935, 1961), *Piano Concertos for Children: Middle Grades*

Furthermore, besides his work as an editor, Rubbakh was writing piano arrangements of Bach, Haydn, Mussorgsky, Tchaikovsky, and Gluck works adapted for children. For example, he arranged *Intermezzo* from Tchaikovsky's *Orchestral Suite No. 1*, Op. 43 for two pianos.[39]

NK: I remember his arrangement of Chopin's »Heroic« Polonaise (Op. 53 in A flat major). Yet, it was written in A major because it's easier to play on the piano.
YT: Did he arrange it for his students?
NK: Yes. But the main thing for him of course was pedagogy.

As a lector Rubbakh used to travel to different cities in Russia to give masterclasses and lectures in different musical institutions and to demonstrate his principles of teaching piano. Thus, in 1952 he did a pedagogical lecture-recital in the city Ufa (capital of the Republic of Bashkortostan) in Musical School No. 1 for teachers of Bashkiria.[40]

Rubbakh would be one of the key figures in Kapustin's life influencing him in many different ways: as a teacher, pianist, educator, and as a person. After Kapustin entered the class of Rubbakh his life changed forever.

NK: The four years that I spent around Rubbakh (1952 through1956) were the most interesting and productive years of my student life.

(Moscow: Soviet Composer, 1989), *Polyphonic Pieces* (Moscow: Soviet Composer, 1970*), Polyphonic Works of Soviet Composers* (Moscow: Soviet Composer, 1976), *Selected Etudes of Foreign Composers* (Moscow: Muzgiz, 1960, 1962, 1965), and more. Accessed November 9, 2017. https://search.rsl.ru/en/search#q=руббах аврелиан григорьевич.

[39] Moscow: Muzgiz, 1956, 1962.

[40] Evgeniya Pupkova, »Pereigravshaya vsego Baha«. Accessed November 9, 2017. http://pupkova.ru/biography/.

Nikolai Kapustin, student of the Moscow Musical College, ca. 1954-1955

Despite the fact that Rubbakh was Kapustin's third piano teacher, Kapustin referred to Rubbakh as a »very first real teacher«.[41]

NK: He taught me how to play the piano.

Rubbakh was in his late fifties when Kapustin began to study with him. Undoubtedly, being an experienced teacher, Rubbakh noticed serious potential in a young Kapustin. Although, at the same time he probably also noticed things that Kapustin needed to work on, but that did not frighten Rubbakh. The main factor for Rubbakh in his decision to take Kapustin in his class was the talent of a young performer.

YT: Did Rubbakh give you the pieces to work on after you entered the college?
NK: Yes, the piece that Rubbakh assigned to me to work on during the summer break was Arensky Fantasia on Russian Folksongs, Op. 48.
YT: Really? I played this piece too, it's very beautiful music.
NK: Yes, especially the closing passages at the end of the piece. That was the very first piece that I played after I entered Musical College.

---

[41] Interview with the author, June 17, 2015, Ruza, Russia.

YT: Who accompanied you?
NK: Rubbakh. He always accompanied me.

Kapustin remembered his impression from the first lesson with Rubbakh, which was in September of 1952.

NK: The most interesting thing is when I came to him on my first lesson. I was completely shocked at how beautiful his sound was on the piano. He had an amazing touch. Unlike Saint Petersburg's performers, he played with the real sound. This was a clear example of the Moscow school of playing.

It is always quite interesting to know what the teacher's philosophy is and how the teacher envisions the lesson.

YT: Did Rubbakh play for you during the lesson?
NK: If he would not play it would be extremely difficult to understand everything. He played just short episodes, as an example, but it was magical. His instrument had a live sound, and mine refused to be alive. By the way, he had an exceptional instrument in his class – Bechstein grand piano.
YT: So, Rubbakh's major direction in the lessons was to work on the sound?
NK: Yes, that was the main thing.
YT: Was he a demanding teacher? I remember Evgeniya Pupkova wrote in her biography that she was crying on the lessons trying to get away from the »dirty« pedal.
NK: I don't recall this. Even when I deserved a serious critique I don't remember that he raised his voice to me.
YT: It looks like he had different behavior to different students.
NK: As it should be.
YT: Did Rubbakh have a specific time for each student for the lesson or it was just an order of students?[42]
NK: I think there was something very general. What I clearly remember is that there were always many visitors attending the lessons.
YT: Is that true? That means that right on the first lesson you have to come already well prepared.
NK: Yes, from the first lesson everything should be memorized, but it was allowed to play with some minor mistakes.

---

[42] Note by the author: Remembering my own experience of study in Musical College in Russia I can tell that some teachers determine only the order of the students but not the actual length of the lesson. An individual lesson would last as long as it needed to be (forty-five minutes to one hour and thirty minutes), depending on the student's preparation and ability to work in the lesson.

There was a special atmosphere on the lessons with Rubbakh. Many of his students used to come earlier to the class and stay longer, listening to the lessons of their classmates.

NK: It was always a very friendly and fun atmosphere.
YT: I think if you would be afraid of your teacher you wouldn't come earlier to the lesson.
NK: Of course. We were good friends. I remember Rubbakh tried to quit smoking at that time and he asked me secretly to get the cigarettes for him.
YT: Did you help him?
NK: Sure, I did.

Rubbakh was an excellent virtuoso pianist, especially known for his fine technique of the left hand, which can be quite rare. He treated his own students in a same way he treated himself – always with the highest expectations.

YT: How did Rubbakh work on the technique with his students?
NK: I don't remember that I played scales or technique exercises with Rubbakh. He gave us etudes – Czerny, Moshkovsky, and others. In addition, I worked independently to develop my technique. Through my study in college I probably learned somewhere around ten or more Chopin etudes by myself.
YT: Did Rubbakh used to perform on the concerts?
NK: Not really. I remember when I studied on the third-fourth course of the Musical College he started to prepare himself very seriously for some performances but then said that his heart is not strong enough to continue doing that. However, what he learned he played for us.
YT: How did that happen?
NK: We begged him to play and he finally agreed to play for us in the classroom.
YT: What did he play?
NK: He played one of the Bach-Busoni organ fugues. It was a brilliant performance.
YT: Did you have concerts of the teachers of Musical College?
NK: I don't recall that. On the other side I remember there were concerts and masterclasses of different famous pianists and composers. That was very interesting. I attended the masterclass of Heinrich Neuhaus[43] and his son Stanislav Neuhaus. Also I

---

[43] Heinrich Neuhaus (1888-1964) was a famous Russia pianist and pedagogue. He taught at the Moscow Conservatory from 1922 until 1964. His pedagogic book »The Art of Piano Playing« (1958) is regarded as one of the most authoritative and most widely used treatments on the subject. His students were Sviatoslav Richter, Emil Gilels, Lev Naumov, Vera Gornostayeva, Eliso Virsaladze, Aleksey Nasedkin, Vladimir Krainev, Berta Maranz, and Evgeny Mogilevsky. Accessed November 9, 2017. http://www.mosconsv.ru/ru/person.aspx?id=121143.

remember the lecture-recitals of Anatoly Alexandrov,⁴⁴ Dmitry Kabalevsky, and pianist Tatiana Nikolaeva.⁴⁵

YT: You attended so many masterclasses!

NK: How could you miss events like that? I was very curious about it.

Rubbakh's authority as a pianist and as a teacher in musical circles of Moscow was set so high that some eminent pianists would come to him to discuss issues and ask for suggestions, even though they were not his students.

NK: I remember once Lazar Berman⁴⁶ came to Rubbakh. He came to discuss the topic of his dissertation during his study in Moscow Conservatory, which he decided should be Liszt's Twelve Transcendental Etudes. He was supposed to write about etudes, do a presentation (Lecture-Recital), and perform. Hearing this idea Rubbakh said: »But then you will have to play all twelve etudes,« where Berman answered: ›This is a small detail, the question is – what to write?‹

In the winter of 1955 Rubbakh celebrated his 60th birthday. Traditionally, his students came to congratulate him with this significant event. Nikolai Kapustin was among them.

NK: I remember we all came to his class at the same time. He was pleased to see us.

---

⁴⁴ Anatoly Nikolayevich Alexandrov (1888-1982) was a Russian composer and pianist. He attended Moscow Conservatory, where he was a student of Sergei Taneyev and Konstantin Igumnov. Alexandrov wrote orchestral works, chamber, vocal, and piano music. Accessed November 9, 2017. https://dic.academic.ru/dic.nsf/enc_biography/2047/Александров.

⁴⁵ Tatiana Petrovna Nikolaeva (1924-1993) was a Russian Soviet pianist, composer, and teacher. She graduated from the Moscow Conservatory in 1947 (class of Professor Alexander Goldenweiser). In 1950 she won the first International Johann Sebastian Bach Competition (Leipzig, Germany). She made over fifty recordings during her career, notably the keyboard works by J.S. Bach. She also was famous for her premier of Shostakovich's cycle »24 Preludes and Fugues« in 1952. Nikolaeva was teaching at the Moscow Conservatory from 1959. She also sat as a jury member on many international competitions, including the Leeds International Piano Competition (1984-1987). Starting from the early 1980s Nikolaeva began to perform internationally - in Europe, Japan, and in the United States. Among her students were Nikolai Lugansky and Oxana Yablonskaya. Accessed November 9, 2017. http://www.mosconsv.ru/ru/person.aspx?id=41223, http://musicseasons.org/tatyana-petrovna-nikolaeva/.

⁴⁶ Lazar Naumovich Berman (1930-2005) was a Soviet Russian virtuoso pianist. He graduated from the Moscow Conservatory and completed his post-graduate studies in 1957 (class of Professor Alexander Goldenweiser). Berman became a laureate of Queen Elisabeth International Music Competition and International Frantz Liszt Piano Competition in 1956. Berman was known for his superb performance of Liszt's »Transcendental Etudes«, which was recorded on Russian record lebel »Melodiya« in the 1960s. Accessed February 13, 2018. https://www.allmusic.com/artist/lazar-berman-mn0002041344.

Rubbakh used to invite his students to his house to spend time together.

NK: Usually it was only his close students. Jenia (Evgeniya Pupkova) lived in his house[47] and I was going everywhere with Andrei Mikhalkov.[48]
YT: How often were these evenings happening?
NK: There was no specific system or order – just whenever he wanted he invited us.
YT: Did anyone perform on those evenings?
NK: All the time. I remember I learned the Rossini/Ginzburg transcription of Mozart's »Aria Figaro.« This is a brilliant transcription, and extremely difficult technically. In my practice it sometimes didn't come out well but I still played it for my friends.
YT: What a great tradition – to play for each other.
NK: In the college we used to do it on a regular basis.

Rubbakh was a person with a wide range of musical interests, beginning from the works of J. S. Bach and finishing with the recordings of the Count Basie Orchestra. It is an interesting detail of his life that Rubbakh and Alexander Tsfasman[49] both studied with Felix Blumenfeld.

NK: Rubbakh was a curious man; he was always interested in something new. That's why he had a positive attitude towards jazz.

Rubbakh supported Kapustin's interest in jazz music. Probably Rubbakh couldn't predict that his student would go so far in his desire to put these two vastly different musical trends together – classical and jazz music. Indeed, Rubbakh was one of the few people in Kapustin's life who influenced him tremendously, supported him, and helped him through his entire life.

There are no doubts that Rubbakh was an extremely influential teacher not only for Kapustin but for all people who had a chance to study with him. For example, Evgeniya Pupkova, Marina Marshak, and Isaac Katz would become very successful pianists and teachers.

---

[47] Engeniya Pupkova would become one of the nationally known performers of J. S. Bach's music. After Samuel Feinberg and Tatyana Nikolaeva, she was the third pianist in Russia who performed almost all works written by J. S. Bach. Accessed November 9, 2017. http://pupkova.ru/biography/.

[48] Conversation about Andrei Mikhalkov-Konchalovsky will be presented at the latter part of Chapter II.

[49] Alexander Tsfasman (1906-1971) graduated from Nizhny Novgorod Musical Technicum in 1923 and from Moscow Conservatory in 1930 (class of Professor Felix Blumenfeld). Tsfasman became an important figure in Soviet Jazz from the middle 1920s until the late 1960s. Accessed November 9, 2017. http://www.jazz.ru/mag/372/tsfasman.htm.

YT: Knowing that Rubbakh was interested in many different activities, being a teacher, performer, editor, and composer, have you ever thought about following the path of your teacher?

NK: I don't know. For some reason for me it was always interesting to compose the music. I wanted it the most.

YT: Have you ever tried to study composition?

NK: Never. I am a self-taught composer, same as J. S. Bach.

Kapustin never stopped his relationship with his deeply beloved teacher even after study in Musical College. He used to visit Rubbakh from time to time.

NK: I remember once I even came to visit him with Alla (Kapustina); that was long after my conservatory graduation. We got acquainted with his young wife Lilia (Safronova), who was his student in the past. I knew his first wife too. Elionora Iogannovna was a very good woman.

Connection to the Family and Teachers Frantsuzova and Vinnichenko

Another source of big support and inspiration for Kapustin was his family and two of his teachers, Piotr Vinnichenko and Lubov' Frantsuzova, who never disappeared from the horizons of his life. Kapustin used to come back to the Ukraine to visit his parents twice a year, during Christmas and summer breaks.

YT: Did you continue your relationship with Vinnichenko after you started to live in Moscow?

NK: Of course, we never lost our connection. I remember he even came to visit me in Moscow in the late 1970s. I was already married to Alla, we lived in our own flat, and had our first son Anton. He even tuned my piano during that visit.

Lubov' Frantsuzova, who was still teaching at that time in Artemovsk Musical College, was limitlessly happy for her young student, who reached that highest level of accomplishment – to study in Moscow Musical College.

YT: Do you know any other students of Frantsuzova who had a chance to study in Moscow?

NK: I think I was the only one. I remember she used to prepare students mostly to enter the conservatories in the Ukraine such as Kiev Conservatory and Kharkiv Conservatory.

YT: Did you visit Frantsuzova after your acceptance to Musical College?

NK: Oh, yes. Right after the first year of my study in Moscow, in the summer of 1953, I visited her with my mother in her house in Artemovsk. I remember I was playing the piano and they were talking about Moscow. Lubov' Borisovna (Frantsuzova) kept saying: »Kolia, how great you are playing, and what progress you have made!«

YT: Did she feel jealous about the fact that you studied with Rubbakh?

NK: What jealousy are you talking about? Of course she understood that I made a huge achievement – the boy from the province who was chosen to study in Moscow. It doesn't happen too often.

Kapustin's parents lived in Nikitovka through their whole life, waiting for the visits of their children – Nikolai and Fira.

YT: Did you come to visit your parents during all that years of your study in Musical College and Conservatory?

NK: Yes, even later when I started to work. Alla used to come too. We even left our children for the summer in Nikitovka. For us it was a big relief because life was difficult.

Every time Nikolai came back home for the vacation, he had all the necessary conditions around him for productive practice. His new instrument »Chernigov«, that his parents bought for him not long before his entrance to the Musical College, was always tuned and ready for use. Nikolai used to practice piano a lot during these visits back home. This was understandable; because the unspoken rule of study in Moscow was that every student of Musical College was supposed to learn a new program over the summer, memorize it, and play it close to the final tempo right from the beginning of the new semester.

Nikolai's sister, Fira Kapustina, studied in the Lviv University as a chemist from 1948 until 1953.

YT: *How often did she come to Nikitovka?*
NK: *Not often. I used to come more frequently than she. I remember Fira used to go camping with her friends a lot. She had her own life by that time.*
YT: *What did she do after she graduated from the university?*
NK: *After she graduated she moved to Torzhok,*[50] *and then to Tver' (now Kalinin). This small city of Torzhok is very interesting. It was the place of inspiration for many Russian writers and poets of the nineteenth century.*

Torzhok, Russia

---

[50] Torzhok - one of the Russian ancient cities of upper Volga-river area. Situated on the river Tvertsa, it was founded in the XII century. It is famous not only as the city-museum, but also as a resort for its mineral springs. The great Russian poet Alexander Pushkin used to visit Torzhok to see the nature and to enjoy the view of many churches and monasteries around the city.

YT: *What is so special about this city?*

NK: *Its nature. It has a very unique landscape and atmosphere. Once we wanted to go there with Alla but something stood in our way and we had to change our plans.*

YT: *Did Fira come to Moscow to visit you?*

NK: *All the time. Torzhok and Tver' are not that far from Moscow.*

YT: *Did she ever play piano or violin after her lessons when she was a teenager?*

NK: *Yes. She got her PhD in chemistry but she used to perform on the piano and violin from time to time in some of the concerts that were organized in their institute. She worked as an inorganic chemist but she loved music through her whole life.*

YT: *Did Fira have any family?*

NK: *She was never married.*

During his first years of study in Moscow Nikolai missed his home very much and was writing letters to the Ukraine asking his parents to come and visit him. This is the letter from Kapustin to his father Grigory Efimovich Kapustin written in Ukrainian language (ca. 1953-1954):

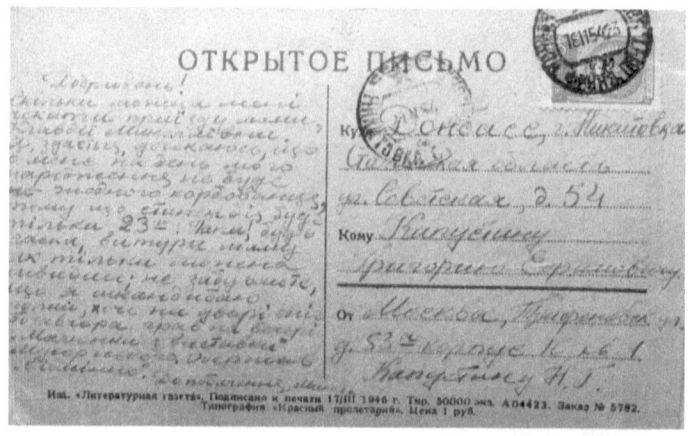

Good Day! How long should I wait for my mother, Klavdia Nikolayevna[51], *to visit? I think I will get to the point when I will have no money by the time of my birthday, because the stipend is coming only on the 23rd. Father, do me a favor – can you force mother to come here as soon as possible? Please, don't forget I am living here without any clothes, and it's snowing here already. A few days ago I played »Pictures at an Exhibition« of Mussorgsky. It was a successful performance, I got an »A.« Until I see you again, Mikola (Ukranian way of saying Nikolai).*[52]

---

[51] Note by the author: Kapustin referred to his mother with her middle name (Klavdia Nikolayevna), which was considered to be a sign of the biggest respect and adoration to his parents.

[52] The author's translation of this letter is unable to convey the inflections of the Ukrainian language in which it was written.

In spite of the fact that Nikolai missed his home immensely, he knew that the major goal of his new life was to study in the Musical College. This would make his parents proud. The very first thing in this study was performance on the piano. Generally, all the performances happened in the hall of the Musical College and only the best students were given the opportunity to perform in the Small Concert Hall of the Moscow Conservatory. Kapustin was one of those students.

Nikolai Kapustin, Small Concert Hall of the Moscow Conservatory, ca. 1955-1956

Recitals at the Musical College

Kapustin's first performance in the Small Concert Hall of the Moscow Conservatory happened on March 29, 1953 when Kapustin, being a student of the first course of Musical College, played Arensky's *Fantasia on Russian Folksongs*, Op. 48, accompanied by Rubbakh.

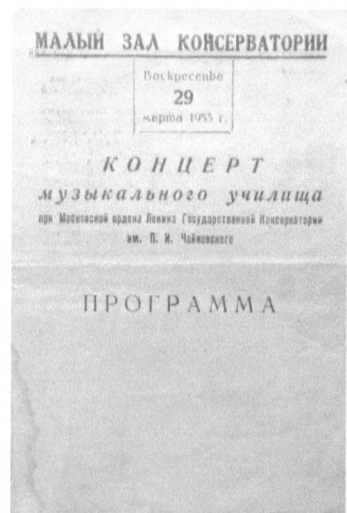 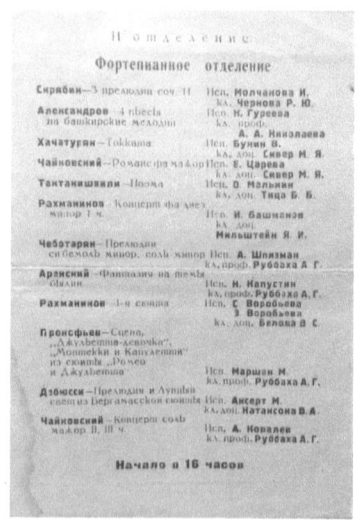

Concert Program: Students of Moscow Musical College, Small Concert Hall, Moscow Conservatory, March 29, 1953

NK: That was my very first performance in Moscow; I was fifteen years old.
YT: What did you feel that day knowing that your teacher is playing with you?
NK: I felt honored.

Being a student of Rubbakh, Kapustin studied a variety of different repertoire. Some of those pieces he would perform on the juries and some he would study for his own growth. One of those works was the Mozart's *Piano Concerto No. 25* in C major (K. 503).

NK: With Rubbakh I played just the first movement of Mozart's concerto. This was allowed in the Musical College. I played the complete concerto a few years later as a student of Goldenweiser in the Small Hall of the Conservatory. Goldenweiser preferred to play pieces in the length and form it was written. So, if you are playing a large work it should be performed in all movements.
YT: Do you remember other pieces that you played with Rubbakh for your growth?

NK: A few days ago I was listening Saint-Saens' Second Concerto in G minor (Op. 22), which reminded me that I studied this concerto with Rubbakh, also just the first movement.

On December 27, 1953, being a student of the second course of the Musical College, Nikolai Kapustin was selected to participate in the concert dedicated to the 60th Anniversary of the death of Piotr Iliyich Tchaikovsky. The concert took place in the Small Hall of the Moscow Conservatory. Kapustin played Tchaikovsky's *Russian Scherzo* from *Two Pieces for the Piano*, Op. 1.

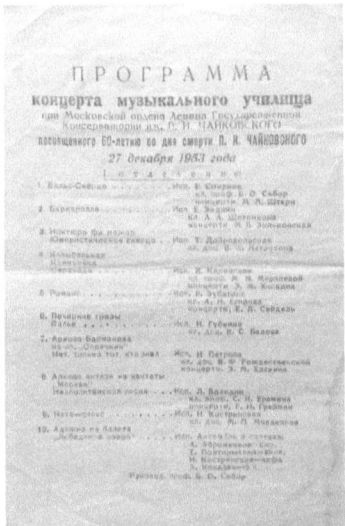 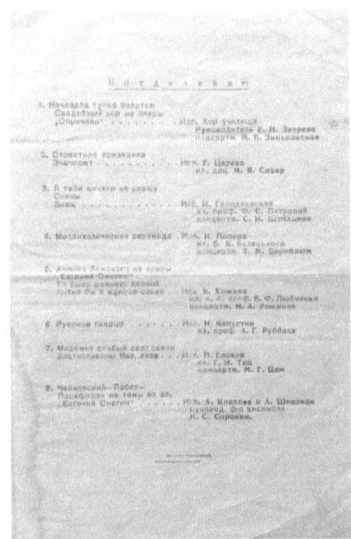

Concert Program: Concert of Students of Musical College, Small Concert Hall of the Moscow Conservatory, December 27, 1953

Only the best students of the Musical College had the honor to participate in such a significant event. These students were awarded travel to Tchaikovsky's House-Museum in Klin.[53]

NK: That trip to Klin happened right after the concert. Only the students who deserved it were brought to Klin. It was a very fun trip. We saw Tchaikovsky's house, walked through his rooms, saw his grand piano and the place where he used to work, and we also listened to his music.
YT: What a wonderful experience!

---

[53] Klin – city in Russia situated 50 miles northwest of Moscow. Tchaikovsky lived in the country house in Klin from 1892 until his death in 1893. This house is now a museum.

NK: Even more – later I played the Tchaikovsky Russian Scherzo live on the television program.

On May 3, 1955, being a student of the third course of Musical College, Kapustin played Prokofiev's Concerto No. 1, again accompanied by his teacher – Avrelian Rubbakh.

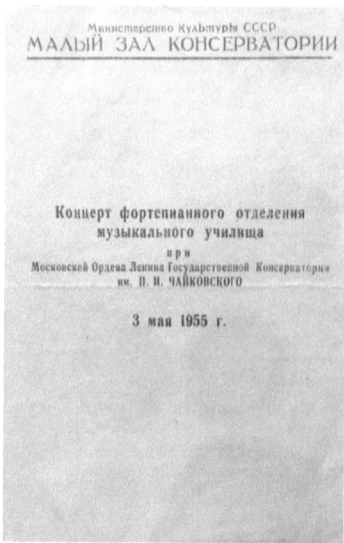 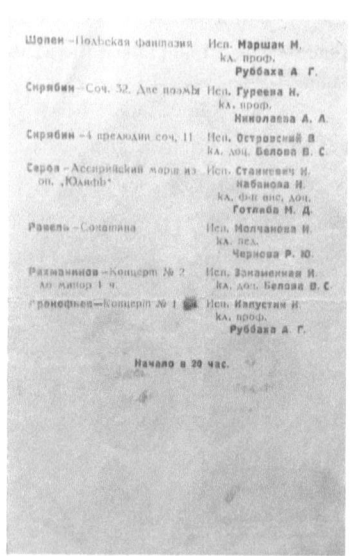

Concert Program: Concert of Piano Performance Majors of the Musical College, Small Concert Hall of Moscow Conservatory, May 3, 1955

NK: That was a big event. Rubbakh was thinking whether or not to give me this concerto. Before that I studied a few Prokofiev pieces with Rubbakh but never tried a large-scale piece.
YT: What was the reason of Rubbakh's hesitations?
NK: It is very difficult piece. Now pianists don't feel shame playing difficult pieces very poorly. Rubbakh wanted to be sure that I was ready for that work.
YT: Did you ask him to give you this piece or was that Rubbakh's decision?
NK: I asked Rubbakh to give it to me. In my opinion, the first concerto is Prokofiev's finest one out of all five. Prokofiev was just twenty-one years old when he wrote this piece, so young, but so brilliant.
YT: Wasn't that approximately your age when you played it?
NK: I was seventeen.
YT: How did the performance go?
NK: I think Rubbakh was happy about it.

In the winter of 1955, being a student of the fourth course of the Musical College, Kapustin again performed in the Small Concert Hall of the Moscow Conservatory. It was a very special concert since it was dedicated to his beloved teacher Avrelian Rubbakh, celebrating Rubbakh's sixtieth Jubilee and the forty years of his teaching career. In the first part of the concert, current students of Rubbakh played, and in the second half, his students from the past. One of the pieces that Kapustin performed on that concert is still considered to be one of the most difficult pieces ever written for solo piano – Liszt *Reminiscences de Don Juan* (S. 418).

> *YT: Was it your choice to play this piece or it was suggested by Rubbakh?*
> *NK: I begged him to give me that piece. During that last year in college I played »Don Juan« in the Small Hall, the Great Hall, and on the entering exams to the Conservatory.*

From Kapustin's letter to Kapustin's parents in the winter of 1955:

> Здравствуйте все !!
>
> В течение этого месяца со мной было порядочно приключений. С военкоматом я покончил только 20 февраля. Все в порядке: осенью – в армию. Недавно у Михалковых был вечер памяти Шаляпина. Был Козловский, и теперь я с ним хорошо знаком. Неделю назад мне довелось пить вино с Хачатуряном. Я даже играл ему свои сочинения, после чего он сказал, чтобы я поступал в консерваторию на композиторское отделение.
> Числа 16 приехал Сергей Владимирович (из Италии). Он подарил мне много вещей : итальянский мундштук, в который вкладываются стеклянные цилиндрики с антиникотином, две пачки антиникатина (не вата, а соль), итальянских и американских сигарет, спички, зажигающиеся обо все предметы, значок участников олимпийских игр, жевательную резинку.
> Костюм я еще не купил. Вчера играл в малом зале в старом костюме. Этот концерт был посвящен 60-летию со дня рождения Рубаха и 40-летию его педагогической деятельности. В первом отделении играли его настоящие ученики, во втором – бывшие. Я должен был заканчивать первое отделение, но вышло, что последней играла Женя, которая специально для этого пришла по-позже. Свинья !
> Я играл целые пол-часа - « Игру воды" Равеля и, конечно, « "Дон Жуана". Сыграл, как-будто, ничего: пять раз вызывали. Кроме этого я еще аккомпанировал Андрею концерт Хачатуряна. Так-что я торчал на сцене 45 минут! Скоро, может быть, пришлю фотографии (дело в том, что всех игравших снимали как из зала, так и со сцены. Со сцены, обычно, снимают больших мастеров, так-что это было немного анекдотично).
> Если и в этом письме Фира найдет ошибки, то оно явится ПОСЛЕДНИМ.
>
> Всего хорошего.
>   Главный наборщик – / Н. Капустин /.

Hello to all! During this past month I had enough adventure. I finished the story with the recruitment office just now on February 20th. So everything is alright – I am going to the army in autumn (it's a joke)… I did not buy the new suit yet. Yesterday I played in the Small Hall of the Conservatory wearing the old suit. The concert was dedicated to Rubbakh's sixtieth Jubilee and the forty years of his pedagogical career. The first part of the concert involved his current students' performance. The second part was his former students. I was supposed to finish the first part of the concert, but it ended up that Jenia (Evgeniya Pupkova) came late on purpose so she would end the first half. I played Ravel's Play of Water [Jeux d'eau] for a half hour and, of course, Don Juan [Liszt's Reminiscences de Don Juan]. It turned out to be okay. They asked me to come on stage to bow five times. In addition, I accompanied Andrei [Mikhalkov] in Khachaturian's Piano Concerto, so I was on stage for forty-five minutes! Soon, maybe, I will send you the pictures. The thing is - they were taking pictures from the hall and from the stage. Usually, only the »big« masters get pictures from the stage. So, it was a little comical. If Fira will find mistakes in this letter, then it will be the last one. All the best. Main typewriter, Nikolai Kapustin.[54]

---

[54] The letter translated by the author.

Andrei Mikhalkov and Nikolai Kapustin performing Khachaturian's Piano Concerto on Rubbakh's Jubilee, Small Concert Hall of the Moscow Conservatory, 1955

An interesting episode happened in the green room right before that concert started.

NK: As you know, the Small Hall of the Moscow Conservatory is a very serious place. Right before the concert started I began playing jazz in the green room.
YT: Why did you do that?
NK: To make the atmosphere less stressful.
YT: What was the reaction of the other students to your playing?
NK: Everybody was in shock – how can you allow yourself to play boogie-woogie, another definition of jazz, before that serious performance?
YT: That only means that you were absolutely ready for that performance.
NK: Yes, I wasn't stressed at all.
YT: I guess you were the only one.
NK: Maybe.

Teachers and Courses at the Musical College

Talking about teachers that Kapustin had a chance to study with in Musical College, it is important to mention pianist Maria Solomonovna Nemenova-Lunts, who was teaching an accompanying class.

Maria Nemenova-Lunts

Maria Solomonovna Nemenova-Lunts (1879-1954) was a student of Alexander Scriabin. In 1922 she graduated with the golden medal from Moscow Conservatory, and became a Professor of the Moscow Conservatory the same year, teaching private piano, chamber music, and accompanying class.[55] Also, Nemenova-Lunts was the author of the memoires of Scriabin.[56]

NK: It was pleasant to realize that she was a student of Alexander Scriabin.
YT: What kind of teacher was Nemenova-Lunts?
NK: She was a very kind teacher, and I liked her a lot. Although, she was quite old.

Kapustin studied in the class of Nemenova-Lunts, which was modeled upon the idea of accompanying a singer or instrumentalist. Her vision about the nature of the piano sound was similar to Scriabin's view, who was trying to find the appropriate sound for each and every note.

---

[55] Maria Nemenova-Lunts. Accessed February 13, 2018.
https://dic.academic.ru/dic.nsf/enc_music/5438/Неменова.
[56] Maria Nemenova-Lunts, »Memories about Alexander Scriabin«, *Muzikalnii sovremennik*, no. 4/5 (1916): 97-110.

Nemenova-Lunts:
The sound itself was the main concern for Scriabin. He asked us to play the same note over and over again trying to find for him the only known sound, and helping us to find it too.[57]

Nemenova-Lunts used to play quite often for her students, demonstrating and at the same time shocking them with her beautiful sound, brilliant technique, and the ability to »speak« through the music. Unfortunately, Nemenova-Lunts passed away in 1954 when Kapustin studied on the third course of Musical College. That's why Kapustin had to graduate accompanying in the class of Nathan Fisher.

Kapustin always felt his passion and interest in collective performance, which led him to the class of piano duets. This class was led at the beginning by Mikhail Gotlib and later by Konstantin Sorokin.

NK: Both Gotlib and Sorokin were students of Konstantin Igumnov.[58] *I remember we were playing Rachmaninov Russian Rhapsody with Gotlib.*
YT: How about Konstantin Sorokin?
NK: Like Rubbakh, Sorokin was also an editor and very good composer. He was also a great admirer of Ravel's music. I remember once we played Ravel's Spanish Rhapsody in the Great Concert Hall of Moscow Conservatory with Jenia (Evgeniya Pupkova).
YT: How did it go?
NK: We played well. Rubbakh invited Andrei Eshpai[59] *to this concert and Eshpai came up after our performance to congratulate us. Later, in the 1980s, we even met with him a few times. He asked me to record a CD of my Concerto for Alto-Saxophone and Orchestra (Op. 50) together with his Concerto for Soprano Saxophone and Orchestra. Unfortunately, the CD of these two concertos was not released until almost twenty-five years later (2002) in Japan.*

---

[57] Maria Nemenova-Lunts. Accessed November 9, 2017. http://aquarius-classic.ru/person?sid=129.
[58] Konstantin Nikolayevich Igumnov (1973-1948) was a celebrated pianist and a teacher. Igumnov studied under Nikolai Zverev, and at the Moscow Conservatory under Alexander Ziloti and Pavel Pabst. He took theory and composition courses from Sergei Taneyev, Anton Arensky, and Mikhail Ippolitov-Ivanov. From 1899 he was a Professor at the Moscow Conservatory. Among his students were: Lev Oborin, Maria Grinberg, and Rosa Tamarkina. Accessed February 13, 2018. http://www.mosconsv.ru/ru/person.aspx?id=121136.
[59] Andrei Yakovlevich Eshpai (1925-2015) was an ethnic Mari (Russian and Soviet) composer. He studied piano at the Moscow Conservatory under Vladimir Sofronitsky, composition under Nikolai Rakov and Nikolai Myaskovsky, and performed his postgraduate study under Aram Khachaturian. Among his works are symphonic, chamber, piano, and vocal music, as well as music written for Russian Soviet movies and theater. Accessed February 13, 2018. http://www.mosconsv.ru/ru/person.aspx?id=9012.

During the study in Musical College each student had to complete a specific set of subjects for each course.[60] The program of study was set up in a way that students did not have the right to choose subjects; it was completed by the musical institution. A wide range of different subjects, providing versatile growth and development of young musicians, was studied at the Musical College. They included private piano, chamber ensemble, accompanying, piano duet, folk art, orchestration, ear-training, musical literature, harmony, theory, form analysis, English language, Russian language, Russian literature, history, and more.

NK: In Musical College there were many more subjects than in the Conservatory. I ended up thinking that study in the Musical College would be enough for me. I had the opportunity to study with such a wonderful teacher – Avrelian Rubbakh. In general, all the teachers in Musical College were on a very high level.
YT: So you enjoyed study in the college.
NK: Very much. There was a very warm atmosphere; I had a lot of friends. It is easier to get friends when you are young.

Talking about Kapustin's classmates, there were around fifteen to seventeen students in the group who studied with him. Coming from different backgrounds, they all had one thing in common – the desire to study, to learn, and to be great performers.

YT: Were the students who studied with you generally from Moscow or from other cities?
NK: In general, they were students from Moscow but there were a few, like me for example, who came from the other cities. I remember that Slava Ovchinnikov was from Voronezh.[61]

The subject »Methods of Teaching Piano« was about different methods of teaching piano for young students and adults. The students of this class were also expected to take part in a teaching practicum.

YT: How did you study in that class?
NK: With this class I had serious issues.
YT: Why is that?
NK: I was professionally ill-equipped. I would have to teach the students there and it was the most painful for me.

---

[60] This system is functioning in all three steps of musical education in Russia – Music School, Musical College, and Conservatory.
[61] Voronezh is an administrative center of the Voronezh region of Russia which is situated on the banks of the Voronezh River. Voronezh is situated around 300 miles from Moscow.

In addition to the musical subjects, one of the general education subjects that Kapustin had to take was English language.

YT: Was that a surprise for you?

NK: Yes, it was a big surprise... again! As I told you, I studied French in the Ukraine as a foreign language. When I moved to Moscow it turned out that they taught only English.

YT: What did you do in this difficult situation?

NK: I started quickly to refresh my memory in the English language. I was pleasantly surprised – I had good knowledge even after having such a long break.

YT: Now, when all your education is over, which language do you prefer?

NK: For me even now it is easier to read in French, where one word is connected to the next, and in a way you are always going forward. English is more like Russian, slower language.

Based on test results, Kapustin was selected to the group of advanced students studying English.

YT: So, the years of English study was not in vain.

NK: Yes, the years of my self-study were quite productive.

Self-Education

Here in Moscow, as well as in Nikitovka, self-education became one of the major directions in Kapustin's musical study. He used to go weekly to the *Muzgiz* (Moscow Publishing House) to buy music scores.

NK: They knew me very well and reserved the newest music scores for me that were just published. Name me the piece I didn't have, I had everything.

In this post-war period it was very difficult to get the music scores. However, Nikolai was persistent in his desire to achieve his goals.

NK: Starting from the time when I lived in the Ukraine I used to order scores in Moscow. They sent it to me by mail. I tried to get the scores by any means possible. I remember the neighbor of Lubov' Borisovna (Frantsuzova) was a famous pianist. He passed away and his relatives started to sell his music scores. That day I chose a lot of music, and my parents paid it all off.

Kapustin's training in the Musical College was at a very high level, which gave him a strong background for composing music on his own. He educated himself. Kapustin used to spend hours in the library studying the scores of different composers.

NK: I remember I studied all thirty-two Beethoven's sonatas, five concertos, all on my own. I went through tons of literature.
YT: Did you study the scores of famous composers only during the years at the college?
NK: I studied the scores through my whole life. I remember I studied a lot of Bach's music, Bartok, Prokofiev, Britten, many other composers too.

In addition, Kapustin used to learn to play the piano music in order to see how these pieces were put together.

NK: I played a lot of Rachmaninov's music – for example, Etude-tableau in Eb minor (Op. 39 No. 5) and Piano Concerto No. 4 in G minor (Op. 40), one of my favorite pieces. All these I learned by myself; that's how I studied as a composer. I didn't show this to Rubbakh or Goldenweiser – that was specifically for me.

It is always interesting to see the development of the compositional style of a particular composer: which music he is listening to, which composers he likes or dislikes, and why.

YT: Did you hear about the music of Shostakovich, Prokofiev, and Stravinsky at that time?

NK: *I heard but my classmates did not.*
YT: *What was the attitude towards Shostakovich?*
NK: *Back then as well as now the attitude is not too positive.*
YT: *What do you mean by saying »not too positive«? Is this attitude from the government side or from the musical society in Moscow?*
NK: *No, from my side. My music is absolutely different from what Shostakovich had composed.*
YT: *How about the attitude from the musical society of that time towards Shostakovich? Was it positive or not?*
NK: *More than positive, but this doesn't relate to me. Actually, I studied in the Conservatory with his son – Maxim Shostakovich. He was also a pianist but ended up becoming a conductor.*
YT: *Did you talk with Maxim about his father?*
NK: *It sounds strange, but for some reason we never talked about him.*
YT: *Did you happen to have favorite composers when you studied in the college?*
NK: *Yes. My first big time favorite composer was Sergei Prokofiev. The second one was Ravel, and the third one was Bartok. The last two were already in the Conservatory.*
YT: *Why Prokofiev?*
NK: *I got this love from my teacher – Rubbakh. The thing is that Rubbakh knew Prokofiev, they were friends, and Rubbakh wanted to introduce me as his admirer, but Prokofiev died so unexpectedly in March 1953.*
YT: *This is something really fascinating – to meet with Prokofiev.*
NK: *Although, Prokofiev had a very difficult character.*
YT: *I heard that he was very ill at the end.*
NK: *Yes, this looks strange to me. He was a man of the sport type, and for some reason he started to have issues with his heart. He died so young – he was just sixty-two years old.*

A strange coincidence happened on the day of Prokofiev's death. On the same day, March 5, 1953, the leader of Soviet Union, the »father« of the nation, Joseph Stalin died of a massive heart attack. The whole country was plunged into suffering and mourning. This caused enormous difficulties in the organization of Prokofiev's funeral.

YT: *Did you know about Prokofiev's death?*
NK: *Nobody knew. Of course, his close friends and family knew, but we all found out about it later. We loved Prokofiev very much and were dumbfounded by this shocking news. It is a shame but there were just a very few people at his funeral.*
YT: *Yes. It is quite interesting that he returned to Russia right before WWII, a very difficult time for the country. Despite this he composed a great amount of significant*

music – Symphony No. 5, String Quartet No. 2, Flute Sonata in D, Piano Sonatas No. 7 and 8, and much more.

NK: *People don't understand that it doesn't matter where you are living. If he did not return he would continue writing genius music. If you have it inside of you it's there.*

Composition

After Kapustin's first piece *Sonata* that he composed in 1950 in Nikitovka Kapustin continued composing intensively during all years of study in the Musical College and the Moscow Conservatory. The years of study at the Musical College were a period of observing and perceiving the jazz style. Kapustin used to listen to and transcribe jazz especially when he lived in the Mikhalkov house. This music would gradually become a part of Kapustin's musical language.

YT: Based on what is officially known, you composed the first piece in 1950 and the next one, which is Op. 1, in 1957. Is that true?

NK: Surely not. I was composing all this time in between the 1950 and 1957. My opus 1 is written for the big band (Concertino for Piano and Orchestra, Op. 1) but that was not the first piece I wrote for the big band. There were a few before that opus.

YT: Where are they?

NK: I considered them as exercises, so I didn't give them the opus numbers.

YT: Are they preserved somewhere in your archives?

NK: Unfortunately, not all.

During the years of study at the Musical College Kapustin continued composing solo piano music. He wrote *Sonatina* (1954), *Romance in F major* (1954), *Polka-Rondo* (1955) and *Czech Rhapsody* for two pianos (1956).

In 1954 Kapustin composed a piece called *Sonatina*. It was a work in three movements (fast/slow/fast).[62] Rubbakh, being the biggest supporter of Kapustin's talent as a composer, decided to publish *Sonatina*. Coincidently, in the qualifying committee for publishing the scores were people who would play an important role in Kapustin's life: Alexander Goldenweiser and Tatiana Nikolaeva. Unfortunately, their decision was quite a disappointment for Kapustin. The committee suggested publishing only the last movement of the *Sonatina* – Finale.

NK: And I said – all or nothing at all.

Now, more than sixty years later, Kapustin still believes that it was right decision, although, he noted once,

NK: If I would publish any of my works earlier, I would be like Shostakovich, who published his first piece at the age of thirteen.[63]

---

[62] Note by the author: The full copy of the original score was archived in Rubbakh's house.
[63] Shostakovich Op. 1: Scherzo in F-sharp minor for Orchestra (1919).

YT: Do you have any sketches left in your home?

NK: Unfortunately, the score of this Sonatina was lost. I know for sure that Rubbakh had the original score of this Sonatina at his home, but who knows where it is now. You have no idea how much pain I feel every time I think about this work. The only thing that survived is the section of the Sonatina that was intended to be the slow movement called Romance. Rubbakh didn't like it, as well as me, by the way, so I didn't use this material. How ironic is it that this is the only material I have left!

Romance in F major, Moscow, 1954

YT: I like the harmonies in that piece and the way the music moves from one tonality to another. It reminds me about the music of Arno Babadjanian.

NK: Yes, I love his harmonies too. Although, I went much further than Babadjanian in my harmonic approach.

YT: Yes, in your next piece Polka-Rondo (1955) I see a more complex harmonic plan, modulations to distant keys. In other words, very intense harmonic language but still I don't hear the jazz yet.

NK: It was not the time for jazz, very close but not there yet.

Polka-Rondo, 1955

YT: *This desire to write beautiful harmonies was with you from the very beginning, even before the jazz influence.*
NK: *Yes, harmonic language was always something that I liked to explore.*
YT: *And another thing that you had from the very beginning was your desire to play fast.*
NK: *Not always but to some extent yes, I like the technical approach in my works.*
YT: *So, it looks like even after sixty-five years of composing music, those two aspects, harmonic language and technique, are still the main elements of your style.*
NK: *Yes, it is.*

The last piece that Kapustin composed in Musical College was *Czech Rhapsody* for two pianos (1956).

 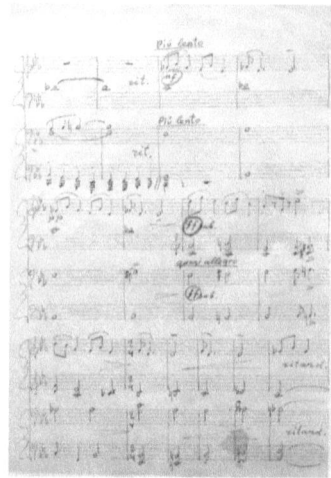

Czech Rhapsody for two pianos, 1956

YT: I keep thinking – why did you decide to call this piece Czech Rhapsody but not Hungarian or Ukrainian Rhapsody for example?
NK: At that time I was listening to a lot of jazz music, and Czech jazz was no exception.
YT: So, in a way it was a gesture of the respect to jazz culture in the Czech Republic?
NK: In a way yes, plus we were always friends with the Czech Republic.
YT: I noticed that the first piano has jazz chords in the left hand.
NK: Yes, this piece has a lot of jazz chords.
YT: Can we say that the Czech Rhapsody was your turning point – the piece that signified the beginning of your jazz musical language?
NK: Yes, it was the first piece where I started to use a jazz approach to composition. Just remember – that transition from classical to jazz language happened gradually and this piece stands right in that period of change.
YT: So, in other words, it has both classical and jazz elements.
NK: Correct. I remember we even performed Czech Rhapsody with Andrei (Mikhalkov-Konchalovsky) in Mikhalkov's house for Khachaturian. Khachaturian didn't like those jazz harmonies. It was too much for him.
YT: Yes, but Khachaturian wasn't a jazz composer.
NK: No, he wasn't.
YT: I noticed also that the second piano part was easier than the first part. Did you do it on purpose – to make Andrei's life less stressful?
NK: No, I didn't intend this. I guess it just happened that way.

New Friends of Nikolai Kapustin

On November 22, 1953, studying on the second course of the Musical College, Nikolai Kapustin celebrated his 16th birthday. Unexpectedly, his friends, the students from Rubbakh's class, prepared a surprise for him.

NK: Rubbakh organized a surprise party to celebrate my birthday. They even sang a song for me.

The song was well rehearsed and performed with the Isaac Katz[64] accompanying. There were several verses and the main material was taken from the famous Soviet song »Nasha sila v dele pravom« (Our Strength in Our Right). The original lyrics of this song were written by Sergei Mikhalkov but were rewritten by students in honor of Kolia Kapustin.

NK: The song began with these words: »Kolia got his sixteen years, all the adults and children are happy.«
YT: Was Katz also a student of Rubbakh?
NK: Yes, he even lived in Rubbakh's house for a while. At that time, in 1953, he was working as an assistant to Rubbakh in the Musical College. When I graduated Musical College in 1956 he graduated from the Moscow Conservatory. Actually, he also studied with Goldenweiser. After graduation Katz moved immediately to Nizhny Novgorod to teach at the conservatory there.
YT: That's where I graduated from.
NK: I know.
YT: Did you ever meet with Katz after that?
NK: Ohhh, sure. I met with him a few times. First, we met when I was on tour with the Lundstrem Big Band in Nizhny Novgorod. I think even Alla (Kapustina) accompanied me at that time. I was telling them my jokes, some with »bad« Russian language. Katz said: »Kolia, please, don't be shy, tell us everything you have.«
YT: When was that?
NK: At the beginning of 1960s, right after my graduation from conservatory.
YT: Did Alla Semionovna go on tour with you often?

---

[64] Isaac Iosifovich Katz (1922-2009) was a Russian/Israeli pianist and teacher. He graduated from Moscow Conservatory (class of Alexander Goldenweiser) in 1946, and during 1954-1990 was the chairman of the piano faculty in Nizhny Novgorod Conservatory. Some of his influential students, Professor Ekaterina Flerova and Professor Galina Blagovidova, are currently teaching at Nizhny Novgorod Conservatory, continuing the tradition of Moscow school of playing. Accessed November 8, 2017. http://nnovcons.ru/obrazovanie/fakultety/fortepiannyy-fakultet/, http://famous-birthdays.ru/data/22_sentyabrya/katz_isaak_iosifovich.html.

NK: Very often, especially at the beginning. Then, when she got a job teaching German she stopped travelling with us.
YT: How was that meeting with Katz?
NK: Very fun, we were friends. The last time we met accidently in Moscow on the Seventh Tchaikovsky International Competition in the 1980s. I came to listen to Vladimir Ovchinnikov,[65] who also graduated from Moscow Conservatory. It turned out that Ovchinnikov shared the second place with Peter Donohoe, and the first place was not given to anyone. Nobody knew Ovchinnikov before that competition. That's how his name appeared on the international musical stage.

From the moment Kapustin began to study in Musical College a new life opened its doors towards the future achievements, success, and new flow of life for Nikolai.

YT: Was it difficult for you to adapt yourself to a new condition of life?
NK: I was expecting it. Yes, everything was different in Moscow, but I liked that difference.

From the autumn of 1952 Nikolai began to live in the dormitory of the Musical College. This building had four floors and was quite old, but it had a serious advantage – it had instruments.

NK: Each room where the students lived had an instrument. Also, there was a rehearsal hall on the last floor where there were grand pianos.
YT: I can't believe – grand pianos in the dormitory!
NK: At any time, no matter if it is early morning or late at night, we always had a chance to practice there. Of course, the condition of those instruments was very poor, but it still helped. If you would be willing to practice on the better instruments then you might try going to the Musical College, but there you would have a chance of not finding a practice room. So, it was all up to you. Also I remember we used to go to the Gnessin Institute to use their practice rooms. These schools were situated close to each other.
YT: In other words, each student used all his possible opportunities in practicing the piano.
NK: Absolutely. It was a normal flow of life.

---

[65] Vladimir Pavlovich Ovchinnikov (born 1958) is a Russian pianist, graduated from the Moscow Conservatory in 1981 (class of Aleksey Nasedkin). He won International VII Tchaikovsky Competition (Russia, 1982) and Leeds International Piano Competition (England, 1987). Accessed February 13, 2018. http://www.mosconsv.ru/ru/person.aspx?id=31514.

Nikolai lived in a room of the dormitory with other students.

YT: How many people lived with you in the same room? Somewhere like four or three?
NK: I would consider this as happiness.
YT: Really? Happiness is to have four people in the room?
NK (laughing): We had seven.
YT: This is like in the army!
NK: We got used to it. I actually liked it. That was a fun life; I had many friends.

In the 1950s, as well as now, students in Russia used to have a monthly stipend based on their grades. Kapustin had the highest grades during all four years of his study in Musical College, so he always received the top stipend.

YT: Was it possible to live on your stipend?
NK: Oh no, of course it was impossible to live on that stipend. Although later, when I moved to Mikhalkov's house, it was absolutely enough. I had great accommodations in their house, tasty food, and everything you would need. We used to go often with the Mikhalkov family to Sergei Mikhalkov's favorite restaurant - »VTO« (»Russian Art Society« restaurant).

Life at the Mikhalkov House

That new turn of Kapustin's life happened in spring of 1954 when Nikolai studied on the second course of the Musical College. Andrei Mikhalkov,[66] who was also a student of Rubbakh, had become a close friend to Nikolai.

NK: Andrei entered the college as a student of Chernov but within a few months transferred to Rubbakh.

One day Andrei came to visit Nikolai in his dormitory. Here's where the new story began.

NK: Andrei was completely shocked about the conditions of life in the dormitory. He promised that he was going to talk to his parents to see if they would allow me to live for a while in their house.
YT: How did the conversation go?
NK: Andrei talked to Sergei Vladimirovich (Mikhalkov) and he allowed me to stay. Even more, all those years that I lived in Mikhalkov's house they treated me very well, like I was their adopted son.

That is how Kapustin's life dramatically changed to something fascinating, something unexpectedly great and memorable. Mikhalkov's family was a part of Kapustin's life for just a few years, but the memory of these people has stayed with him even now.

---

[66] Andrei Mikhalkov-Konchalovsky (b. 1937) is a famous Russian-American film director, film producer and screenwriter. His first full-length feature »The First Teacher« (1964) was favorably received in the Soviet Union and screened by numerous film festivals abroad. His most popular Hollywood releases are »Maria's Lovers« (1984), »Runaway Train« (1985), and »Tango & Cash« (1989), starring Sylvester Stallone and Kurt Russell. In the 1990s he produced »The Odyssey« (1997) and the award-winning remake »The Lion in Winter« (2003). Accessed November 9, 2017. http://konchalovsky.ru/life/biography.

Natalia Konchalovskaya and Sergei Mikhalkov

Andrei was a son of the famous Russian poet and writer Sergei Mikhalkov.[67] Due to his profession Sergei Mikhalkov used to travel abroad from time to time. Kapustin mentioned Sergei Mikhalkov's trip to Italy in one of his letters to his parents in 1955:

> On the 16*th* (of March) Sergei Vladimirovich [father of Andrei Mikhalkov] came back from his trip to Italy. He presented me with many different things: Italian mouthpiece cigarette holder to which you can insert glass cylinders with the anti-nicotine (filters), two

---

[67] Sergey Vladimirovich Mikhalkov (1913-2009) was a Soviet and Russian poet and writer. In 1942, at the time when the country was deeply embroiled in World War II, Joseph Stalin commissioned Mikhalkov to write lyrics for a new National Anthem of the Soviet Union to emphasize the Russian theme for the national anthem instead of the international one (music was composed by Alexander Alexandrov). The new anthem was introduced to the country on January 1, 1944 and continued until 1991, when it was retired by President Boris Yeltsin after the USSR disintegration. However, when Vladimir Putin took over from Yeltsin in 2000, Putin pushed to restore the music of old anthem with the new lyrics written by Sergei Mikhalkov. The result was the National Anthem of Russia, which was officially adopted in 2001. Apart from the national anthem, Mikhalkov produced a great number of satirical plays and provided scripts for several Soviet comedies. He was also the author of numerous children books. On Mikhalkov's 90th birthday in 2003, Putin personally visited him at his home to present him with the 2nd class Order for Service to Fatherland for his contributions to culture of Russia. Accessed November 9, 2017. https://bigenc.ru/literature/text/2219410.

packages of the anti-nicotine (not cotton but salt – higher quality),[68] *Italian and American cigarettes, matches that light up from any object, a badge from the Olympic games, and chewing gum.*

YT: *This is interesting – you described everything Mikhalkov brought to you from abroad in such a detail in your letter.*
NK: *Do you think people in Russia knew about Italian cigarettes or chewing gum in the middle 1950s?*
YT: *Of course not! I see what you are saying – it all was very special for you.*
NK: *Of course. This family was far ahead of time.*

The heart of Mikhalkov's family was the mother – Natalia Petrovna Konchalovskaya.[69] One of the fascinating facts about Natalia Konchalovskaya is that she was the granddaughter of one of the most famous Russian painters – Vasily Surikov.[70] Her father, Piotr Petrovich Konchalovsky[71] was also a noted Moscow painter.

NK: *Piotr Petrovich (Konchalovsky) used to visit Mikhalkov's family from time to time. They lived very close, within walking distance. Piotr Petrovich loved to listen to Bach's music. I remember once Rubbakh asked his students to come to Konchalovsky's house to play Bach's works for him. There were four or five of us on that performance. Please, don't ask what piece I played because I don't remember, probably something from the Well-Tempered Clavier.*
YT: *Rubbakh was quite a figure!*
NK: *Yes. It also worked very well for us because it was like an additional performance before the juries. It worked for both sides.*
YT: *What do you remember about Natalia Konchalovskaya?*

---

[68] Note by the author: In Russia in the 1950s people smoked Russian cigarettes with no filter. The cigarette holder and filters represented a new generation of cigarettes that were not available in Russia at that time.
[69] Natalia Petrovna Konchalovskaya (1903-1988) was a notable children's writer, poet, and translator. Accessed November 9, 2017. https://www.pravda.ru/culture/culturalhistory/personality/24-01-2003/35059-konchalovskaja-0/.
[70] Vasily Ivanovich Surikov (1848-1916), the foremost Russian painter of large-scale historical subjects. His major pieces are among the best-known paintings in Russia. Some of them are: Morning of Streltsy's Execution (1881), Boyarynya Morozova (1887), Menshikov in Berezov (1883), and Conquest of Siberia by Yermak (1895).
Accessed November 9, 2017. http://artsurikov.ru/.
[71] Piotr Petrovich Konchalovsky (1876-1956) was a Russian painter. During the sixty years of creative work he completed nearly two thousand paintings. Accessed November 9, 2017. http://www.artcyclopedia.ru/konchalovskij_petr_petrovich.htm.

NK: She was a notable children's writer. She even wrote poetry for young children based on the alphabet.

YT: It seems she was a well-educated person.

NK: Oh yes. I remember she translated Auber's opera »Fra Diavolo« from the French language to Russian.

YT: What was the character of Natalia Konchalovskaya? What kind of person was she?

NK: She was quite a capricious person but always had a very good attitude towards me. I remember once I broke a mirror in the hallway. As you know, it is a bad sign to break mirrors. I thought to myself – just wait; now she goes… but she kept silent, like it was nothing special, like nothing happened. That was her upbringing.

That's how, starting from the spring of 1954 until 1956, Kapustin lived in the house that was situated on the Vosstaniya Square, the center of Moscow. Even more, the house was within walking distance to the Musical College, while the dormitory was situated very far from the music building.

NK: We kept going back and forth all the time. It was very convenient.

The house was very big, with numerous rooms, and Andrei and Nikolai had their own room. These friends became so close that they used to go everywhere together.

YT: You were like two brothers, weren't you?

NK: Exactly. He was just three months older than me. I remember on one of my birthdays Andrei presented the score of Ravel's Piano Concerto for the Left Hand to me. It was very difficult to find new music scores at that time. Not only did I love the music of Ravel but I would later play that concerto at the conservatory.[72]

YT: So, Andrei's present came in handy.

NK: Yes, also this was the time when I got acquainted with Nikita (Mikhalkov),[73] Adrei's younger brother. We were like fifteen years old and Nikita was something around seven or eight.

YT: Did Mikhalkov's family have an instrument at home?

---

[72] Note by the author: Kapustin would play Ravel's *Piano Concerto for the Left Hand* at the jury during his first year of study at the conservatory.

[73] Nikita Mikhalkov (born 1945) is a Russian film-maker, actor, and the head of the Russian Cinematographers' Union. Mikhalkov established an international reputation with his »A Slave of Love« (1976), »An Unfinished Piece for Player Piano« (1977), »Station for Two« (1980), and »A Cruel Romance« (1984). Mikhalkov's most famous production to date, »Burnt by the Sun« (1994), received Grand Prize at Cannes Film Festival (1994) and the Academy Award for Best Foreign Language Film (1995). The most epic venture to date is his film »The Barber of Siberia« (1998). In 2007 Mikhalkov directed and starred in »12«, which was nominated for Best Foreign Language Film for the 80th Academy Award. Accessed November 9, 2017. https://24smi.org/celebrity/287-nikita-mikhalkov.html.

NK: Yes, they actually had three grand pianos – two in their house in Moscow and one in their summer house in the Moscow suburb.

YT: Two grand pianos in the house? That sounds very rare to me.

NK: Yes, one instrument was a new Bluthner, which was in the living room. They used it only for special occasions, for example when guests were in the house. The other instrument was in our room and we used it for practice all the time.

YT: This is very convenient – to practice at home.

NK: Yes. Although, sometimes we needed to practice at the same time, so I used to go to the dormitory to play piano. Of course it was more pleasant to practice in the Musical College but I didn't want to take a chance and end up waiting for the practice room.

Acquaintance with Jazz

Something new happened in Kapustin's life when he moved into Mikhalkov's house. It was the long nights of listening to the radio programs of the »Voice of America.«

> NK: *It was possible to listen to »Voice of America« only late at night. During the day the radio waves were blocked out and it was very difficult to hear anything. Andrei used to listen to the radio every night, during the whole night, and didn't give me the chance to sleep. That's how I became a part of this whole thing.*
>
> YT: *How about Andrei's parents? Did they know that you were listening to »Voice of America« at night?*
>
> NK: *I am not sure if they ever heard it. Mikhalkov had a very big house; I suspect that they heard nothing.*
>
> YT: *So, you listened to it secretly.*
>
> NK: *Yes.*
>
> YT: *Is it possible that, had you not come to live in Mikhalkov's house, you may not have gotten acquainted with jazz?*
>
> NK: *I wouldn't be that dramatic, I would probably hear it sometime later. Although, I have to tell you, that first impression of jazz music in Mikhalkov house was very strong and made a huge impact on me.*
>
> YT: *Were any of your friends from Musical College interested in jazz?*
>
> NK: *Yes, many of my friends were listening to jazz music, it was a modern trend.*

The truth is, Kapustin got involved in jazz music not by choice, but ended up dedicating his entire life to a close relationship with jazz music. In the 1950s jazz was prohibited and not accepted by the official musical directives of USSR culture. At that time, the predominance in music was given to the nationalistic regime of the Soviet Union. That may be one of the reasons why jazz attracted the attention of so many young hearts who were searching for something new and fresh; something that was not dictated by the central authority of the country.

> YT: *Isn't it true that it was dangerous to listen to jazz, for example programs of the »Voice of America«? I remember there was a very well-known Russian saying – »Today you are playing jazz and tomorrow you will be a traitor of your Motherland.«*
>
> NK: *Yes, it was a difficult situation. We had to listen to jazz. Without listening there would be no musicians. For me, if the musician doesn't understand jazz in detail he is not a jazz musician.*
>
> YT: *Which performers did you listen to on the »Voice of America«?*

> NK: Most of the music that we listened to was traditional jazz. I remember there was a lot of big band music, such as the Duke Ellington Orchestra, the Count Basie Orchestra, the Glenn Miller Orchestra, the Benny Goodman Orchestra, and many others. Concerning the individual instrumentalists, I can recall Erroll Garner, Oscar Peterson, Ornette Coleman, Billy Taylor, and Lenny Tristano.
> YT: Was it only music or were there additional programs?
> NK: Most of the programs were hosted by Conover, but I remember that sometimes the famous jazzmen would also lead the programs. It could be Louis Armstrong, Count Basie, or possibly others. It was so fascinating to hear their voices and listen to what they were saying.
> YT: How did you study these recordings? Just by listening?
> NK: Oh, no. We used to record these performances on the magnetic tape, listened to them many times, and transcribed the music so it would be possible to see what they played.
> YT: So, you transcribed all these recordings?
> NK: Yes, I did.

At the beginning of 1950s it was very rare to have the magnetic tape recorder at home. This kind of the equipment would become more widespread in Russia much later, in the late 1960s-beginning of 1970s.

> YT: Is it true that the tape recorder was a rare thing during that time even in Moscow?
> NK: Yes, that was a unique thing. That tape recorder was a big help for us.

In addition to listening to the jazz programs on the »Voice of America« Kapustin tried to get the jazz vinyl records by any means possible.

> NK: Our friends used to go to Europe and we would ask them to bring jazz recordings. I remember Sergei Mikhalkov was in Italy once and he bought jazz vinyl records for us. He wasn't very experienced in jazz. That's why, for some reason, he bought recordings of the Stan Kenton Big Band, which was very popular at that time, and also Frankie Laine, who was not even a jazz artist. Originally, Laine was a classical tenor, who later attempted singing jazz.
> YT: Did you transcribe Stan Kenton?
> NK: Surely, I did.

Starting from the middle 1950s Kapustin was not only transcribing jazz but also began to perform jazz.

> NK: As a jazz pianist I didn't perform a lot. I learned how to play jazz deliberately for myself. Of course, I played a lot of jazz music in the Lundstrem Big Band later in the 1960s; I transcribed so much music for them and we played it all.

Music in Mikhalkov's House

In the 1950s, as well as probably even now, Mikhalkov's house was one of the main centers of cultural and musical life in Moscow. The »brightest colors« of Russian arts circles were invited to come to their house. Some of those acquaintances made important contributions to the life of all those who attended those evenings.

YT: *Who did Mikhalkov invite to their house?*
NK: *I remember Ivan Kozlovsky[74] came once.*
YT: *Ivan Kozlovsky?!?*
NK: *Yes. There was an evening dedicated to Feodor Chaliapin.[75] Kozlovsky was there and I even played for him. Kozlovsky said: »Kolia (Nikolai), can you play for us something catchy?« I played something in a jazz style and they were dancing.*
YT: *Did you meet Kozlovsky after that evening in Mokhalkov's house?*
NK: *Yes, at the beginning of 1990s I attended Nikolai Petrov's concert and Kolia (Nikolai Petrov) said that Kozlovsky was in the audience and that he would like to meet with me. I was surprised that after all these years he (Kozlovsky) remembered me. It was very pleasant to see him, but at that time he was very old.*

A life-changing meeting happened with Kapustin when he was living in Mikhalkov's house. On one of the evenings in 1956 Kapustin became acquainted with Oleg Lundstrem.[76] Lundstrem would become an important figure in Kapustin's career as a composer and a jazz musician in the 1960s.

---

[74] Ivan Semyonovich Kozlovsky (1900-1993) was a Ukrainian lyric tenor and one of the most well-known performers of Soviet Opera. Kozlovsky was one of the leading tenors at the Bolshoi Theatre in Moscow (1926-1954). He sang over fifty operas as the leading tenor at the Bolshoi Theatre and was especially famous for his role as Vladimir Lensky in Tchaikovsky's opera »Eugene Onegin«, Berendey in Rimsky-Korsakov's opera »The Snow Maiden«, and Levko in another Rimsky-Korsakov's opera »May Night«. In 1940 Kozlovsky was awarded the prestigious designation of People's Artist of the USSR. Kozlovsky was well-known as a favorite singer of Joseph Stalin, but he was never allowed to leave the border of the USSR. Kozlovsky gave many concerts throughout the Soviet Union, singing Russian and Ukrainian songs and romances. Accessed February 13, 2018. http://www.belcanto.ru/kozlovsky.html.

[75] Fiodor Chaliapin (1873-1938) was a famous Russian opera singer whose career began at the St. Petersburg Imperial Opera in 1894 and continued at the Mamontov Private Opera between 1896 and 1899. He sang at the Bolshoi Theatre in Moscow from 1899 until 1914, and in 1901 began touring in the West, making sensational performances at La Scala, the Metropolitan Opera, and elsewhere. Accessed February 13, 2018. http://www.aif.ru/culture/person/fedor_shalyapin_maloizvestnye_fakty_i_vehi_tvorchestva.

[76] Oleg Leonidovich Lundstrem (1916-2005) was a Soviet composer, the leader and the conductor of the Oleg Lundstrem Orchestra, one of the earliest officially recognized jazz bands in the Soviet Union. Lundstrem received numerous honors and awards, some of them are: Honored Artist of the RSFSR (1973), People's Artist of the RSFSR (1984), State Prize of the Russian

YT: How did you happen to meet Lundstrem?

NK: He brought some of his big band recordings and we listened to them. This was a Soviet jazz sound, not American.

YT: What would be the difference between Soviet and American jazz?

NK: Soviet jazz is quite far away from the American jazz.

YT: In what sense – professionally or stylistically?

NK: Stylistically.

YT: So, in Russian jazz you can hear the influence of Soviet music. Is that right?

NK: Something like that. Russian jazz sounds rudimentary, not as well developed to my ear.

YT: Did someone introduce you to Lundstrem?

NK: I don't think, although later he remembered me and took me as a jazz pianist to play in his big band.

Another significant meeting for Kapustin in Mikhalkov's house was his acquaintance with Aram Khachaturian.[77]

NK: I knew Khachaturian very well. He was invited to Mikhalkov's home. Andrei (Mikhalkov) and I performed my composition Czech Rhapsody for two pianos that day.

YT: Did Khachaturian enjoy your music?

NK: He liked it but said there were too many »spicy« harmonies for his taste.

YT: What did he mean by that?

NK: The Czech Rhapsody I composed at the end of my study in Musical College, so it was already a jazz piece with jazz harmonies. That's why it was too much for Khachaturian.

YT: From what I remember – you didn't assign an opus number for this Czech Rhapsody, correct?

Federation (1998), and the 3rd Class Order of Merit for the Fatherland. Conversation about the Lundstrem Orchestra will be presented in the Chapter III.

[77] Aram Il'yich Khachaturian (1903-1978) was a Soviet Armenian composer and conductor. He is considered to be as one of the leading composers of the Soviet period. Raised in Tbilisi (capital of Georgia), Khachaturian moved to Moscow in 1921. He studied in the Gnessin Institute and then at the Moscow Conservatory (class of Nikolai Myaskovsky). Khachaturian's first major work, the Piano Concerto (1936), popularized his name within and outside the Soviet Union. In 1944 he wrote the Anthem of the Armenian SSR. In 1948 Khachaturian, along with Sergei Prokofiev and Dmitry Shostakovich, was officially denounced as a »formalist« and his music dubbed as »anti-people« music. From 1951 he taught at the Gnessin Institute and the Moscow Conservatory. Khachaturian is the best known for his ballet music »Gayane« (1942) and »Spartacus« (1954). His most popular piece, the »Sabre Dance« from »Gayane«, has been used extensively in popular culture and has been covered by a number of musicians' worldwide. He travelled to Europe, Latin America, and the United States with concerts of his own works. Khachaturian was the most renowned Armenian composer of 20th century. Accessed February 13, 2018. http://www.mosconsv.ru/ru/person.aspx?id=45795.

NK: This is true. I didn't assign the opus number for this piece, since it was composed during my study in Musical College.
YT: Did Khachaturian talk about his own music?
NK: Yes. He said he doesn't like when people are constantly performing his Sabre Dance and whistling at the same time. He then imitated that kind of performance for us. We were laughing. Khachaturian, as well as Prokofiev, had a special sense of humor. They liked to joke with their friends, but only with close people, not everyone.

Another famous person, who used to visit Mikhakov's house in the middle 1950s, was an Armenian composer and a pianist Arno Babajanian.[78]

YT: Did you get acquainted with Babajanian on one of those evenings?
NK: No, that day he just came to visit Sergei Vladimirovich (Mikhalkov). I remember he sat at the grand piano and started to play a few notes. He was a brilliant pianist.
YT: What happened next?
NK: He came to our room just to say hello. At that time I had already played his Heroic Ballad. I loved his music so much, especially his harmonies.
YT: Did you tell him that you were impressed by his Heroic Ballad?
NK: No, I didn't.

Many eminent people from different areas of Russian culture used to visit the house of Sergei Mikhalkov. Once Kapustin played Mussorgsky's *Pictures at an Exhibition* for a very well-known Russian movie director – Yuri Zavadsky.[79]

YT: Did Zavadsky enjoy listening to your performance?
NK: I think yes. I finished playing Pictures at an Exhibition and was given five rubles by Natalia Petrovna (Konchalovskaya) for the good performance as a sign of reward.
YT: I think five rubles at that time was a serious amount of money.
NK: Oh, yes it was, and I knew how I was going to spend it – we went to the restaurant with Andrei the same day.

---

[78] Arno Babajanian (1921-1983) was a Soviet Armenian composer and pianist. In 1928, at the age of seven, Babajanian started to study in the group for talented children at the Yerevan State Musical Conservatory. In 1938 he moved to Moscow to continue his studies in Gnessin Institute and then in Moscow Conservatory (class of Konstantin Igumnov). One of his masterpieces is considered to be the Piano Trio in F# minor (1952). In 1971 he was named People's Artist of the Soviet Union. Babajanian wrote many popular songs in collaboration with the leading poets of Soviet Union, such as Yevgeny Yevtushenko and Robert Rozhdestvensky. His music is rooted in Armenian folk music. Babajanian was also a noted pianist and often performed his own works in concerts.
Accessed February 13, 2018. http://babajanyan.ru/biography_arno_babadzhanyana.html.
[79] Yuri Alexandrovich Zavadsky (1894-1977) was a Russian actor, teacher, and movie director. Starting from 1940 he was a director of Mossovet Theatre in Moscow and Professor in the Russian Academy of Theatre Arts. Accessed February 13, 2018.
https://www.britannica.com/biography/Yury-Alexandrovich-Zavadsky.

YT: Since Andrei became a very well-known movie director, do you remember if Andrei Tarkovsky[80] visited Mikhalkov's house?

NK: Yes, he did, although, that happened a few years later. At that time I was not living at the Mikhalkov house. I knew Adrei as a pianist. When he dropped out from the second course of the Conservatory, our relationship gradually diminished.

YT: Did you perform Pictures at an Exhibition at any other occasions?

NK: I played Pictures at an Exhibition a few times more. I remember one of the performances was in the Columned Hall of the House of Unions.[81]

YT: How did it go?

NK: There was a celebratory event and I came to play Mussorgsky in a very strange outfit.

YT: What do you mean?

NK: I performed on stage at the Columned Hall of the House of Unions in an extravagant jacket of bright yellow color.

YT: You performed in the Columned Hall in a yellow jacket [82]?!?

NK: Yes (laughing). This all happened because of Andrei. Sometime before that we went to the private tailor, a very rare thing at that time. The tailor was supposed to sew a yellow jacket for Andrei. We found out that there will be enough material to sew not one but two yellow jackets. That's how I got my new jacket. I decided to wear that jacket for the performance of Mussorgsky. I thought it would be better that way. By the way, I started to play this piece from The Ballet of Unhatched Chicks in their Shells until the end.

YT: There is your color connection!

NK: Exactly. Although, the very next day the director of our college asked me to visit her. She said that I should never do that again. I was very young.

YT: You were very modern and brave.

NK: Yes, everybody at that time wanted to look like Elvis Presley and everybody had a hair flip on the head.

YT: And you too?

---

[80] Andrei Arsenyevich Tarkovsky (1932-1986) was one of the greatest Russian film-maker, writer, film editor, film theorist, and thearte director. Tarkovsky's films include »Ivan's Childhood« (1962), »Andrei Rublev« (1966), »Solaris« (1972), »Mirror« (1975), »Stalker« (1979), »Nostalghia« (1983), and »The Sacrifice« (1986). Accessed November 10, 2017. https://www.britannica.com/biography/Andrey-Arsenyevich-Tarkovsky.

[81] Columns Hall of the House of Unions (also called Palace of Unions) is a historical building in the Tverskoy District of central Moscow, which was built in 1780 for Prince Vasily Dolgoruky-Krymsky. During the first half of the 19th century it was visited by Alexander Pushkin and Yevgeny Baratynsky. From the 1840s it increasingly became a venue for concerts, and from 1860 it annually played host to cycles of symphonic concerts, conducted by such outstanding figures as Piotr Tchaikovsky, Nikolai Rimsky-Korsakov, Nikolai Rubinstein, and Antonin Dvorak.

[82] It is an unspoken rule to perform classical music mostly in black or in dark colors.

NK: And me too. I have a picture from my Komsomol membership card[83] with that look.

YT: I remember my parents were mentioning about wearing the striped trousers in the 1950s-1960s.

NK: Oh yes, striped pants was the norm for a modern man at that time. We used to buy all these Western clothes with Andrei in the second hand shop. I remember I had an English suit and then later an American suit.

Coming back to Mikhakov's house in the middle 1950s, it is important to mention an interesting tradition of this house, the opportunity to perform the entire piano recitals.

NK: I remember Isaac Katz performed his program in Mikhalkov's house before his final recital at the Conservatory. At that time he was finishing his postgraduate studies. One piece I remember from that program – Ravel's »Alborada del Gracioso« from »Mirrows«.

Kapustin recalled a memorable moment of his life, which was getting acquainted with prominent Russian pianist Vladimir Sofronitsky.[84] Natalia Konchalovskaya and Vladimir Sofronitsky were childhood friends and Sofronitsky used to invite Natalia to visit him once in a while. One day she came with Andrei and Nikolai.

NK: Sofronitsky was an unsociable person, but he was a friend of Natalia Petrovna (Konchalovskaya). Once we spent the entire evening in Sofronitsky's house.
YT: Can you tell me about this meeting?
NK: A few days before that meeting we attended Sofronitsky's concert where he played works by Schubert.
YT: What did you do when you came to visit Sofronitsky at his house?
NK: When we came to visit we asked him to repeat a section from the last Schubert's Sonata in B flat major (D. 960) and he played a slow movement of that sonata.
YT: What happened next?

---

[83] Komsomol (All-Union Leninist Young Communist League) was a political youth organization in the Soviet Union. It is sometimes described also as the youth division of the Communist Party of the Soviet Union.

[84] Vladimir Vladimirovich Sofronitsky (1901-1961) was an outstanding Soviet Russian classical pianist, best known as an interpreter of Alexander Scriabin, whose eldest daughter Elena he married in 1920. Sofronitsky graduated from the Saint Petersburg Conservatory (class of Professor Leonid Nikolaev) in 1921, where his classmates were Dmitry Shostakovich, Maria Yudina, and Elena Scriabina. Sofronitsky taught at the Saint Petersburg Conservatory (1936-1942) and then at the Moscow Conservatory (1942-1961). Sofronitsky recorded a large number of Scriabin's works and also works by Beethoven, Schubert, Chopin, Schumann, Liszt, Rachmaninov, Medtner, and Prokofiev. Accessed February 13, 2018. http://www.mosconsv.ru/ru/person.aspx?id=130953.

NK: He asked us to perform something and I played my Sonatina, all three movements.
YT: So, you didn't expect that you are going to perform your Sonatina when you were going to Sofronitsky's house?
NK: Of course not. This piece was already in my fingers, I could play it at any time.
YT: What did he tell you about your Sonatina?
NK: Sofronitsky said he liked the slow second movement the most. That was surprising because I thought the power is in the first movement and in the finale. Afterwards Sofronitsky treated us to a glass of wine. I still remember that it was a very good Georgian grape wine »Tsinandali.«
YT: Did you meet with Sofronitsky later?
NK: No, that was the only time, we never meet again. He died young, within five or six years after our meeting.
YT: Did you know who Vladimir Sofronitsky really was when you came to that meeting?
NK: Later, when I studied in the Conservatory, I kept thinking how I could have come to his house, and drink wine with him, just like that…

One of the most favorite places where Mikhalkov's family loved to travel was their summer house on the Nikolina Gora (Nikolin's Hill).[85] The house belonged to the family of Natalia Konchalovskaya.

NK: I remember Sergei Vladimirovich (Mikhalkov) was driving the car and we were all sitting in the back. Nikolina Gora is situated very close to Moscow so it was a short trip.
YT: What did you do in the Nikolina Gora?
NK: Their house was situated very close to the Moscow River, so we used to go swimming a lot. We had a great time.
YT: Did you perform on the Nikolina Gora?
NK: Sometimes yes. They had a new Bechstein (grand piano). Sergei Vladimirovich and Natalia Petrovna used to invite their friends to come visit them to Nikolina Gora. Rubbakh used to come to Nikolina Gora as well.

---

[85] Nikolina Gora is a fashionable region of the Moscow suburb, a place surrounded by beautiful landscape. In the 1950s this place was the home for people who represented the best of Russian science and art. Sergei Kapitsa, Vasily Livanov, Nikolai Slichenko, Yuri Bashmet, Nikolai Petrov, Sviatoslav Richter, and many others lived in Nikolina Gora. The house of Konchalovskaya was one of the highest rated houses in that area. Accessed November 10, 2017. https://utro.ru/articles/2004/03/31/293600.shtml.

The Visit of Kapustin's Parents to Moscow

In 1955 Kapustin's parents, Klavdia Nikolayevna and Grigory Efimovich, came to Moscow to visit their son together for the first time. During that visit they tried to spend as much time as possible together.

NK: We went to the restaurant with my parents and Andrei. I still remember that day. That was the restaurant »Bird's Flight« in the hotel »Moscow,« one of the most respected places in Moscow at that time.
YT: How long did your parents stay in Moscow?
NK: They stayed for a few days. As you know, time flies by very quickly when you are with someone you love.
YT: Did your parents come back to visit you later?
NK: The last time my father came alone, that was in the early 1960s.
YT: So they came just three times during those nine years of study in Moscow?
NK: Yes, it looks that way.
YT: Did you think about living in Moscow with all your family?
NK: Unfortunately, I didn't have that opportunity, I lived in the dormitory.

As all things come to an end, Kapustin's life at Mikhalkov's house also had come to an end one day and transform into something different, something new.

YT: When did you move back to the dormitory from Mikhalkov's house?
NK: I can't say that I completely moved from their house to the dormitory. For a while I used to stay in Mikhalkov's house most of the day and just went back to the dormitory to spend the night, but somehow I gradually moved back to the dormitory. During those two or three years of my life spent in Mikhalkov's house I lived very well.

Final Exams of the Musical College and Entering the Moscow Conservatory

In June of 1956, being a student of the fourth course, Kapustin was going through the final stage of his study in the Musical College. That was the time of final exams. Something absolutely disastrous happened with Kapustin on the day of his piano performance exam.

>   NK: *That day Andrei invited me to Gorky Park to have a little rest before the serious performance. We had a little beer and went back home. Then we felt tired and decided to take a short nap. The moment we woke I realized that I had slept over! I was in shock. We called to the college and someone told us that the jury committee was waiting for me. I don't remember if I ran any faster in my entire life than on that day.*
>   YT: *As I remember you told me that the Musical College was situated within walking distance from Mikhalkov's house.*
>   NK: *Yes, but they were waiting!*
>   YT: *Did you play immediately after that run?*
>   NK: *Yes, I rushed in like crazy right into the performance hall and without catching my breath started to play. That's what it means to be young; you could do something like this.*
>   YT: *Do you remember what you played?*
>   NK: *Very well. The first piece was »Aurora« (Beethoven Piano Sonata No. 21 Op. 53, also known as »Waldstein«). I also played »Don Juan« (Liszt »Reminiscences de Don Juan«, S. 418).*
>   YT: *I guess the »Aurora« started right at the pulse of your heart beating. How did the jury committee grade your performance?*
>   NK: *They gave me »A.«*
>   YT: *So, they were not upset with you?*
>   NK (smiling): *No, they were not.*

In August of 1956, the time had come and changes in Kapustin's life were knocking at the door. That was the time of his entering exams to the Moscow Conservatory. Just before the entering exams Rubbakh and two of his students, Nikolai Kapustin and Evgenia Pupkova, went to Alexander Goldenweiser[86] for an audition.

>   NK: *We went with Rubbakh to Alexander Goldenweiser's house to play for him. I played Liszt's »Don Juan« (Mozart-Liszt, Reminiscences de Don Juan, S. 418) and*

---

[86] Alexander Goldenweiser was one of the leading teachers at the Moscow Conservatory. The full conversation will be presented in Chapter III.

> *Jenia (Pupkova) played Liszt's »Fantasy on Themes from Mozart's Figaro and Don Giovanni« (Mozart-Liszt-Busoni, Fantasy on Two Motives from Mozart's »The Marriage of Figaro«, S. 697).*
> *YT: It is interesting that Rubbakh decided to give Liszt's piano transcriptions of Mozart to both of you. Did you know what Jenia would play for Goldenweiser?*
> *NK: Yes, I knew that. We were close friends with Jenia. We would consult each other with some technical issues and giving suggestions.*
> *YT: Did you feel nervous or afraid about your performance?*
> *NK: I never was afraid to play piano, not until the point when I graduated from the Conservatory.*
> *YT: So, I guess your audition went well.*
> *NK: Very well. Goldenweiser said to Rubbakh: »Where do you find such pianists?«*

The entering exams to the Moscow Conservatory began at the end of July 1956. The most important part of the entering exams was the performance of the prepared program.[87]

> *NK: I prepared a very difficult program – Prokofiev's Concerto No. 2 in G minor (Op. 16), Liszt's »Don Juan«, Bach's Prelude and Fugue, and few other pieces. The entering committee asked me to play only »Don Juan«.*
> *YT: Only one piece?*
> *NK: Yes, that was it. Although, it's a long piece, I think around twenty minutes in length. I wanted so badly to play Prokofiev's Concerto. We rehearsed it with Andrei, who accompanied me on this concerto, and were ready to play but they didn't ask.*
> *YT: Were you upset about it?*
> *NK: Of course I was. At that time nobody played Prokofiev Second Concerto. I found the score with the big difficulties, learned it, and planned to perform it.*
> *YT: How did you find out that you would have to play only one piece?*
> *NK: Rubbakh came to me backstage and told me.*
> *YT: They probably decided to hear just one piece from you because of the amount of enrollees to the Conservatory.*
> *NK: Could be.*

It is known, that the competition to study in the Moscow Conservatory was always set on a very high level.

> *YT: Do you know how many people tried to enter the Moscow Conservatory that year?*
> *NK: I don't. Mostly there were pianists from Moscow, but there were some people from other cities too.*

---

[87] The standard length of the program is approximately 35-40 minutes, which usually consists of four pieces.

YT: I can't imagine how many hearts were broken that day.

That performance of Liszt's Reminiscences de Don Juan was the beginning and the end of Kapustin's entering exams at the Moscow Conservatory. Due to the fact that Kapustin graduated Musical College with the highest honor he was released from the remaining part of the exams.

NK: I didn't know about that and spent my entire summer preparing myself for the Soviet history exam.
YT: It is so bad that you did not know you would be released from that exam.
NK: I had no idea. The fact is, right after my graduation from the Musical College I left to Nikitovka (Ukraine). I was in such a hurry to leave that I did not have a chance to talk to anyone about the entering exams. I wanted to get home as fast as possible. When I found out that I worked for nothing I got so mad – why did I suffer?
YT: How about the theory and harmony exams?
NK: None, I didn't do any of those.
YT: So, the only thing that you actually did to enter the Moscow Conservatory was to play »Don Juan«?
NK: Yes, that was it!

At the beginning of August 1956 Kapustin successfully enrolled in the Moscow Conservatory. Even more, he was selected to study in the class of legendary teacher Alexander Goldenweiser.

YT: How did you celebrate your successful exams?
NK: Right after my exam I had a nice vacation with my friends. We travelled to the coast of the Black Sea to the city of Khosta.[88] It was a long journey; we were there for three weeks or even longer.

---

[88] Khosta – micro district in the city Sochi, it is primarily known as a spa and a resort on the Black Sea coast of Russia.

Nikolai Kapustin (first row, first from the right) with his friends, Khosta, August 22, 1956

The experience and knowledge that Kapustin gained from study in the Musical College would help him through his entire life. Even now, sixty years after his graduation, he still believes that study at the Musical College would be absolutely enough for his future life as a composer.

YT: What do you feel about your teacher – Avrelian Rubbakh?
NK: I love and respect him very much. His wife told me that not long before he passed away he kept looking at the picture of his teacher, Felix Blumenfeld, and cried. He had a big heart.

Chapter Three: Study at the Moscow Conservatory (1956-1961)

Alexander Goldenweiser

Nikolai Kapustin, during his five years of study at the Moscow Conservatory, had the honor of being a student of one of the most celebrated teachers in the history of Russian piano performance – Alexander Goldenweiser.

Alexander Borisovich Goldenweiser (1875-1961) was a highly influential teacher, talented pianist, composer, editor, writer, music critic, and social leader. Goldenweiser is considered one of the founders of the Russian Soviet School of piano performance.

Alexander Borisovich Goldenweiser

Alexander Goldenweiser graduated from the Moscow Conservatory in 1895 as a pianist, where he was a student of Alexander Ziloti and Pavel Pabst, and in 1897 as a composer, where he was a student of Mikhail Ippolitov-Ivanov, Anton Arensky, and Sergei Taneev. Goldenweiser taught at the Moscow Conservatory for fifty-five years, starting from 1906 until his death in 1961. During the years of 1922-1924 and 1939-1942 Goldenweiser was the director of the Moscow Conservatory. Among his celebrated students were Samuil Feinberg, Grigory

Ginzburg, Roza Tamarkina, Tatiana Nikolaeva, Dmitry Bashkirov, Dmitry Kabalevsky, and Nikolai Kapustin.[89]

One of the most interesting aspects of Goldenweiser's biography was the fact that Goldenweiser was a classmate of Sergei Rachmaninov, Alexander Scriabin, Nikolai Medtner, and Alexander Goedicke.[90] This had a serious effect on his students and the people who were in his life. Another interesting fact of Goldenweiser's biography was that he was a close friend of the great Leo Tolstoy.[91] As a writer, in memory of Tolstoy, Goldenweiser wrote a two-volume memoir called »Vblizi Tolstogo«[92] (»Living Near Tolstoy«). In this memoir he described his close relationship with the eminent Russian writer and their conversations during the last fifteen years of Tolstoy's life.

> *NK: Goldenweiser used to visit Tolstoy very often and even stayed overnight in Tolstoy's home. He also used to play piano for Tolstoy. Of course, for the most time, they talked a lot about life.*

As a composer, Goldenweiser wrote three operas,[93] two orchestral suites, chamber, vocal, and piano works. However, he was most widely known for his work as an editor. Goldenweiser edited works of Tchaikovsky, J. S. Bach, Mozart, Beethoven, Domenico Scarlatti, Schumann, Rachmaninov and others.[94] As a music critic, Goldenweiser wrote an immense number of articles about Anton Rubinshtein, Nikolai Rubinshtein, Alexander Ziloti, Sergei Rachmaninov, Nikolai Myaskovsky, Lev Conus, Mikhail Gnessin, and others. As a pianist, Goldenweiser performed as a soloist as well as a member of chamber ensembles. He collaborated with such famous musicians as Pablo Casals, David Oistrakh, Lev

---

[89] Alexander Goldenweiser. Accessed November 13, 2017.
https://dic.academic.ru/dic.nsf/enc_music/2110/Гольденвейзер.
[90] Ibid.
[91] Count Lev Nikolaievich Tolstoy (1828-1910) was a Russian writer who is regarded as one of the greatest authors of all time. Two of his masterpieces, »War and Peace« (1869) and »Anna Karenina« (1877), received the highest critical acclaim. Tolstoy also wrote autobiographical trilogy »Childhood«, »Boyhood«, and »Youth« (1852-1856), several novellas, and religious-philosophical essays. Accessed February 14, 2018.
http://enc-dic.com/colier/Tolsto-lev-nikolaevich-6464.html.
[92] Alexander Goldenweiser, *Vblizi Tolstogo*, M.: Goslitizdat, 1922-1923, 1959.
[93] Goldenweiser composed three operas: »The Singer« (based on Ivan Turgenev's novel), »Torrents of Spring« (based on Ivan Turgenev's novel), and »A Feast in Time of Plague« (based on Alexander Pushkin's drama). Accessed February 10, 2016.
http://www.mosconsv.ru/ru/person.aspx?id=121142.
[94] Goldenweiser edited works of Piotr Tchaikovsky (concertos, trio, Concert Fantasia, sextet), J. S. Bach (partitas, inventions, »Well-Tempered Clavier«), Mozart (sonatas and concertos), Beethoven (32 sonatas, concertos, variations), Domenico Scarlatti (sonatas), Schumann (complete collection of the piano works), and more. Accessed February 10, 2016.
http://www.mosconsv.ru/ru/person.aspx?id=121142.

Kogan, and Mstislav Rostropovich. It is noted that Goldenweiser was a pianist of the intellectual style of piano performance. He had a subtle yet exquisite sense of musical style, an elevated level of simplicity, and superb craftsmanship. He gained a broad reputation for his interpretations of works by Mozart, Beethoven, Schumann, Grieg, and Russian composers, such as Arensky, Medtner, and the early works of Scriabin.[95]

Along with his many activities, there is no doubt that the pedagogical aspect of piano performance was one of his major priorities. As a Professor at the Moscow Conservatory he spent the greatest part of his life teaching students. At the same time, Goldenweiser was the initiator and the co-founder of the Central Music School for Gifted Children (CMS), which existed from 1932 under the Moscow Conservatory.[96] In other words, Goldenweiser was not only interested in working with developed pianists but also in the area of childhood musical education.

---

[95] Alexander Goldenweiser. Accessed November 13, 2017. http://www.mosconsv.ru/ru/person.aspx?id=121142.

[96] Note by the author: The major goal of the CMS was the preparation of the talented children to study at the Moscow Conservatory. This musical school is considered to be one of the most prestigious educational institutions in the world. Accessed November 13, 2017. http://cmsmoscow.ru/about/.

Study in the Class of Goldenweiser

It is always interesting to observe the inside atmosphere of the students within the class of a particular teacher. Some of the classes are extremely friendly, some are more independent.

YT: How was the atmosphere within Goldenweiser's class? Were you friends?
NK: Of course we were. I can't say that we were all very close, but we were friends. You see, Jenia [Pupkova] and I lived in the dormitory so that already put us aside from the other students who were from Moscow. On the other hand, I was a good friend with Oxana Yablonskaya, who was born and raised in Moscow.

Right from the beginning of Kapustin's study with Goldenweiser, he was put into a difficult position since Goldenweiser's expectations for his students were set much higher than Kapustin had ever experienced.

NK: On the first lesson everything should be memorized and performed at the final tempo. There was no place for error or uncertainty. Goldenweiser expected to hear the complete version of the piece, preferably with the student's own interpretation.

In addition to that »stressful« position for each student, there were always many people who attended the lessons of Goldenweiser. They were his current students, former students, or just visitors.

NK: Goldenweiser's wife Elena Ivanovna,[97] who was his student from the past, also attended all of his lessons. She was like his secretary, writing down everything that Goldenweiser talked about. Every lesson was like a masterclass.
YT: Why did she do that?
NK: For the history. She knew that it would be important material for the next generation of pianists.
YT: Did you ever visit Rubbakh after you started to study with Goldenweiser?
NK: At the beginning I used to go very often, then less and less later.
YT: Did you ask his suggestions on the pieces you worked on?
NK: Surely I did. It was a tradition - his students from the past used to come to play for him and ask his advice. It is difficult to find a teacher as great as Rubbakh.

---

[97] Elena Ivanovna Goldenweiser (Grachiova) was the second wife of Alexander Goldenweiser. In the middle of the 1990s she published some Goldenweiser's diaries: »Dnevnik A. B. Goldenweizera. Tetrad' pervaya (1889-1904)« [Diary of A. B. Goldenweiser. Notebook One (1889-1904)]. Moscow: Muzyka, 1995 and »Dnevnik A. B. Goldenweizera. Tetradi vtoraya-shestaya (1905-1909)« [Diary of A. B. Goldenweiser. Notebooks Two-Six (1905-1909)]. Moscow: Muzyka, 1997.

It is quite interesting to compare these two pedagogues of Nikolai Kapustin – Rubbakh and Goldenweiser. Living at the same time in Moscow, they represented two different approaches in teaching and two different understandings of the pedagogical process.

YT: If we would compare the teaching of Rubbakh and Goldenweiser, would you see any similarities between them?

NK: They were absolutely different. Goldenweiser worked on the large picture, Rubbakh worked on every small detail of the piece.

YT: Can you explain this?

NK: There are many nuances in our pianistic work. Rubbakh taught me all the details that made the good pianist different from the »poor« one. He worked with us as like a potter works with clay.

YT: How about the choice of the repertoire for the students?

NK: Goldenweiser preferred to work on large dimension pieces, for example if you are playing a concerto it must be all movements, not just the first. I remember I played all three movements of Chopin's Concerto in E minor (Op. 11) and Goldenweiser accompanied me. He also liked to do the cycles, for example a concert dedicated to all Prokofiev's sonatas.

YT: Would you say that Goldenweiser expected the students to do the major part of the work by themselves?

NK: Yes, I think so. I remember once that Nika Grinberg had a very stressful lesson with Goldenweiser. That day she played with some mistakes and stopped a few times forgetting the score. Goldenweiser got so upset with her that he threw the score on the floor in front of all those people who attended the lesson. I was not there that day but I was informed later about that incident.

YT: So, it was a dangerous thing.

NK: Sure, it was. His good relationship with her mother, Maria Grinberg,[98] did not help »poor« Nika to solve the problematic situation.

YT: Can we say that Goldenweiser was a severe teacher?

NK: He raised his voice to me only once. That was when I studied in my first year of the Conservatory. I was playing Prokofiev's Piano Sonata No. 7 and decided to try Horowitz's interpretation in the middle part of the sonata. He raised his voice to me and

---

[98] Maria Grinberg (1908-1978) was a student of Felix Blumenfeld and Konstantin Igumnov at the Moscow Conservatory. Grinberg was an important figure in the Russian piano school. Critics compared her performances to those of Vladimir Horowitz and Arthur Rubinstein. Grinberg was the first Russian pianist to record the complete set of thirty-two Beethoven piano sonatas. However, in 1937 both her father and husband were arrested and executed as »enemies of the people«. After the death of Stalin she was finally allowed to travel abroad. Accessed February 14, 2018. http://magazines.russ.ru/znamia/1999/5/inger.html, http://www.alefmagazine.com/pub1630.html.

forbid me to play that way. You know, at that time we were not closely acquainted yet. Also, I have a suspicion that Goldenweiser, in a way, disliked Horowitz's playing. I have no idea why.

YT: *How did your relationship with Goldenweiser change after you studied with him for a few years?*

NK: *I became closer to him, he liked me. I even used to help him go down the stairs at the conservatory at the end of his working day. His class No. 40 was situated on the fourth floor and for some reason he enjoyed using the stairs instead of the elevator.*

YT: *Did you talk during these small trips »down to the earth«?*

NK (smiling): *Ohhh yes, we talked.*

It is obvious that students selected by Goldenweiser were already experienced performers by the time they entered the Moscow Conservatory.

YT: *Did any other students of Rubbakh, besides you and Evgeniya Pupkova, ever try to enter the class of Goldenweiser?*

NK: *Yes, Rubbakh thought that Goldenweiser was one of the best teachers at the Moscow Conservatory. I remember I accompanied Arnold Shpizman and Arkady Kovaliov, both students of Rubbakh who tried to enter the Conservatory a year before me in the summer of 1955.*

YT: *Which pieces did you accompany?*

NK: *I played Rachmaninov's Piano Concerto No. 1 with Arnold (Shpizman) and Babajanian's »Heroic Ballad« with Arkady (Kovaliov).*

YT: *Were both pianists accepted to Goldenweiser's class?*

NK: *No, only the one who performed Rachmaninov's Concerto (Shpizman). The student who played the »Heroic Ballad« (Kovaliov) played very well but forgot the score because of the high level of stress.*

YT: *What did you do when Kovaliov forgot the score?*

NK: *I stopped too and waited a while until he began to play the second time.*

YT: *What a horrible situation for you!*

NK: *Yes, it's a big responsibility to accompany someone to the entering exams at the Moscow Conservatory.*

Nikolai Kapustin, late 1950s

It is always difficult to predict the result of an important audition or entering exam, especially if this is a decision about your study and your future at the Moscow Conservatory.

> *YT: Did you ever think about any other teacher at the Moscow Conservatory in the event Goldenweiser would not take you to his class? Did you have a »Plan B«?*
> *NK: I have a story on this matter. It happened right at the beginning of my study at the conservatory, when I studied the first year. My friend Andrei Mikhalkov got married, and I was invited to his wedding. There were so many famous people at that wedding. Just try to name someone who was not invited, everybody was there. Somehow I ended up sitting at the table with Boris Zemliansky, Heinrich Neuhaus' assistant. Zemliansky suggested that I switch teachers and study with Neuhaus. He said: »There is nothing wrong with that. There are many examples when students change their professor«.*
> *YT: What did you think in that case?*
> *NK: First of all, I would never do something like this to Goldenweiser. And second – I don't think I would survive it. Neuhaus would not like me, let's start with that. Although, we used to talk with him every time we would occasionally meet at the conservatory.*
> *YT: Why did you think he would not like you?*

NK: He would not like me because I was different. Neuhaus was romantic.
YT: So you decided that you didn't want to do this?
NK: I didn't decide anything, I knew from the beginning that I was not going to do this. Goldenweiser was the perfect teacher for me.
YT: And it seems like Goldenweiser liked you very much.
NK: Looks that way.
YT: How often did you go to the lessons with Goldenweiser?
NK: At the beginning I was coming once a week, like everybody, but later I got lazy and stopped going every week. By the way, to play for Goldenweiser was a big deal – everything should be memorized and performed in the »final edition«, final tempo, and everything. You need time to learn all of this.

It is important to note that even between the professors of the Moscow Conservatory there was a big difference in the way they approached the teaching process.

YT: I remember when I studied at the Nizhny Novgorod Conservatory we were talking about the differences in teaching between Alexander Goldenweiser and Konstantin Igumnov.[99] For example, Goldenweiser allowed anyone to attend his lessons, visitors and his students, and Igumnov taught with »closed« doors. Another difference was that Igumnov taught students to »speak« through music. On the other hand, Goldenweiser put the style of the composer as the major priority.
NK: Not only that, even more – they were big time enemies, always feuding with each other. Once their disagreements ended up with Igumnov's exclaiming: »I will not even attend your funeral.« It was known that Goldenweiser had a special sense of humor. His answer surprised with its' sharpness. Goldenweiser said: »But I will come to yours.«
YT: Why did they feud?
NK: They were incompatible. Igumnov was a romantic[100] and Goldenweiser was dry and scholastic. However, Goldenweiser used to compose music and Igumnov never composed anything.

There is a large amount of material written by former students of Goldenweiser, who became famous musicians and teachers, about his style of work in

---

[99] Konstantin Nikolaievich Igumnov (1873-1948) was a great pianist and one of the major professors at the Moscow Conservatory. He studied piano with Nikolai Zverev and Alexander Ziloti, and composition with Sergei Taneyev and Anton Arensky. In 1894 Igumnov graduated from the Moscow Conservatory with the highest honor. Starting from 1899 Igumnov became a professor of the Moscow Conservatory at the same time touring Russia and abroad. His students were: Lev Oborin, Yakov Flier, Maria Grinberg, Rosa Tamarkina, and Arno Babadjanian. Accessed February 15, 2018. http://www.mosconsv.ru/ru/person.aspx?id=121136.
[100] Note by the author: Here, the word »romantic« indicates the romantic way of music interpretation, emotional approach to composition in opposition to the intellectual interpretation.

the lessons. Among them are Alexander Nikolaev,[101] Alexander Alekseev,[102] Lazar Berman,[103] Isaac Katz,[104] Evgeniya Pupkova,[105] and Dmitry Blagoi.[106]

It is noted that the primary pedagogical principle of Goldenweiser was the development of the musician as a deep and widely-educated individual:

The performer must aim for reaching the level of spiritual growth and internal significance of the composer.[107]

Goldenweiser put serious attention to his work with rhythm as he stated:

Almost everybody has the ability to hear pitch, developed or not, but bad rhythm is a universal disaster.[108]

Since the music is the organization of sound in time, the unit of time (the pulse) should be unchangeable through the piece. Goldenweiser noted:

Unfortunately, because of the change of texture, the students often lose the pulse and begin to speed up or slow down, without even noticing.[109]

Being a teacher at the Central Music School, Goldenweiser was also working with young pianists. One of the major areas of his work with children was attention to the hand position and relaxed hand motion. Goldenweiser noted that we should proceed from the natural hand position:

Nobody would play with tension in the hand if we could establish a naturally comfortable position. For example, each person will take a pencil from the table with a naturally free motion in his hand unless he would want to do it differently on purpose… There is only

---

[101] Nikolaev, Alexander. »Ispolnitel'skie i pedagogicheskie printsipi A. B. Goldenweizera« [Performance and Teaching Principles of A. B. Goldenweiser]. In *Mastera sovetskoi pianisticheskoi shkoli*. Moscow: Muzgiz, 1954, 1961.

[102] Alekseev, Alexander. »Jizn' muzikanta« [Life of the Musician]. In *Pamiati A. B. Goldenweizera*, 7-51. Moscow: Sovetskii kompozitor, 1969.

[103] Berman, Lazar'. »Moi uchitel' A. B. Goldenweizer« [My Teacher Alexander Borisovich Goldenweiser]. In *Godi stranstvii. Razmishleniya pianista*. Moscow: Classica XXI, 2006. 240 pp.

[104] Katz, Isaac. *A pomnish kak…?* [Do You Remember How?] Jerusalem: Philobiblon, 2007.

[105] Evgeniya Pupkova, »Pereigravshaya Vsego Baha«, http://pupkova.ru/biography. Accessed February 8, 2016.

[106] *In the Class of A. B. Goldenweiser*, compiled by D. D. Blagoi, E. I. Goldenweiser. Moscow: Muzyka, 1986. 210 pp.

[107] Alexander Goldenweiser. »About Performance«. In *The Questions of the Piano Performance*, 62. Moscow: Muzyka, 1965.

[108] Pupkova, »Pereigravshaya Vsego Baha«. Accessed February 8, 2016. http://pupkova.ru/biography/.

[109] Ibid.

one way to solve this problem – you should establish conditions for your hand in which it will be impossible to be tense or strained.[110]

Goldenweiser suggested starting to work on easy musical material and gradually developing good working habits. Also, he had a strong belief in the connection of the motoric hand motion with our brain system:

I am convinced that hands do not play an important role in the process of the performance, as most people think. Everything depends mostly on the neuro-brain center.[111]

At the conservatory Goldenweiser had four assistants, all his former students, who helped him work with his students. These assistants were Ludmila Sosina, Liya Levinson, Dmitry Bashkirov, and Dmitry Blagoi. Their role was to prepare students for the lessons with Goldenweiser.

Nikolai Kapustin was guided towards study with Dmitry Bashkirov.[112]

---

[110] Anna Blagaya, »Alexander Goldenweiser - O postanovke ruk i borbe s napriajeniem« [The Hand Position and the Fight with Tension]. Accessed February 8, 2016. http://blagaya.ru/skripka/violin_azbuka/ruki/gold-o-postanovke/.
[111] Ibid.
[112] Dmitry Bashkirov (born 1931) is a Russian pianist and educator. He was born in Tbilisi (Georgia), where he studied at the music school (class of Anastasia Virsaladze, the grandmother of Eliso Virsaladze). In 1950 Bashkirov moved to Moscow to study at the Moscow Conservatory (class of Alexander Goldenweiser). In 1957 he finished his post-graduate study (class of Alexander Goldenweiser) and began teaching at the Moscow Conservatory. In 1987 Bashkirov became co-founder and professor at the »Queen Sofia College of Music« (Madrid, Spain). Bashkirov is a great interpreter of Mozart, Beethoven, Shubert, Brahms, and Prokofiev. Accessed February 15, 2018. http://www.mosconsv.ru/ru/person.aspx?id=8936.

Class of Alexander Goldenweiser and other professors of the Moscow Conservatory: Alexander Goldenweiser (first row, third from the left), Elena Goldenweiser (first row, second from the left), Liya Levinson (first row, fourth from the left), Dmitry Bashkirov (first row, third from the right), Nodar Gabunia (first row, first from the right), Nikolai Kapustin (second row, fifth from the right), Oxana Yablonskaya (second row, fourth from the right)

YT: Did the assistants attend the lessons with Goldenweiser?
NK: No, they did not.
YT: How did your lessons go with Dmitry Bashkirov?
NK: He said to me right from the beginning: »What can I teach you?« His suggestion was do not bother to attend the lessons with him.
YT: Did you go?
NK: Of course I did not, I followed his suggestion. I attended only the lessons with the »Old Man«.
YT: The »Old Man«?
NK: Yes, that's how his students referred to Goldenweiser.[113]

As a teacher, Goldenweiser had a connection to some specific composers. Interestingly enough, being a modern day composer himself, he had a preference towards more traditional music, especially the Viennese School composers and

---

[113] Note by the author: That was a sign of the big respect to the teacher, similar to what we would call in the United States »Doc«.

the Romantic composers.[114] On the other hand, he wasn't against his students' interest in music of twentieth century composers, such as Prokofiev, Scriabin, Rachmaninov, and Shostakovich.

> YT: *Did Goldenweiser like the music of Bartok?*
> NK: *The music of Bartok was not on the list of his favorites. I remember once I played Bartok's Sonata for Two Pianos and Percussion[115] with Nodar Gabunia[116] for Goldenweiser. We just started to play it, stopped at the end of the section and Goldenweiser said: »What can I say? The music in the unison always sounded good.« That piece started from the unison part.*
> YT: *It looks that he didn't appreciate it.*
> NK: *He didn't like modern music, although he himself was a modern day composer.*
> YT: *Yes, this piece is extremely difficult technically and complicated as ensemble work.*
> NK: *For me, with the exception of the finale, it was not a difficult work.*
> YT: *I was a little surprised, when I listened to the piece, that there are two percussionists involved in the piece.*
> NK: *We even decided that having two percussionists was not enough for us, so we used three, although in Bartok's score there are just two.*
> YT: *Whose idea was it to play that piece?*
> NK: *Nodar (Gabunia) suggested that piece.*
> YT: *So, when Goldenweiser's students wanted to play modern pieces he was not against it.*
> NK: *He didn't refuse working on modern pieces.*
> YT: *How about Goldenweiser's attitude towards Medtner?*
> NK: *He loved Medtner, but I didn't. Did you know that Medtner was a Russian composer who didn't graduate as a composer? So, he was like me, a self-taught composer.*
> YT: *What about Prokofiev?*
> NK: *Goldenweiser and Prokofiev knew each other very well and Prokofiev even took a few composition lessons with Goldenweiser in his early years.*
> YT: *I can't believe!*

---

[114] Skype conversation with Nikolai Kapustin, March 4, 2016.
[115] Bartok »Sonata for Two Pianos and Percussion« (1937) was composed for the 10th Anniversary of the International Society of Contemporary Music in Basel (Switzerland). The piece combined the idea of classical structure and unusual scoring for two pianos and percussion. Accessed February 18, 2018. https://www.britannica.com/topic/Sonata-for-Two-Pianos-and-Percussion.
[116] Note by the author: Nodar Gabunia was a close friend of Nikolai Kapustin during his study at the Moscow Conservatory. The conversation about Gabunia will be presented in the latter part of the Chapter III.

NK: Yes. Then Prokofiev's parents decided to find the »real« composer for their son and Prokofiev started to take private lessons with Glière.[117]

YT: So, Goldenweiser liked Prokofiev's music?

NK: As you see, we played Prokofiev sonatas. I think Goldenweiser considered Prokofiev as his former student, that's why.

YT: I found out that Dmitry Kabalevsky also studied with Goldenweiser.[118]

NK: This is true.

YT: Did Goldenweiser ever mention Kabalevsky during the lessons?

NK: Never.

YT: So, is it true that the general attitude towards Kabalevsky was different from that of Prokofiev? (silence) Is that because Kabalevsky wrote music that embraced the ideas of socialist realism?

NK: Not only Kabalevsky, everybody made a mark on this matter. Prokofiev even composed a cantata »Zdravitsa« (Hail to Stalin) Op. 85 in honor of Stalin.

---

[117] Reinhold Glière (1875-1956) was a composer and the professor at the Moscow Conservatory. His output includes works in various genres of orchestral, chamber, vocal, and solo piano music. Accessed February 15, 2018. http://www.mosconsv.ru/ru/person.aspx?id=34741.

[118] Dmitry Kabalevsky (1904-1987) was a Russian composer. In 1929 Kabalevsky graduated from the Moscow Conservatory in composition (class of Georgy Katuar) and in 1930 in piano performance (class of Alexander Goldenweiser). Accessed February 15, 2018. http://www.mosconsv.ru/ru/person.aspx?id=37115.

Concerts of Goldenweiser's Students

Goldenweiser had a tradition in his class to organize concerts dedicated to specific composers.[119] For example, Kapustin participated in the concerts dedicated to Prokofiev sonatas, Beethoven sonatas, Medtner piano works, as well as concerts dedicated to the Soviet composers.

In autumn 1956 Goldenweiser organized a cycle of three concerts dedicated to all Prokofiev's sonatas. This happened right at the beginning of Kapustin's first year of study at the conservatory. Kapustin played one of the most famous Prokofiev sonatas – Piano Sonata No. 7 in B flat major Op. 83, which belongs to a group of his three »War Sonatas.«

> *YT: Did you choose the Prokofiev sonata or did Goldenweiser assign it to you?*
> *NK: He didn't assign it to me and I didn't choose it either.*
> *YT: Then how did you end up playing this piece?*
> *NK: Actually, there was a story concerning that Prokofiev sonata. Goldenweiser assigned one sonata to each of his students to learn over the summer. Since I had just entered his class I was not supposed to be a part of this concert. One of my friends, Arnold Shpizman, to whom I accompanied Rachmaninov's concerto during his entering exams at the conservatory, was supposed to learn Sonata No. 7. However, he didn't complete his summer assignments and didn't learn the piece. He begged me to play it instead of him. He said: »Kolia, this is a piece in your style, you are the modernist. I don't understand anything in this music.« I never played this sonata before, although I heard it many times, so I knew the music.*
> *YT: Did you agree?*
> *NK: Yes, I was very interested in that sonata and decided to work on it. I learned it in a very short period of time, even though it is a very difficult piece. I don't think I could do something like that now.*
> *YT: How did Arnold Shpizman react on your agreement?*
> *NK: He was very thankful. I saved his life! Unfortunately, there was a side effect out of this productive work – I started to skip classes and because of this, I had some serious problems with attendance, but that was my choice.*
> *YT: Oh, no... How did the performance go?*

---

[119] Note by the author: These were additional performances of Goldenweiser's students organized aside from their jury performances every semester.

NK: It went very well. Vladimir Ashkenazy[120] was in the audience and liked my performance.

Another concert that Kapustin participated in during his first year of study with Goldenweiser was dedicated to the works of Soviet composers. Kapustin performed two pieces from Goldenweiser's Polyphonic Notebooks and three etudes of Alexander Goedicke.

NK: After the concert Goldenweiser came into the green room with a smile on his face. He said to me: »Did you know that Tatiana Nikolaeva played the same characterpiece as you, when she studied with me, and stumbled over the same spot?« (laughing)
YT: I guess it is an honor to make the same mistake as Tatiana Nikolaeva. Great job!

During the study at the conservatory Kapustin also participated in a concert of Goldenweiser's students dedicated to the piano music of Nikolai Medtner. Goldenweiser profoundly respected the music of Medtner and regarded this composer as underrated.

NK: I remember that I played a piece of Medtner in the Small Hall of the Moscow Conservatory. I didn't enjoy playing it. That's why I probably don't remember the actual name of this piece, although, I think it was one of his sonatas. There is one thing about his sonatas that strikes me the most – he used to select very poetic names for his pieces, for example he had Sonata-Reminiscence, Sonata-Tragica, Sonata-Minacciosa.[121]

On April 13, 1959, during Kapustin's third year of study at the Moscow Conservatory, he participated in the concert of Goldenweiser's students dedicated to Beethoven sonatas. It was one of the concerts from the cycle of »Thirty-Two Beethoven Piano Sonatas«. Goldenweiser assigned Piano Sonata No. 22 in F major Op. 54 to Kapustin.

---

[120] Note by the author: Vladimir Ashkenazy was one of Kapustin's friends at the Moscow Conservatory. The conversation about Ashkenazy will be presented in the latter part of Chapter III.
[121] Some of other Medtner sonatas called *Fairy-Tale Sonata* (Op. 25 No. 1), *Night Wind Sonata* (Op. 25 No. 2), and *Sonata-Idyll* (Op. 56).

Program: Concert of students of Goldenweiser.
Cycle »Thirty-Two Sonatas of Beethoven«, Small Hall of the Moscow Conservatory,
April 3, 1959

YT: Is this a two-movement sonata?

NK: Yes, the first movement is like a minuet and the second one is very technical.

YT: Do you remember how Goldenweiser worked on Beethoven's sonata?

NK: I remember I had to work mostly on my own, preparing my interpretation. He would give some suggestions, but it was our responsibility to prepare the piece.

YT: Since you were preparing the sonata on your own, did you listen to performances of other pianists?

NK: I asked Goldenweiser to give me this sonata after I heard Richter's performance. I liked everything – the music and the performance itself.

YT: Did the students of Goldenweiser play all thirty-two sonatas?

NK: Yes, there were five or six concerts. Goldenweiser wanted to play the whole cycle. The only thing is that the sonatas were not performed in order. Schnabel also played that way, not in order.

YT: This is a very serious project – you have to have students who can play all of these sonatas.

NK: That's true, especially sonatas like Hammerklavier (Op. 106 in B flat major). By the way, Nodar (Gabunia) played this sonata on the concert.

YT: There are two completely opposite ways of learning a new piece: first – do not listen to any performances before you form your own interpretation. Second – to listen to the recordings, study them, and only after that form your own interpretation.

NK: It seems very strange to hear that you can't listen to other performances. As a student you must listen. There is nothing frightening in that; in any case, your performance will be different from others.

YT: I agree. It is the same as if you want to become a composer and decided not to listen to any music so it would not affect your originality.

NK: Exactly. Although, lately I stopped listening to the music of other composers.

YT: Of course you had a period when you were growing as a composer. Then, when you formed your style, you didn't need to listen any more.

NK: Yes, at the beginning I was listening to everything I could possibly listen to.

There was another good tradition at the Moscow Conservatory – to organize the series of free concerts. These concerts took place in the performance halls of Moscow which were situated outside of the conservatory and were open to any public audience.

YT: Were the students obligated to perform on these concerts?

NK: There was no obligation, but it was suggested; plus, the students mostly played pieces that they studied during the year and were preparing to perform on the jury. It was a benefit for both sides.

YT: Did you study these pieces with Goldenweiser?

NK: I remember on one of those patronage concerts I played Kreisler-Rachmaninov's waltz Love's Joy. This is a brilliant piece; Rachmaninov wrote this arrangement when he was living in the United States. I found the music score and learned it.

YT: How was the performance?

NK: I played it very successfully, although this is a very difficult piece. I think I played it for Goldenweiser just a couple of times, in case there were suggestions, since Goldenweiser and Rachmaninov were friends.

YT: Just a couple of times?

NK: He didn't ask for more.

YT: So, in a way you learned the piece on your own.

NK: Yes, it looks that way.

YT: How often did you perform on these concerts?

NK: There were a lot of these performances. They asked us to participate in these events because it was considered a social activity. I also played Stravinsky's Petrushka on a similar patronage concert. I played this piece later for my final exam at the conservatory.

YT: *Who was in the audience for those charity concerts?*
NK: *It sounds a little strange, but it was mostly children.*
YT: *Really?*
NK: *Yes, it was the students of musical schools.*[122] *I remember when I played Petrushka the speaker explained to them that Petrushka is a kind of doll.*
YT: *She made them interested in what you were going to perform.*
NK: *Exactly. It was not just a music performance but also it was kind of an educational process where their teacher would talk about the composers and the pieces they were going to hear.*
YT: *So it was a lecture-recital.*
NK: *Yes.*

---

[122] Note by the author: The age of students of musical schools in Russia varies from seven to fifteen years old.

Kapustin's Piano Repertoire and Interest in Atonal Music

During Kapustin's study at the conservatory he learned a wide variety of pieces in different genres and musical styles. An interesting example of one of the pieces he studied was Scriabin's *Three Etudes*, Op. 65, which is considered one of his last piano works.

NK: This is a very notable set of etudes – all three are written in different intervals. The first one in 9th, second one in major 7th, and the last one in 5th.

YT: I keep thinking about that first etude on the 9th. There are not many performers can do that because you need to have a very good stretch in your hand or just simply need to have a large hand.

NK: Not really. It's not a very big stretch, just a little more than an octave.

YT: But the whole etude is built on the 9th.

NK: Yes, but it is somehow comfortable to play all those 9^{th}s. Of course if you have a small hand it would be impossible to play that etude. You would be able to play it.

YT: I am not sure about that statement.

NK: I am sure.

YT: This is a very hard piece.

NK: It seems that it is hard to play but once you start playing you will feel different, much better. So, all it takes is just to begin working on the piece. My friend Volodia Ashkenazy liked how I played these etudes very much. By the way, the first time I heard these etudes they were played by Richter. I liked them enormously, especially the first one.

YT: Did you hear Richter's playing in one of the concerts that you attended?

NK: Maybe even during some radio programs. I listened to a lot of music during that period.

YT: It seems that Richter is one of your favorite pianists.

NK: Yes, this is true.

YT: Do you agree that in Russia musicians keep comparing Richter and Gilels[123]? Some people like Richter more, some Gilels.

---

[123] Emil Grigoryevich Gilels (1916-1985) was a Soviet pianist, widely regarded as one of the greatest pianists of the twentieth century. In 1935 he graduated from the Odessa Conservatory (class of Berta Reingbald) and in 1938 he completed his postgraduate study at the Moscow Conservatory (class of Professor Heinrich Neuhaus). Gilels premiered works of Prokofiev, Khachaturian, and Kabalevsky. He had an extensive repertoire from Baroque to the late Romantic and twentieth century classical music. Gilels was one of the first Soviet artists allowed to travel and concertize in the West. Accessed November 14, 2017.
http://www.emilgilels.com/, http://www.mosconsv.ru/ru/disk.aspx?id=22188.

NK: Yes, I remember in his book Neuhaus talks mostly about Richter; Gilels is somehow aside from the mainstream. I don't agree with that. Gilels is also a genius performer. They were very different from each other.
YT: Interesting detail, both Richter and Gilels played Scriabin's late pieces.
NK: Yes, I like late Scriabin too - his Op. 65 and everything that came after that. He did not write a lot though. His last opus was 74, Five Preludes for Piano.
YT: What do you like about those etudes Op. 65?
NK: At that point Scriabin started his experiments with atonality.
YT: It is known that Scriabin came so close to the twelve-tone system that he could potentially have been the founder of this system had he not passed away.
NK: It is a good thing that he didn't make it.
YT: I like his music a lot – it sounds very beautiful to my ear, even experimenting with the atonality.
NK: In opposition to Schoenberg.
YT: I heard that Scriabin was a mystical person.
NK: Yes, this is true.
YT: Do you believe in supernatural things?
NK (with a smile): Of course not. His friend Sergei Rachmaninov did not believe in these things either. In this sense I am closer to Rachmaninov.

As a student at the conservatory Kapustin was open to everything new, innovative, and unknown. In Russia in the middle 1950s, as well as in the United States, one of the trends of the day was experimenting with the twelve-tone technique in compositional and performance circles.

NK: I remember I even played Schoenberg's Suite for Piano Op. 25[124] for Goldenweiser.
YT: Really? What was Goldenweiser's reaction to Schoenberg pieces?
NK: Of course he didn't like dodecaphonic music. This is an interesting fact – Schoenberg was just one year older than Goldenweiser.
YT: The same generation.
NK: Yes.
YT: How did you find the strength to play this music for Goldenweiser if you knew ahead of time that he would not like it?

---

[124] Arnold Schoenberg (1874-1951) was an Austrian Jewish composer, music theorist, and painter. He was a leader of the Second Viennese School of composers. Schoenberg developed a twelve-tone technique, an influential compositional method of twentieth century music. The *Suite for Piano*, Op. 25 (1924) is considered to be the first twelve-tone piece composed by the Schoenberg. Accessed February 15, 2018.
https://www.britannica.com/biography/Arnold-Schoenberg.

NK: I decided to play it for courage. Additionally, they asked me to play this piece for the Nauchno-Studencheskoe Obshestvo (The Student Research and Creative Society),[125] so I wanted to perform it first for my teacher.

YT: How did the performance go?

NK: Unfortunately they were so interested in the piece that they asked me to give them the score. I was not sure if I could play that piece by memory, but I did.

YT: You have a phenomenon memory!

NK: Yes, at that time I was pretty good.

YT: How long did you study that piece? The score looks very frightening.

NK: In the pianistic matter there is nothing dangerous in there. The main difficulty is how to remember all those notes.

YT: I keep thinking – how to remember twelve-tone music? On one hand, you should understand how the notes are connected between each other, but, on the other hand, if the only connection between them is based on a mathematical approach, then how to hear them?

NK: You should listen for the music too, no matter how strange it may be.

YT: Do you have to feel the music?

NK: No, that's not that kind of music that you have to feel.

YT: Then what approach should you take in order to play twelve-tone music?

NK: It will come on its own.

YT: Is this the only piece by Schoenberg that you played?

NK: Oh, no. On the same concert I also played a piece called *Waltz* from Schoenberg's *Five Piano Pieces*, Op. 23, also a dodecaphonic[126] piece. This opus is his first dodecaphonic piece, not the Op. 25.

YT: For some reason I thought that it was Op. 25.

NK: Yes, because in the suite the entire piece is dodecaphonic but in Op. 23 just one section – waltz.

YT: If you would compare these two opuses, 23 and 25, how would you express the differences or similarities between them?

NK: It sounds pretty much the same to my ear.

YT: Did you play the pieces of any other Second Viennese School composers?

NK: I remember at some point I was very much interested in Webern's *Variations*, Op. 27.

YT: How did you find this piece?

---

[125] The Student Research and Creative Society is a voluntary student group within the Moscow Conservatory. The function of this society is the organization of different educational events, such as concerts, seminars, lecture-recitals, and festivals, in order to maintain and continue further development of students of the conservatory as intellectual and knowledgeable personalities. Accessed July 19, 2016. http://www.mosconsv.ru/ru/groups.aspx?id=139436.

[126] Dodecaphony or twelve-tone technique is a method of musical composition devised by Austrian composer Arnold Schoenberg.

NK: I attended Gould's concert at the conservatory during his very first visit to Russia when nobody knew who Glenn Gould[127] was.
YT: Lucky you. Could you tell me please about this concert?
NK: The concert was in May of 1957 when I was finishing my first year. It was a lecture-recital. Gould finished this recital with the performance of Webern's variations. I liked it terribly right from the beginning. Later I found the score, played a little, and then, for some reason, stopped playing it.
YT: Why?
NK: I guess I didn't like it as much as when I first heard it at Gould's concert.
YT: Yes, this is very complicated music – matrixes, retrogrades, inversions, retrograde-inversions.
NK: And none of these you can hear.
YT: I agree. What else did he play on that concert?
NK: He also played Bach, of course, Berg's piano sonata, and Schoenberg's music. The other interesting thing that I remember was his lecture. The funny thing, his translator couldn't understand what »atonal music« means. Is it music without tonality? (laughing) I also remember how he took off his sweaters... He was so young, just twenty-five years old.
YT: I read that he stopped performing live concerts at the age of thirty one.
NK: Yes, he stopped performing live very early. He had his own recording studio where he spent all his time. I guess he had a great instrument there, maybe more than one.
YT: How about the audience – did they like Gould?
NK: Oh, at his first concert in Moscow there were not so many people, I would say – very little, he was unknown to the Russian audience. However, after the rumor spread out about this superb Canadian pianist, it was impossible to get tickets for his second concert.
YT: How about your reaction to Gould?
NK: We were walking home with a friend of mine Igor Krukov, discussing Gould's playing all the way. We understood right from the beginning that in front of us was a genius... Believe it or not, we never heard dodecaphonic music before Gould.
YT: So, the first time you heard dodecaphonic music you were twenty years old.
NK: Correct.

---

[127] Glenn Gould (1932-1982) was a Canadian pianist who became one of the best-known and the most celebrated classical pianists of the twentieth century. He was particularly renowned as an interpreter of keyboard music of J. S. Bach. Gould rejected most standard Romantic piano literature, although his repertoire was diverse, including works of late Beethoven and Arnold Schoenberg. Gould stopped giving concerts at the age of thirty one to concentrate on studio recordings and other projects. Gould was also known as a writer, composer, conductor, and broadcaster. Accessed February 16, 2018.
https://www.britannica.com/biography/Glenn-Gould.

YT: *I am not sure if you would agree with me or not, but my teacher from the Musical College, Tamara Sammuilovna Brodskaya, used to say that Gould was a genius pianist but don't ever try to imitate him.*

NK: *I totally agree. He was so unique that it is worthless to try playing like Gould.*

YT: *Yes, when you are listening to Richter or Gilels, for example, you can study their recordings and use some ideas for yourself but Gould…*

NK: *He was so different and unique at the same time so there was no reason to even try.*

YT: *Did Gould play an encore on that concert?*

NK: *How do you know this?*

YT: *I am just guessing.*

NK: *Good guess. Yes, he played a section from Bach's Goldberg Variations. It was a brilliant performance; I got so excited about this piece that I found the score later. The most fascinating thing for me is what miracles Bach could do with his canons!*

YT: *Did you play any of Berg's pieces?*

NK: *Yes, I accompanied Berg's Violin Concerto. I had to actually learn the piece because the music like this is impossible to sight-read.*

YT: *This is so fascinating, in the middle of 1950s you were already acquainted with music written by all three Second Viennese School composers – Schoenberg, Webern, and Berg!*

NK: *To tell you the truth, the first time I saw dodecaphonic music was a long time before that when I was still living in Nikitovka. That was Six Little Piano Pieces, Op. 19 by Schoenberg. Of course, it's not that Schoenberg style that we all know about, but still…. it was Schoenberg.*

YT: *How did you find it? Did Lubov' Frantsuzova or Piotr Vinnichenko give it to you?*

NK: *A friend of Lubov' Borisovna (Frantsuzova), also a pianist, passed away and they were selling his music scores. I remember that was when I saw the scores of Cyril Scott*[128] *for the first time too. He was a well-known composer for a while but then for some reason disappeared.*

YT: *How did you choose which scores to take? Did anyone help you?*

NK: *No, they just let me look through the scores and I chose based on my intuition.*

YT: *And you were around twelve years old at that time.*

NK: *Something like that.*

YT: *Did you know who Schoenberg was when you were choosing his score?*

NK: *I had no idea whatsoever. I was very young at that time.*

YT: *Why did you take it then?*

---

[128] Cyril Scott (1879-1970) was an English composer, writer, and poet. He showed a talent for music from his early age and began to study piano at the Hoch Conservatory (Frankfurt, Germany) at the age of twelve. He composed orchestral, chamber, piano music, as well as vocal and choral music. Accessed February 16, 2018. http://www.cyrilscott.net/.

NK: I was curious about the composer and his music. Interesting fact, at that point Schoenberg was still alive. Did you know that Schoenberg and Gershwin[129] were friends? They even used to play tennis together.
YT: Really? The American popular composer and the composer of atonal music?
NK: I have Schoenberg's book of articles where he was writing about his relationship with different people. He considered Gershwin to be an extraordinarily talented person. I think it's up to the composer to determine which style of music he is going to explore.

It is known that Schoenberg was an important figure in the musical education of the United States. Furthermore, during the 1940s-1960s the students of the compositional departments of educational institutions of the United States were supposed to compose atonal music in order to complete their degree program.

YT: Did you have any directions for composition students at the conservatory in the 1950s?
NK: Yes, we did. It was prohibited to compose atonal music.
YT: What a coincidence! It was just the opposite in the United States during the same time.
NK: If it would be my will I would prohibit it also. All atonal music sounds very similar.
YT: Since you played some pieces of Schoenberg and Berg, you had some interest in that music.
NK: You could play whatever you like; only composing atonal music was prohibited. You may continue composing that music but it will never be performed. I had two close friends who studied at the conservatory as composers. They were Nikolai Sidelnikov[130] and Viacheslav Ovchinnikov.[131] Viacheslav Ovchinnikov composed music for the film »War and the Peace« and became famous because of this movie.

---

[129] George Gershwin (1898-1937) was an American composer and pianist of Ukrainian Jewish ancestry. Gershwin's compositions spanned both popular and classical genres. Among his best-known works are the orchestral compositions »Rhapsody in Blue« (1924), »An American in Paris« (1928), and the opera »Porgy and Bess« (1935). Accessed February 16, 2018. https://www.britannica.com/biography/George-Gershwin.

[130] Nikolai Nikolayevich Sidelnikov (1930-1992) was a Russian Soviet composer. Sidelnikov graduated from the Moscow Conservatory in composition (class of Ekaterina Messner) in 1957 and finished his post-graduate study in composition (class of Yuri Shaporin) in 1961. Beginning from 1981 he was a professor at the Moscow Conservatory. His works include operas, ballet »Stepan Razin«, six symphonies, an oratorio, cantatas, choral, chamber, and vocal music. Accessed February 16, 2018.
https://dic.academic.ru/dic.nsf/enc_biography/112490/Сидельников.

[131] Viacheslav Aleksandrovich Ovchinnikov (born 1936) is a Russian composer and conductor. He graduated from the Moscow Conservatory in 1962. Ovchnnikov has composed symphonies, symphonic poems, as well as works for chamber orchestra, small ensemble, and solo instruments. He is best known as a composer of music for such films as »War and Peace« (1967),

YT: *Oh, yes. This is a very famous movie!*

NK: *I don't know a lot about movies.*

YT: *What kind of music did Nikolai Sidelnikov write?*

NK: *He wrote music that would be closer to my music.*

YT: *What interesting friends you had at the conservatory!*

NK: *Yes, we were friends. Talking about the composers – I performed a piece with Gubaidulina for four hands.*

YT: *Were you acquainted with Sofia Gubaidulina[132]?*

NK: *Of course I was; we studied together.*

YT: *How did you know her?*

NK: *We had to play Schnittke's piece with her on the piano for four-hands. Schnittke was unknown for a long time. We couldn't expect that he would become so famous. That was a surprise. He was definitely one who composed atonal music.*

YT: *So, you were acquainted with Alfred Schnittke[133] also?*

NK: *Yes, I knew him very well. Sofia and I played his graduation piece called Nagasaki.[134] It was a very heavy piece, about the horrors of the war.*

YT: *This is so fascinating, Sophia Gubaidulina, Alfred Schnittke, all these famous people around you.*

NK: *Yes, I got lucky. Many famous people studied with me at the conservatory. Everybody who studied at the conservatory or was doing a post-graduate course knew each*

»Ivan's Childhood« (1962) and »Andrei Rubliov« (1966). Accessed February 16, 2018. http://vyacheslavovchinnikov.ru/ru/content/?id=26.

[132] Sofia Asgatovna Gubaidulina (born 1931) is a Russian composer. In 1963 she finished her post-graduate study at the Moscow Conservatory (class of Professor Vissarion Shebalin). Since 1992 Gubaidulina has lived in Germany. She has written orchestral works, vocal music, music for chamber ensemble, piano music, as well as music for films. Gubaidulina received numerous awards, among them Prix de Monaco (1987), The Russian State Prize (1992), Koussevitzky International Record Award (1989, 1994), and Living Composer Prize of the Cannes Classical Awards (2003). Accessed February 16, 2018. https://www.britannica.com/biography/Sofia-Gubaidulina, http://www.biografija.ru/biography/gubajdulina-sofya-sofiya-azgatovna.htm.

[133] Alfred Schnittke (1934-1998) was a Soviet Russian composer. Schnittke's early music shows the strong influence of Dmitry Schostakovich. Schnittke created a new style, which has been called »polystylism«, where he juxtaposed and combined music of various styles from past and present. His first piece composed in polystylistic technique was his Second Violin Sonata »Quasi una Sonata« (1968). Schnittke's output includes orchestral music, choral, chamber music, operas, ballets, and the music for films. Accessed February 16, 2018. https://www.britannica.com/biography/Alfred-Schnittke.

[134] »Nagasaki« is an oratorio, composed by Schnittke in 1958. The work was considered formalistic, and Schnittke was accused of forgetting the principles of Realism in music. »Nagasaki« was recorded by the Moscow Radio Symphony in 1959 but wasn't printed and didn't receive any subsequent performances. It was finally given its public premiere in its original form in Cape Town by Cape Philharmonic in 2006. Accessed February 16, 2018. http://intoclassics.net/news/2009-09-15-2454, http://americansymphony.org/alfred-schnittke-nagasaki/.

other. The only person I was not acquainted with was Edison Denisov.[135] *He was older than me.*

YT: What do you think about the music of Edison Denisov? Once somebody asked me to accompany his saxophone concerto but I decided to refuse after looking at the score.

NK: When you see the name of Edison Denisov on the score it would be wise to refuse to play it immediately. All the music of these composers is not mine.

---

[135] Edison Denisov (1929-1996) was a Russian composer in the so-called »alternative« division of Soviet music. Denisov graduated from the Moscow Conservatory in 1956. In 1979 he was blacklisted as one of the »Khrennikov's Seven« at the Sixth Congress of the Union of Soviet Composers for unapproved participation in some festivals of Soviet music in the West. By 1991 four composers out of »Khrennikov's Seven« left the USSR. Denisov immigrated to France. Accessed February 16, 2018. http://www.musicologie.org/Biographies/d/denissov.html.

Courses at the Conservatory

One of the most favorite subjects Kapustin studied at the Moscow Conservatory was called the »History of Piano Performance«. The course was led by the eminent Professor Alexander Nikolaev.[136]

NK: I was interested in this subject long before I started to study it officially at the conservatory. At the time I still lived in Nikitovka I had a lot of books on famous pianists, I loved reading about them.

YT: It is fascinating that you became interested in this topic at that early age.

NK: How could you not be interested in that if you are a pianist?

YT: And you had a great teacher.

NK: Oh yes, I got lucky again. By the way, Alexander Nikolaev was also a student of Goldenweiser.

YT: How did you progress in his class?

NK: Very well, I got an »A« for his class. I didn't prepare much for this class because I already knew most of the material we were talking about in the lectures. I remember once he asked us to perform one of the Clementi sonatas. I had to play the one that is in D major. I liked that sonata. Later I even played it in the Small Performance Hall of the conservatory on a concert. Interesting detail, Nikolaev kept insisting that I should record it in the studio at the conservatory.

YT: Why did he insist?

NK: I guess he liked how I played this sonata. He said: »Let's preserve it for the next generation of pianists.«

YT: Did you record it?

NK: Unfortunately I did not.

YT: How long were those lectures with Nikolaev?

NK: It was a two-hour class. Most of the classes at the conservatory were two hours long.

YT: So long?

NK: Yes, but after a while you get used to it.

---

[136] Alexander Alexandrovich Nikolaev (1903-1980) was a famous Russian music theorist. In 1934 he graduated from the Moscow Conservatory as pianist (class of Professor Grigory Ginzburg). In 1937 Nikolaev finished his post-graduate study in the history and theory of pianism (class of Professor Kogan). Starting from 1937 he taught at the Moscow Conservatory. Nikolaev was the general editor of the journal »Questions of the Musical-Performance Art« as well as the editor of »Essays on the Methodology of Teaching Piano«. Nikolaev wrote numerous books, essays, and articles on the subject of piano performance art, musical education in USSR, and pedagogical and performance principles of leading teachers of the Russian piano school. Accessed November 14, 2017. http://www.musenc.ru/html/n/nikolaev.html, https://dic.academic.ru/dic.nsf/enc_biography/91502/Николаев. The beginning of conversation on Nikolaev was presented in Chapter I, pp. 44-45.

YT: I just had a thought – is Nikolaev the one who auditioned you before the entering exams to the Musical College in 1952?
NK (smiling): Yes, that was him.
YT: Oh no... Did he remember you from that audition?
NK: I don't think so. I studied with him on the third course of conservatory (1958-1959), so six or seven years had passed since my audition.
YT: But you remembered him.
NK: Oh, yes. I felt excited when I found out that Nikolaev was going to teach a course for us. Fate brought me back to him.

Another class that Kapustin enjoyed at the Moscow Conservatory was the class of »Chamber Ensemble«. This class was led by Professor Konstantin Adzhemov.[137]

Konstantin Khristophorovich Adzhemov

---

[137] Konstantin Khristoforovich Adzhemov (1911-1985) was a Soviet pianist, teacher, music critic, and classical music commentator. He graduated from the Moscow Conservatory in 1937 (class of Professor Igumnov). In 1940 he finished his post-graduate study in chamber ensemble and the history of the piano performance. From 1944 he began teaching at the Moscow Conservatory and from 1953 in the Gnessin Institute. In 1941-1958 Adzhemov was the editor of the symphonic programs of the Russian USSR radio. Starting from 1955 for more than twenty five years he hosted the programs »The Evenings of the Sound Recordings« and from 1959 the program »The Conversations about Piano Performance«. Accessed November 14, 2017. http://www.mosconsv.ru/ru/person.aspx?id=9038.

NK: Adzhemov was not only a great teacher; he was also a well-known interpreter of Rachmaninov and Debussy's works. He was a very well educated person. He could easily speak in French and German languages.

YT: Was your relationship with Adzhemov like between student and teacher or was it something more?

NK: Of course it was more than just student and teacher; we used to talk about many things in our lessons. I remember during my last year of study at the conservatory, in the spring of 1961, Yuri Gagarin[138] flew to space. Right after this happened I came to the lesson with Adzhemov and he asked me: »Kolia, is it true that Gagarin went into space?«

YT: What did you say?

NK (smiling): I said: »Yes, this is true!« Adzhemov was shocked with that news, and we all felt the same way. It was world news, and especially in the USSR people celebrated it with every possible highest honor.

YT: This is so cool that you were a witness of this global historic moment. I wish I had lived in 1961.

NK: I remember at the beginning there was just the news on TV that Gagarin landed successfully in the Saratov region. We were waiting a few days after that until the official celebration started.

YT: I keep wondering about that strange accident when Gagarin crashed during the training flight.

NK: This whole story about Gagarin's tragic accident is totally unknown; it is hard to tell now what actually happened that day, on the March 27, 1968. Personally, I don't believe in accidents.

YT: You saw a lot of history during your life. Coming back to your lessons with Adzhemov, who were your ensemble members and what instruments did they play?

NK: I had a permanent ensemble member – her name was Danielle Arthur, a violinist. So, it was a duo.

YT: Was she a French student?

NK: Yes. She began her study as a violinist in Paris and was doing some additional study at the Moscow Conservatory.

YT: Did you speak with her in French?

NK: I possibly could, but she spoke Russian quite well, I think she studied Russian in France before coming to Moscow. Adzhemov, however, spoke to her in French quite often.

YT: How long did you play with Danielle?

---

[138] Yuri Alekseyevich Gagarin (1934-1968) was the Soviet cosmonaut, who first completed the journey into outer space on April 12, 1961. *The Anniversary of Yuri Gagarin's 80th Birthday*, RIA News. Accessed February 18, 2018. https://ria.ru/spravka/20140309/998590852.html.

NK: I think at least two years. Did I tell you that she was a student of David Oistrakh[139]*?*
YT: David Oistrakh? This is another big name.
NK: Yes, he was a very well-known violinist. I remember once we even went with Danielle to play for Oistrakh. At that time we worked on Beethoven's »Spring« Sonata (Sonata for Violin and Piano No. 5 in F major, Op. 24). There was one complicated spot, the ritenuto in the trills in both violin and piano parts. Danielle complained to Oistrakh that it is very difficult to play this spot together. He was surprised a little, he said: »What is special about this spot?« He asked me to play it with him and we played it a few times. It was so comfortable and simple to play with him, no difficulties at all. After that he turned to Danielle and said: »You see, everything is not difficult, just don't be afraid.«
YT: Did she understand?
NK: Yes, after that lesson with Oistrakh, this spot started to come out pretty well.

One of the classes that each student is supposed to complete at the conservatory is »Methods of Teaching Piano«, which includes a teaching practicum. Kapustin was never strongly interested in the teaching aspect of study.

NK: When I studied in the college I understood that teaching was not my thing; I was absolutely not suited for this. At the conservatory they allowed me to substitute accompanying in the conducting class for the teaching classes. This I enjoyed a lot.
YT: Is this a standard procedure to allow students to switch subjects? To be precise, to switch a course to a practicum?
NK: Not really.
YT: That's what I think. They made an exception for you. From my experience the plan for normal students would end pretty dramatically, especially knowing that this was the Moscow Conservatory.
NK: They didn't want to let me go.
YT: Did anyone help you with that? Goldenweiser for example?
NK: Not that I know of…
YT: They knew that your destination is in a different area – to compose music.

---

[139] David Fyodorovich Oistrakh (1908-1974) was a renowned Soviet classical violinist and violist. Oistrakh collaborated with major orchestras and musicians from the Soviet Union, Europe, and the United States. Numerous violin works were dedicated to him including both of Dmitry Shostakovich's violin concerti, and the violin concerto by Aram Khachaturian. From 1937 he was the professor at the Moscow Conservatory. Oistrakh is considered one of the preeminent violinists of the 20th century. Accessed February 16, 2018. http://www.mosconsv.ru/ru/person.aspx?id=126114.

NK: Richter[140] *never was a teacher; this was not for him. At the same time, he was a genius pianist.*
YT: *I agree. What did you accompany in that conducting class?*
NK: *It was mostly symphonies – Beethoven, Myaskovsky, some other composers. We played almost all Myaskovsky's symphonies.*[141]

One of other subjects on the list of classes was a harmony class.

YT: *What did you think about the harmony class?*
NK: *I didn't open any harmony books, not even once.*
YT: *Why is that?*
NK: *It was terribly boring to read everything. I knew that material long before. Sometimes I got a feeling that I wrote those books myself.*
YT: *How about »History of Western Music« or »History of Russian Music« classes? Did you have them at the conservatory?*
NK: *Of course I did. I didn't enjoy them much because they studied history, which is about the composers or about the music, but not the music itself. The music itself is what I was most interested in.*

One of the classes that Kapustin remembers in a »special way« was a class called »Dialectic Materialism«.

YT: *Even the name of this class sounds scary to me.*
NK: *I remember that those two-hour lectures were especially long. Our teacher was Sammuil Rapoport, he was famous for giving everyone an »F.« Somehow I got a »B« in this class, but for the »History of the KPSS« (History of the Communist Party) I got »C.« The rest of my grades are mostly »A«, but here is my remarkable »C.«*
YT: *When I studied at the conservatory we didn't have the history of the communist party or dialectic materialism.*
NK: *No luck, you missed it!*
YT: *Did you have any other »interesting« classes?*
NK: *Another one? Sure. We had a »Military Training« class. Here I got an »A.« That was a very rare thing in the conservatory (with the smile).*

---

[140] Sviatoslav Richter (1915-1997) was a Russian pianist known for the depth of his interpretations, virtuoso technique, and vast repertoire, which included the works of Bach, Schumann, Liszt, Prokofiev, and Mussorgsky. He is considered as one of the greatest pianists of the twentieth century. Accessed February 16, 2018.
https://www.britannica.com/biography/Sviatoslav-Richter.
[141] Nikolai Yakovlevich Myaskovsky (1881-1950) was a Russian Soviet composer. He is referred to as the »Father of the Soviet symphony«. Myaskovsky was awarded the Stalin Prize five times, more than any other composer. He composed orchestral music (twenty seven symphonies), chamber, choral, and piano works. Accessed February 16, 2018.
http://filarmonia.kh.ua/nikolaj-myaskovskij/.

YT: How did you make it happen?
NK: I am still wondering how I made it to an »A.« I remember I was a part of the infantry group. One day we had training outside the conservatory. During the time I responded to one of colonel's questions, heavy rain began. I wasn't wearing the cloak but I continued answering him and kept pretending that the rain didn't really bother me. I guess he regarded that as a good thing, he respected that gesture.

One of the most difficult periods at any educational institution is during juries and exams. In the Moscow Conservatory it was especially dramatic but not for all the students.

YT: I read from the Pupkova's notes[142] that during juries students were working in groups, preparing for their exams, and constantly drinking black coffee. Did you prepare in groups or by yourself?
NK: What should I prepare for?
YT: For the exams. Didn't you prepare for that?
NK: Yes I did, but without any enthusiasm. Jenia (Pupkova) did better than me, she got all straight »As.«
YT: In other words, you were doing only the things that you were interested in.
NK: Of course.

---

[142] Pupkova, »Pereigravshaya vsego Baha«. Accessed April 15, 2016. http://pupkova.ru/biography/.

Accompanying

One of the things that Kapustin enjoyed doing at the conservatory, but was not a part of his curriculum, was accompanying other musicians. It is worth mentioning that these were not just any musicians, but some very special performers. One of the first collaborations happened in the autumn of 1956 when Kapustin accompanied one of the well-known pianists of Russian piano performance school – Tatiana Nikolaeva.[143]

NK: Tatiana Nikolaeva was an outstanding pianist; she enjoyed enormous respect at the conservatory.
YT: How did you get acquainted with Nikolaeva?
NK: From what I remember, close to the performance date, her original pianist suddenly became very ill and was not able to accompany her. She needed to find another pianist in a very short amount of time but had trouble and couldn't find anyone.
YT: I understand that. Who would take that responsibility?
NK: At that moment I entered the conservatory. Nikolaeva was a former student of Goldenweiser, I guess he suggested that she talk to me. That's how we got acquainted. Later, Tatiana and I became very good friends. I remember she used to come to Goldenweiser to play for him quite often.
YT: On which piece did you accompany her?
NK: We played Prokofiev's Fifth Piano Concerto for the Studying Student Society performance.
YT: Did you learn the whole concerto?
NK: Of course I did. I had very good sight-reading skills, so I could do that. Plus, Sergei Prokofiev was one of my favorite composers.
YT: What was Nikolaeva's reaction?
NK (smiling): She was surprised that I could learn the concerto that quickly. Actually, I remember we played this concerto twice.
YT: Was it an encore the second time?
NK: Not really. After we played it the first time she turned to the audience and said: »This is very difficult music, and, if Kolia (Nikolai Kapustin) does not mind, we will play it a second time.«
YT: Did you play the whole concerto again?
NK: Yes, we did. This is not a very long concerto, even though it has five movements.
YT: Did you feel stress playing the concerto a second time?

---

[143] See page 57.

NK: No, I didn't. I was absolutely calm, as if we were playing it for the first time. I knew that she was going to play this concerto later with the orchestra, so she needed to be ready for that.
YT: That seems a little unusual to me – to play the whole concerto a second time.
NK: I guess, the first time we played she didn't feel quite right. That's all.
YT: Why did she choose to play Prokofiev's Fifth Concerto?
NK: This concerto was not one of the most known concertos of Prokofiev. In fact, Prokofiev's first three concertos are well known. The Fourth Concerto, for the left hand, was not well received. The Fifth Concerto was also not very popular.
YT: Why is that?
NK: I think maybe the audience didn't like the music… It is hard to tell why some pieces are not well received.
YT: So, in a way Nikolaeva decided to perform this concerto in order to attract interest in this piece?
NK: Yes. Although by that time Prokofiev had not been alive for quite some time.

Another interesting collaboration of Kapustin was when he accompanied eminent pianist Maria Yudina.[144]

NK: I played Stravinsky's Piano Concerto (Concerto for Piano and Wind Instruments) with Yudina. She was trying to find a good pianist to accompany this concerto and through a friends' connection she found me. I think we played it two or three times for sure. As with Nikolaeva, Yudina played this concerto later with orchestra.
YT: Was she teaching at the Moscow Conservatory?
NK: For a short period of time. Yudina had a bad relationship with the Soviet authorities because she was a very religious person.

During the middle years of Kapustin's study at the conservatory he had the experience of playing J. S. Bach *Double Harpsichord Concerto in C major* (BWV 1061) in the Small Hall of the Moscow Conservatory with the Moscow Conservatory Student Orchestra.

---

[144] Maria Yudina (1899-1970) was a Soviet pianist. She graduated from the Petrograd Conservatory (now Saint Petersburg Conservatory) in the class of Anna Esipova. Her classmates included Dmitry Shostakovich and Vladimir Sofronitsky. Starting from 1921 until 1960 Yudina was teaching at different times in the Petrograd Conservatory, Tbilisi State Conservatory, Moscow Conservatory, and the Gnessin Institute. In 1960 Yudina was thrown out of the Gnessin Institute because of her religious attitudes and her advocacy of modern Western music. Yudina was an uncompromising critic of the Soviet regime. Among her friends were Boris Pasternak, Osip Mandelstam, Mikhail Bakhtin, Dmitry Shostakovich, Pierre Boulez, and Karlheinz Stockhausen. Richter refers to Yudina as the immensely talented pianist, who played Stravinsky, Hindemith, Krenek, and Bartok at the time when these composers were not only unknown but banned in the Soviet Union. Accessed February 18, 2018. http://www.bach-cantatas.com/Bio/Yudina-Maria.htm, http://www.classicfm.com/discover-music/latest/maria-yudina-stalin/.

> NK: I remember I played this concerto with Leonid Blok. He was a year older than me. Leonid later became the accompanist of violinist Viktor Tretiakov.[145] There was an interesting episode about this performance – I played the first piano part and Leonid the second. He asked me to sit on the second piano for some reason. I still don't understand why... Of course I agreed with no problem.
> YT: This is strange – playing the first piano part and sitting on the second piano?
> NK: Exactly.
> YT: Did you enjoy playing this concerto?
> NK: Of course I did. I found out that the beginning of the last movement (third movement »Vivace«) that the 8*th* notes sound exactly the same as »Sweet Georgia Brown,«[146] of course in different rhythmic setting.
> YT: I can't believe it! There is the connection of Baroque music and jazz.

On one hand, all the additional performance projects, that Kapustin was involved in during his years at the conservatory outside his educational program, made this time more intense. On the other hand, he had the experience of playing with some of the best Russian pianists of the twentieth century, such as Tatiana Nikolaeva and Maria Yudina. There are no doubts that this experience made Kapustin a better pianist.

> NK: Of course it was difficult. Plus, in addition to that I was a very responsible person. I could not just play as if I were sight-reading the score. I felt that everything should be done at the proper level.
> YT: You still remain a responsible person.
> NK: That's probably why it is so hard for me now to compose music.
> YT: I understand, but on the other hand – if you are in the process of composing something then it is going to be an extraordinary piece.

---

[145] Viktor Viktorovich Tretiakov (born 1946) is a Russian violinist and conductor. In 1966, at the age of nineteen, he won the first prize in the third International Tchaikovsky Competition, and after that has performed with almost every major orchestra in the world, including Berlin, Vienna, Moscow, St. Petersburg, London, Los Angeles, Munich and many others. Tretiakov taught for many years at the Moscow Conservatory. In 1996 he took the teaching position in Cologne (Germany). Accessed February 18, 2018. http://web.archive.org/web/20110910195253/http://www.biograph.ru/bank/tretyakov_vv.htm.

[146] »Sweet Georgia Brown« is a famous jazz standard written in 1925 by Ben Bernie, Maceo Pinkard (music), and Kenneth Casey (lyrics).

Kapustin's Injury of the Right Hand

Right at the beginning of Kapustin's study at the conservatory he got into a situation which could have potentially affected his entire life, moving him away from piano performance.

NK: *Everything started the very next day after I performed Prokofiev's Piano Concerto No. 5 with Tatiana Nikolaeva. I started to feel something uncomfortable in the third finger of my right hand. At that time, as it always happens, Nikolaeva asked me to begin working on a new piece. She wanted me to accompany her on one of Golubev's*[147] *symphonies. We were supposed to perform this piece in the »Union of Soviet Composers«*[148] *but this performance never happened.*
YT: *Is it because of your injury?*
NK: *Unfortunately yes. It ended up being a very serious case. It is called a hangnail, something that precedes gangrene. The person who helped me in this horrible situation was Natalia Konchalovskaya. Her friend was able to organize surgery for me in the »Vishnevsky Institute of Surgery.«*[149]
YT: *How did the surgery go?*
NK: *It went very well; they saved my finger. I experienced very severe pain before and after the surgery.*
YT: *Did this affect your study at the conservatory?*
NK: *At that time I didn't see myself as a composer, I wanted to be a classical pianist. So it was a complete tragedy for me. If the surgery would have gone badly, they would have to amputate my finger.*
YT: *And in addition to that – everything happened right when you entered the conservatory.*
NK: *Yes, during my first semester. I was not able to use my right hand at all for almost half a year. Because of that situation I had to play Ravel's Piano Concerto for the Left Hand for my first jury.*
YT: *Did you play only one piece?*
NK: *Yes. By the summer of 1957 I could already play a little with my right hand and I learned one of Bach's Prelude and Fugues. Goldenweiser suggested not performing it for*

---

[147] Evgeny Kirillovich Golubev (1910-1988) was a Russian Soviet composer. He was teaching composition at the Moscow Conservatory. Some of his known students were Tatiana Nikolaeva and Alfred Schnittke. His own compositions include orchestral, chamber, piano, and choir music. Accessed February 18, 2018. http://www.music-dic.ru/html-music-keld/g/1855.html.
[148] »Union of Soviet Composers« is a Russian public organization uniting professional composers and musicologists from forty-eight regions of Russia. It was founded in 1960.
[149] Note by the author: Vishnevsky Institute of Surgery is considered to be one of the best surgical institutions in Russia even today.

> *my exam because I still experienced pain in my right hand so I played only the concerto. Nodar (Gabunia), my friend, accompanied me. There was one interesting fact about that exam – it is that Gilels was on the committee.*
> *YT: Emil Gilels?!?*
> *NK: Yes. I remember that a while ago I heard Gilels playing this concerto in the Great Hall of the conservatory. I liked it very much. Although, to tell you the truth, my favorite interpretation of this concerto is by Richter.*
> *YT: Did you have a chance to talk to Gilels afterwards?*
> *NK: This is what I am wondering myself – how did it happen that I was acquainted with neither Gilels nor Richter? I was one of a few people who attended Gould's first performance in Moscow, I knew the elusive Sofronitsky, but these two…everybody was acquainted with Gilels and Richter except me.*
> *YT: So, you decided to play Ravel's concerto after listening to these two giant pianists?*
> *NK: Yes, I started to think about that piece during my last year of study at the musical college. I asked my friend Andrei (Mikhalkov) to help me with finding the score of this concerto. Andrei presented it to me on my eighteenth birthday on the November 22, 1955 (with a smile). It was very easy for him to get the score; he had all kinds of connections. That's how I decided to play this concerto on my first jury at the conservatory – I already knew the piece. By the time I started my second year of study I was able to use both hands.*

There was one positive benefit that Kapustin had to deal with because of his injury – during his first year at the conservatory he composed the Piano Sonata for the Left Hand (1957) that remains unpublished to this day.[150]

> *NK: I composed it in Mikhalkov's house in the Nikolina Gora (suburb of Moscow). I still have the score of this sonata somewhere in our house.*
> *YT: Why don't you want to publish your early works?*
> *NK: I would like to keep them unpublished. I was very young at that time.*

---

[150] The conversation about Kapustin's *Sonata for the Left Hand* will be presented in the latter part of Chapter III.

Nikolai Kapustin, Moscow Conservatory, ca. 1957-1958

Master-Classes and Concerts at the Moscow Conservatory

As we all know, one of the most important aspects of our development as serious performers comes from our ability to listen and absorb other performances in order to create your own style of playing. Kapustin attended dozens of different concerts and masterclasses during his period of study at the Moscow Conservatory. Some of Kapustin's favorite concerts were the concerts of Vladimir Sofronitsky.

> *NK: I attended all of his concerts. I did not miss even one. I remember he had a kind of superstition – he always scheduled his performances on the same date almost every year. He was a mystical man. I guess that's why he played Alexander Scriabin so well. He also had a great sense of humor and was extremely talented in composing palindromes.*[151] *Actually, I do that too. I have a whole collection of palindromes. Although, I can't read all of them because of the content; some of them include »dirty« language. This is a good one: Vodila vniz invalidov (translation: she was helping invalids to go down).*
> *YT: Who was helping the invalids and down where?*
> *NK: This we don't really know.*

One of the bright moments in the history of piano playing in Russia was the Van Cliburn[152] triumph on the 1st International Tchaikovsky Competition in Moscow in the spring of 1958. At that time Kapustin was finishing his second year of study at the conservatory.

> *NK: Goldenweiser used to talk about Van Cliburn on the lessons. I remember he said once that Van Cliburn reminded him of Sergei Rachmaninov. I didn't attend Van Cliburn's very first performance in Moscow. He was completely unknown to the Russian audience at the beginning. Although, after he played the very first day, the rumors appeared on the air about the genius pianist from the United States.*
> *YT: That was at the time of the »cold war« between the USSR and the US.*
> *NK: Yes, nobody knew how it was going to end.*
> *YT: Oh yes, to let the American pianist win on the biggest Russian competition was probably a very serious thing.*

---

[151] A palindrome is a word, phrase, number, or other sequence of characters that reads the same backwards or forward, for example »race car« and »Was it a car or a cat I saw?«

[152] Van Cliburn (1934-2013) was an American pianist who achieved worldwide recognition in 1958 when he won the International Tchaikovsky Piano Competition in Moscow. Cliburn performed and recorded through the 1970s. He played for royalty and heads of state from dozens of countries and for every US president since 1958. Accessed February 18, 2018. https://www.britannica.com/biography/Van-Cliburn.

NK: And it was the very first Tchaikovsky Competition.
YT: I remember he had a Russian teacher – Rosina Lhevinne,[153] who prepared him for the competition.
NK: Yes, you could feel the Russian school of playing in his performance. Gilels, who was the head of the competition committee, regarded Cliburn's performance in the highest regard. When I heard Cliburn the last time at the end of the1980s in Moscow I liked him very much. I think he played later even better than at the time of the competition. I remember he came to Russia with his mother and was granted $10,000. I guess that was for his contribution to the Russian musical culture. That was serious money!

It is quite interesting that in addition to the classical concerts that were organized in the performance halls of the Moscow Conservatory there were also rare jazz concerts. The most memorable concert happened in 1959. It was the duet of the jazz pianist Dwike Mitchell[154] and bassist/French horn player Willie Ruff.

NK: I especially remember that concert of two improvisers. They were both African-American musicians, a pianist Dwike Mitchell and a double bass/French horn player Willie Ruff. Ruff mostly played the double bass that night. Mitchell surprised us with his technique. They played so well that we couldn't stop clapping. Later, I found out that they were completely unknown in the US.
YT: What did they play?
NK: Generally, modern jazz.
YT: I read that some of the professors from the conservatory left the concert.[155]
NK: That's true. Why would they like it? Jazz was not appreciated at the conservatory.
YT: Although, you liked the musicians.
NK: Yes, they were highly virtuoso performers. I remember a friend of mine, Vladimir Ashkenazy, also attended that concert. On the way home we were talking about our impression from those amazing improvisers. He said: »I am pretty sure that if they would be asked to play any of Chopin's etudes they wouldn't be able to play it with their technique.«

---

[153] Rosina Lhevinne (1880-1976) was a pianist and famed pedagogue. She graduated from the Moscow Conservatory in 1898 (class of Vasily Safonov). In 1919 Lhevinne immigrated to the US and joined the faculty of the Juilliard School. Among her students were many of the best young pianists of the 1940s-1960s, including Van Cliburn, who arrived in her class in 1951. Accessed February 18, 2018. http://enc-dic.com/enc_music/Levina-R-4072.html.
[154] The Duo Mitchell Dwike and Willie Ruff toured Soviet Union and China in 1959 with Yale University Russian Chorus. During this tour they were able also to perform some jazz music. Accessed November 14, 2017.
https://www.allmusic.com/artist/dwike-mitchell-mn0000132649/biography.
[155] Evgeniya Pupkova, »Pereigravshaya Vsego Baha.« Accessed February 8, 2016. http://pupkova.ru/biography.

YT: What did you say?

NK: I said that I think that those jazzmen are playing something that is so comfortable for them to play. If they would play something less comfortable the result could be different.

YT: Yes, as everywhere else. It's a big question for me if those classical pianists who can play Chopin's etudes would ever be able to improvise as well as Mitchell and Ruff did.

Being a student at the conservatory Kapustin started to attend the jazz concerts of big band music outside the conservatory, for example concerts of the Oleg Lundstrem Orchestra.

NK: I had no idea that I was going to be a part of the band. We did meet a few times with Lundstrem. In the middle 1950s the band didn't come to Moscow too often because they were based in Kazan.[156] I remember attending their concerts twice.

YT: What did you think about the Lundstrem Orchestra at that time?

NK: The first time I went to their concert I thought they were old-fashioned. There were musicians from the original band who played from the time when the band was in China. When I came to their second concert the sound of the band was different. A new group of musicians had joined the band, younger people, and it was the musicians with whom I would later play.

YT: In a way you joined the band with a new generation of musicians, which created the new modern sound.

NK: Yes, this is exactly what it was. All members of the new band were improvisers, not like in the previous setting where they didn't improvise at all.

---

[156] Kazan is the capital and the largest city of the Republic of Tatarstan, Russia. It is situated in the European Russia territory, 500 miles away from Moscow.

Student Life at the Moscow Conservatory and Kapustin's Friends

Life in the dormitory of the Moscow Conservatory was very exciting for Kapustin. He made a lot of new friends. One of his friends, Manashir Yakubov, remembered his experience of listening to Kapustin's virtuoso playing. In one of his articles about Kapustin he wrote:

We used to pack into the dormitory room when he was playing something amazing, technically unreachable, in the way our jazz idols would, with a completely calm demeanor. He demonstrated the highest technical achievements that put us into emotional shock. Kolia [Nikolai] was showing us the basic ideas for the boogie-woogie playing and was sincerely surprised when we could not understand it so quickly.[157]

The big advantage of the dormitory, in comparison to the dormitory of the Musical College, was that during Kapustin's second year of study the Rehearsal Hall opened. This hall is situated on the top floor of the building where students could practice on grand pianos in addition to having upright pianos in each room.

Although, living away from his parents had some disadvantages too. For example, one incident that Kapustin was a part of almost ended up with him being expelled from the conservatory.

NK: I remember there was a dangerous virus in Moscow, and the situation got so bad that the conservatory was placed under quarantine. No one was allowed to attend the lectures and we were required to stay in our dormitory. We quickly got bored. My friend and I decided to draw abstract pictures. He was a choir conductor but had experience in painting. There were a few students who joined us. After we finished the drawings we put them on the walls of the dormitory for fun, like an exhibition. That was it.
YT: What happened next?
NK: We were put onto the list of students who were supposed to be expelled from the conservatory.
YT: Because of what?
NK: Because of those pictures. It was considered bourgeois art. We tried to explain that it was just as a joke, students' foolery, but it didn't work.
YT: What happened next?
NK: I thought that it's all over for me but Goldenweiser rescued me. He talked to the director of the conservatory about this incident. He said: »I knew in my life just two

---

[157] Yakubov, Manashir. »Kontsert v djazovom stile [Concert in Jazz Style]«. *Utro Rossii*, June 8-14, 1995, p. 9. Translated by Yana Tyulkova.

people equally talented, these are Sergei Rachmaninov and Tatiana Nikolaeva. Now I know the third one – Nikolai Kapustin.« After this conversation we were all forgiven, and our whole group of »modern painters« was rescued.
YT: It looks like you initiated this entire thing and you also saved everyone.
NK: Not I, Goldenweiser helped us.

Talking about Kapustin's friends at the conservatory, it is necessary to begin with a person with whom Kapustin would have a life-long relationship, Nodar Gabunia.[158]

YT: How did you get acquainted with Gabunia?
NK: We both were students of Goldenweiser. Furthermore, he was also a student from the outside of Moscow, like me. He was from Tbilisi (Georgia) and I was from Nikitovka (Ukraine).
YT: Did he live at the dormitory?
NK: No, he rented the apartments. He lived very close to the conservatory. I was a frequent guest at his place.
YT: Did he become a famous composer in Tbilisi?
NK: Even before he left Tbilisi to study in Moscow he already had a great reputation as a talented Georgian composer. He was a student of Khachaturian at the conservatory. Actually, I also attended Khachaturian's classes quite often. I knew Khachaturian very well.
YT: Could you please tell me about it?
NK: I remember he smoked a lot, and even during his classes there was smoke all over the place.
YT: Was it individual lessons or a group?
NK: There were a few of us. Nodar invited me to join this class.
YT: What kind of music did Nodar Gabunia compose?
NK: Very good music. I liked his compositions. He was a very good composer and a very good pianist also.
YT: Did Nodar know that you were composing music?
NK: Of course he did. I played all the pieces that I was composing at that time for him. I remember I composed my Sonata in C minor and asked Nodar his opinion about

---

[158] Nodar Gabunia (1933-2000) was a composer and a pianist who dominated Georgian music in the latter decades of the twentieth century. He studied at the Tbilisi Conservatory (Georgia). In 1957 he graduated from the Moscow Conservatory as a pianist (class of Alexander Goldenweiser) and in 1962 as a composer (class of Aram Khachaturian). Right after his graduation he began teaching at the Tbilisi Conservatory, and starting from 1984 he was appointed Rector of the conservatory. Gabunia's works are strongly influenced by the Georgian sound. His works include orchestral, chamber, vocal music, as well as solo piano pieces. Gabunia was also a film score composer; one of his famous works is the theme from the film of Ivane Kotorashvili »Story«. Accessed February 18, 2018. https://dic.academic.ru/dic.nsf/enc_music/1801/Габуния, http://www.nodargabunia.com/start.html.

showing this piece to the »old man« (Goldenweiser). He was also a composer, as you know. Nodar suggested not showing it because Goldenweiser was far from jazz and not interested at all. I remember once Goldenweiser said: »Yes, jazz invigorates me.«
YT: *Did you visit Gabunia in Georgia?*
NK: *Yes, I came twice to Tbilisi – in 1958 and at the beginning of the 1960s, when I was already working with Oleg Lundstrem. Both times I stayed in his house. We were close friends. It was a very good time – we used to visit our friends every evening and perform our music for each other. I enjoyed very much being there. I remember right after my second visit to Tbilisi I went from the airport straight to the rehearsal with the big band. It was a very busy time for me.*

Kapustin visiting Nodar Gabunia, Tbilisi, 1958. From the right: Nodar Gabunia, Manana Gabunia (Nodar's sister), Nikolai Kapustin, and Mishiko

NK: *A few months ago my other friend from the conservatory Oxana Yablonskaya, also a student of Goldenweiser, called me on my birthday (November 22, 2016). She* told me about Nodar's last years of life. He lived in the US and passed away in Amsterdam because of cancer in 2000.

The pianist Oxana Yablonskaya[159] was another good friend of Nikolai Kapustin at the conservatory.

NK: She was from Moscow, as were many students of Goldenweiser, and began to study piano at a very young age, something like six, at the CMS (Central Music School for the Gifted Children). By the way, we both had Dmitry Bashkirov as a Goldenweiser assistant.

YT: So, she had a connection to Goldenweiser from a very young age.

NK: Yes.

YT: Did you attend the lessons of other students of Goldenweiser?

NK: Not really. I was constantly in a hurry there for some reason. I remember once Oxana attended my lesson where I was playing Liszt's Transcendental Etude No. 5 Feux Follets. We talked about some technical issues of this piece and she was also interested in the size of my hand. It is known that Liszt had a large hand, but Liszt himself claimed that his hand was absolutely normal in size, and I believe him.

YT: So, you were helping each other.

NK: Of course. I remember we both played another piece – Beethoven's Eroica Variations, Op. 35 and used to discuss it. I also accompanied her with Tchaikovsky's Piano Concerto No. 2, Op. 44, all three movements. We were very good friends. She lives now in Israel, but before that she lived in the United Stated and Canada. The last time I talked to her she said that her Canadian students are playing my compositions, particularly my Etudes Op. 40. I was very pleased to hear that.

YT: Did she dedicate her life to teaching?

NK: Yes, she is an internationally well-known teacher. When she lived in the US she taught at the Juilliard School for many years. To tell you the truth, I think she was one of the best students of Goldenweiser. I remember after she graduated she continued her study and completed post-graduate study under Tatiana Nikolaeva.

---

[159] Oxana Yablonskaya (born 1938) is a Russian pianist who has had an active international performance career since the early 1960s. Yablonskaya graduated from the Moscow Conservatory in 1962 (class of Alexander Goldenweiser) and completed her post-graduate study in 1965 (class of Tatiana Nikolaeva). She began teaching at the Moscow Conservatory from 1962. Yablonskaya won the top prizes in the Marguerite Long-Jasques Thibaud Competition (1963), Rio de Janeiro Piano Competition (1965), and the Vienna Beethoven Competition (1969). She immigrated to the USA in 1977. Yablonskaya went on to appear with many of the world's finest symphony orchestras. She taught as a member of the piano faculty at the Juilliard School for more than thirty years, until 2009. Yablonskaya is a Yamaha Performing Artist. Accessed November 14, 2017. https://www.puigcerdamusic.com/oxana-yablonskaya.

I feel so delighted that Oxana Yablonskaya agreed to say a couple of words about her friend from the conservatory, Nikolai Kapustin:

It is easy to talk about the music of Nikolai Kapustin, and it is not as easy to talk about Kolia as a person.

When we studied at the conservatory, Kolia seemed a little strange to me – everybody was talking all the time, laughing loudly, missing classes (of course not often and not the private piano lessons) but he was different. Goldenweiser himself never missed classes and was never late. I remember Nikolai's performance of Beethoven's Variations, Op. 35 very clearly. He never came to the lessons with Goldenweiser unprepared. His performances were always well planned, and all technical difficulties of the pieces were worked out. Between the classes he played jazz... I remember very often he played one of his compositions, I think it's now called Sonatina, Op. 100. It was written in the style of Mozart, and we all tried to play it by ear. It starts as an easy piece, but it changes quickly.

I remember his performance with Nodar Gabunia of Bartok's Concerto for Two Pianos and Percussion very well – it was a sensation at that time... In general, he reminded me Goldenweiser himself – always prim, seasoned, and never any kind of sloppiness that students often allow themselves.

Once I found the phone number of Kapustin and called him from the United States. We didn't talk probably for fifty years (!!!). I invited him to Italy. Unfortunately, he refused to come, he said that he is no longer travelling long distances. He was surprised that I was talking about his music. He said: »How do you know about my music?« I answered that the whole world knows his music, that he made a revolution in classical music, and that everybody admires his music, including me. To tell you the truth, he was surprised to hear that... sincerely surprised.

The music of Kapustin made a revolution – his music is easy to recognize, performed everywhere, and very popular. Although, it is difficult to perform his music the way he plays it himself. I remember I was listening to someone else's performance of Kapustin and was delighted by them until the point when I heard Nikolai playing his compositions... No one can even get close to his interpretation. He is a brilliant pianist, who can play with the real jazz rhythm that is necessary for the performance of his music. I adore his music, play it myself, and assign it to my students. In the whole world you can constantly hear his solo piano compositions on international competitions, festivals... everywhere.[160]

Another close friend of Kapustin from the Moscow Conservatory, who gained world-wide recognition as a classical pianist, was Vladimir Ashkenazy.[161]

---

[160] From the correspondence with Oxana Yablonskaya, February 27, 2018.

[161] Vladimir Ashkenazy (born 1937) is a well-known Russian pianist. He was born in Gorky (Nizhny Novgorod) and was accepted at the CMS (Moscow) at the age of eight. Ashkenazy graduated from the Moscow Conservatory (class of Lev Oborin). In 1955 Ashkenazy won second prize in the International Chopin Piano Competition in Warsaw, in 1956 the first prize in the Queen Elisabeth Music Competition in Brussels, and in 1962 he shared the first prize with John

YT: I remember you told me that Ashkenazy listened to your performance of Chopin's Concerto No. 1 in E minor, accompanied by Goldenweiser, in one of your exams, and he liked it.

NK: Yes, he appreciated my performances.

YT: Who was his teacher at the conservatory?

NK: He and Andrei Mikhalkov studied together with the same teacher – Lev Oborin, although, Adrei didn't survive long at the conservatory.

YT: Did you attend Ashkenazy's concerts?

NK: Of course I did. We had a ritual to walk after the concerts and to talk about the music. I knew his father, David Ashkenazy, very well. He was also a virtuoso pianist. I guess the virtuosity was in their blood. David Ashkenazy worked mostly in the area of popular music. I remember he accompanied Klavdiya Shulzhenko.[162]

YT: Did you attend the Second International Tchaikovsky Piano Competition in 1962 when Ashkenazy shared the first prize with John Ogdon?

NK: I didn't go. He told me he didn't want to perform on that competition but he was pressured to do it.

YT: Did Lev Oborin, his teacher, push him?

NK: Oh no! It was the Ministry of Culture of the USSR. After Cliburn's victory on the First Tchaikovsky Competition our country needed a winner.

YT: So, it was politically necessary.

NK: Of course.

YT: I read that Vladimir Ashkenazy had some questions concerning his citizenship.

NK: He had only one question – his relationship with Yekaterina Furtseva, the Minister of Culture of the USSR. He was a very popular pianist, who was invited to play many concerts, which gave him serious income. Ashkenazy refused to give the biggest part of his income to the government, when most of the artists of that time did. Finally, he had to immigrate to England. He was forced to leave.

YT: There is information that he now resides in Switzerland.

NK: This I don't know, I lost the connection with him.

Ogdon in the International Tchaikovsky Competition. From 1970s to the present time Ashkenazy has received six Grammy Awards for the Best Instrumental Soloist Performance, Best Instrumental Soloist Performance with Orchestra, and for the Best Chamber Music Performance. Accessed February 18, 2018. https://www.britannica.com/biography/Vladimir-Ashkenazy, http://www.vladimirashkenazy.com/biography.php.

[162] Klavdiya Ivanovna Shulzhenko (1906-1984) was a well-known popular singer from the Soviet Union. She started singing with jazz and pop bands in the late 1920s. During WWII Shulzhenko performed about a thousand concerts for Soviet soldiers in besieged Leningrad and elsewhere. In 1945 Shulzhenko was awarded the Order of the Red Star and was named People's Artist of the USSR in 1971. Accessed November 14, 2017. http://www.peoples.ru/art/music/stage/shulzhenko/, http://telegrafua.com/country/13888/.

Another friend of Kapustin, with whom he studied together for nine years, was Evgeniya Pupkova. Furthermore, they studied with the same teachers – Avrelian Rubbakh and Alexander Goldenweiser.

NK: I played a lot of music with Jenia (Evgeniya Pupkova). I used to go to the music store to buy the piano scores for four hands so we would play together. I remember during the first year of our study at the conservatory, Jenia and I listened to Gershwin's Rhapsody in Blue for the first time, performed by Alexander Tsfasman. Neither of us felt a strong admiration to this interpretation of Gershwin's piece.
YT: Why didn't you like it?
NK: It didn't move me.
YT: What did Pupkova do after graduation?
NK: She returned to the city where she was born – to Ufa and remained there.
AK (joining the conversation): I keep asking him to reconnect with all his friends from the past but Kolia keeps postponing that.

Another person with whom Kapustin got acquainted with during his study at the conservatory, and whose friendship would be life-long, was Nikolai Petrov.[163]

NK: I got acquainted with Kolia (Nikolai Petrov) in 1961. At that time he was finishing his study at the Central Music School. His teacher was Tatiyana Kestner. I knew her son, Yuri Kestner, who asked me to listen to Nikolai's performance of Liszt's Transcendental Etude Fleux Follets. That's how our friendship started. Later he would also study with Goldenweiser at the conservatory.
YT: I remember from the time I studied at the conservatory that Nikolai Petrov was one of a few pianists who could play classical music and jazz. Is that true?
NK: Yes, he played jazz with the score, but he didn't improvise like jazz pianists do on a regular basis.
YT: He played a lot of your music.
NK: Yes, he premiered my Piano Sonata No. 2 Op. 54 in Russia before Marc-André Hamelin played a Western premier of this piece. He also premiered my Piano Concerto No. 5, Op. 72 that I dedicated to him and Piano Quintet, Op. 89. We have a long history to share.

---

[163] Nikolai Arnoldovich Petrov (1943-2011) was an eminent Russian pianist. In 1966 Petrov graduated from the Moscow Conservatory. He gave regular performances in Moscow, US, England, France, and other European countries. The continuation of the conversation about Petrov will be presented in the Chapters VI and VII.

Composing Music at the Conservatory

There are three composers who Kapustin considers to be his favorites. They are Sergei Prokofiev, Béla Bartók, and Maurice Ravel. Sergei Prokofiev was his »first big love«. Interest in Prokofiev's music started from the time he studied at the Moscow Musical College. As it was mentioned earlier, his teacher, Avrelian Rubbakh, was a friend and a big admirer of Prokofiev's works. The interest in Béla Bartók appeared from the conservatory period when his friend, Nodar Gabunia, was investigating the music of the Hungarian composer.

YT: I remember Bartok was one of the innovative composers of his time.
NK: Actually, I don't like everything in Bartók. For example, I don't like his Sonata.
YT: How about his cycle Mikrokosmos?
NK: This work I like.
YT: How did you get your third influence – the music of Ravel?
NK: It came from myself. I played a lot of Ravel's music, Jeux d'eau, Le tombeau de Couperin, and also his Piano Concerto for the Left Hand. I didn't play his Violin Sonata No. 2, which was influenced by American jazz and blues, but I was very well acquainted with this piece.
YT: Do you also like some specific works in Ravel's music like in Bartók for example?
NK: In Ravel I like absolutely everything. This is actually a very unique thing about Ravel – it's hard to identify the difference between his early or late works.
YT: So, his style didn't change through the years?
NK: It did not. His style formed right from the beginning and stayed that way.
YT: I have read that a lot of jazz pianists, like Oscar Peterson and Bill Evans, were also interested in Ravel's music because of his harmonies.
NK: Yes, I agree – his harmony is what strikes you the most.
YT: I always wanted to ask you – when you studied at the conservatory did Goldenweiser chose the pieces to play for you or it was your choice?
NK: Most of the time it was my choice.
YT: That's why you played your favorite composers!
NK: Of course.
YT: For some reason when we talk about impressionist composers the first composer on the list is Debussy and Ravel the second. Do you agree with that?
NK: No, I don't agree. For me Ravel is a more interesting composer than Debussy. To tell you the truth, I don't like Debussy.

It is known that during Kapustin's last year of study at the Musical College he was asked by Khachaturian to study as a composition major at the conservatory. Surprisingly enough, Kapustin refused.

> YT: *Why didn't you want to study composition and piano performance, like some of your friends did, or just composition?*
> NK: *Everybody suggested that I do that but I was afraid, like being afraid of the fire. I believe that it is impossible to teach how to compose the music. It's either there or not.*

During the period of study at the conservatory (1956-1961) Kapustin kept composing his own music. Those compositions exist now without any opus numbers. As a summation, the piano pieces that were composed during his study at the musical college and earlier included *Piano Sonata* (Nikitovka, 1950), *Romance in F major* (Moscow, 1954), *Sonatina* (1954), *Polka-Rondo* (1955), and *Czech Rhapsody for two pianos* (1956). The pieces that appeared during his study at the conservatory included *Piano Sonata for the Left Hand* (1957), two *Sonatinas* (ca. 1957-1958), and the *Piano Sonata in C minor* (ca. 1958-1959).

> YT: *Interesting detail – the first piece that you composed at the conservatory was the Sonata for the Left Hand. I don't hear the jazz elements in there.*
> NK: *This sonata was the last piece that I composed in traditional classical style. After that piece there was no way to go back.*

Sonata for the Left Hand (1957)

YT: *Can you tell a little more about this Sonata for the Left Hand?*
NK: *This sonata was written for the left hand at the time when I couldn't use my right hand because of injury during my first year. I remember once I even played this sonata to Karen Khachaturian, the nephew of Aram Khachaturian, also a composer. He enjoyed it very much.*
YT: *I tried to play a little bit of your Sonata for the Left Hand. It looks that this is a difficult piece.*
NK: *No, it's not. The only difficult part for this sonata is the finale.*
YT: *How about the two Sonatinas that you composed during the same period of time – are they difficult?*
NK: *Not really. The first Sonatina was lost but the second one was reworked into my Sonatina (Op. 100) that I composed in 2000, and which is now very popular. Not many people know that this opus was rewritten from my very early works.*
YT: *How did that happen?*
NK: *I had a friend who worked at the publishing company and he asked me to write something easy for the piano, not as complicated as I usually do. I didn't think too long and decided to rearrange my early Sonatina. I did that especially because we were friends*

from the conservatory period. We used to live in the same room in the dormitory. I knew that he would remember that piece.

YT: *How much did you change the original score?*

NK: *I made it more complex, especially harmonically.*

The most affective piece that Kapustin wrote during his years at the Moscow Conservatory was *Piano Sonata in C minor* (Big Sonata), which was composed around 1958-1959.

YT: *Beginning from this sonata you started intensively using harmonies and rhythmic idioms of jazz and blues.*

NK: *Yes, that was my new beginning. I remember I performed this Sonata in C minor extensively for my friends.*

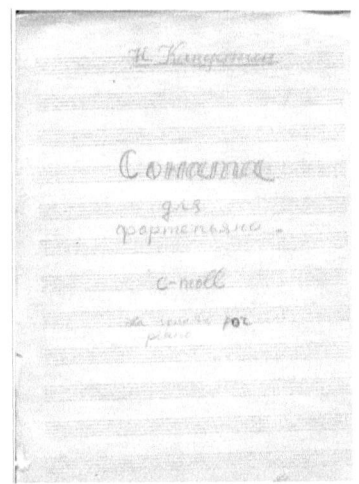 

Piano Sonata in C minor (ca. 1958-1959)

YT: *What about the form and style of this work?*

NK: *This sonata is a three-movement work. Stylistically, in this piece the jazz elements appeared most noticeably.*

YT: *We talked with you earlier that jazz elements started to appear already in the Czech Rhapsody (1956) during your last years of study at the musical college.*

NK: *Yes, it happened gradually.*

YT: *Did you have an idea to rewrite your Piano Sonata in C minor and publish it, same as you did with one of your Sonatinas?*

NK: To rewrite a sonatina is one thing, but to rewrite a whole sonata – this is a completely different thing. There would be too many things to do. It was easier for me to compose a brand new sonata instead.

YT: I remember you mentioned there were some moments that you really liked in that piece. Why don't you publish it as your early work the way it was written?

NK: Yes, some people asked me why I didn't include this work in the list of my compositions and didn't give it an opus number.

YT: Yes, why didn't you do it?

NK: I felt that this sonata is not perfect in its form; I still don't like a couple of transitions in there. Chopin also had the same issue sometimes in his works. Overall it's a good piece.

YT: It looks like before your collaboration with Oleg Lundstrem you were composing mostly solo piano pieces.

NK: It looks that way, but I also composed orchestral music during that time and chamber music too.

YT: Do you have any scores for orchestral or chamber music from that period preserved in your house?

NK: Unfortunately not. Although, I am sure that some of them still exist somewhere. I remember I met Sergei Mikhalkov, the younger brother of Andrei Mikhalkov, at the Moscow Movie Production Company »Mosfilm« and he told me that there are still some of my scores left in their house. This made me feel relief. Who knows, maybe some of them are still there?

The Festival of Youth and Students (Moscow, July 1957)

The Sixth World Festival of Youth and Students (WFYS) was held in Moscow starting July 28, 1957. The festival attracted 34,000 people from 130 countries,[164] which was the highest number of attendees since the First WFYS in Prague in 1947.[165]

The Sixth World Festival of Youth and Students, Moscow, USSR, July 1957

People brought music from many world cultures to the USSR to participate in this international event. Nikolai Kapustin was asked to compose an orchestral piece to be performed on the festival with the Yuri Saulsky Big Band. This band was one of the groups that represented Russian big band jazz. It is interesting that this big band was organized specifically for the performance on that festival. The piece they performed, composed by Kapustin, was called Concertino for Piano and Orchestra.

---

[164] The Sixth World Festival of Youth and Students was one of the results of the political reforms in the USSR organized by its leader Nikita Khrushchev, known as »Khrushchev's Thaw«. Foreigners could come for a visit, and Russian people were allowed to meet foreigners, but only in groups under supervision. Accessed July 7, 2016.
http://all-that-is-interesting.com/moscow-1957-host-world-festival-youth-students.
[165] The First World Festival of Youth and Students was held in 1947 in Prague and attracted 17,000 people.

YT: *The Concertino for the Piano and Orchestra* is listed as your Op. 1.
NK: Yes, I decided that since this piece would be presented on such a significant event it would be appropriate to have it as my first opus. Saulsky[166] asked me to compose this piece.
YT: Yuri Saulsky was an important figure in Russian music. How did you get acquainted with him?
NK: I knew him before the summer of 1957. In the middle 1950s I used to attend the rehearsals of a jazz combo led by a friend of mine, pianist Boris Richkov. That's where I got acquainted with Saulsky. We became good friends with Yuri Sergeevich (Saulsky).
YT: What kind of music did Richkov's combo play?
NK: I remember once I came to their rehearsal and they were playing In the Mood of Glenn Miller (smiling). They got the scores somewhere and were rehearsing. That was a rare thing; mostly we had to transcribe the music on our own.
YT: How did your rehearsals with the Saulsky Big Band go? Did you rehearse a lot?
NK: Since this was a very significant performance, we rehearsed this piece very intensely. As we got closer to the day of our performance we rehearsed every day. In addition to that, the music was not as simple as they expected. It needed serious work.
YT: How did the premier performance of the *Concertino for the Piano and Orchestra, Op. 1* go?
NK: It was very well received. The audience was very appreciative.
YT: Did someone happen to record that performance?
NK: Yes, somebody recorded it but I didn't get a copy at the beginning, and then all the contacts were lost.
YT: Oh, this is so sad – that was the first public performance of your piece.
NK: Yes, it was.
YT: What was your impression of the festival in general?
NK: There were so many people.
YT: Did you get acquainted with some of musicians from other countries?
NK: Of course. I remember we became good friends with the classical musicians from Ireland. It was a very interesting and new experience for us.
YT: What do you think – what was the result of your appearance on the festival?
NK: The result was that people became familiar with my music and me.
YT: Do you think that it became a starting point for your future collaboration with the Oleg Lundstrem Orchestra?

---

[166] Yuri Sergeevich Saulsky (1928-2003) was a Russian film composer and author of musical educational articles and essays. In 1954 he graduated from the Moscow Conservatory with a major in theory and composition. In 1962 Saulsky became a member of the »Union of Composers«. He was an author of the ballets, musicals, and songs for jazz and sympho-jazz groups. Accessed February 18, 2018. http://www.amumgk.ru/pages/people/people_10693.html.

> NK: *I think so. For sure that was one of the factors that made him recommend me as a pianist and composer for the band.*

It is known that jazz musicians in the world are very supportive of each other. Russia was not an exception in this matter. In the summer of 1957 a meeting of two big bands, Saulsky Big Band and Lundstrem Orchestra, was organized.

> NK: *I remember the Lundstrem Big Band came to Moscow to perform a concert as a part of their tour and we organized a meeting with them. At that time they were still based in Kazan'. The meeting was held in a famous restaurant »Aragvi«, a very good Georgian food restaurant. We respected musicians of the Lundstrem Big Band very much; they were Western people for us.*
> YT: *Why is that?*
> NK: *They were Russian musicians who lived in China. You could see quite easily the influence of the Western culture on them.*

After Kapustin's first official public appearance as a composer on the festival he continued to compose music for the big band. He did not assign opus numbers to those works.

> NK: *I remember at the end of my study at the conservatory (ca. 1960-1961) I even started to compose music for commissions. For example, for Lundstrem I composed at least three pieces during that time.*
> YT: *These are not the works that we know of, correct?*
> NK: *Yes. The only question I have is where is all this material now?*

Jazz Quintet Experience

Another advantage of Kapustin's appearance on the festival of 1957 is that he started to perform as a jazz pianist in small jazz ensemble groups and combos. Even more, Kapustin organized a jazz quintet with the musicians who originally played with him in the Saulsky Big Band.

YT: Who were the members of your quintet?
NK: We had Aleksey Zoubov on tenor saxophone, Konstantin Bakholdin on trombone, Alexander Garetkin on drums, Igor Berukhshtis on the double bass. Did I miss anyone?
YT: Yes, you on the piano!
NK: Oh yes.
YT: Whose idea was to organize the band?
NK: It was our common decision. It happened right after the festival; that's when we started to rehearse with the quintet.
YT: What did you rehearse for?
NK: For getting gigs. In the autumn of 1957 we were asked to work as the house band in the restaurant of the hotel »National«, one of the most well-known places at that time in Moscow. It was a big deal and we agreed. However, later it created all kinds of problems. First of all, I had to get permission from the conservatory administration allowing me to work because I was still a full-time student. Believe it or not, that was just the beginning of my second year of study at the conservatory. Second, we were supposed to play there every evening with only one day a week off, and every session was four to five hours long, which was quite exhausting. Therefore, in a while I realized that this is almost impossible to handle this job together with the conservatory's commitments.
YT: So, that's why you decided to resign from that work?
NK: Yes. Also, there was one more thing that kept bothering me – we had to play exactly the same repertoire from one night to another. That was also very painful.
YT: What was in the repertoire of your quintet?
NK: It was mostly jazz standards.
YT: How long did you survive that crazy life?
NK: I played in the »National« for only one month but that was absolutely enough for me. I got the experience.
YT: After you left the band, did you perform with these musicians from the quintet?

NK: *Of course I did. We would play with Bakholdin and Zoubov together in the Lundstrem Orchestra. Actually, after I left the band they also didn't last long. I think within a month or two they decided to stop. It was a very hard job.*[167]

Something extraordinary happened during that month that Kapustin played in the »National«. The fact is that this hotel was one of the highest rated places in Moscow, so people who stayed at that hotel were not just ordinary people. There were a lot internationally known people in that place. One day, some of the visitors of the restaurant were Americans. They listened to the Russian jazz quintet, enjoyed it, and even recorded their performance. A few months later, at the beginning of 1958, this recording reached the radio program of the »The Voice of America« and was broadcasted in the US.

YT: *How did you find out about your quintet being broadcast on »The Voice of America«?*
NK: *Aleksey Zoubov had a connection to those Americans and he spoke English fluently. He even gave me that recording to listen to.*
YT: *Really? What did you play on that recording?*
NK: *We played a few compositions but the one that I especially remember was called The Man from Mars. It is a blues. The form of this blues is quite interesting – it is a two-part form with twelve bars for each part.*
YT: *What do you feel about that fact that American audience heard your performance on »The Voice of America« in the 1958?*
NK: *We were lucky.*
YT: *The next question that comes in mind is - did Goldenweiser know about the jazz festival and jazz quintet?*
NK: *He did not know about either. That would create a big problem for my existence at the conservatory. Jazz was not appreciated at the Moscow Conservatory, especially at that time.*
YT: *I understand.*
NK: *Of course, he may have heard something but we never talked with him about that.*
YT: *Goldenweiser was a man from the classical world.*
NK: *Absolutely. The thing is I am pretty sure that he didn't know about the existence of Miles Davis and Herbie Hancock.*
YT: *I guess it was because people from the classical world don't want to listen to anything different than classical music. In this sense people from the jazz world have more open minds.*

---

[167] According to Alexei Zoubov the hotel performances were stopped by the Moscow special office due to inappropriate repertoire. See »Memories of Alexei Zoubov«, Appedix E.

NK: I am not sure about that statement. The people from jazz are also closed to classical music. There are not many musicians who are capable of doing both, as we are with you.

Last Exams at the Moscow Conservatory

The time had come and in the summer of 1961 Kapustin was standing in front of a serious challenge, the final exams at the Moscow Conservatory. The most difficult exam was piano performance. Kapustin played an extensive and technically difficult program, which was an hour and thirty minutes in length.[168] The pressure was on.

YT: *Which pieces did you play at your final exam?*
NK: *I played Stravinsky's Petrushka, Liszt's Sonata in B minor (S. 178), Beethoven's Sonata No. 22 in F major (Op. 54), one of Bach's Preludes and Fugues, and I finished my program with Bartók's Piano Concerto No. 2, accompanied by Nodar Gabunia.*
YT: *What an intense program! Did you play the entire concerto?*
NK: *That would be too long for the jury. I played the whole concerto for myself but for the exam I had to perform only the second and third movement. I didn't like that idea because I had to start with the slow second movement, but Goldenweiser probably thought that the first movement itself would not be long enough for my program. I remember there was an interesting episode with Goldenweiser that happened right before my exam. He was preparing the list of pieces of my final program, a document that he was supposed to submit to the jury before my performance. Goldenweiser decided to put the Piano Sonata of Yuri Yatsevich as a twentieth century piece that was one of the requirements for the final program. The fact is that I played this sonata a while before, on one of my previous exams in the Small Hall, but I did not prepare this piece for my final exam. Goldenweiser assured me that jury would not ask me to play this piece.*
YT: *Did you agree to do it???*
NK: *Yes, I agreed.*
YT: *Did the jury ask you to play Yatsevich?*
NK: *Why would they? Of course they did not.*
YT: *What would happen if they would ask you to play it? This was an extremely risky situation, not to mention the fact that this was your final exam.*
NK: *I knew that this would never happen. Goldenweiser was a giant figure at the conservatory; everything that happened always happened in the way he envisioned it.*
YT: *How did your performance go?*
NK: *It went very well. At that time I was not afraid to play, so I felt confident about myself. I got an »A«. By the way, I was asked to continue my education at the*

---

[168] Note by the author: Standard length of the final program at the Conservatory was 45-50 minutes; Kapustin's program was twice longer.

conservatory and begin my post-graduate study. It was a big deal back then to receive a proposal like that. Just a very few students were selected for that position and I was one of them.

YT: Did you accept the offer?

NK: No, I did not.

YT: You did not accept the offer to complete the post-graduate study at the Moscow Conservatory with having no expenses? Why did you do that?

NK: I got tired of study. Looking back at all my years of study at the musical college and the conservatory I keep thinking that musical college would be absolutely enough for me. By the end of my study at the musical college I was eighteen years old, which is the same age as Scriabin and Rachmaninov when they were finishing their study. So, those five years that I spent at the conservatory you can consider already a loss of time. The post-graduate study would add three more years to that.

YT: It looks that you made your choice towards the work with the Lundstrem Orchestra.

NK: Yes, I didn't hesitate a moment.

A Serious Conversation

At the end of the study at the conservatory, Kapustin, as with each graduate student, was supposed to begin his teaching career. Interestingly enough, in the 1960s the educational institution had the right to determine the students' place of work. Kapustin was directed to the city Alma-Ata.[169]

NK: My situation was quite interesting. I had two options. First, I could continue my education at the conservatory and complete my post-graduate study or second, I could begin working as a piano instructor in Alma-Ata Musical College. Neither of those options was good for me. The third option, as a freelance musician, didn't exist at that time. By the way, I remember I even called to that musical college in the Alma-Ata and had a conversation with them. They said that they would preferably like to have a piano instructor who could also play accordion. At that moment I understood what was waiting for me there. If I would go I would experience complete ruination of my skills as a musician.
YT: What did you do then?
NK: I talked to the managing director of the Lundstrem Orchestra, his name was Mikhail Tsin, and explained him my situation. The fact is – the conservatory administration didn't want to give me the diploma without my agreement to work in the Alma-Ata. The fact that I was planning to work with the jazz band didn't give me any additional points either. It was inappropriate for a graduate student of the Moscow Conservatory. Tsin decided to visit Goldenweiser and talk to him. I told Tsin that I anticipated the conversation would not be one of the pleasant ones.
YT: What was the result of this conversation?
NK (smiling): As you see – he made it through very successfully. Goldenweiser helped me again – I received the diploma and did not go to Alma-Ata nor continued my post-graduate study at the Moscow Conservatory. Instead, I began working with the Oleg Lundstrem Orchestra.

---

[169] Almaty (also known as Alma-Ata) is the largest city in Kazakhstan, which situated in the south of Russia.

Postlude: Goldenweiser

Alexander Goldenweiser retired from teaching at the Moscow Conservatory in the summer of 1961. Kapustin was one of his last students.

YT: *How do you remember your teacher?*
NK: *He was a man of few words. Although, sometimes he liked to talk to some of us.*
YT: *I feel that he was an austere teacher.*
NK: *This is true. Actually, Rubbakh was also a severe teacher, but he was warm to his students.*
YT: *So, Rubbakh was closer to his students, and Goldenweiser was more like at a distance.*
NK: *Yes.*
YT: *Have you ever been to Goldenweiser's home?*
NK: *I was there twice. The first time I came with Rubbakh, when I played Liszt's Don Juan for Goldenweiser before my entering exams to the conservatory. The second time I was there with my friend Alexander Zagorinsky[170] many years later, in the 1990s, when we performed my Cello Sonata No. 1, Op. 63.*
YT: *Is that true that Goldenweiser's house on Gorky Street became a museum?*
NK: *Yes, this is absolutely true. His house became a museum from the middle 1950s. Goldenweiser himself helped in the creation of it, and even guided excursions through the house until the end of his life. There were many concerts organized at his house, it became a concert venue.[171] Actually, that's how I ended up playing my cello sonata at his house.*

Alexander Goldenweiser passed away on November 27, 1961 in his summerhouse on the Nikolina Gora, in the suburb of Moscow.

YT: *How did you find out about Goldenweiser's death?*
NK: *I was already playing at that time with the Lundstrem Orchestra. Igor Lundstrem, the brother of Oleg, told me about that sad news. Later, I found out that Alexander Borisovich (Goldenweiser) died in his sleep.*
YT: *Isn't that what we all wish for ourselves?*

---

[170] Conversation about Alexander Zagorinsky will be presented in the Chapter VI.

[171] Starting from 1955 until the present the house of Goldenweiser functions as a museum. The house is divided into memorial and musical areas. Goldenweiser's archives consist of memorial objects (paintings, graphics and sculptures), and the library with Goldenweiser's manuscripts, letters, music scores, books, and pictures with Rimsky-Korsakov, Taneev, Rachmaninov, Medtner, Chekhov and others. The musical part of the house functions as a place for performances of instrumental and vocal music. Accessed July 15, 2016. http://progulkipomoskve.ru/publ/muzei_moskvy/muzej_kvartira_pianista_a_b_goldenvejzera_v_moskve/27-1-0-1766.

NK: Could be. Nobody expected his death so early, although he was already eighty-six years old. At about the same time as Goldenweiser, Grigory Ginzburg, another genius pianist, was slowly getting ready to leave us because of brain cancer. It's a horrible thing... Goldenweiser and Ginzburg used to joke with each other, like playing a game, about who was going to live longer. Ginzburg passed away about a week after Goldenweiser. I guess he won this game.[172]

---

[172] Note by the author: Grigory Ginzburg passed away on December 5, 1961.

# Chapter Four: Years of Work with the Oleg Lundstrem Big Band (1961-1972)

History of the Oleg Lundstrem Big Band – The Beginning

The history of the Oleg Lundstrem Big Band goes back to the early 1930s when the group of musicians, who were also friends, decided to organize the band. Their main goal was to perform jazz music, which was becoming very popular in the dance halls at that time.[173] The best way to introduce the leader of the group, Oleg Lundstrem, was made by Jason Ankeny:

»*The father of Russian jazz, Oleg Lundstrem, helmed the nation's first big band, keeping the group afloat for more than seven decades despite the fierce opposition of Soviet leaders.*«[174]

Oleg Leonidovich Lundstrem

Oleg Leonidovich Lundstrem (1916-2005) was born on April 2, 1916 in Chita, Russia. In 1921 the family moved to Harbin (China) where his father, Leonid Frantsevich Lundstrem, was invited to work as a middle school physics

---

[173] Oleg Lundstrem Big Band: http://journal.jazz.ru/2016/04/01/oleg-lundstrem-centennial/, http://www.allmusic.com/artist/oleg-lundstrem-mn0001230706/biography, http://www.russia-ic.com/people/general/1/381/, https://www.theguardian.com/culture/2005/oct/28/russia.jazz, http://info-jazz.ru/community/blog/?action=show&id=101, http://journal.jazz.ru/2016/09/30/oleg-lundstrem-orchestra-02/.

[174] Jason Ankeny, Biography of Oleg Lundstrem. Accessed on August 10, 2016. http://www.allmusic.com/artist/oleg-lundstrem-mn0001230706/biography.

teacher and then as a lecturer at the Harbin Polytechnic Institute. As a teenager, Lundstrem had a wide range of interests and passions. On one hand, he was interested in technical science. Thus, in 1932 he graduated from the college of commerce and entered the Polytechnic Institute. Later in 1944, Lundstrem graduated from the French Technical Center as an architectural engineer. On the other hand, he was very much interested in music. Thus, in 1935 he graduated from the Musical College as a violinist. His interest in jazz big band music began in 1934 when he first heard the recording of the Duke Ellington Orchestra playing the piece called »Dear Old Southland.« The 1930s in the United States was characterized by the rise of the swing era, the time of such famous jazz orchestras as Count Basie, Duke Ellington, Benny Goodman, Glenn Miller, and many others. Soon after that time, Lundstrem and his eight friends, among them his younger brother Igor Lundstrem decided to form a jazz band. Basically, it was a group of amateur young musicians who had a strong desire to play jazz music. The band gained popularity in Harbin and very soon after that, in 1935, moved to Shanghai (China). Shanghai was the city which could be called »Asian New York« where there was always a need for good, high quality big band music. At the beginning of the 1940s, just five years after the group moved to Shanghai, the band reached a high level of popularity. They performed in the most popular dance halls of Shanghai, such as the ballrooms »Paramount« and »Majestic«.[175]

The repertoire of the band included not only American jazz music but also the jazz arrangements of Russian songs[176] and original compositions by the leader of the band, Oleg Lundstrem.

YT: Do you know how musicians chose who was going to be the leader of the band?
NK: I think they choose Oleg by voting. At that time it was already a full big band with nineteen musicians on board.

In 1947 the band, along with their families, decided to return to the USSR. That was a difficult period of post-World War II, which was not the best time for the jazz musicians to return to their native country. On the other hand, they had brought with them new American instruments and a large big band library of scores gathered through years of living in China. Unfortunately, the band did not receive the permission to settle in Moscow or Saint-Petersburg.[177] That's why

---

[175] Oleg Lundstrem. Accessed February 21, 2018.
http://journal.jazz.ru/2016/04/01/oleg-lundstrem-centennial/.
[176] One of the Russian Soviet songs that Lundstrem arranged for the big band was the famous »Katyusha« (Blanter), »The Song of Captain Brave« (Dunaevsky), »Foreign Cities« (Vertinsky) and many others. Accessed February 20, 2018.
http://journal.jazz.ru/2016/04/01/oleg-lundstrem-centennial/.
[177] History of the Lundstrem Big Band. Accessed July 15, 2016.

they decided to settle in the city of Kazan,[178] which is geographically the closest large city to Moscow. Here in Kazan, the Lundstrem Big Band was supposed to become the jazz band of the Tatar Autonomous Soviet Socialist Republic. Unfortunately, this did not happen. On February 10th, 1948 the Central Committee of the Communist Party of the Soviet Union issued a decree on the opera composed by the young Georgian composer Vano Muradeli »The Great Friendship.« The opera, that was supposed to mark the 30th Anniversary of the October Revolution, was described as »an inartistic work, faulty both musically and in regards to its subject matter.«[179] Muradeli was denounced for embarking on a »faulty formalistic path, fatal to the work of a Soviet composer.«[180] As a further result of this decree, the three leading composers of the Soviet Union, Sergei Prokofiev, Dmitry Shostakovich, and Aram Khachaturian, were also called »formalists« composers, with all the expected negative consequences.[181] There was no definite negation of jazz music in that document. However, just the use of the word »jazz« in an official context, as something alien that contradicts with the spirit of the Soviet nation, was enough to put the jazz music on the back burner for a long seven years.[182]

This decree signified the early stage of the Cold War[183] between the two biggest countries in the world – the Soviet Union and the United States. During this time in the Soviet Union, in agreement of the nationalistic path, all contemporary Western influences were forbidden. As a result of this, it was announced that Russian people do not need jazz music anymore, as it was coming from the West.

---

http://info-jazz.ru/community/blog/?action=Show&id=101.

[178] Kazan is the capital and largest city of the Republic of Tatarstan, Russia. It is the eighth most populous city in Russia. Kazan' is 500 miles away from Moscow.

[179] The Central Committee's decree of 10 February 1948, 'On Muradeli's opera *The Great Friendship*,' translated by Nicolas Slonimsky, ed., *Music Since 1900*, 5th ed. (New York: Schirmer Books, 1994), pp.1055-1057. Originally published as 'Postanovlenie TsK VKP (b) ob opere »Velikaia druzhba« V. Muradeli', 10 February 1948, Russian State Archive of Social and Political History, Moscow (Rossiiskii gosudarstvennyi arkhiv sotsial'no-politicheskoi istorii – RGASPI), fond. 17, op. 3, delo 1069, I. 12, 42-49. Published in *Pravda*, 11 February 1948.

[180] Ibid.

[181] Syncope of the Jazz Life: Creative Path of Oleg Lundstrem and His Orchestra, Part II. Accessed February 2, 2018. http://journal.jazz.ru/2016/09/30/oleg-lundstrem-orchestra-02/.

[182] Cyril Moshkow, »Jazz in the USSR. Chronology«, appendix to journal »Time Out Moscow«, Moscow, 2007. Accessed December 18, 2017. http://journal.jazz.ru/2017/10/01/russian-jazz-timeline/.

[183] Cold War was a state of political and military tension after World War II between powers in the Western Bloc (the United States and its NATO allies) and powers in the Eastern Bloc (the Soviet Union and its satellite states). A common time frame is the period between 1947, the year the Truman Doctrine was announced, and 1991, the year the Soviet Union collapsed.

NK: The »Iron curtain« fell onto the Soviet Union and not even one serious composer dared to touch the jazz music.[184]

Oleg Lundstrem and his musicians from the band were forced to find jobs in the opera theatre, cinema hall orchestras, or any other places that would earn them any kind of income. Thus, Oleg Lundstrem started to work as a violinist at the Theatre of Opera and Ballet, returning to his first musical instrument. In 1948 he entered the Kazan Conservatory along with his brother Igor Lundstrem and some of his friends who came from China. In 1953 Oleg Lundstrem graduated from the Kazan State Conservatory receiving a degree in composition and a degree in symphonic conducting.

Through all these years Lundstrem tried to keep the big band together performing for different occasions. Happily, in 1955 the orchestra recorded a series of songs by Tatar composers arranged by Oleg Lundstrem. That same year the band performed several concerts with great success at the Kazan Drama Theatre. These events attracted the attention of the Moscow Concert Society. The turning point was when the orchestra hired their first managing director, Mikhail Ilyich Tsin, who joined the band in 1956 and stayed with the group for many years. Tsin, being at that time an administrator of the Moscow State Concert Association »Mosconcert,«[185] helped the Lundstrem Orchestra to become the official Russian State Concert Orchestra.

On October 1, 1956 by order of the Ministry of Culture of the Russian Soviet Federative Socialist Republic, a performance orchestra was organized in the system of the All-Russian State Concert Orchestra (later Rosconcert) under the direction of Oleg Lundstrem on the basis of the collective that had arrived from China.[186]

This was the beginning of »The Khrushchev Thaw« as well as the beginning of the remarkable history of the Oleg Lundstrem Big Band. In 1957, as a result of this incredible change, the big band and their families moved to Moscow to settle there forever. The time had come for the band to experience huge success in touring inside and outside of the Soviet Union.

---

[184] Iskander Gafarov, »Nikolai Kapustin. Shtrihi k portretu«, Molodoi *uchionii*, no. 2 (2013): 445-446. Accessed December 18, 2017. https://moluch.ru/archive/49/6252/.

[185] The Moscow State Association »Mosconcert« is the oldest and the biggest concert organization in Moscow. It was founded on January 25, 1931. The main goal of the association is to bring the art to people and to support and develop modern art movements. Accessed August 12, 2016. http://www.mosconcert.com/aboutus/.

[186] Oleg Lundstrem Jazz Orchestra. Accessed August 12, 2016. http://journal.jazz.ru/2016/04/01/oleg-lundstrem-centennial/.

Nikolai Kapustin Joins the Big Band

In the summer of 1961 Nikolai Kapustin joined the Lundstrem Big Band which was already on the wave of its popularity in the Soviet Union. Interestingly enough, it was just a few years after the band's relocation from Kazan. This fact proves that the speed of growing success of this big band exceeded all possible expectations.

NK: I joined the band at the moment the »old« Shanghai musicians were changed for a new generation of young performers who lived in Moscow.

YT: What happened to the »old« Shanghai musicians? I thought they all moved from Kazan to Moscow.

NK: Not all. Some of them were not able to move to Moscow since they already settled in Kazan – they had their jobs in Kazan, families and everything, so here's that. Then there is also such a thing called »time of change.« So, I guess it was time for the band to begin a new stage of their growth, that's all.

YT: You came perfectly in time. This is a special talent – to appear at the right place at the right time!

Nikolai Kapustin (piano), Oleg Lundstrem Big Band, 1964[187]

---

[187] »Jazz.ru.« Accessed August 12, 2016.
http://journal.jazz.ru/2016/04/01/oleg-lundstrem-centennial/.

NK: Yes, I got lucky.
YT: What was the difference between the Shanghai musicians and the Moscow guys?
NK: The thing is, the Shanghai musicians did not improvise at all and almost all Moscow musicians improvised very well.
YT: So in a way this new generation of young performers from Moscow was more advanced in jazz.
NK: Yes, this is exactly what it was.
YT: Did you improvise also?
NK: What a strange question, of course I did! Otherwise I would not be a part of this big band.
YT: Do you think the change of members of the orchestra was made on purpose?
NK: Of course no, but as you know, everything comes to an end at some point. It was time for natural changes to come to the band, to give the new blood, new feel, and a new modern sound. Also, don't think that all of the Shanghai musicians were gone. Some of them were still playing with us in the 1960s and 1970s, for example the bass player Alexander Gravis. However, the majority of the power in the band belonged to a new generation of Moscow musicians.
YT: Did the members of the orchestra keep changing after that?
NK: Not really. I think once the young performers came to the big band it stayed that way for a long time. Of course, there were some insignificant changes, as it always happens in the band, but the main cast of the band stayed the same.
YT: Why do you think Lundstrem choose you but not someone else?
NK: As you know, it didn't happen by accident. I composed for Oleg (Lundstrem) earlier during my last years of study at the conservatory. Plus, we knew each other very well from the time when I lived in Mikhalkov's house in the middle 1950s. Lundstrem visited Sergei Vladimirovich (Mikhalkov) from the time when they lived in Kazan. So, I guess there were many different reasons why he chose me.
YT: Do you remember how it happened?
NK: Nothing special. Lundstrem just asked me if I would be interested in working with him in the big band, that's all.
YT: Oh my – nothing special! Did he ask you at the time when you still studied at the conservatory?
NK: Yes, it was planned long before I joined the band. I think he had this idea in mind right from our first meeting in Mikhalkov's house.
YT: So, he noticed you right from the beginning.
NK (with the smile): I guess so.

In other words, Lundstrem offering Kapustin the position in the big band gave the young man his »ticket« to life. That was the beginning of a new turn in the flow of Kapustin's life, not unexpected, but highly anticipated and completely different from what he had before.

> *YT: Did you know the former pianist of the big band who you replaced in 1961?*
> *NK: Of course, I remember him very well. That was Estonian pianist Leo Tauts. He was informed long before it happened that I am going to join the band after my graduation. Plus, he knew that he wasn't the »sharpest knife« in the drawer.*
> *YT: So, he understood the situation and did not feel jealous or upset.*
> *NK: Of course not. Even after he left the band we continued to be good friends. He had a very special sense of humor. I remember he was famous because before the performances he used to shave only one cheek – the one that is towards the audience, the right one (laughing).*
> *YT: Oh no… He was probably the only one in this matter, a unique individual.*
> *NK: I liked his sense of humor. I remember when we were on tour in Estonia with Lundstrem we even met with him and he introduced us to all his friends and showed some historical places in Tallinn. He was a good man.*

Kapustin and His Duties in the Big Band

Nikolai Kapustin, ca. 1961-1962

Oleg Lundstrem, being a great musician and experienced band leader, undoubtedly noticed the level of talent of a young twenty-three year old man named Nikolai Kapustin. He decided to use Nikolai's abilities in all ways possible. Therefore, right from the moment Kapustin joined the band, he had a wide range of responsibilities as a pianist, arranger, transcriber, and composer.

YT: What was the main focus for you in the band concerning these responsibilities?
NK: I had two major directions – I was a pianist and a composer.
YT: Did the work in the Lundstrem Big Band meet your expectations?
NK: Yes, especially in the beginning. I couldn't expect more then what I had. To tell you the truth, at that time I thought I had reached the top of my dreams, something I had been searching for.

As a jazz pianist, Kapustin had developed a brilliant technique that he acquired during all his years of study at the Musical College and the Moscow

Conservatory. He was the only member of the band with a degree in performance from the Moscow Conservatory.[188]

> YT: *How did you feel in comparison with other musicians in the band when you joined them?*
> NK: *In the beginning, of course, there were some musicians who were more experienced than me, for instance Alexei Zoubov and Konstantin Bakholdin. Although, I was ready for that.*
> YT: *How did they look at the person who just graduated from the Moscow Conservatory with the diploma in classical music?*
> NK: *The thing is – I knew the majority of the musicians from the past. For example, with Zoubov[189] and Bakholdin[190] we played together in the Saulsky Big Band and then even later, in our quintet. So, I was not a foreign element in the band. However, Bakholdin considered me as a »hopeless classicist«. In reality, I equally loved both classical and jazz music which is reflected in my own music.*

By the beginning of his work with Lundstrem, Kapustin already had his style of playing that came out of his endless hours of listening to »The Voice of America« and occasionally rare vinyl recordings. His ability and desire to transcribe music of the great jazz pianists, and the experience of performing with the Yuri Saulsky Big Band and his own Quintet, shaped his musical tastes.

> YT: *Can you recall some names of the musicians who influenced you?*
> NK: *There are so many of them. I listened to a lot of Oscar Peterson's improvisations. Bill Evans I felt at the beginning was a little far from me. He seemed to be too lyrical, but later I changed my attitude towards him and began to really appreciate his music. In general, I listened to a lot of different styles of music, for example the music of Herbie Hancock, Lennie Tristano, McCoy Tyner, and Quincy Jones. By the way, Lundstrem*

---

[188] The other members who had degrees in music were Oleg Lundstrem and his brother Igor, who both graduated from the Kazan Conservatory.

[189] Alexei Zoubov (born in 1936) is a Russian jazz saxophonist and composer. Zoubov graduated from the Moscow University with a degree in Physics but his passion was jazz. Zoubov worked with many Russian jazz collectives, for example with the Oleg Lundstrem Big Band, the Crescendo Quartet, and also played duo with Igor Saulsky. In 1984 he moved to Los-Angeles. During the years of living in the United States he worked with jazz greats like Gary Burton, Chick Corea, Paul Gonsalves, Charlie Haden, »Tootie« Heath, Dick Hyman, Keith Jarrett, and Milcho Leviev. Zoubov's last CD »Rejuvenation Project« was released in 2006. Accessed November 23, 2017. http://alexeiz.com/bio.php.

[190] Konstantin Bakholdin (1936-1987) was a Russian trombonist, one of the first improvisers in the late 1950s in Russia. Bakholdin played in the Oleg Lundstrem Big Band (1960-1965), Vadim Ludvikovsky Big Band (1966-1973), and in the instrumental ensemble »Melody« (1973-1987). Accessed November 23, 2017. https://www.findagrave.com/memorial/108410686.

suggested that I listen to Quincy Jones. I didn't plan to do that, but later I became really interested in his music.

YT: Did your understanding of jazz change once you joined the band?

NK: I have to admit that as a jazz pianist I played differently before I joined the band.

YT: How so?

NK: I enjoyed my experiences playing with the Saulsky Big Band and with my friends in the quintet, but I think the Lundstrem Big Band was my real jazz conservatory, my real jazz school. Lundstrem taught us how to play jazz, how to feel it. You don't receive a diploma from this kind of study but it counts even more. By the way, I didn't need the diploma because I already had it.

YT: Did you play the keyboard instrument with Lundstrem?

NK: I didn't play the keyboard because it did not appear until later, but I did play the electric organ.

YT: Could you expand a little about your experience of playing the electric organ?

NK: We did not use a lot of the electric organ sound with Lundstrem but if we did I played simultaneously on the organ and piano – with my right hand on the organ and with my left hand on the grand piano.

YT: Where did you learn this type of technique – at the musical college or conservatory?

NK: It is not a big difference from playing just on the piano; I learned to play this way with the big band.

YT: Right away?

NK: Right away.

As a composer, most of the material that Kapustin wrote during the years 1961-1972 (Opus 2 through Opus 13), was for the Lundstrem Big Band.

NK: I started to compose music for the big band during my last years of study at the conservatory. That was actually the main reason I decided to join the band – to be able to play the music that I composed, serious jazz music for the big band, and have experience as a jazz pianist. Unfortunately, within a few years I realized that I would not be able to get what I originally planned for this band.

YT: Can you tell who also composed the music for the Lundstrem Big Band?

NK: Of course Lundstrem himself used to compose, and then there was also Georgy Garanian,[191] who composed for the band too.

YT: Did you work with Garanian?

---

[191] Georgy Garanian (1934-2010) was an ethnic Armenian Russian jazz saxophonist, bandleader and composer. He was one of the first Russian musicians who attracted attention of the Western world as part of jazz from the USSR. As a musician, conductor, and composer, he was the leader of the ensemble *Melodiya* (1970s–1980s) and the Moscow Big Band (1992–1995). In the 1990s Garanian toured regularly as a trio with pianist Daniil Kramer and guitarist Aleksey Kuznetsov. Accessed November 23, 2017. http://www.jazz.ru/pages/garanian/, http://garanian.ru/en/.

NK: Yes, we were very good friends. Actually, we both used to write arrangements and transcribe the music for Lundstrem. Later, in the middle 1970s, we both worked at the Moscow Cinematography Orchestra, so we have some history to share.
AK (joining the conversation): Garanian was the first person who started to call him »Koliasha«, very friendly with love and big respect (smiling). After that Lundstrem himself and all the other musicians from the band referred to Kolia as Koliasha.
YT: Yes, tradition is a serious thing. What can we do about it? So, it was three of you – you, Lundstrem, and Garanian.
NK: Generally yes, but there was also Estonian composer Uno Naissoo[192] and Russian composer Igor Yakushenko,[193] who used to compose music for the big band. In reality, of course there were many more, but the three of us were predominant composers, since we were also a part of the big band.

During the years of work with the Lundstrem Orchestra, Kapustin took part in two recordings of vinyl discs. On the first disc called »Oleg Lundstrem Orchestra« Kapustin participated as a pianist. The disc was released by Melodiya in 1966.[194]

---

[192] Uno Naissoo (1928-1980) was a famous Estonian composer, pedagogue, musical theorist, and jazz musician. Naissoo graduated from Tallinn State Conservatory in 1952 as a choral conductor. He became a member of the Estonian Composers' Union in 1954. He was one of the founders of the Estonian Radio Male Quartet (1960) and Tallinn Chamber Choir (1962). In 1947 Naissoo established the first Estonian jazz organization »Swing Club« and was one of the artistic directors of Tallinn jazz festivals (1949). Accessed November 23, 2017. http://www.emic.ee/uno-naissoo.
[193] Igor Vasil'evich Yakushenko (1932-1999) was a Russian jazz composer and a pedagogue. Yakushenko graduated from the Gnessin Institute in 1956 (class of Aram Khachaturian). He led the composition class at the Central Music School for the Gifted Children under the Moscow Conservatory and the Music School under the Gnessin Institute. Yakushenko composed orchestral music, jazz and popular music, music for children, music for the movies, theatre, radio, and TV. Accessed November 23, 2017. http://kkre-17.narod.ru/jakushenko.htm.
[194] Melodiya (33C 01333-4), 1966.

Cover of the vinyl disc »Oleg Lundstrem Orchestra«, Melodiya, 1966

On the second vinyl disc of the orchestra, recorded in 1970, Kapustin participated as a pianist and composer. The disc included two compositions of Kapustin – *Variations for Piano and Orchestra*, Op. 3, and *Aquarium*, Op. 12.[195]

 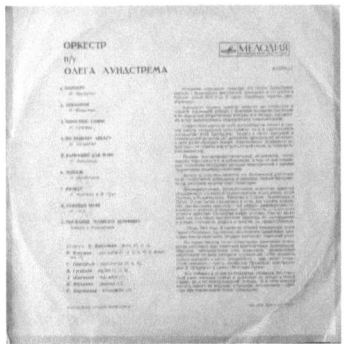

Vinyl disc »Oleg Lundstrem Orchestra«, Melodiya, 1970

YT: *Do you remember how you recoded those two pieces for the disc in 1970?*
NK: *It was a long time ago, so I don't remember how we recorded it but what I remember is that those two pieces we performed quite often with Lundstrem.*
YT: *I see that on that disc there were also compositions written by Lundstrem, Yakushenko, Kunsman, and Gruz.*
NK: *Yes, this orchestra always had a very creative group of composers who worked for the band.*

---

[195] Melodiya (D 027931-2), 1970.

YT: I also see that for the last composition on that vinyl disc you recorded a cover of the famous jazz standard »On Green Dolphin Street«.

NK: Now, after you said that, I started to remember it… Yes, we always wanted to finish our concerts and recordings with something memorable and powerful.

YT: Did you know at that time about Miles Davis' recording of this tune?

NK: Yes, I think his album »Kind of Blue« was one of the iconic recordings in Russia that we used to listen to.

As an arranger, Kapustin began to write jazz arrangements of famous Russian songs, songs written by the Soviet composers, and even themes from Classical music repertoire for the big band.

YT: Did you like writing arrangements?

NK: Writing arrangements was not one of my favorites. Very soon they understood that my thing is composing serious music. Although, I have to admit that at some point arrangements helped me greatly because it became an additional source of income. I have no idea what I would have done during our first years of marriage with Alla. We would not survive just on the income from touring with Lundstrem. I guess that's how it always goes with young families – we had much love, but did not have much money.

YT: Can you tell a little bit about your arrangement of the popular song of Soloviov-Sedoi »In the Boat«?

NK: I remember that song. This one came out very well.

YT: Did you like writing the jazz arrangements of the popular Russian songs?

NK: Only if I liked the song itself. Usually, Solovyov-Sedoi had very good songs.

YT: How many songs did you arrange approximately?

NK: A million or more.

YT: So, let me clarify this – are those song arrangements that you did for the Lundstrem Orchestra primarily instrumental compositions?

NK: No, there were singers in there too.

YT: Ohhhhh, so some of your arrangements did include the vocal parts?

NK: Of course, many of my arrangements included vocalists, but I never considered this writing as something serious.

YT: Maybe that's why your attitude towards songs was that negative – because it's all connected to the entertainment?

NK: Yes, that may be right. I always wanted to compose serious instrumental music, but not something that would entertain the audience today and will be forgotten tomorrow.

YT: Do you remember who was also writing arrangements for the Lundstrem Big Band?

NK: In addition to myself and Garanian there was also Latvian composer and arranger Vitaly Dolgov[196] and later saxophonist Nikolai Panov,[197] who was a member of the Lundstrem Big Band in the 1980s.

YT: It looks like Lundstrem used the artistic resources from the entire USSR collaborating with composers and arrangers from Estonia and Latvia.

NK: Of course. Since all the countries at that time belonged to the USSR the geography of our collaborations and the performances were quite extensive.

YT: As we know many of your friends from that time immigrated to other countries. Have you ever thought about the opportunity of living in another country?

NK: Yes, I did. A good friend of mine, Vladimir Gruz who was a very talented arranger, immigrated to the United States at the beginning of the 1970s. He asked me to join him but I refused. I was right because he couldn't find his place there in spite of the fact that he was a gifted musician.

YT: Was Gruz a member of the big band?

NK: Yes, we worked together in the Lundstrem Big Band, he played French horn. Alla knows him very well. So, going to another country, there are absolutely no guarantees on anything.

As a transcriber, Kapustin spent hours transcribing orchestral parts of the music of the Count Basie Orchestra, the Duke Ellington Orchestra, and other eminent big bands of the 1930s-1950s.

NK: At that time it was very difficult to find the scores for jazz big band in Russia, so we had to transcribe it. Most of the jazz standards that we played with Lundstrem were transcribed material.

YT: Did you transcribe all the instrumental parts of the piece?

NK: Yes, absolutely everything. Why?

YT: This is a gigantic pain! How long did it take you to transcribe one piece? I think this kind of work should last for months.

NK: I've always been in a hurry because they didn't give me enough time for transcribing. Of course, I had approximately no less than a month. Also, it depends on the piece specifically. It is like a puzzle.

---

[196] Vitaly Dolgov (1937-2007) was a Latvian jazz arranger, composer, saxophonist, and conductor. In 1960s he was writing and arranging the music for the Eddie Rosner Big Band, Vadim Ludvikovsky Big Band, and the Oleg Lundstrem Big Band. In 1999 he was the conductor and musical manager for the Igor Butman Big Band. Accessed November 23, 2017. http://www.km.ru/muzyka/encyclopedia/dolgov-vitalii, http://info-jazz.ru/community/jazzmen?action=show&id=53.

[197] Nikolai Panov (born in 1945) is a Russian jazz saxophonist, composer, and arranger. In 1984 he became a soloist and arranger for the Oleg Lundstrem Big Band. Later, he toured extensively with his own band called »Jazz Gallery«. Since 1999 Panov lives in the United States. Accessed November 23, 2017. http://www.persona.rin.ru/eng/view/f//20907/nikolai-panov.

YT: *Plus, the length of the pieces was probably very long.*

NK: *Not really. The length was pretty much standard – no more than five minutes for one piece.*

YT: *In this situation that five minutes could seem like a life-long song. Do you remember which orchestras you transcribed the most?*

NK: *I remember I was doing a lot of Count Basie music, but also of course Duke Ellington and Glen Miller compositions.*

YT: *So, it is the big band music of 1930s-1940s.*

NK: *Not necessarily. I was also transcribing the Stan Kenton Big Band, and this is already 1950s. It was many of them, hard to remember all their names.*

YT: *Were you the only transcriber in the band?*

NK: *We shared this duty with Garanian.*

YT: *I can't imagine what kind of ear the person should have to do this work.*

NK: *I had absolute pitch but it was developed from my childhood on the instrument that we had at home. That instrument was made before WWII and it was tuned on purpose a half step lower. I guess they were just afraid to tune it higher since the strings were old.*

YT: *Did you know about that?*

NK: *Of course I did not, I found out about that later. So, due to this fact I still hear everything a half step lower, for example I hear Beethoven's Fifth Symphony in B minor.*

YT: *Instead of C?*

NK: *Instead of C.*

The Musicians of the Lundstrem Big Band

Oleg Lundstrem Big Band, 1960s

The story of the Oleg Lundstrem Big Band was unique in many ways and one was the band's instrumentation. Traditionally, the instrumentation of the jazz big band included five saxophones, four trumpets, four trombones, rhythm section of piano, bass and drums, and some optional instruments, such as guitar and percussion. Surprisingly, the Lundstrem Big Band had a non-traditional instrumentation as sometimes they had six saxophones and five trumpets.

YT: Why did you have an additional saxophone and trumpet?
NK: For some reason it was always that way right from the beginning. I don't understand this either. I didn't always know what to do with the sixth saxophone. That was especially hard when I was transcribing. I ended up composing a specific part for those instruments since all the pieces I was transcribing only had five saxophones. That was slowing down my transcribing process.
YT: Maybe more instruments make it sounds more dense?
NK: I don't know. Even Lundstrem didn't know what to do with those additional instruments when he was composing his music.
YT: Did any of your instruments double the parts of the others?
NK: Oh, no. Doubling is not a good thing for the instrumentation; each instrument has to have its own part. The good thing is that the fifth trumpet could potentially be a second conductor. So, sometimes when Lundstrem did not conduct for some reason, that fifth trumpet was in his place; but that happened not so often.
YT: Did you have any additional instruments like guitar or percussion?

NK: *Of course, we had a permanent guitar player. We also had percussion but this instrument did not appear right from the beginning. I think they did not have percussion in the early period of the band.*

YT: *So, you had many musicians in the band, all in maximum numbers.*

NK: *Yes, many musicians, more then we needed probably.*

YT: *How then was it possible to retain specific members of the band?*

NK: *Lundstrem never tried to hold or persuade anyone, his authority was set so high that musicians did not want to leave the band. Although, if something like this happened he would never take offense with you. He was a very practical man; he knew that the main thing for the jazz musician is to survive. So, one of the reasons musicians could leave was for financial stability. Although, I have to tell you, in general the membership of the band stayed stable for a long time.*

Oleg Lundstrem carefully selected the musicians for his band, choosing the ones that would add uniqueness and individuality to it. It was noted many times that the Lundstrem Orchestra played with uplifting emotions and always with drive and positive energy. It is obvious that Lundstrem himself generated that spot of light and that specific feel, conducting the band. Also, Lundstrem was a great example of the band leader who led the band in a democratic way where nobody was restricted in their desire to show their own opinion on any topic.

YT: *Were you allowed to show your opinion about the piece or some topic that needed to be discussed concerning the music you played?*

NK: *Why are you even asking this question? Of course yes. We all were equal members of the band. If it helps the band to be better why not discuss it?*

YT: *I think this is the best scenario of working within the big band but this does not always happen. Sometimes the leaders of the band are dictating the main direction.*

NK: *I can see that. Luckily, that was not our case.*

YT: *I read that at the beginning, in the 1940s, Lundstrem himself used to play piano in addition to conducting the band.*[198] *Is that true?*

NK: *Yes, absolutely true. I even remember when I played with the big band in the 1960s, Lundstrem would occasionally play solo piano improvisations. However, that didn't happen too often. For the most part he was conducting. I remember once we were playing a concert in Czechoslovakia (now the Czech Republic) and the audience was surprised that Lundstrem conducted us all the time. He conducted even at the places when he may not need to do that, for example during my improvisation where the rhythm section is only playing with me.*

YT: *Why did he do that?*

---

[198] Oleg Leonidovich Lundstrem. Accessed August 16, 2016.
http://journal.jazz.ru/2016/09/30/oleg-lundstrem-orchestra-02/.

NK: *Let's start with that, he always conducted very well and it was pleasant just to observe him conducting.*

YT: *How did you react to the fact that he was conducting during your improvisation?*

NK: *Calmly. I remember we often performed a composition of the Count Basie Orchestra called »Not Now, I'll Tell You When«. The first part of that piece is just the rhythm section – piano, bass, and drums. He could simply not conduct us because it was unnecessary, but he still did.*

The members of the Lundstrem Big Band were like a big family where partnership, friendship, and care were the major components of their intense life.

YT: *Can we talk about some of the musicians from the band who were especially close to you?*

NK: *Sure. Let's talk about two of my closest friends – tenor- saxophonist Alexei Zoubov and trombonist Konstantin Bakholdin. Alexei and Konstantin are both legendary musicians; everybody from the jazz world knows these names. The thing is – they were some of the first improvisers not only in the Lundstrem Big Band but also in Russia in the early 1950s.*

Left picture: Konstantin Bakholdin (left side, third from the top), Alexei Zoubov (left side, fourth from the top); Right picture: Igor Lundstrem (right side, fourth from the top)

YT: How did they learn to improvise? I don't think they had study books on improvisation.

NK: Of course not. At that time there was no books on improvisation, they improvised by ear.

YT: Where did they study? Did they graduate from the Musical Colleges?

NK: None of the musicians from the Lundstrem Big Band were professional musicians based on their diplomas. Most of them had high education diplomas, but that was from other areas, for example from a science or technical field. I know that Zoubov graduated from the Moscow State University with the degree in physics, Bakholdin from the Moscow Institute of Communications.

YT: Oh, really? Then how did they turn to jazz?

NK: Jazz was their passion, their major interest. So, at some point they all left their professions, some of them right after graduation day, and dedicated themselves to the career of being touring jazz performers.

YT: So, it looks to me that they taught themselves.

NK: Yes, exactly. What else could it be? They played jazz, listened to jazz, and sometimes even tried to transcribe jazz. That was their jazz education.

YT: How did their careers develop after the Lundstrem Big Band?

NK: Zoubov now lives in the United States for more than thirty years. I think he moved to Los Angeles in the middle 1980s. I heard recently that he just got back from his tour in Israel. I guess he is doing very well; Beverly Hills is not the place for losers to be around.

YT: It is so good that you are keeping in contact with your old friends.

NK: Of course, especially with the ones who were so close.

YT: I remember you said that you had opportunities to immigrate but decided not to do it.

NK: Yes, there were many situations when I could potentially leave Russia. Those were my friends who were leaving the country and asked me to join them. Although, they knew in advance that I would not go.

YT: Why is that?

NK: I don't see myself living anywhere else except Russia.

YT: You are a deeply Russian man.

NK: Yes, I am.

YT: How about Konstantin Bakholdin? What kind of musician was he?

NK: He was another legendary musician, very gifted… He was a great improviser. Konstantin passed away in 1987.

YT: Did Bakholdin work only in the Lundstrem Big Band?

NK: Oh no. He was also a part of the Ludvikovsky Big Band and the famous ensemble »Melody« later in the 1970s. He was a highly in demand musician. I miss him a lot.

Fortunately, I was able to contact Mr. Zoubov, who now lives in Beverley Hills, CA (USA), and he kindly agreed to share his memories of his friend Nikolai Kapustin:

> *I don't remember how I first heard about Kapustin – it was so long ago, probably somewhere in the middle 1950s. The rumors started to flow by then that there is a piano student at the conservatory that has enormous technique and talent and was quite a novelty. He writes and plays real jazz compositions. For us, who just started to play jazz, the music that wasn't much appreciated and even considered dangerous by the Soviet regime, every new musician appearing in this field, especially of Kapustin's caliber, was a source of excitement.*[199]

The musicians from the big band were for the most part originally from Moscow. However, there were some who were from other cities, same as Nikolai Kapustin. These new circumstances of Kapustin's life as a jazz musician led him into a new adversity.

> YT: *Where did you live after your graduation from the conservatory?*
> NK: *That was a big question. Many people asked me to tell them my home address so they would send things to me and I was ashamed to say that I didn't have an address. I had to hide it somehow.*
> YT: *How did you survive then?*
> NK: *Starting from 1961 I was literally a wanderer. I lived sheltered in the apartments of my friends. These were very difficult years in my life.*
> YT: *I can't believe it! How long did this horrible situation last?*
> NK: *It lasted three years, until 1964, when Lundstrem helped me to receive my own flat.*
> YT: *How did that happen?*
> NK: *First of all, Lundstrem had a lot of good friends who appreciated him and his jazz music. Secondly, we had a very knowledgeable manager, Mikhail Tsin, who stayed with the band for many years. So, somehow after we became the official big band of the »Mosconcert« it worked out that Lundstrem and Tsin were able to get flats for some of the musicians in the band.*
> YT: *Were those flats to rent?*
> NK: *No, these were our own flats. Remember, at that time everything in the USSR was for free – education, medicine, and living properties too. I remember that flat, actually it was a studio, was very small but it was all mine.*
> YT: *I think there are no words to express how happy you were when you finally got it.*
> NK: *Oh, don't even start that... I was in heaven! The interesting thing was we all got flats in the same building.*

---

[199] The continuation of Zoubov's memories on Kapustin will be presented in the Appendix E.

YT: What do you mean?

NK: I mean exactly what I said – it was a brand new building and Lundstrem was able to get all our flats in the same place. Leonid Lundstrem, the brother of Oleg, also lived with us. There were seven or eight musicians who lived with their families at that place.

YT: You had a fun life – you guys played together and lived together!

NK: Yes, I didn't complain - I liked it that way.

YT: Did all musicians who needed a place to live receive the flats in 1964?

NK: Of course not.

YT: How did Lundstrem decide which musicians would get the flats first?

NK: I guess based on their importance in the band and the age too of course. By the way, I was the youngest member of the band at that time.

YT: That means that Lundstrem highly respected your appearance in the group.

NK: It looks that way.

On the Road with the Lundstrem Big Band: Repertoire and Performances

Nikolai Kapustin. During one of his tours with the Lundstrem Big Band, 1960s

Oleg Lundstrem Big Band had a wide range of repertoire that was performed during their tours in the USSR and abroad. It is interesting that ninety percent of their repertoire consisted of popular music and just ten belonged to jazz. In order to understand why it worked that way I would like to introduce one memorable episode from the history of the Lundstrem Big Band. This story happened in 1960 when the band performed a concert in the Russian north city of Ussuriisk. That was just a few months before Kapustin joined the band:

In July 1960 the newspaper »Komsomolskaya Pravda« [Komsomol Truth] received the letter from the audience who attended the concert in Ussuriisk. This letter was directed to the Russian Touring Concert Society about the experience that people had attending the concert. The letter was signed by people from the military, education, political leaders, and many others. The essence of this letter was the fact that during those concerts people felt like they were in some kind of American cabaret. Even the opening piece, composed by Lundstrem himself, reminded listeners of the »meaningless, screechy sounds« of jazz in the

191

West. *The whole program was accused with its connection to formalism. Listeners also noted that the MC tried to induce sympathy to this big band music. In fact he said that Lundstrem was writing the light music seriously. At the end of this letter, the listeners asked the leaders of the Russian Touring Concert Society to reconsider the repertoire of this big band and put special attention to the pieces that would be played by this group. In addition it was pointed out that the repertoire that listeners had heard in Ussuriisk on May 28 and May 29 concerts did not call for any clean and happy emotion and that listening to this music should be prohibited for the Soviet people, especially the younger generation.*[200]

YT: Had you heard about that story in Ussuriisk from 1960?
NK: I did not hear that. You are the first person who told me about that episode.
YT: Do you agree that the Ussuriisk incident proves that the Lundstrem Big Band had to go through some impediment from the people who thought that jazz is the bad influence from the West?
NK: Of course yes. Sometimes we had to go through some contradictions. Although, overall there were not many of the situations like in Ussuriisk because of Lundstrem's authority and respect from many people in Russia. He knew how to smooth out all questionable situations.

In order to survive and function well in this politically unstable surrounding, the Lundstrem Big Band appeared on the programs as »Concert Popular Big Band« but not a »Jazz Big Band«. The band collaborated with the most famous popular singers and vocal groups of that time of the USSR, for example with Maya Kristalinskaya, Valery Obodzinsky, and the vocal quartets »Accord« and »Lada«.

---

[200] Oleg Lundstrem. Accessed August 8, 2016.
http://journal.jazz.ru/2016/04/01/oleg-lundstrem-centennial/.

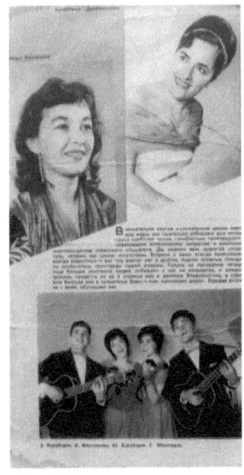

Lundstrem Big Band with Quartet »Accord« (bottom of the left side) and Quartet »Lada« (bottom of the right side)

YT: *How often was the repertoire of the big band renewed?*
NK: *I think once in two years the program was completely changed, but you have to remember that our main direction was the work with vocalists, so they had to learn new repertoire as well.*
YT: *What do you think about the vocalists with whom you collaborated?*
NK: *Not extremely high, if not to say something worse. Although some of them sometimes even tried to sing jazz. The most advanced in this regard was Estonian vocalist Aino Balina.*[201] *She had a very low voice, a timbre that would sound perfect for jazz music.*
YT: *Did you like her singing?*
NK: *Yes, I did.*
YT: *Do you remember how she joined the band?*
NK: *We met her at one of our performances in Latvia. At that time she worked with the Egil Schwartz Big Band.*[202] *We lured her. Lundstrem offered her a position with us and she agreed.*
YT: *So, she toured with the band in the USSR.*
NK: *Yes.*
YT: *Did she improvise?*
NK: *Yes, she did, but not often.*

---

[201] Aino Balina, Accessed November 7, 2017.
http://lr2.lsm.lv/lv/raksts/muzikju-jubilejas/dziedatajai-aino-balinai-80.a51573/.
[202] Egil Schwartz. Accessed November 7, 2017.
http://www.kino-teatr.ru/kino/acter/m/ros/380891/bio/.

YT: *How would you put the instrumental music in comparison with the vocal as a part of the big band repertoire?*

NK: *It was a dominance of popular vocal music.*

YT: *So, were you suffering from that dominance?*

NK: *Of course I was. To tell you the truth, when I joined the big band I didn't expect that amount of vocal popular music in our repertoire.*

YT: *What did you expect?*

NK: *I thought that we would be playing the pieces of Count Basie or Duke Ellington. We did play them but not as often as I would wish. I remember once I decided to count how many jazz pieces we have in our program. It ended up being just four pieces! Overall, it was never more than six, unfortunately.*

YT: *How many pieces did you have in the program approximately?*

NK: *The programs were always very long. I think we had more than twenty compositions, could be even up to twenty-five.*

YT: *So, it looks like a fifth of the program was dedicated to jazz.*

NK: *Something like this. We always started and finished our program with jazz music for some reason.*

Concert program of Oleg Lundstrem Big Band. Nikolai Kapustin (forth picture, left top corner)

In addition to the intense schedule of the big band's performances, another important aspect of the band's activities was their rehearsals.

YT: How often did you rehearse with the big band?
NK: We rehearsed every day, but we also had time off after the tours, sometimes for quite extensive periods.
YT: Can you give an approximate timetable of your tours and the time for rest?
NK: Sure. We would tour for a month and then we would have three weeks off.
YT: During those tour periods with Lundstrem how often would you play concerts?
NK: Very often.
YT: Something like two-three times a week?
NK: Something like two-three times a day.
YT: A day???!!! This is ridiculous!
NK: Of course there were some days off, but there were not many of them.
YT: How did you survive such intense trips?
NK: You need to be very healthy in order to tour with this big band. I always barely survived to the end of the trip.
YT: How about the rest of the band?
NK: This is an interesting thing – the older members of the band for some reason survived better than we did. I guess they were hardier.
YT: Do you remember any conflict situations inside of the band during the tour periods?
NK: I don't think so. Looking back, I keep thinking even through the hard and difficult time of our touring we were able somehow to maintain that warm atmosphere inside of the band. We were young, healthy, and happy. We were friends.
YT: What did you do during those three weeks' rest?
NK: What would you expect me to say? Of course I had all kinds of gigs during that »time of rest«. When you are a jazz musician you never stop playing.

Over the years that Kapustin worked with the Lundstrem Big Band they toured in hundreds of cities in Russia and in all the surrounding countries of the Soviet Union, such as Latvia, Estonia, Ukraine, Lithuania, Bulgaria, Rumania, Poland, Czechoslovakia (now the Czech Republic and Slovakia), and many others.

YT: I saw in one of the TV programs about the Lundstrem Big Band that the invitations for the band came from many countries in Europe and the United States. The only thing is that all this information did not reach Oleg Lundstrem since it was blocked by the »Rosconcert.«[203] The »Rosconcert« used to write them very friendly letters back with

---

[203] Rosconcert. Accessed November 23, 2017.
https://dic.academic.ru/dic.nsf/enc_music/6580/Росконцерт.

the refusal. They explained it as the busyness of the big band at the present time. Can you comment on that?

NK: *This possibly could have happened. We lived at the time when many things were prohibited and travelling abroad was one of them. The country was closed for many years.*

YT: *How about the festival in 1957?*

NK: *That was the first sign of the freedom, the very first one. These kinds of changes do not happen quickly as you know.*

In June 1965 Kapustin, being a part of the Oleg Lundstrem Orchestra, took his first tour abroad. The band participated in the International Jazz Festival in Prague. Quoting from the album cover from 1970 recording of the Lundstrem Big Band:

> For the first time in history Soviet jazz was presented in Prague; on the stage is the Oleg Lundstrem Orchestra. The brilliant performance of the jazz compositions of Soviet composers and their imaginative interpretations won the audience. »This ensemble represents a very high level of performance, only the best jazz musicians can compete with a group like that«, wrote the Professor of the Prague Conservatory Y. Prishkril (newspaper »The Evening Prague«).[204]

YT: *Do you remember your first trip abroad with Lundstrem?*

NK: *Yes, I do. We travelled to the Czech Republic. It was the time when this country was called Czechoslovakia.*

YT: *Where did you perform?*

NK: *We were a part of the big jazz festival and played in one of the biggest jazz halls of Prague named »Lucerna«.*[205]

YT: *How did your performance go?*

NK: *We had big success.*

YT: *Did Alla Semionovna (Kapustina) go with you on that tour?*

NK: *No, at that point I was not yet married.*

YT: *Did she travel with you after you got married?*

NK: *Oh yes, especially during the first few years. She got acquainted with all my friends very quickly. Alla even became good friends with Aino Balina, the vocalist.*

YT: *How did you feel during those concerts with Lundstrem? Did you feel stress or did you adjust yourself and later on stopped feeling the pressure?*

NK: *How can you do that – adjust yourself to the stress? Of course you would feel stress all the time. The material was not simple at all.*

---

[204] Cover article on the vinyl disc »Oleg Lundstrem Orchestra«, Melodiya (D 027931-2), 1970.
[205] Lucerna Concert Hall. Accessed December 24, 2017. https://goout.net/en/concert-halls/great-hall-lucerna/ckf/.

Another memorable performance of the Lundstrem Big Band happened in September 1965 when the Lundstrem Big Band was touring in Warsaw (Poland).

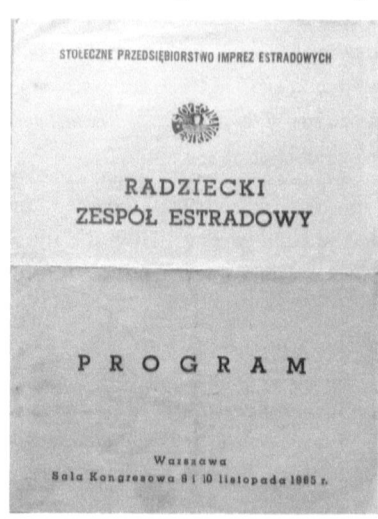

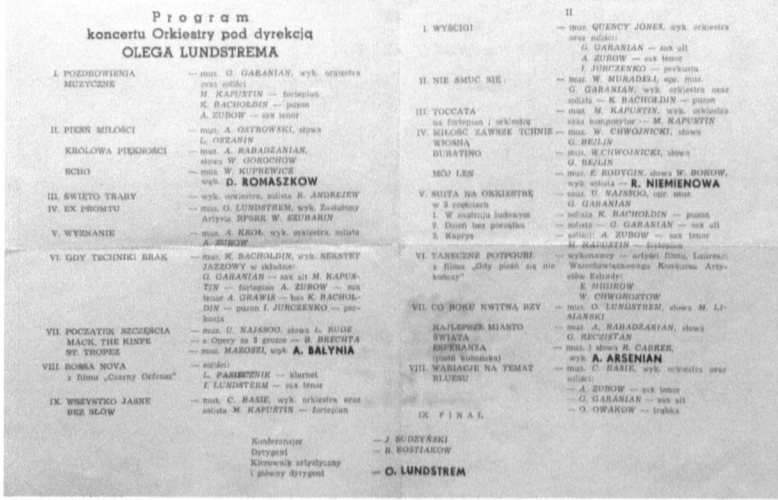

Lundstrem Big Band in Warsaw, Poland, September 9-10, 1965

YT: *Can you tell about the pieces that you played at that concert in Warsaw?*
NK: *I remember on that concert we performed my arrangement of Count Basie's song »Everything is Clear Without Words«.*
YT: *How often did the band perform your arrangements?*
NK: *Very often.*

YT: *Were you satisfied with the band's performances of your arrangements?*
NK: *Of course I was. Our band was one of the best ones in Russia, they played well.*
YT: *I noticed that on that concert in Warsaw the band also performed your composition – »Toccata« Op. 8.*
NK: *Yes, »Toccata« was a part of many of our performances, which I am thankful for. I remember we even recorded »Toccata« on the television in Warsaw during that visit in 1965. Although, I have to admit, that was a big stress for me, I always had to be in a perfect shape as a classical pianist. As you know, my pieces are very technically demanding.*
YT: *Did the audience appreciate your performance?*
NK: *Everywhere we played concerts we had successful performances, very well received music. We tried to do our best.*
YT: *Did you like touring with Lundstrem?*
NK: *At the beginning yes, very much, but later I got tired of it… very much. It was a hard life touring non-stop with the big band. The repertoire with all of those popular songs made me feel bored. It was difficult for me to quit the band, but I gradually moved towards that decision. I think it was a necessary change for me at that point. Otherwise, it became like a »ground hog day« – every day the same things over and over again.*
YT: *I understand. Do you remember any performances of the big band that were special for some reason?*
NK: *Yes, I remember our performance on the festival in Tallinn in 1967. It was a very good festival.*

The international jazz festival »Tallinn-67« in Estonia was one of a few festivals of the USSR that had a long lasting history. In comparison with other jazz festivals in Tallinn this particular festival, which took place during the May 11-14, 1967, was the 14th festival and it had a special meaning for the history of USSR. This edition of the festival was dedicated to the celebration of the 50th Anniversary of the Russian October Revolution.[206] The jazz festival was held in the biggest sport hall of Estonia called »Kalevi Spordihall«.[207] It consisted of two parts – competition and concert. The competition part included musicians in small and large jazz groups, as well as the big bands. Lundstrem Big Band participated in the concert program only. Among the countries represented at the festival were Russia, Latvia, Estonia, Finland, and the USA.

---

[206] October Revolution, which also known as the Great October Socialist Revolution, happened on October 25, 1917 (Old Style calendar, which is the November 7, 1917 in the New Style calendar).
[207] »Kalevi Spordihall« is multi-purpose arena in Estonia which holds up to 1,000 people.

YT: Which performers struck you the most?

NK: During that festival in Tallinn I remember I got acquainted with Zbigniew Namyslowski.[208] *Namyslowski is a very well-known Polish alto-saxophonist. He performed the program with his quartet. Also, there was a young Keith Jarrett*[209] *with the Charles Lloyd Quartet.*[210] *It was just the very beginning of the career for Jarrett; he was just twenty two years old back then. That was his first visit to the USSR, but how he played... Interesting thing, Charles Lloyd's career for some reason went down later, which you would not say about Keith Jarrett.*

YT: Was that the first time you saw Keith Jarrett's live performance?

NK: Yes, that was my first time; and I liked him tremendously. He played different back in 1967.

YT: How so?

NK: Better. Early Jarrett is more like a post-bob performer, but later he moved towards avant-garde music.

YT: And you don't like avant-garde music.

NK: I don't.

---

[208] Zbigniew Namyslowski. Accessed November 23, 2017. http://culture.pl/pl/tworca/zbigniew-namyslowski.

[209] Keith Jarrett. Accessed November 23, 2017. https://www.keithjarrett.org/.

[210] Charles Lloyd Quartet. Accessed November 23, 2017. https://www.charleslloyd.com/.

Other Musical Projects of Nikolai Kapustin

Despite the fact that Kapustin was highly involved in working with the Lundstrem Big Band, he was still able to find time to have the experience of working with other musical projects, playing and composing for other bands.

YT: Did Lundstrem know about your other projects?
NK: Sometimes yes, sometimes no. I didn't inform him what I was doing with my free time.
YT: What was his reaction concerning those additional projects? Was he upset with you?
NK: Of course not. He knew if we wanted to do something it would happen anyway. He was a flexible man, he could adjust. Actually, Lundstrem was also the initiator of some projects aside from our big band.
YT: What do you mean?
NK: Lundstrem asked me to participate in a smaller setting of the big band, in his combo. The goal for this group was similar to the orchestra – to participate in jazz festivals and jazz concerts. In other words, that would be exactly the same idea as a big band except with a smaller group.
YT: Oh, that's interesting. Did you agree?
NK: I played a few times with them but then refused to participate. By that time it was already too much work for me, plus this additional work would move me completely away from composition. Also I needed to have the rest, at least sometime. There was no such thing called »rest« in my life during those years of work with this big band.
YT: When did you join Lundstrem's smaller group?
NK: This happened at the beginning of 1970s. At that time I was close to finishing my collaboration with Lundstrem, I was thinking seriously about leaving the band.
YT: What was Lundstrem's reaction on your refusal to play in the smaller group?
NK: He was really surprised. He could not understand how you would be against playing in the smaller groups with musicians at that level. He said: »But this is jazz!« I still remember that time – every morning we had rehearsals and every evening we had performances with the big band. He wanted me to do those small groups in addition to this crazy schedule. That was overwhelming.
YT: Just in theory, do you see yourself playing only in the smaller groups and not with the big band?
NK: I came to Lundstrem to play with the big band, that's what I enjoyed the most.
YT: Did you play in any other jazz groups besides Lundstrem's combo?
NK: Of course I did. We used to come back to Moscow from our tours to have rest, but during that time we usually played somewhere else. I had many friends, and they asked me to play a lot.

> YT: *You said you didn't want to do that.*
> NK: *Yes, I did that with no special enthusiasm. I realized by then that being a jazz musician is not my thing.*
> YT: *How about at the time when you came to Lundstrem – were you interested in jazz?*
> NK: *At the beginning yes, but not for a long time. My desire to play jazz disappeared very quickly after I began playing with the band. Unfortunately, I had to continue doing that for quite a bit of time, eleven years, because of the income. It was not big money, but still it was something.*

In addition to collaborations with different jazz combos Kapustin also worked with some big bands as an arranger.

> YT: *What was your most memorable collaboration with some other bands?*
> NK: *That was my work with the Leonid Utyosov Big Band.*[211]
> YT: *Wow!!! Leonid Utyosov – he is a legendary musician and actor. Nikolai Grigorievich, you knew everybody!!!*
> NK: *Almost everybody.*
> YT: *How did you get acquainted with Utyosov?*
> NK: *I remember he was one of the guests at the wedding of Andrei Mikhalkov in 1956, but I can't tell how I got acquainted with him, I just can't… It was such a long time ago… I think I knew him earlier.*
> YT: *What piece did you arrange for the Utyosov Big Band?*
> NK: *It was a famous operetta by Friml and Stothart »Rose-Marie«.*
> YT: *How is it possible you can remember all these names?*
> NK: *I am telling you it's a well-known piece, they became worldly famous for it, everybody knows it.*

---

[211] Leonid Osipovich Utyosov. Accessed November 7, 2017.
http://russiapedia.rt.com/prominent-russians/music/leonid-utyosov/.

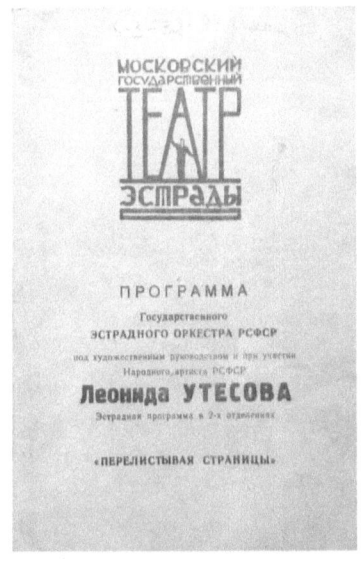 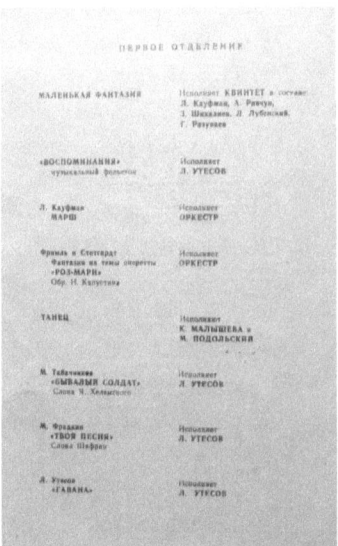

Program of the concert of the Leonid Utyosov Big Band »Turning the Pages« with Kapustin's arrangement of Friml-Stothart operetta »Rose-Marie«

YT: Was it originally your idea to write the jazz arrangement of a piece from the classical genre?
NK: No, Utyosov asked me to write this arrangement.
YT: So, he picked the piece.
NK: Yes and no. Utyosov had a trombone player who also worked with us in the Lundstrem Big Band. Utyosov had an idea to write a modern arrangement for the classical piece. I guess they talked and decided to ask me to be a part of this project.
YT: Then you decided which piece to do?
NK: I came to their rehearsals, listened to the band, and liked them a lot. Then we decided that the piece is going to be the operetta »Rose-Marie«. I didn't know that operetta very well to begin with, so we went with that trombonist to the library, got the original score and I began to work.
YT: Did Lundstrem know about this project?
NK: No, he did not.
YT: So, you never performed this piece with Lundstrem.
NK: No, I didn't. Although, it would sound better if the Lundstrem Big Band would perform it, more in the jazz style. There was a strange situation around this whole story.
YT: What was the story?
NK: Around that time Utyosov fired one of his musicians from the band, the bass player, for no serious reason, undeservedly, because he decided to get another gig outside of

the Utyosov Big Band. I don't know all the circumstances, but some of the musicians as a sign of solidarity decided not to collaborate with Utyosov.

YT: There are many musicians who work at different places. You can't just belong to one orchestra; you need to have a decent income.

NK: You would think. Plus, my friend Georgy (Garanian) kept warning me that I should not take that project no matter what, in case of Lundstrem's negative reaction.

YT: But still you did it.

NK: Yes, in spite of all those reasons not to do, I still did it. I believe that I made the right choice because I did it for the music, music that was interesting for me.

YT: Do you know if anyone recorded the performance of »Rose-Marie«?

NK: Yes, there is a recording of it on youtube performed by the Utyosov Big Band.

YT: When did you hear the performance of your arrangement of »Rose-Marie«?

NK: I remember we were on a vacation in Yalta[212] in the middle 1960s and I saw the concert of the Utyosov Big Band on TV with my arrangement of »Rose-Marie«.

YT: So, that happened by accident.

NK: Yes, I saw it accidently. I remember I saw for the first time that they had two conductors, which really surprised me.

YT: How is this possible? I never knew that it's possible to do.

NK: Utyosov conducted the string group and the second conductor – the big band.

YT: Do you know the approximate date when you collaborated with Utyosov?

NK: It was in 1963.

YT: Was Utyosov happy about this arrangement?

NK: I think so. He said he was always dreaming about doing something like this – taking the classical piece and bringing it back to a modern life. Funny thing, back in 1963 my arrangement sounded modern. Of course you can't say that now.

YT: So, your experience of work with Utyosov was not very stressful.

NK: Yes, we had a very good relationship with Utyosov in spite of the fact that he was not an easygoing person; he had a very complex character. If you look at him in the movie »Jolly Fellows« (1934) he is a very funny and happy guy. This was not true in real life. In reality he was a very difficult person, sometimes even rude. I remember I even got acquainted with his daughter during our rehearsals. Her name was Edit Utyosova. She was a singer. I think she worked with the Utyosov Big Band for quite a long period of time.

YT: She was a very pretty woman.

NK: Yes, she was.

---

[212] Yalta – a resort city on a south of Russia, which situated on a coast of the Black Sea.

In the 1970s, as well as now, there was another direction for the composer-arranger to supplement his income. This was the opportunity to write music for movies.

YT: Did anyone ask you to compose music for the movies?
NK: This happened a million times.
YT: What did you say?
NK: I didn't write a single note for the movies. I said a million times no.
YT: Why did you do that?
NK: I don't like movies in general and I don't like the idea of writing music for the movies. This is not me.
YT: But your friends did that, as well as some famous composers, such as Prokofiev, Shostakovich, or Khachaturian for example.
NK: My story is different.
YT: They used your »Toccata« Opus 8 in the movie »When the Song Does Not End« (1964).
NK: Yes, but this was a different thing. They asked me to use a section of my piece for this movie; I did not compose this piece originally to use in the movie.
YT: Did you agree?
NK: How could I say no? They knew that I would agree.
YT: Do you watch movies when you have free time?
NK: Never. I don't like movies from the time when I was young.
YT: So, you don't watch TV at all.
NK: This is not true. I watch the news.
YT: Ahhhh, so you would like to be informed what happens in the world.
NK: Yes.
YT: What do you like to do in your free time?
NK: I like to read books. It's more interesting than watching movies.
YT: I agree. What kind of books do you read?
NK: Lately I like only books on physics, but earlier I enjoyed reading books on linguistics and biology. Of course, I read a lot of books about music.
YT: Books on linguistics?
NK: Yes, but after I read a few French books on linguistics I stopped being interested in it.
YT: Really?
NK: Yes, it was boring. I remember when I was reading our old editions of Russian books on linguistics – you can't stop reading it, that's how interesting it was. My son, Anton, took them all to the United States. No wonder why.
YT: So, you don't read the fiction books.
NK: Oh no.

Jazz Environment of USSR in the 1960s-1970s

The period of the middle 1950s to the early 1960s in Russia, known as the »Khrushchev Thaw«, was marked by the appearance of new educational and cultural contacts, festivals, art shows, new fashions, foreign movies, and many other modern trends.[213] In the world of jazz, this was evidenced by the tours in the USSR of some significant musicians that deeply influenced the development of jazz traditions in Russia. The most celebrated concerts that Kapustin was involved in were the concerts of the Benny Goodman Big Band and the Duke Ellington Big Band.

In 1962 the great Benny Goodman[214] visited the Soviet Union, giving concerts in Moscow, Saint-Petersburg, Kiev, and other cities of the USSR.[215] It was the first American jazz band that received permission from the Russian government to tour in the USSR.[216]

There were two interesting details about Goodman's biography. First, he had Ukrainian ancestry as his parents emigrated from the Ukraine to the USA at the beginning of twentieth century. Second, Goodman had a proletarian origin since he was the son of a worker at the garment factory. Those two factors probably played a major role in the decision of the Russian government to allow the Goodman jazz band to tour the USSR.[217] In addition, the fact that John F. Kennedy became the president of the USA in 1961 helped to diminish the polarity between these two countries and turned into the direction of a warmer relationship.

The reception that Benny Goodman received was with a high level of respect, adoration, and love from the Russian audience. It got to the point that it was difficult to get tickets for his concerts.[218] Goodman would visit the USSR

---

[213] Khrushchev Thaw. Accessed December 12, 2016.
http://www.newworldencyclopedia.org/entry/Khrushchev_Thaw.
[214] Benny Goodman Big Band. Accessed December 10, 2016.
https://www.britannica.com/biography/Benny-Goodman.
[215] During this visit to the USSR the Benny Goodman Big Band played in Saint-Petersburg, Moscow, Kiev, Tashkent, Tbilisi, and Sochi. The concerts were attended by over 180,000 people. Accessed December 10, 2016. http://www.gorzvuk.com/enciclopedia/history/1962/.
[216] In order to choose which band to invite to the USSR Dmirty Kabalevsky visited the USA and listened a few big bands, among them were the Benny Goodman Big Band and the Louis Armstrong Big Band. Kabalevsky made the choice towards Benny Goodman. Accessed December 10, 2016. http://www.gorzvuk.com/enciclopedia/history/1962/.
[217] Ibid.
[218] Concerts of Benny Goodman in the USSR (documentary movie). Accessed December 8, 2016. https://www.youtube.com/watch?v=BLUZFVY7_uk.

many times after that first tour in 1962. He made repeated trips in 1963, 1967, and 1970.

YT: Do you remember your impression of the appearance of the Benny Goodman Big Band?

NK: I have a story on this matter. The fact is, Goodman's schedule was extremely intense. They did a million things a day – concerts, interviews, attendance of exhibitions, meetings with different people. Everybody wanted to meet with Benny Goodman. One thing that they started to do, but did not finish, was a movie about Goodman's visit to the USSR. Unfortunately, they did not record enough musical material during that visit for the movie, so the solution was quite unusual. They asked us, musicians from the Oleg Lundstrem Big Band, to imitate the playing of Goodman's musicians.

YT: Could you please repeat the last sentences?

NK: Yes, this sounds like a joke but this is true. We were asked to play Goodman's music imitating the Americans. In our part of the movie, they filmed using just silhouettes of our guys.

YT: How about yourself?

NK: With me it was more complicated – they decided to film only my hands.

YT: What???!!!

NK: Since Goodman's pianist, Teddy Wilson, looked quite a bit different from me, they painted my hands in darker color and I played Wilson's improvisation. Of course I listened to it before the recording and learned it exactly the way Wilson played it.

YT: Was it difficult for you to learn Wilson's improvisation?

NK: Not at all. I had no difficulties in learning his manner of playing. He was the permanent pianist for Benny Goodman. Actually, as a pianist I knew Teddy Wilson for quite some time – we listened to his recordings at the Mikhalkov house in 1950s. At that time I appreciated his playing enormously, but later on I became disappointed – he was playing too old-fashioned for me.

YT: It is fascinating how much music you've listened to during the time you lived at the Mikhalkov house!

NK: Yes, that was a lot. In addition to Benny Goodman we listened to quite an extensive amount of big band music, not only big band music but jazz in general.

YT: Do you remember what you played for that movie?

NK: I remember it was the blues.

YT: This whole thing sounds like an episode from the movie.

NK: No wonder why, for me too.

YT: How did you find out about your »movie debut« as Teddy Wilson? Did it come up very suddenly or were you informed about it in advance?

NK: We were on tour at that time, and it just happened to be that we were in Saint-Petersburg at that particular moment. That's where they were filming the movie about Benny Goodman.

YT: So you just appeared at the right time in the right place again.

NK: Exactly. Lundstrem told us about this idea and said that we need to help our friends from the movie. That's how it all started. I remember right after that recording I went straight to the hotel room, and the first thing I did was wash my hands.

YT: Did something like this happen to you again in your life?

NK: Playing for somebody else? No. I think that was my first and very last experience of doing something like this, and that was enough!

YT: Did you attend the concerts of Benny Goodman?

NK: Of course we did. Actually, I remember it was very hard to get the tickets to that concert – everybody wanted to see the legendary American jazz musicians.

YT: Did you happen to meet Goodman during his visit to the USSR?

NK: Unfortunately not. First of all, we were also busy. We had our own performances going on. Second, if you want to meet Benny Goodman then you need to speak English, which I was not ready for.

YT: Oh, no…

NK: I always felt that the language »barrier« was something that stopped us from communicating with people from other countries. Of course, some of our guys »tried« to speak English, as you know, gestures, some words and so on. I just decided for myself that I am not going to do that, I didn't want to look funny in Goodman's eyes.

YT: If not for the language thing would you be interested in the communication between the American and Russian musicians?

NK: What a strange question – of course yes!

In 1971 another legendary American band visited the USSR with a series of concerts. That was the Duke Ellington Big Band.[219] The tour included concerts in Moscow, Saint-Petersburg, Rostov, Minsk (Belarus Republic), and Kiev (Ukraine). The fact that Ellington's plane was met at the Saint-Petersburg airport with a Dixieland band marching on the tarmac speaks about the level of popularity of these musicians. On each concert of Ellington's band in Moscow there were more than twelve thousand people. There is no need to mention that all the tickets for Ellington's performances were sold out long before the actual concert dates.[220]

---

[219] Duke Ellington Big Band. Accessed December 8, 2016.
https://www.britannica.com/biography/Duke-Ellington.

[220] Duke Ellington. Biography. Accessed December 8, 2016.
http://sevjazz.info/index.php?option=com_content&view=article&id=444:2012-04-28-12-40-04&catid=48:jazz-stars&Itemid=50.

NK: Duke Ellington came to the USSR at the time when I was already thinking about leaving the Lundstrem Big Band.
YT: Did you attend his performance?
NK: I did. The thing I remember most was his concert at the smaller venue »House of Composers« in Moscow (Moscow Composer House).
YT: Yes, I remember that's the place where the Saulsky Big Band met with the Lundstrem Big Band in the late 1950s.
NK: Yes, this is correct. Only this time we were meeting Duke Ellington.
YT: Could you please tell me about this event?
NK: For some reason it felt short to me, I think the meeting lasted less than an hour. Ellington talked about jazz and then he played a little bit on the piano for us.
YT: Did the members of his band also take part in this meeting?
NK: No, that was a meeting only with Ellington.
YT: Do you remember what he played?
NK: He played his famous piece »Take the A-Train«. After that he played with our jazz musicians, it was something similar to a jam session. I felt very special that day.
YT: Why is that?
NK: I was standing right behind the piano when Ellington played »Take the A-Train«. If I would reach out my hand I could easily touch him.
YT: Oh, my… You were so close to that legendary person!
NK: Yes, I was lucky. He was already in his seventies.[221]

Aside from the American jazz experience, Nikolai Kapustin had an interesting insight into being acquainted with the European jazz tradition. Specifically, he had an opportunity to collaborate with jazz bands from Czechoslovakia and West Germany.

NK: I remember in the middle 1960s we went on tour with the Lundstrem Big Band to Czechoslovakia. It just happened that we had a chance to attend the concert of the famous Karel Vlach Big Band.[222] Karel Vlach was a key-figure of the jazz tradition in Czechoslovakia. Another musician who is considered to be one of the major jazz band leaders in that country was Karel Krautgartner.[223] In 1961, when I was still a student at the conservatory, Krautgartner visited the USSR with his big band and we attended one of his concerts.

---

[221] Note by the author: Duke Ellington passed away three years later in May 24, 1974.
[222] Karel Vlach. Accessed November 24, 2017. http://jazz-jazz.ru/?category=download&altname=karel_vlach__vte345iny_v_lloydu_i._19391942_1994.
[223] Karel Krautgartner. Accessed November 7, 2017. http://www.jazz.ru/mag/171/krautgartner.htm.

YT: Did you have a chance to communicate with the musicians from the Krautgartner band?

NK: Yes, we did. We got acquainted with musicians from the band. Even more, it turned out that we became good friends with Krautgartner's bass player. We even invited him to one of our apartments and did a little jam session there.

YT: During the day time I hope?

NK: What do you think?

YT: Then how about the neighbors?

NK: We tried to stay quiet. That was a fun time.

YT: It looks like you had a good relationship with Czech musicians.

NK: Yes, another big name from the Czech jazz tradition was Gustav Brom.[224]

YT: Did you know him too?

NK: Yes, I knew him very well. I remember during our tour with Lundstrem we visited Brom at his house with Zoubov and Bakholdin. We spent a wonderful time with him; we were drinking a very fine wine.

YT: It is amazing how many jazz musicians you were connected to.

NK: I remember meeting the jazz musicians from West Germany as well – Kurt Edelhagen Big Band.[225] *Do you know this name?*

YT: Unfortunately not. When did that meeting happen?

NK: That was in the middle 1960s, I believe, during their concerts in Moscow. I remember we went to that meeting together with Oleg Lundstrem. Of course, traditionally, they played for us a little bit, and then we organized the meeting with his band in our »House of Friendship«.[226]

YT: This is a great tradition – to play for each other!

NK: Yes, it is. Edelhagen even presented me with great quality German staff paper. I was so thankful to him for this surprise.

YT: So, he knew that you are composer.

NK: Of course he did. I played my »Toccata« Opus 8 for him. We performed this piece very often with Lundstrem. It had a great effect on the audience.

YT: Do you remember any other bands that visited Moscow in the 1960s?

NK: There was a jazz big band from Japan, who performed in Moscow. Please, don't ask me what was the name of that big band because it's in Japanese. In other words, there were many concerts of jazz big band music in the 1960s... maybe too many.

YT: Do you have any regrets attending or not attending some concerts?

---

[224] Gustav Brom. Accessed November 24, 2017. http://www.radio.cz/es/rubrica/musica-clasica-jazz/gustav-brom-de-cometa-del-swing-a-rey-del-jazz.
[225] Kurt Edelhagen. Accessed November 24, 2017. http://jazzprofiles.blogspot.com/2013/07/orchester-kurt-edelhagen.html.
[226] The full name of this place is »House of Friendship with People of Foreign Countries«.

NK: I regret not attending one concert. That was in the autumn of 1962; we were on tour with the Lundstrem Big Band and I was not able to attend to the concert of Igor Stravinsky, who visited Moscow at that time.[227]
YT: The concert of Igor Stravinsky?!?
NK: Yes, I missed his concert, and that was after his forty-eight years of living away from Russia. He came as a conductor. Interesting thing – Oleg Lundstrem left our tour for a couple of day to attend that concert but we were not allowed to do the same.
YT: What a nice guy!
NK: The sad thing – that was Stravinsky's last visit to Russia.

Aside from the experience of meeting with jazz musicians from the USA and Europe, Kapustin had many contacts inside the Russian jazz tradition. There were many other big bands functioning at the same time as Lundstrem including the Eddie Rosner Big Band,[228] Alexander Tsfasman Big Band,[229] Vadim Ludvikovsky Orchestra,[230] Anatoly Kroll Orchestra,[231] and the new orchestra of Yuri Saulsky.

YT: Were you acquainted with Eddie Rosner?
NK: Yes, I knew him; we met a few times.
YT: Was the music of the Rosner Big Band similar to the Lundstrem Big Band or different?
NK: Of course the music was different. Rosner jazz sounded earlier in style to my ear. In comparison with Rosner, Lundstrem had a more modern sound. Also, Rosner played a lot on trumpet with his orchestra as a soloist; Lundstrem just conducted the big band.
YT: How about Alexander Tsfasman?
NK: Tsfasman performed a lot during World War II.
YT: So, in a way Tsfasman and Rosner were a generation before the Lundstrem Big Band.
NK: Yes, Tsfasman was known as one of the first jazz performers in Russia. He started his musical career as a jazz performer as early as the middle 1920s. On the

---

[227] Stravinskaya, Ksenia. »Priezd I. F. Stravinskogo v SSSR (sentyabr'-oktiabr'1962)« [The Visit of I. F. Stravinsky to the USSR, September-October 1962], Muzyka, Saint-Petersburg, 1978, pp. 84-164. http://www.opentextnn.ru/music/personalia/stravinsry/?id=3566.
[228] Eddie Rosner. Accessed November 7, 2017. http://www.jazz.ru/mag/78/reading.htm.
[229] Alexander Tsfasman. Accessed November 7, 2017. http://www.jazz.ru/mag/372/tsfasman.htm.
[230] Vadim Ludvikovsky. Accessed November 7, 2017. http://nashenasledie.livejournal.com/121134.html.
[231] Anatoly Kroll. Accessed November 7, 2017. http://www.jazzmap.ru/rus/bands/Anatolij-Kroll-kompozitor-dirizhur-dzhazovyj-pianist.php.

other side, as a classical pianist, he was a student of Felix Blumenfeld at the Moscow Conservatory.

YT: *So, as well as you, he also had classical and jazz inside.*

NK: *Yes.*

YT: *Did you meet Tsfasman personally?*

NK: *Yes, I did. He was a very good man, very friendly, and in addition to that he was a brilliant pianist. I remember once I came to Gagra[232] for our summer vacation with Alla and the owner of the apartments told me that just a little while ago Alexander Tsfasman stayed in the same apartment as we did (laughing).*

YT: *How is that possible?*

NK: *I have no idea.*

YT: *So, out of a million other apartments in the resort town you both chose the same one?*

NK: *Yes, that was exactly like you said.*

YT: *I guess you had the same taste with Tsfasman not only in music but in life also.*

NK: *Yes, at that time I was not well acquainted with him, although, later we met quite often for different occasions.*

YT: *How about Anatoly Kroll?*

NK: *He was younger than Lundstrem. I got acquainted with Kroll when I worked in the Lundstrem Big Band, somewhere in the middle 1960s. Kroll lived at that time in Tula[233] and then moved at the beginning of the 1970s to Moscow. We were very close friends.*

YT: *Did you know him from the time when he lived to Moscow?*

NK: *I knew him even earlier – when he lived in Tula.*

YT: *Did you hear the new big band of Yuri Saulsky?*

NK: *Yes, I went to their concert. I was very interested in how they were going to sound.*

YT: *What did you think?*

NK: *I liked them a lot.*

YT: *I remember they even had vocalists in that orchestra on a regular basis.*

NK: *Believe it or not, Valentina Tolkunova,[234] who was his wife for a little while, sang with the Saulsky Orchestra as a jazz singer.*

YT: *Really? This sounds quite surprising – she is not a jazz singer.*

NK: *I guess at some point in her career she tried to be a jazz singer. That was a modern trend at that time – to sing jazz.*

---

[232] Gagra is a resort town on the northeast coast of the Black Sea, at the foot of Caucasus Mountains.

[233] Tula is a city in Russia situated 100 miles south from Moscow.

[234] Valentina Tolkunova. Accessed November 7, 2017. http://www.kino-teatr.ru/kino/acter/w/star/4322/bio/.

YT: *Did you hear about the Saint-Petersburg Jazz Orchestra led by Iosif Weinstein[235]?*
NK: *Yes, every time we were on tour in Saint-Petersburg we obviously went to see him. For some reason Weinstein disappeared quite fast from our view. After the 1960s I lost the connection with him.*
YT: *Did you hear about the Vadim Ludvikovsky Orchestra?*
NK: *They were one of the best ones in Russia in the 1960s. I even played with them occasionally.*
YT: *How did that happen?*
NK: *His pianist, Boris Frumkin, asked me to sub for him.*
YT: *What kind of music did they play?*
NK: *Very good music. They played a lot of modern jazz. Ludvikovsky and Garanian were writing music for them, and Frumkin also wrote sometimes. They did a great job. Actually, he visited me a while ago, somewhere in the 1990s.*
YT: *What happened with Ludvikovsky?*
NK: *He got fired from his position as the leader of the band. I guess the leadership of the orchestra didn't like Ludvikovsky and as a result Ludvikovsky lost his position.*
YT: *That sounds strange to me. Did he immigrate to some other country after that?*
NK: *No, he continued to live in Moscow and to write his music. He was a very good composer.*
YT: *This is a very sad story.*
NK: *Sorry, that's life.*

In the history of Russian musical culture, there was always an opposition of the two biggest cities, two cultural centers of the country – Moscow and Saint-Petersburg. Being capitals of Russia at some point in history, these cities made an important impact on Russian classical and jazz music.

YT: *Did you feel the competition between classical pianists in Moscow and Saint-Petersburg?*
NK: *Of course. There is a huge difference in understanding of the sound concept itself between the Moscow and Saint-Petersburg schools of playing. The Moscow sound is the sound of Rachmaninov which is a full, deep, real sound. The Saint-Petersburg sound is weak, like a »bird« sound, which they called »refined«.*
YT: *How about the jazz music? Did you feel the opposition of jazz music in these two cities?*
NK: *Oh no… Jazz is jazz, even on Mars. Here we were all on the same page, no competition or disagreement.*

---

[235] Iosif Weinstein. Accessed November 7, 2017.
http://jazzquad.ru/index.pl?act=PRODUCT&id=296.

YT: So, do you agree with the statement that jazz put people closer to each other?
NK: Yes, jazz music unites people.

Compositions of 1961-1972 (Ops. 2-13)

In spite of the fact that during the 1960s and the beginning of 1970s Nikolai Kapustin was deeply involved in the musical life of the Lundstrem Big Band as a touring jazz pianist, his major interest in music continued to be composition. The 1960s can be considered the early period of creativity for Kapustin as a composer. During this time, he composed twelve compositions, Op. 2 through Op. 13, eleven of which were written for the Oleg Lundstrem Big Band.

> *YT: Do you have some routine that helps you during the compositional process?*
> *NK: Yes, there is one thing – I like to smoke when I compose the music. Both of my parents smoked, so I guess I got it from them. It helps me to compose the music.*
> *YT: What do you smoke?*
> *NK: In the past I used to smoke cigarettes but then switched it to clove cigarettes.*
> *YT: Why is that?*
> *NK: I stopped smoking cigarettes because they didn't last long enough – you just start thinking about one idea and it's already done. Clove lasts longer.*
> *YT: Do you compose the music on the piano or writing at the desk?*
> *NK: Generally at the desk. I remember Glazunov[236] used to compose his symphonies at the piano and didn't like when somebody was listening to him behind the door.*
> *YT: Is that the reason why you compose at the desk?*
> *NK (smiling): Of course not.*

Three of Kapustin's major works from the period with the Oleg Lundstrem Big Band were *Piano Concert No. 1*, Op. 2, *Variations for Piano and Big Band*, Op. 3, and *Toccata for Piano and Big Band*, Op. 8.

The *Concerto for Piano and Orchestra No. 1*, Op. 2 (1961) was the very first piece that Kapustin composed for the Lundstrem Big Band.

> *YT: Why did you decide to compose the piano concerto as the very first piece for Lundstrem? Why did you choose this genre?*
> *NK: I have always wanted to write something serious and extensive for the piano with the big band. We talked with Lundstrem about that and decided that it is going to be the piano concerto and that I am going to perform this concerto with his big band. That sounded very good to me.*
> *YT: How did this turn out?*

---

[236] Alexander Glazunov. Accessed November 7, 2017.
https://www.britannica.com/biography/Aleksandr-Glazunov.

NK: You see, as I understood later, they didn't need that kind of music. They needed songs, something lighter, shorter, not as difficult, and more entertainment value rather than serious material. I didn't know about that at the very beginning.

YT: Did you perform this piece with Lundstrem?

NK: Yes, we performed it just five times, and sometimes even a cut version. The audience would not survive the length that I wrote. That was quite a disappointment for me.

YT: Yes, I noticed there were a lot of songs in the Lundstrem repertoire.

NK: Unfortunately, it was a predominance of songs.

YT: Did you happen to record the Piano Concerto No. 1?

NK: Yes, we recorded it, but this recording was preserved in the Lundstrem archive. I am not sure if it still exists.

In contrast with Piano Concerto No. 1, Kapustin's next opus, the piece called *Variations for Piano and Big Band*, Op. 3 (1962) was performed quite often during concerts of the Lundstrem Big Band.

NK: After that unlucky experience with my concerto, Lundstrem asked me to write the piece for the big band that would be shorter, something like three-four minutes in length, but still effective and musically meaningful. That's how »Variations«, Op. 3 came across, and it ended up becoming a very successful piece.

YT: I have listened to the recording of you playing this piece with the Lundstrem Big Band – the piano part is extremely difficult.

NK: Yes, the piano part is crucially important in this piece.

YT: How often did you perform this piece?

NK: Very often.

YT: I think it's very hard to keep yourself always in a perfect form pianistically, especially during the tours.

NK: I agree. It was hard, but I did it.

YT: I remember that Rachmaninov said getting the income based on your performances as a pianist is challenging, it's a tough life.

NK: Yes. Rachmaninov was mostly famous in the USA as a pianist, but not as a composer, which is a very sad thing.

The *Toccata for Piano and Orchestra*, Op. 8 (1964) was one of the pieces that was extremely popular and became a part of many Lundstrem Big Band performances. This piece also appeared in the movie »When the Song Does Not End« (1964).

NK: Did you know that they used the short version of the »Toccata« for the movie?

YT: No, I didn't. How big was the cut?

NK: The original length of the piece is twice longer, more than four minutes. They took just a half of the piece.
YT: Really? If you would not say that I would never suspect that it was a cut version.
NK: Unfortunately yes, and I knew that.
YT: And you never performed the full version of »Toccata«?
NK: We did. On our concerts we usually played the full version.
YT: Why do you think »Toccata« was so popular?
NK: It was popular because it is a very technical piece. People like when the fingers are running.
YT: Yes, it looks very effective, and your technique is just incredible.
NK: Thank you.

Nikolai Kapustin: Connection to His Family and Old Friends

Being away from his beloved parents and having such an intense life, Kapustin still tried to keep close connections with his family and came to Nikitovka to visit them every free moment.

Nikolai Kapustin, his mother Klavdia Nikolayevna and his father Gregory Efimovich. Nikitovka, Ukraine, 1970s

YT: How often did you come to visit your parents?
NK: Whenever I had free time. It was a very difficult period with all those tours with Lundstrem, I was very busy. Later when I got married, we would visit them with the children. I always remembered my parents. I used to come to them until they passed away. Even now, when they are both gone, I think of them often.
YT: How far was your home in Nikitovka from Moscow?
NK: One night on a train.
YT: Not too far.
NK: No.
YT: Did your parents come to visit you during those years of work with Lundstrem Big Band?
NK: Yes, my father came to visit me in Moscow right at the beginning in the autumn of 1961. That was his last visit to Moscow.
YT: What did you do with your father during that visit?
NK: I invited him to the concert of Lundstrem Big Band. I was sitting at the piano and he was sitting with the audience.

YT: I bet your father was very proud of his son.
NK: Yes, he was. The only thing that I regret now is that I didn't find the right moment to introduce my father to Oleg Lundstrem. You know how things happen.

Kapustin's life as a member of the Lundstrem Big Band moved him away from his old conservatory friends, but with all his activities, concerts and touring, new friends appeared.

YT: I see that your life completely changed with the appearance of the Lundstrem Big Band. Did you miss your time at the conservatory?
NK: No, I did not miss it. As I told you before, those years I spent for nothing. However, I do miss my friends. As we graduated conservatory, Jenia Pupkova went to her home in Ufa, and is still living there. Many relationships with some of my friends from conservatory ended with graduation. Although, Slava Ovchinnikov and Oxana Yablonskaya still call once in a while.
YT: What about Nodar Gabunia?
NK: Nodar... We were big time friends for many years after graduation. I visited him in Tbilisi three times. The first visit was in 1958 and the second in 1961. I remember after the trip in 1961 I went straight from the plane to the rehearsal with the Lundstrem Big Band. We were rehearsing my Piano Concerto No. 1 at that time. The last time I visited Nodar was with Alla (Kapustina) after our marriage at the beginning of 1970s.
YT: So, Alla Semionovna knows Nodar Gabunia?
NK: Of course, she knows him very well. We were on tour with Lundstrem at that time and we were travelling through Tbilisi. Alla was with us too, so we decided to make a stop in Tbilisi to visit my old friend Nodar.
YT: What good friends you were – you used any possible chance to see each other!
NK: That's for sure.

Alla

Alla Baranovskaya

Alla Semionovna Baranovskaya was born on January 30, 1945 in the city of Novokuznetsk (Siberia, Russia). She was the youngest child in the family. Alla had two older brothers, Sergei and Veniamin, and an older sister Aza.

YT: Could you say a few words about your parents?
AK: My mother, Praskovia Ivanovna Baranovskaya, lived at a difficult time – the years of war and suffering; also she had four children to take care of. She was paralyzed when I was thirteen… My mother was gone by the time I was twenty. She was just fifty-nine years old.

Proskovia Ivanovna Baranovskaya

YT: Sorry for my question.
AK: That's ok. So, I didn't have a childhood like most children do. At the time when my girlfriends were running and playing around the garden yard I was taking care of my ill mother. When she passed away my sister Aza became like a mother to me.
YT: What is the age difference between you and Aza?
AK: She was nine years older than me, which at that time felt like a lot. Aza was born in 1936. She was married very early, at just twenty-one years old, so she moved away from our house but visited us very often. This year on October 24th (2016) will be fourteen years since she passed away, my dear Aza.
YT: What about your father?

AK: My father, Semion Naumovich, worked at the Novokuznetsk metallurgical factory as a foreman. He was a calm and reasonable man. I have always listened to and followed his advice. I loved him deeply.

Being born during the final months of World War II, Alla developed a strong character and learned how to withstand the difficulties of life. Despite these difficulties, her life was moving in a positive direction. In the autumn of 1964 Alla was accepted to the Novokuznetsk State Pedagogical Institute, the department of German language. At that time, she couldn't even predict that in a few years one accidental meeting would change her life completely. Because of this meeting she would forever move away from the place she was born and raised.

In the autumn of 1967 Nikolai Kapustin was on tour with the Oleg Lundstrem Big Band. One of the cities where they performed was the city of Novokuznetsk. That was the beginning of Nikolai and Alla's story, a story of deep, selfless, true love.

YT: How did you meet Alla?
NK: We met in a cafeteria.
YT: Really? Could you tell me please about this life changing moment?
NK: I still remember that day very clearly. We arrived with Lundstrem to Novokuznetsk to perform a couple of concerts. Before going to our performance, my friend Vladimir Cherepanov, who played trumpet in the big band, decided we should get a snack in a cafeteria that was just across the street from the performance hall. There sitting at the table we noticed two attractive girls at another table close to us. Cherepanov decided to have a little conversation with them, and that's how it started.

On the road with Lundstrem. From the left – Vladimir Cherepavon, Nikolai Kapustin and one other musician from the band

YT: I guess you started to talk with the girls.

NK: Me? No. I was a very shy person.

AK (joining the conversation): And he still is. During our first meeting Kolia kept mostly silent.

NK: Volodia (Vladimir Cherepanov) handled the conversation; he invited the girls to our evening concert. We were surprised when they said they had already bought the tickets.

YT: Alla, how did you happen to be at that cafeteria?

AK: Same as Kolia (Nikolai Kapustin) - me and my friend decided to take a bite before going to the concert of Lundstrem Big Band. I used to go to the musical concerts all the time through all my life, but this was my very first experience of going to the jazz concert.

YT: Is that true? And after that people do not believe in the fate!

AK: Yes, I had no idea that this jazz concert was going to change my life, and that I would meet Kolia. I guess that was a good call. Actually, I think that was the first visit of Kolia to Novokuznetsk. Is that true?

NK: Yes, we came a few times more with Lundstrem again, but that was the very first one.

YT: Unbelievable!

AK: Of course after this concert Kolia embraced me with the jazz life and now I feel like a part of it, but back then it was an absolutely new experience for me.

YT: Did you notice two gentlemen sitting close to you at that cafeteria?

AK: Of course we did!!! We were thinking – oh, my gosh, just look at that....

YT: Looking at your story you can't stop wondering how unpredictable life is and what surprises she can prepare for us sometimes.

AK: I was telling the story of my life to my friends when I worked in the hotel »Pekin«. They asked me to repeat it a million times, over and over again. I was like a narrator telling my own life's story. Yes, it sounded like the tale that became reality.

YT: What happened next? Did you go to their concert?

AK: Of course we did. The whole concert I was looking at Kolia and talking to my girlfriend: »He is mine«, just in case she would start thinking about him (smiling).

NK (with tears in his eyes): After the concert we met backstage and had another conversation.

AK: Yes, they had to leave Novokuznetsk and travel to Barnaul, their next city on the tour. Barnaul is close to Novokuznetsk, something around five hours by car.

YT: Does this distance feel close for you?

NK: For the Siberian understanding everything in the north feels close.

AK: So, we decided that we were going to Barnaul also.

YT: No way... Really?

AK: Yes, right from the beginning I realized that I wanted to be with Kolia. We had an adventure in Barnaul. The question was – where to spend the night. Kolia of course had the hotel but we didn't. So, we got lucky – with my student ID card we were accepted to stay one night in the dormitory of the Pedagogical Institute of Barnaul.

YT: Did you come to visit Nikolai Grigorievich (Kapustin) in Moscow?

AK: Yes, we met in November (1967) and he invited me to Moscow in December (1967) to celebrate the New Year. This was my very first visit to Moscow. You can imagine how surprised I was seeing the capital of our country for the first time in my life. I was really impressed with everything – the food, the streets, and people who lived in Moscow.

YT: How long did you stay in Moscow during that visit?

AK: Not for a long time, I think I stayed in Moscow for a week. Kolia invited me everywhere; it was a very pleasant time. Then I went back home to Novokuznetsk.

NK: We stayed in contact by writing letters to each other.

AK: Yes, I kept all his letters, each and every one. Then in the summer of 1968 I graduated from the Institute and came to stay with Kolia forever.

NK: Since July 16, 1968 we have never been apart.

YT: Never?

AK: Never. This coming year (2017) on July 16th we will celebrate forty-eight years being together.

NK: Why do you keep repeating forty-eight, forty-eight?

AK: Why?

NK: Because it's forty-nine!

AK: Really?

YT: Alla Semionovna, do you remember July 16th 1968?

AK: I remember the day. I was travelling by the Siberian train Novokuznetsk-Moscow. It was a three-day trip, very-very long, but I knew that I was going to the man I love, and I was ready to do anything to be together with him. My father, sister Aza, and my relatives in Novokuznetsk didn't like the idea of me going to Moscow. They were talking about Kolia, saying that he is a touring musician, an artist who goes around the world, always in the sight of people, and that he may leave me. Also, all my relatives stayed in Novokuznetsk, and they were afraid we would never see each other. I remember my father said to me: »Allochka (gentle way of saying Alla), I know that you are our one and only shining star, our golden lady, but please give serious thought before making your decision.« I didn't listen to even one word that he was saying to me. Although now, looking back, I can tell that there was a lot of truth in those words. You know, the person who is in love is like a deaf person – nothing else matters. The thing that I knew for sure was that I loved Kolia and that he is not the man they thought he was. They did not meet Kolia at that point yet. So, I remember I was going on that three-day trip to Moscow and I kept thinking all that time about all these things… I was worried and didn't know what to expect from my future. At the moment I saw Kolia on the railway station I understood that I made the right decision. He was standing at the railway station with gladiolus flowers in his hands; my Kolia, the man of my life, my one and only love… And I was right, I still feel the same way I did that day.[237]

YT: I see in my imagination all the moments of your life, it's like in a movie.

AK: Yes, it is.

YT: What happened next?

AK: Kolia took me on the tour with Lundstrem to the Russian south. It was a really great time. Kolia introduced me to Oleg Leonidovich (Lundstrem). The thing is, at that time we were not married yet and that caused some problems concerning our accommodation in the hotels. They didn't want to put us together so we stayed in different rooms and used to secretly go to each other.

NK (to Alla Semionovna): Do you remember, in Tbilisi they were watching us very closely?

AK: Yes, that was so funny.

YT: This is so romantic…

AK: It was a serious thing – if somebody would notice us Lundstrem could have a big problem, but he knew that Kolia was not the kind of the man who changed girlfriends like gloves; he knew that this was a serious relationship.

YT: When did you marry each other?

---

[237] Note by the author: I looked at Nikolai Grigorievich at that moment – he was crying… Tears of a happy man who met his love in the middle of nowhere, in the north city of Siberia, but that was the true and very strong love.

NK: *Our marriage was on January 3, 1969. It was not a very big marriage; just a few friends. After the official ceremony of marriage, I remember we went to the restaurant »Praga« to celebrate.*

The marriage of Nikolai Kapustin and Alla Baranovskaya, Moscow, January 3, 1969

AK: *We didn't have a lot of money at that time, so I was wearing a very modest wedding dress that day.*
YT: *It's not about how many people attend your marriage or the cost of your dress; it's about how you really feel that day.*
NK: *Yes, for us it was a very special day in our lives.*
YT: *How did your life change after the marriage?*
AK: *After our marriage I began working at the secondary school as a teacher of the German language.*

On November 10th 1971 a very big happiness came to the Kapustin family when their first child was born. It was a boy. Alla and Nikolai decided to name him Anton Kapustin.

AK: *I was allowed to stay at home just one year after Anton was born.[238] That was a very difficult time for us with Kolia. Unfortunately, since Anton was very young at that point, sometimes he was ill and I had to stay at home with him. So I had to miss a lot of working days. We didn't have grandparents, like most young families, who would help us; everything was on Kolia and me. That's why I had to leave the school and begin working at the hotel »Pekin« as a German translator.*

---

[238] Note by the author: In most official organizations in Russia the women are allowed to stay home with the new born child for two years. During this whole period, she would receive a portion of her salary too.

NK: This is one of the biggest hotels in Moscow.
AK: Yes. The big advantage of the new place was my new schedule of work – I was working one day and had one day off. That was pleasant. I worked in »Pekin« for thirty years.
YT: Very long. So it was a good change.
AK: Yes, I really enjoyed being there. I had good people around me and it was a good job.

Even after the marriage Nikolai and Alla kept writing letters to each other. Reading their letters, you feel immediately the life of two young people who were never bored or unhappy.

NK: Letters were always a very essential part of our life with Alla.
YT: Did you save Alla's letters?
AK: You think he would keep them? Men feel different about these things; they usually do not save them, but women do.
NK: I think I have them somewhere, at least some of them for sure.
AK: Yes, I remember that Kolia was writing that he went to the post office waiting for my letter but for some reason he didn't receive any. He wrote something like: »I did receive the letter from my parents but didn't receive any from you. I feel upset.«
YT: Wait a minute… Since Nikolai Grigorievich was on tour how did he receive the letters from you?
NK: At the post office of the city we were in.
AK: Yes, he was writing the name of the city, the dates that they were supposed to stay, and I was sending them straight to that city.
NK: Yes, then I had to come to the post office with my passport and only then would they give it to me.
YT: Sounds like a slightly complicated plan.
NK: Yes, it was. Sometimes Alla would send them straight to the hotel if we were staying in the city for a while. What can you do? That was the only way we could stay in contact with each other.[239]

---

[239] Note by the author: In our documents for this book I had two letters from Nikolai to Alla. My original plan was to choose one, but then I realized that I would like to include them both; that's how unique, fresh, and touching they are.

Letter No. 1 from Nikolai to Alla (April 11, 1970):

Hello my dear Allochka!
You probably know from Moolya[240] that we are going to finish the tour not on the 18th —

You probably know from Moolya that we are going to finish the tour not on the 18th but on the 17th. That means that I am going to be home on Saturday which makes me very happy — the first two days we will spend completely together.

I don't have anything to write about myself; we are performing two concerts a day. I don't have any more power at all, and I am not the only one who feels this way. I don't want to talk about this.

We are now in the city called Rubtsovka. The name of the city, especially its ending »ka« tells you a lot already. In other words, Nikitovka looks more attractive.

Today at 6 pm is the first concert and the second at 9 pm, tomorrow is the same thing. The next day, just one, thank you. We are then going to Ust-Kaminogorsk for four days. All together we have six days left. One more thing — the letter may not reach you, I don't have any more envelopes with the air mail stamp on it.

I am in a hurry; now is a quarter to five and we are leaving at 5 pm. I have to run.

So, in a week I will be home. We are flying to Alma-Ata on May 7th. I will have twenty days to rest, I thought it would be less.

My pen is going to finish soon (already diluted by the water), that's why I am calling it a day. Wait for me. I miss you like I've never missed you before, more than ever. Kisses, your Kolia.

P.S.: What kind of a joke happened with our house?

---

[240] Note by the author: Moolya Lundstrem was the wife of Igor Lundstrem, the brother of Oleg Lundstrem. Both couples lived in the same apartment building and shared all the news between each other concerning the touring of the Lundstrem Orchestra.

Letter No. 2 from Nikolai to Alla (December 20, 1970):

Hello Allochka!
This night we arrived in Murom.[241] Now is December 20th, 1 pm, and I just woke up. I have to go to the concert at 5 pm. We played eighteen concerts already. If there will be two concerts a day until the end of the tour it will be thirty six altogether. Two of them we will play without any payment, so it is thirty four concerts, and this is already 400 rubles if not more. About our trip in January – it probably will not happen because Dima doesn't want to work again with those people; he suggested we work again in Moscow, but the conditions are very questionable. I need to think about it.
We will stay in Murom for four days, then one day in Arzamas, and one day somewhere close to Gorky. From Gorky we are going to Moscow. If there will be a chance to leave right after the concert, me, Gravis, Igor, and Dima will be taking the taxi and going home to Marina Roscha.[242]
How are you doing there without money my poor dear? You probably sent money to your parents, this is in vain. By the way, for a week already we are travelling without Vadim; he is always going ahead of us organizing the places for our concerts in the next cities. Therefore, we can't get paid until we see him. I keep living on a daily allowance. In other words, see you in five days, maybe only on the railway train station as we pass by. In this case I will send you the telegram. Kisses, your Kolia.

---

[241] Murom is the city in Vladimir region of Russia.
[242] Marina Roscha – place where Kapustin lived in Moscow.

Oleg Lundstrem – Postlude

Oleg Leonidovich Lundstrem passed away on October 14, 2005. In the autumn of 2016, a big event happened in the history of the Oleg Lundstrem Big Band. Due to the 100-years Anniversary of Oleg Lundstrem's birthday a new project began – the filming of the movie about Oleg Lundstrem, his life, and his famous band.

NK: The people from the TV center contacted me and asked my permission to use some of my opuses for the movie.
YT: Did you agree?
NK: Of course. It's an honor to be a part of this celebratory event for me.
YT: I keep thinking about the role of Lundstrem in your life – not only musically, but in general.
NK: Yes, if I would not play in his big band I would never come to Novokuznetsk and would never meet Alla.
YT: Lundstrem was like your godfather.
NK: Yes, and he will always be.

Nikolai Kapustin with the Oleg Lundstrem vinyl disc in his hands, Moscow, July 26, 2017

Chapter Five: Years of Work with the Boris Karamyshev »Blue Screen« Orchestra (1972-1977) and the Russian State Symphony Orchestra of Cinematography (1977-1984)

Boris Karamyshev and His »Blue Screen« Orchestra

Boris Pavlovich Karamyshev (1915-2005) was an eminent Soviet Russian composer and conductor. It is unfortunate that the name of this talented and notable musician is almost forgotten in Russia.

> *NK: Few people remember Karamyshev today and you can't find much information about him on the internet either. Even more, sometimes by mistake they identify my recordings with the Karamyshev Big Band as the Lundstrem Big Band. This happened with my Piano Concerto No. 2 Op. 14, Concert Rhapsody Op. 25, and many of my other works written in the 1970s. Undoubtedly, Karamyshev deserves to be more respected.*

Boris Pavlovich Karamyshev

Boris Karamyshev was born in Petrograd (now Saint-Petersburg) on May 15, 1915. He graduated from the Leningrad Musical College in 1939 with a double major in composition and conducting. During his time in the musical college he began his career as a leader of concert pop and jazz orchestras. In contrast with Oleg Lundstrem, who led his orchestra throughout his entire life, Karamyshev had the experience of working with different orchestras, gradually moving towards the most popular orchestra, the orchestra of Russian Radio and Television called »Blue Screen« Orchestra.

At the beginning, in 1934-1939 during the years of study at the musical college, Karamyshev became the leader/conductor of the Leningrad Youth Pop

Orchestra. Later, in 1939-1941, he became the leader/conductor of the Red Army Music Band. Another period of his life started during the years of World War II in Russia, 1941-1945, when Karamyshev became the conductor of the Front-line Exemplary Brass Bands, traveling and performing at different events connected to places of military operations.[243]

> YT: *Is it true that Karamyshev was performing with his bands in the actual war zones?*
> NK: *Yes, it is true. Because of this participation, after the war he was eligible to have accommodation for a couple of months every year in Ruza[244] for free.*
> YT: *Really? That's a lot of money!*
> NK: *Yes, I remember there were a few of them – the musicians who were a part of World War II and were awarded trips to Ruza without expenses.*

After the end of World War II, Karamyshev moved to Moscow and lived there until the end of his life. While living in Moscow, Karamyshev expanded his interests in composing, leading, and conducting orchestras. As a composer Karamyshev was widely known for writing music for numerous Russian movies, such as »Orlyonok (Eaglet)« (1957), »Vernost' (Fidelity)« (1965), »Vsadniki (Horsemen)« (1972) and others. Altogether, Karamyshev wrote the music for seventeen movies.[245] Aside from writing music for movies he composed a number of songs, highly Russian in nature, patriotic in its good sense, and very sensitive in character.[246]

As a band leader and conductor, during 1952-1955, he was the leader of the Moscow »Hermitage Garden« Orchestra. In the period of 1956-1964 Karamyshev was the conductor of the Instrumental Ensemble of the Soviet All-Union Central Radio SSSR, which was later known as radio »Mayak (Lighthouse)«.

His last orchestra, the most famous project, was the Orchestra of All-Union Central Radio and Television »Blue Screen«, where he was the leader, composer, and conductor during the years of 1965-1977. The »Goluboi Ekran« [Blue Screen] Orchestra was the accompanying band to all major musical events, such

---

[243] The Red Book of the Russian Stage: Boris Karamyshev. Accessed November 24, 2017. http://kkre-4.narod.ru/karamishev.htm; also see Nikolai Minkh, »Zametki muzikanta [Notes of the Musician]«, In *Sovetskii dzhaz. Problemi, Sobitiya, Mastera* [Soviet Jazz. Problems, Events, Masters], ed. Alexander Medvedev and Olga Medvedeva. Moscow: Soviet Composer, 1987, 401.

[244] Ruza is a city in Russia, situated 100 km to the west of Moscow, the summer retreat for musicians and composers. Conversation about Ruza will be presented in Chapter VI.

[245] Karamyshev works in the cinema. Accessed November 24, 2017. http://www.kino-teatr.ru/kino/composer/sov/31415/works/.

[246] The Red Book of the Russian Stage: Boris Karamyshev. Accessed November 24, 2017. http://kkre-4.narod.ru/karamishev.htm.

as the New Year program »Goluboi Ogoniok (Little Blue Light)«, in the USSR on the Television and Radio during the 1960s-1970s.[247]

When Nikolai Kapustin joined the band in 1972, it was in the wave of its' phenomenal popularity in the country.

---

[247] Ibid.

Nikolai Kapustin – Transitional Period

At the beginning of 1972 Kapustin finally made the decision to leave the Lundstrem Orchestra. That was one of the hardest moments of his life.

YT: What did Lundstrem say when you told him about your decision?
NK: He was always on my side, he understood me. He said to remember that his door would always be open for me.
YT: Oh, that would only make it worse I think.
NK: It was very hard for me to leave the band but I had no choice, I needed to move on. I couldn't survive any longer doing the same things over and over again...every day.
YT: Did you know in advance that you were going to work with Boris Karamyshev?
NK: Oh no! I just left and that was it.
YT: Left to where?
NK: To nowhere.
YT: I see it now. So, your story was not that you decided to leave one orchestra because you were invited to work with a different orchestra.
NK: Yes, I had no place to go....At that point I just wanted to stop this thing going in my life. That was enough.
YT: How did you survive financially?
NK: For the few months that I was living without any job we had a very difficult time, but I have to tell you, Alla was always on my side no matter what we were going through.
AK (joining the conversation): I believe in Kolia and everything he does. Sometimes he surprises me, but I know for sure that before he makes a step he is thinking seriously about it. I knew that he would find the way out for us and everything would be ok.
NK: And I was right!

Almost right after Kapustin left the Lundstrem Orchestra a friend of his from the time of the Yuri Saulsky Big Band, whose name was Boris Richkov, asked Kapustin if he would be interested in composing a couple of pieces for the radio »Yunost' (Youth)«.

NK: This call came perfectly in time. I composed three orchestral pieces very quickly (Op. 15-17) for this radio and the income from this work helped us to overcome that period.
YT: How long was that transitional period in your life?
NK: I think a couple of months, maybe something around three months.
YT: Oh good, not very long.
NK: Not very long but very memorable. I had a wife and a three month old son on my hands.

Kapustin Joins the Karamyshev Orchestra

In the spring of 1972 a new opportunity appeared in the life of Kapustin. He was invited to join the Concert Pop Orchestra of Central Radio and Television »Blue Screen« directed by Boris Karamyshev. He decided to take this chance, knowing in advance that he was coming back to his previous type of activity. This job, however, was supposed to be less active.

YT: Did you know Karamyshev earlier?
NK: I had no idea who Boris Karamyshev was.
YT: You are a brave man. How did you find out about that position in the Karamyshev band?
NK: As you know, I've always had many friends. So, one friend, a saxophone player who worked with Karamyshev at that time, mentioned this piano position and I decided to try it for myself.
YT: Lucky you!
NK: Yes, but on the other hand, who knows how many pieces I would write if I would not join the Karamyshev band?
YT: I think you made the right decision, especially for that period of time.
NK: Maybe.

Kapustin's friend, the saxophone player whose name was unfortunately forgotten, did a serious favor for him. He talked to Karamyshev, introducing and promoting Kapustin for the open position, and as a result Karamyshev decided to meet with Kapustin.

YT: Do you remember your first meeting with Karamyshev?
NK: I do remember it very well.
YT: Was it something like »I came, I saw, I conquered«?
NK (smiling): No, nothing like that. I came with my friend, the saxophonist, on their rehearsal. That's how I saw Karamyshev the first time. We talked for a few minutes. It was very clear by then that his original pianist was officially leaving the band and I think Karamyshev was glad that I appeared at the same moment. I think later he didn't regret that he took me in the band.
YT: Why would he? What did you think about Karamyshev?
NK: For some reason my first impression was that I didn't like him much from the first sight but this feeling disappeared quickly and we later became very good friends.
YT: He appreciated you very much.
NK: Of course. Even after the band was dissolved we met every summer in Ruza.

AK (joining the conversation): Yes, Boris Pavlovich (Karamyshev) felt tenderness to Kolia and loved him just like he was a son. They spent many evenings together in Ruza, drinking, smoking, and talking.

NK: I remember Karamyshev liked to stay in house No. 20; Alla and I used to visit him quite often.

YT: What did you talk about?

NK: About everything...about life.

YT: Have you ever been in Karamyshev's home?

NK: Yes, I remember I was there once.

YT: Did you like the atmosphere at his home?

NK: Yes, I did. Everything in his home was quite modest, but it was a big flat. By the way, I visited him to get the staff paper for my Second Piano Concerto.

YT: So, it was at the beginning of 1970s.

NK: Yes.

YT: Did you say – you needed staff paper?

NK: Ohhhh, I guess you may not know this – at this time, during the 1970s in Russia, it was a big deal to get staff paper, it was one of the deficit products. Only composers or people connected to music education were allowed to buy it.

YT: What do you mean? Can't you get it simply in the music store?

NK: Ohhh no! You had to be the member of the composer's union, which I was not at that time. I remember sometimes Varlamov let me borrow his composer's document (smiling) so I would buy the music staff paper for myself.

YT: So, you were cheating!

NK: In a way yes, but what else did I have left to do? I needed the paper to write my music.

YT: What would have happened if they would look at Varlamov's document?

NK: Nothing would really happen... except they would probably see the picture of Varlamov in it (laughing), but I knew that they wouldn't do that.

YT: That's so funny... So, you were helping each other.

NK: Of course.

YT: That's crazy, I can't believe there was a time in Russia when you couldn't buy staff paper.

NK: That's why the attitude to that paper was different – you had to write everything very carefully, knowing in advance that each page of this paper was difficult to get.

YT: Ohhh, you are right! And your handwriting is truly amazing.

NK: Actually, looking back I think that it was the right thing to do.

YT: About the staff paper?

NK: Yes, they can't give the paper to people who can't compose the music. I would do the same.

YT: *Ohhh, that's a statement! So, it would just be a waste of paper.*

NK: *Of course. At least that's what I think.*

YT: *Did Karamyshev have a family?*

NK: *Yes, he had a wife and a daughter. I remember his wife even toured with us once, when we were performing with Robert Young*[248] *in the middle 1970s, although, soon after that she passed away. At that time I was still working with Karamyshev and saw it all happening.*

YT: *How old was she?*

NK: *I think she was in her 60s by then. You know, it's hard to tell the woman's age based on the way she looks.*

YT: *That early?*

NK: *Is the 60s considered to be early now?*

YT: *Of course it is. How did he survive that loss?*

NK: *It was very hard for him. He never remarried and lived the rest of his life on his own... almost thirty years.*

---

[248] Conversation about Robert Young will be presented at the latter part of Chapter V.

Kapustin's Duty in the Karamyshev Orchestra/ A New Life in a New Band

Kapustin's life in the new band was on one hand quite different from his previous life with the Lundstrem Orchestra, but on the other hand, some things remained the same. Kapustin shared the same duties in the Lundstrem Orchestra as well as in the Karamyshev Orchestra. He was the pianist, composer, and the arranger for the band.

YT: *Did you enjoy playing with the Karamyshev Orchestra?*
NK: *Of course I did.*
YT: *Did you improvise there?*
NK: *Not as much as with Lundstrem but yes, I did.*
YT: *So, the skills that you developed working with Lundstrem were helpful.*
NK: *Oh yes, it helped me many times even later, throughout my life.*
YT: *Did you know the pianist that played before you who worked with Karamyshev?*
NK: *Yes, his name was Vagif Sadikhov.*
YT: *Vagif? What an interesting name.*
NK: *He was a native of the Republic of Azerbaijan,[249] a very good pianist. For some reason he decided to leave the band.*
YT: *Why is that?*
NK: *I don't know, probably because of the repertoire – songs, songs, and again songs. The predominance of »entertainment« music in those bands was the biggest problem for me.*
YT: *So, in a way the new band was not much different from the one that you just left.*
NK: *In a way yes. Although, I do believe that my work with Karamyshev was a step forward because I felt more comfortable as a composer.*

During these five years of work with Karamyshev Orchestra (1972-1977) Kapustin composed twelve pieces. Among those were one of his major works – *Piano Concerto No. 2*, Op. 14 and his first solo piano work *Suite in Old Style*, Op. 28.

YT: *Why did you feel more comfortable as a composer with Karamyshev?*
NK: *I had more time and more freedom I guess.*
YT: *Did Karamyshev ask for a specific length of pieces, like Lundstrem suggested for example?*
NK: *That's the thing – Karamyshev never set me for anything, I was free to compose whatever I wanted and how long I wanted. I was open to everything my heart would lead me to.*

---

[249] Azerbaijan is a country in the South Caucasus region, a former Soviet Republic.

YT: That's great! It also looks like you joined the band just seven years after it was formed in 1965.

NK: Yes, and that too. The band was at the early stage of its development, relatively young, nothing was completely set. The thing that I liked the most about that band is that the Karamyshev Orchestra had a string section. I felt it as a big advantage in comparison with Lundstrem for example.

YT: Did you use the string group in your pieces composed during that time?

NK: Of course I did. That's why every time someone talks to me about my recordings I keep saying – if you hear strings then it's the Karamyshev Orchestra, Lundstrem didn't have strings.

YT: Was it Karamyshev's original idea to use the string group in the jazz band?

NK: I don't think so. Leonid Utyosov used the string group in his orchestra back in the 1950s.[250]

YT: So, that was kind of a rebirth.

NK: Yes.

As an arranger Kapustin continued writing arrangements of popular songs for the Karamyshev Orchestra as he did with Lundstrem.

YT: Did you write your arrangements of popular songs or themes in the style it was originally composed, in Russian Soviet style?

NK: Do you think I would do that? Of course not. They wanted me to compose modern day arrangements. Those modern elements would come from jazz. I tried to incorporate all my experience that I had earlier.

YT: So, your style was closer to jazz.

NK: To be more specific – to Count Basie style... some of them.

YT: Did you transcribe the music for the Karamyshev Orchestra?

NK: Not really.

YT: Can we say that in order to write an arrangement of any piece the arranger has to have a well-developed skill as a transcriber?

NK: Of course. You can't go far without this skill.

YT: Did you ever feel your superiority over other musicians who could not transcribe the music?

NK: What is special about that?

YT: Your ability to transcribe the music.

NK: There were many of us who could transcribe the music; I was not the only one.

YT: So, you don't feel special in this context.

---

[250] Note by the author: In 1950 Charlie Parker recorded the CD called »Charlie Parker with Strings«, where he used strings in the band. Accessed November 24, 2017. http://www.allmusic.com/album/charlie-parker-with-strings-the-master-takes-mw0000313067.

NK: Not at all.

YT: But don't you think that there are few people who have this unique ability?

NK: No, I am telling you - there are many of us who could do this.

YT: Alright. Did you write any arrangements of Classical pieces?

NK: No, it was mainly the popular Soviet songs or the themes written by Russian composers, for example I wrote many arrangements of Alexander Varlamov's[251] music.

YT: So, basically you were doing the same work as you were with Lundstrem.

NK: Yes, and no. Yes, I was doing the same work but with Lundstrem I was writing the arrangements precisely for Lundstrem, and during my work with Karamyshev I was writing for Karamyshev and many other people. Anyone who would ask me to work for them I would agree.

YT: Now it is clear. So, you had some projects aside from Karamyshev.

NK: Definitely. I had to expand the scope of my work in order to support my family. I did everything I could possibly do.

YT: Yes, Anton was very young at that time.

NK: Of course. I remember I was working very intensively at the time when Anton was growing.

YT: In the 1970s.

NK: Yes. You may not know but I also got paid for my compositions when I composed for Karamyshev. So, it all depended on how much I was composing in addition to my work as a pianist and arranger.

YT: So, from the financial standpoint the Karamyshev Orchestra was a little step ahead in this matter.

NK: Yes, exactly like you said – a little step ahead. Fortunately, in the late 1970s our life got much better.

YT: How did this happen?

NK: That happened because I started to work with the Ministry for Culture that existed under the Russian Government, composing the music for them. They paid very well for my work. That was something pleasant to remember.[252]

Joining the Karamyshev Orchestra, Kapustin entered a new world of musicians, promoters, and people around the personality of Boris Karamyshev.

YT: Were you acquainted with the musicians from this band earlier or was it all a new experience for you?

---

[251] Alexander Varlamov (1904-1990) was a Russian composer and jazz musician. The conversation about Varlamov will be presented in the latter part of the Chapter V.

[252] The conversation about Kapustin's work with the Ministry of Culture SSSR and RSFSR will be presented in the latter part of the Chapter V.

NK: When you live in Moscow for more than ten years you start to become familiar with some of the people from your area. Yes, of course I knew some of them. With some we even worked together earlier on different projects. They were all very good jazz musicians, that's why the band sounded so good.

YT: So, you didn't feel yourself as a new musician?

NK: No, I didn't need to accommodate, or adjust myself. From the beginning of my work with Karamyshev I felt very comfortable.

YT: Did any musicians from Lundstrem Orchestra play in this band?

NK: Not that I know of.

YT: The reason I asked this question is that it is known that your friends from the Lundstrem Orchestra, Zoubov, Bakholdin, and Garanian, also played in the Vadim Ludvikovsky Orchestra, right?

NK: They would not perform with Karamyshev.

YT: Why would they not?

NK: Because the Karamyshev Orchestra was with strings.

YT: And?

NK: And in general, string players would be classically trained musicians.

YT: Oh, we have some tension in here! Do you remember the musicians from the Karamyshev Orchestra who were like Zoubov or Bakholdin in the Lundstrem Orchestra?

NK: Of course each orchestra has the leading musicians, the backbone of the group who leads the rest of the band. The Karamyshev Orchestra in this context was no exception. There were few of them – all great musicians, very talented people. I enjoyed performing with them.

YT: Can you recall their names?

NK: If I would know in the past that you would ask me this question I would try to remember their names.

YT: Did you find new friends in this orchestra?

NK: Of course I did.

YT: I was thinking that you may not have time now, when you have a family, to spend time with your new friends.

NK: If you really want it, you will make the time.

YT: And that's what you did.

NK: Yes.

Karamyshev Orchestra: Instrumentation and Repertoire

In the 1970s the Karamyshev »Blue Screen« Orchestra was one of the most notable bands in Russia. There were a few reasons for that. First, the level of musicianship was highly rated because Karamyshev carefully selected the members of the band. Second, the personality of the leader encouraged them to try new things. He supported the serious jazz compositions written by Nikolai Kapustin and others, expecting them to experiment with music and to open the further horizons of music as art. Third, the Karamyshev Orchestra was the official orchestra of the Central Radio and Television of the USSR, which appeared quite regularly on television and radio, and was well promoted.

One of the crucially important decisions that was made by the leader of the band, was the idea to use the string section as a part of the big band. In other words, in its instrumentation the Karamyshev Orchestra followed the tradition of the earlier orchestras that existed in Russia in the 1950s, for example the Eddie Rosner Orchestra or Leonid Utyosov Orchestra.

YT: Did you like the sound of the orchestra with the strings?
NK: I see it only as an advantage for the music. The strings give the warmth and the richer sound palette to the orchestra.
YT: Yes, and keeping tradition is also a good thing. How many string players did you have in the band?
NK: I think nine. There were four violins, four violas, and a cello player.
YT: How about the rest of the instrumentation – was it the same as with Lundstrem?
NK: Basically, yes.
YT: Then how would you call this band?
NK: Sympho-jazz band.

In the choice of repertoire for the Karamyshev Orchestra, as with some other progressive orchestras of the 1960s-1970s such as the Lundstrem Orchestra, Kroll Orchestra, and the Weinstein Orchestra, they followed the tradition which came from the 1950s. During this time bands mainly accompanied popular singers, however, in their repertoire there was also virtuoso and lyrical instrumental pieces, some of them in jazz style.[253] Each band had a different percentage of popular music to jazz. In the 1960s-1970s it was a necessary step to maintain the audience interest and to entertain during the concert. It was not yet

---

[253] Saulsky, Chugunov. The Brief History of Soviet Jazz. Accessed November 24, 2017. http://www.norma40.ru/articles/sovetskiy-dzhaz-istoriya.htm.

the time when the big band could perform an exclusively jazz instrumental program because the Russian audience was not ready for that. Accordingly, the Karamyshev Orchestra included a combination of popular material with the jazz music in their repertoire.

> YT: *If we would compare the Lundstrem and Karamyshev Big Bands in the proportion of popular and jazz material what would you say?*
> NK: *Lundstrem had more American jazz in his repertoire.*
> YT: *And Karamyshev?*
> NK: *Karamyshev had jazz too, of course, but less since this orchestra was centered on the Russian audience interested in Russian popular music of that time.*
> YT: *So, basically it was songs written by Soviet Russian composers.*
> NK: *Yes. However, when we played jazz it sounded almost authentic. I remember somebody mentioned that when they were listening to us playing Basie's music it sounded like it was actually the Count Basie Orchestra. I was pleased to hear that!*
> YT: *Yes, that is really cool! Is it true that during the 1960s-1970s dance music was quite popular in USSR?*
> NK: *Of course this is true.*
> YT: *You would record entire discs of dance music with Karamyshev.*
> NK: *On those discs we also recorded compositions in jazz style.*

The Karamyshev Orchestra, being one of the leading orchestras of 1960s-1970s, gave Boris Karamyshev an opportunity to be selective and to choose the musicians as well as the composers he wanted to collaborate with.

> YT: *Do you remember composers who presented their pieces for Karamyshev?*
> NK: *There were so many of them… some more important, like Alexander Varlamov, some less.*
> YT: *So, there were many people around Karamyshev who worked with him, same as with Lundstrem, correct?*
> NK: *I think Karamyshev had a larger field of activity.*
> YT: *It is very sad that the Karamyshev Orchestra is not as famous now as the Lundstrem Orchestra.*
> NK: *At his time Karamyshev was extremely famous, but with the passing of time, for some reason, the memory of him was almost lost.*
> YT: *Did you play any material written by Karamyshev himself?*
> NK: *Yes, sometimes we played his compositions. I think we even recorded some of his works.*
> YT: *What do you think about his music?*
> NK: *From my point of view composition was not his strongest side. He was a great leader of the band, a very good conductor, and a very good person.*

YT: But he composed the music for seventeen movies! So, he was in demand.
NK: I didn't say that he wasn't.

A new step was made by Karamyshev when he decided to include serious instrumental jazz pieces composed by Nikolai Kapustin.

YT: Did you play all the pieces that you composed during this time with Karamyshev?
NK: Yes, all of them. I composed those pieces for Karamyshev.
YT: It looks like instrumentation and repertoire-wise your work with Karamyshev was different from Lundstrem. Is there anything that stayed the same?
NK: Yes, songs… predominance of the popular, light music. This is very sad to realize but it is what it is.
YT: In other words, you got what you were trying to escape from.
NK: Yes. Although, I tried to concentrate my attention on something that was more interesting for me.
YT: That was your music.
NK: Yes, I had a very good orchestra to play my music. That was the main thing.
YT: Oh, that was a political step, kind of negotiation so to say.
NK: Yes. Have you ever done that in your life?

Karamyshev Orchestra: Recordings on Radio and Television, Touring

The major field of activity with the Karamyshev Orchestra »Blue Screen« was centered upon live performances on the radio and television, live recordings, and touring.

YT: Did you perform more live or recorded on the radio with Karamyshev?
NK: We did both equally – live performances and recorded sessions.
YT: I think I would feel a little scared to play live on the radio or television.
NK: When you are young nothing scares you.
YT: In which settings did you record on the radio?
NK: Mostly I played with the Karamyshev Orchestra but sometimes I also recorded just the piano by myself, but not that often.

Over the course of twelve years of its existence the orchestra performed with the most famous Russian singers, such as Gelena Velikanova,[254] Tamara Miansarova,[255] as well as with some famous singers from abroad.

YT: These are all top rated singers in the USSR, names that everybody knows.
NK: Yes, these were very famous singers.
YT: Can you recall any vocalist that you remember the most for some reason?
NK: I remember Tamara Miansarova. She was the wife of a friend of mine, who was a very good pianist. By the way, she was also a pianist to begin with, but then started to sing and eventually gained popularity as a singer.
YT: I guess it's a modern trend of our time – for a pianist to become a singer. Did you perform with Muslim Magomayev?
NK: Muslim had his own band. I never performed with him. It was the time when he was extremely popular in the USSR.
YT: How about the programs on Television dedicated to the New Year celebration? Is it possible that you may be a part of the same program with different musical pieces?
NK: That could possibly have happened. All the famous musicians of that time were participating in those programs – singers, bands, and Karamyshev, and Lundstrem... all.
YT: So, your main work at that time was on the radio and television.
NK: More on the television than on the radio. I remember our neighbors kept saying to me that they kept seeing me on TV... That was funny.

---

[254] Gelena Velikanova. Accessed November 8, 2017.
http://www.kino-teatr.ru/kino/acter/w/star/283859/bio/.
[255] Tamara Miansarova. Accessed November 8, 2017. http://miansarova.narod.ru/bio.htm.

YT: Did they ask for an autograph?
NK: I don't think they knew about this thing.
YT: Did you get paid for all your broadcasts on the television?
NK: If I would get paid for all my appearances on the television in the 1960s and 1970s I would be a millionaire by now! Of course not.
YT: In the US musicians get paid for every single appearance on the TV. Even more, depending on how long the shot and how close the camera gets to you, it's calculated differently. For example, my husband, saxophonist Curtis Johnson,[256] keeps receiving a nice check every year on Christmas.
NK: Lucky Curtis! I heard about this but don't think that something like this could ever happen in Russia. People pay to appear on the television – this sounds familiar, but people getting money because of their appearance on the television – this is something new... Yes, especially at that time, in the 1970s, I wouldn't mind a nice check for Christmas time... I had Alla and two children by then.

To this day a very special place on Russian television belongs to the program »Golubio Ogoniok« (Blue Light). Russian people remember this from their childhood, watching this program on New Year's Eve with parents and friends. This program was something you grew up with and stays with you for a long time. Only the best musicians, dancers, and humorists participated in these memorable events. Nikolai Kapustin was a part of these programs for a number of years.

YT: When was the first time you played on the »Goluboi Ogoniok«?
NK: I played there with Lundstrem in the 1960s and with Karamyshev later in the 1970s.
YT: Did you play live on these programs?
NK: Oh no, it was all recorded. Somewhere around two-three weeks before the New Year we would record our performance. It would be impossible to do it all live – so many famous people had to be at the same time at the same place for such a long time.
YT: Yes, plus it was New Year's Eve.
NK: Exactly, and live performance is a dangerous thing, not everybody can do that.

---

[256] Curtis E. Johnson, a Pittsburgh based saxophonist, former Associate Professor of Music at West Virginia University. Johnson has performed as a soloist with the West Virginia Symphony Orchestra, the Wheeling Symphony Orchestra, the Pittsburgh Symphony Orchestra, and the Pittsburgh Jazz Orchestra. He is a renowned R&B and jazz performer, having backed such star performers as Christian McBride, Ahmad Jamal, Benny Golson, Ray Charles, Aretha Franklin, The Temptations, Dionne Warwick, and many others. Johnson served as Artistic Director for the Krakow Summer Jazz Academy. He is currently featured in the book »Legendary Locals of Wheeling« as an artist and as an expert on the career of Leon »Chu« Berry. The PBS special »They Died Before 40« includes Johnson speaking about the life of »Chu« Berry. He has been twice nominated for the Grammy Educator Award. Johnson is a Yamaha Performing Artist/Clinician.

YT: *This is so true. Talking about the television – this is an interesting fact – at the beginning of the 1970s Russian television was in black and white but at the end of the 1970s it was in color!*

NK: *For some reason I was not thinking about that.*

YT: *Yes, and you were on television exactly at that time – revolutionary time. This is kind of a cool thing!*

NK: *Kind of cool.*

Apart from performances on the radio and television the Karamyshev Orchestra toured in the Soviet Union. Since Kapustin could not refuse participation in touring, this put additional pressure in his life.

YT: *It looks like the main function of the Karamyshev Orchestra was different from what you did with Lundstrem, when Lundstrem did a lot of touring and Karamyshev did mainly performances on the Radio and Television. What do you think?*

NK: *Yes, it looked that way too when I joined Karamyshev. I thought my life would be less active now, more settled in Moscow, the life of a touring artist is a hard bread… But you know what? I was wrong. One day I realized that I can see calm life only in my dreams.*

YT: *In general, can you say that Karamyshev toured less than Lundstrem?*

NK: *In general yes. Especially when I joined the band in the beginning of 1970s – we didn't tour much, but later, in the middle 1970s, touring was pretty intense.*

YT: *On the other hand, if the band does a lot of touring that means its popularity is growing and the band is becoming more famous.*

NK: *Maybe.*

YT: *Where did you tour? Did you go abroad?*

NK: *No, we toured only in the USSR… And nothing like Lundstrem – jazz festivals or something like this.*

YT: *Did you tour as an accompanying orchestra for famous singers or as an orchestra on its own?*

NK: *I think both – sometimes with the singers, sometimes alone. There were many different settings for our tours – sometimes even with a few singers or singing groups. Even when we toured with singers there was always a place for our instrumental pieces in the program.*

YT: *So, it was a combination of singing and instrumental music, like with Lundstrem in a way.*

NK: *Exactly.*

YT: *Do you remember any artist you toured with in the 1970s?*

NK: *Yes, my very first big tour with the Karamyshev Orchestra was with Robert Young.*

Robert Young on the cover of his vinyl disc recorded in Moscow studio »Melodiya«, 1977

The British singer Robert Young was born in 1943 in Newcastle upon Tyne. He gained popularity at the beginning of 1970s when in 1971 he was awarded »Most Outstanding Vocal Act Award« by the English newspaper »Stage and Television Today«. Internationally, he gained his popularity through winning the first prize at the Yugoslavian Song Festival the »Ljubljana Grand Prix«.[257]

Russian audiences became acquainted with Young in October of 1973 when he visited the USSR for the first time. Young gave concerts in Moscow, Leningrad, Kiev, and other cities of the USSR with the big success.

YT: I see that the geography of your performances with Young in 1973 was quite impressive.

NK: Yes, we went to many different cities in USSR, performed in the Ukraine and Latvia.

YT: Did you perform only in the big cities?

NK: Everywhere. I remember at the beginning of our tour we played a concert with Robert Young in Novosibirsk.

YT: I guess it was cold there.

NK: Yes, it is Siberia.

YT: How did the audience react to Young?

NK: He was a star… People loved him. He had that type of personality, like Tom Jones, the Russian people would fall in love with – tall, great looking man, singing the

---

[257] Robert Young. Accessed November 8, 2017.
https://www.thestage.co.uk/features/obituaries/2011/robert-young/.

songs with simple harmonies and easy memorable melodies that go straight to your heart and stay there for a while.

YT: Style wise where would you put Robert Young – as a jazz or popular singer?

NK: Popular singer. He did sing a couple of songs in kind of a jazz style, but I didn't like it.

YT: How long did you tour with Robert Young?

NK: It was quite long; I think somewhere around three weeks.

YT: Something like ten concerts or more?

NK: I think much more.

YT: What do you especially remember about that tour?

NK: I remember how Alla was meeting me at home after we returned from that tour.

YT: Did she meet you as a hero?

NK: Yes, as a hero.

YT: Did Alla cook a million different tasty things for you?

NK: Yes, she was waiting for me. I was happy to get back home.

YT: Did you get tired during this tour?

NK: You know, all those tours always ended in a similar way - with the big party at the end, where everybody wants to celebrate, and you have to be a part of it… That's what made me tired. I thought to myself – enough cheering, didn't drink a sip and went straight home to my family.

New Acquaintances of Nikolai Kapustin: Varlamov, Lyadova, and Silantiev

Alexander Varlamov

One of the close friends of Nikolai Kapustin during his work with the Karamyshev Orchestra in the 1970s and later in the 1980s was Alexander Varlamov.

YT: Did your friend Alexander Varlamov have any connection to the XIX century composer Alexander Varlamov,[258] the founder of the Russian art song that we know from the music school textbooks?
NK: I thought about that too.
YT: Did you ask him about it?
NK: Yes, I did. He said that I am not the first person to ask this question and that this is true – he is a distant relative of the great Alexander Varlamov.
YT: That's impressive!

Alexander Vladimirovich Varlamov (1904-1990) was Russian composer, conductor, band leader, and jazz pianist. Varlamov is considered one of the founders of the Russian Soviet jazz musical tradition.[259] Russian jazz theorist Yuri Chugunov and the eminent composer Yuri Saulsky in their essay »Short History of Soviet Jazz« placed Varlamov in a significant position in the history of Russian jazz:

> *In Russia, in the early 1930s, there appeared a number of orchestras that played jazz music, such as the Skomorovsky Orchestra, the Landsberg Orchestra, the Tsfasman Orchestra, and the Varlamov Orchestra. Organized in 1933, the Varlamov Orchestra was considered the band that came closest to the American jazz tradition in their understanding of jazz style in comparison with other jazz bands of that time. The Varlamov Orchestra performed mostly instrumental music, however, the band also accompanied American jazz singer Celestina Cole.*[260]

---

[258] Alexander Egorovich Varlamov (1801-1848). Accessed November 24, 2017. http://files.school-collection.edu.ru/dlrstore/fce0a0ac-d965-0f7e-bc0b-a5c5faa33405/Varlamov bio.htm.
[259] Alexei Nikolayev, »Alexander Varlamov«. *Sovetskii dzhaz. Problemi. Sobitiya. Mastera* [*Soviet Jazz. Problems. Events. Masters*], ed. Alexander Medvedev and Olga Medvedeva (Moscow: Soviet Composer, 1987), pp.346-49; also see Vladimir Feiertag, *Dzhaz. Entsikopedicheskii spravochnik* [*Jazz. Encyclopedic Guide*], (Saint Petersburg: Skifia, 2008), p.104.
[260] Yuri Chugunov, Yuri Saulsky, »Short History of Soviet Jazz«. Accessed November 8, 2017. http://www.norma40.ru/articles/sovetskiy-dzhaz-istoriya.htm.

А.Варламов. 1937 г.

Alexander Varlamov Septet, 1937

The personality of Varlamov and his life as a jazz musician was so extraordinary that it led to some interesting facts of his biography. For example, it's a fact that many episodes of the legendary film of Karen Shakhnazarov »We are from Jazz« (1984) were modeled after the life of Alexander Varlamov.[261] Another fascinating fact from the biography of Alexander Varlamov is that his father,

---

[261] Around the movie »We are from Jazz«. Accessed November 25, 2017, https://www.vokrug.tv/product/show/my_iz_dzhaza/.

Vladimir Varlamov, was a friend and classmate of Vladimir Ulyanov (Lenin)[262] in the Simbirsk (Ulyanovsk) School.[263] The city was renamed to Ulyanovsk from Simbirsk in 1924 in honor of Vladimir Ulyanov-Lenin who was born there in 1870. In addition to Vladimir Lenin, Alexander Varlamov was born in Ulyanovsk, although Varlamov spent the biggest part of his life in Moscow.

YT: Did you know that the father of Alexander Varlamov, Vladimir, was a classmate of Vladimir Ulyanov-Lenin?

NK: I had no idea. This is a very interesting fact.

YT: Do you have any information on where Varlamov studied?

NK: He had great teachers – he was a student of Gnessin[264] himself.

YT: Is this Gnessin, the father of sisters Gnessin, the founders of Gnessin Academy of Music in Moscow?

NK: Yes, that's him. Gnessin was also a composer.

YT: So, Varlamov studied composition with Gnessin.

NK: Correct.[265]

YT: I read that Varlamov also had his own jazz orchestra in the 1930s.

NK: This is true, although, that band didn't survive long.

---

[262] Vladimir Ulyanov (Lenin). Accessed November 25, 2017.
https://www.biography.com/people/vladimir-lenin-9379007.
[263] Valentin Yankovsky, »Alexander Varlamov – Standing at the Roots of Soviet Jazz«. Accessed November 25, 2017. http://shanson-e.tk/forum/showthread.php?p=506261.
[264] Online Jewish Encyclopedia: Mikhail Gnessin. Accessed November 25, 2017. http://eleven.co.il/article/11216.
[265] Varlamov graduated from the Gnessin Musical Technicum (Moscow) as a composition student. Some of his professors were Gnessin, Glier, and Rogal-Levitsky. Accessed November 25, 2017. http://shanson-e.tk/forum/showthread.php?p=506261.

Cover of the vinyl disc »Jazz Orchestras Led by Alexander Varlamov. Recordings of 1930s-1940s«

YT: *I listened to one of Varlamov's early recordings. He sang the famous popular song »Blue Moon« (Rodgers/Hart) translated in Russian language. I didn't know that he was also a singer. He had a very beautiful, charming voice.*
NK: *This was not serious. He was a much better composer.*

During the time of World War II the Varlamov Jazz Orchestra, as well as many other orchestras, travelled and performed on the front lines for the Russian troops, supporting and helping Russian people overcome the suffering and the horror of the war.

Varlamov, however, was arrested by the KGB[266] in January 1943 and spent eight years in a Siberian Correctional Facility. This story remained unknown for many years and only after 1985, during »Perestroika«,[267] was it officially revealed to the public. The official reason is still concealed, although, there are a few assumptions that might lead Varlamov to this highly tragic moment. One of the assumptions was his recording of the foxtrot named »Iosif« on the vinyl disc in the late 1930s. At that time there was only one person in the USSR with this name – Iosif Stalin. First, Varlamov decided to use the violin as a solo instrument for the improvisation, and second, he decided to insert the Jewish intonations in the melody of the improvisation. That may have been enough for the KGB to

---

[266] Soviet Security Service KGB. Accessed February 26, 2018.
https://www.britannica.com/topic/KGB.
[267] Perestroika in the USSR. Accessed February 26, 2018. http://russiapedia.rt.com/of-russian-origin/perestroika/, https://www.britannica.com/topic/perestroika-Soviet-government-policy.

arrest Varlamov right from his rehearsal and destroy eight years of his life.[268] Another version of Varlamov's arrest was the fact that he didn't report that his wife's nephew deserted from the Soviet Army during WWII.[269]

> NK: *Many people were arrested during that time (the 1940s) in Russia, not only musicians, everybody. It was a very difficult time for our nation.*
> YT: *Have you ever talked to Varlamov about the fact that he was arrested and lived away from Moscow for so many years?*
> NK: *Somehow I knew about it, but since he never started this conversation with me I never asked.*
> YT: *I guess he just wanted to forget about it, like it never happened.*
> NK: *You would think.*
> YT: *Not to change the subject – how did you get acquainted with Varlamov?*
> NK: *I met him at the house of Karamyshev. That was the time when I worked with Karamyshev, in the middle 1970s. Varlamov was well known among the jazz musicians in Moscow, a highly respected figure. By that time he had some vision problems, so it was very difficult for him to compose. I started to write the arrangements for him of his music, first I was one of a few people doing this for Varlamov, and then ended up as the only person continuing. I wrote tons of arrangements for Varlamov.*

One of the vinyl discs of Varlamov's compositions arranged by Kapustin was called »Compositions in Dance Rhythms«, which was published in Melodiya in 1980.[270] The disc included the compositions recorded over the period of 1975-1979.[271]

---

[268] Valentin Yankovsky, »Alexander Varlamov – Standing at the Roots of Soviet Jazz«. Accessed November 25, 2017. http://shanson-e.tk/forum/showthread.php?p=506261.
[269] Kirill Moshkov, »95th Anniversary of Russian Jazz. Part II: Chronology of Jazz in Russia«. Accessed December 18, 2017. http://journal.jazz.ru/2017/10/01/russian-jazz-timeline/.
[270] Melodiya (33 C 60-13717-48), 1980.
[271] Some of the recordings of Varlamov's arrangements made by Kapustin. Accessed November 25, 2017. http://www.nikolai-kapustin.info/audio_1.html.

Cover of the Varlamov disc »Compositions in Dance Rhythms«, 1980

Note on the back side of the disc:
To dear Kolia [short from Nikolai] Kapustin with deep gratitude for the magnificent arrangements and delightful improvisations that will forever remain on this record. Sincerely yours, A. V.

YT: *Do you remember that disc?*
NK: *I do, I have that vinyl disc, signed by Varlamov for me somewhere at the house*[272]... *I played piano also on some of those compositions... although, it was many years ago.*
YT: *Do you have any favorite compositions from that Varlamov disc?*
NK: *My favorite one from that disc is »Sail in the Sea«.*
YT: *I remember that piece – it has a piano part in chords with the melody on top, as some of the other pieces from that disc. I asked my husband, Curtis Johnson, to listen to it. He said the first thing that came to his mind was the blind jazz pianist George Shearing.*[273] *Do you know this pianist?*
NK: *Of course I do! Curtis is right (smiling), at that time I was very much interested in Shearing, listened to a lot of his music, and played in his style. Shearing was blind by birth, they asked him if he wanted to have surgery but he refused. He said – then I would not be able to play the way I do it now.*
YT: *How did you find the recordings of Shearing? Did you buy his discs?*
NK: *My friends presented some of his recordings to me, so I didn't need to buy anything.*
YT: *You have good friends!*
NK: *Yes, I can't complain. Which compositions do you like from that Varlamov disc?*

---

[272] Note by the author: The face of Kapustin turned into a big and happy smile since the conversation turned into the area of vinyl discs – the relic of a jazz musician.
[273] George Shearing. Accessed November 25, 2017. http://www.georgeshearing.net/.

YT: *My favorite one is »Going behind the Horizon«. I especially like the piano improvisation part. Did you improvise there in real time or compose a version of the improvisation earlier? Every note is so well placed.*
NK: *That was a real improvisation.*
YT: *Your piano improvisation sounds perfect to me. Why did you decide to stop your career as a jazz pianist?*
NK: *At that time I decided to do something else – to compose the music. I think even if I would be continuing my career as a jazz pianist, finally becoming a great jazz improviser, I still would be one of many.*
YT: *And there is no other Nikolai Kapustin – a composer!*
NK: *Yes.*
YT: *I remember you told me the other day that sometimes you refused to take some additional work as a pianist because you knew that you needed the time for composition. So, you were thinking about it.*
NK: *I always did.*
YT: *Do you believe in predestination?*
NK: *In what?*
YT: *In predestination – no matter what you do you would end up composing your music.*
NK: *I never thought about that. It just happened that way.*
YT: *That's how serious things usually happen – on its own. Which orchestra is performing on that Varlamov disc? Is it the Karamyshev Orchestra?*
NK: *It's a collection of different pieces played by different orchestras at different times during the middle 1970s; the Karamyshev Orchestra was one of them.*
YT: *This is understandable. Since he was so well-known in Russia in the field of jazz music, he probably had many connections.*
NK: *Of course... and everybody knew about Varlamov.*
YT: *Did you play a lot of Varlamov's works with Karamyshev Orchestra?*
NK: *Yes, we performed them quite often.*
YT: *Why did he ask you to do the arrangements of his own works? Why wouldn't he perform it in its' original version or arrange them by himself?*
NK: *I don't know, I guess he didn't like how his works sounded in its original version.*
YT: *Why is that?*
NK: *He thought they didn't sound modern, that they sounded old fashioned.*
YT: *Did you agree with him?*
NK: *Yes, I did. His music sounds in pre-WW II style, like 1930s. Why would I write arrangements for him if they would sound nice to begin with? I think he even tried to write the arrangements of his own compositions on his own but didn't like the result.*
YT: *He then decided to ask the young generation of arrangers to make them sound more modern.*

NK: Yes, to involve »new blood«. That's how I started to work with him.

YT: Just wanted to clarify – did Varlamov already write orchestrated works or just piano versions of them with the accompaniment?

NK: The way it usually happens is that he would play the themes for me on the piano and I would write them down.

YT: In other words, you wrote melody and harmonic chords that corresponded with each other?

NK: Correct.

YT: Did you record it on the tape?

NK: No, I did it without tape recorder.

YT: Then how did you do it? Just writing right away?

NK: Yes. Why would I need the recorder if I have the composer sitting in front of me? It is much simpler and faster.

YT: So, in other words you did a sketch of his composition.

NK: Yes, by pencil, just the sketch of the main ideas, so you would have the melody with the numbers.

YT: What numbers?

NK: The numbers that are usually used in jazz, like a lead sheet.

YT: Do you mean – how the chords function?

NK: Yes.

YT: That's intense work!

NK: Not really. From this work with Varlamov we became good friends. I feel sad that our friendship had come to an end.

YT: Why is that?

NK: I used my original ideas writing arrangements for Varlamov. Let's start with the fact that the first thing I usually did was to re-harmonize his music… his harmonies were too simple for me, very primitive.

YT: I see. So you made his harmonies more interesting, more complex.

NK: Yes. It got to the point when my friends started to tell me to stop writing arrangements and putting these ideas into my own pieces, which I ended up doing anyway.

YT: Yes, it's a fine line, very fragile one, when the arranger becomes the composer.

NK: That's the thing. I guess I was too inventive… I never tried to hold my ideas for something else, once it came to me, I immediately used it.

YT: Did you only do arrangements for Varlamov?

NK: No. I actually composed my »Fantasia for Jazz Quartet«, Op. 27 on the themes of Varlamov. He was a very good composer, the real one. I remember I was working a lot for him.

Alexander Varlamov, late 1980s

YT: Do you remember any episodes from your friendship with Varlamov that have special meaning for you?
NK: I remember one summer we went to Ivanovo[274] with Varlamov and my son Anton for our summer vacation. There was a »House of Composers« in Ivanovo and we spent a very memorable time at that resort.
YT: When was that?
NK: It was in the late 1970s. I remember we went there to celebrate Varlamov's 75th Birthday.
YT: So it was in 1979.
NK: Yes, correct. I remember my youngest son, Pavel, was just born not long before that trip in 1978.
YT: How long did your vacation with Varlamov last?
NK: As usual, something like three weeks... maybe twenty five days.
YT: That's a long period of time.

---

[274] Ivanovo was a summer resort for Russian composers, situated 155 miles away from Moscow. Among the composers, who spent their time in Ivanovo were Prokofiev, Schostakovich, Myaskovsky, Glier, Shaporin, and many others. Accessed November 25, 2017.
https://books.google.com/books?id=tNjPg1HgxZ0C&pg=PA55&lpg=PA55&dq=ivanovo+composers+vacation&source=bl&ots=MI_uCb_jxD&sig=SRGzPp-mIWrrA1MVbdZ1dewxUMns&hl=en&sa=X&ved=0ahUKEwiTt5bF3pDTAhWL2YMKHVO iCZUQ6AEIGjAA#v=onepage&q=ivanovo%20composers%20vacation&f=false.

NK: Yes, it is.

YT: Did you have any river around that resort in Ivanovo?

NK: Of course, there was a big lake out there. We spent most of our time on that lake... swimming, talking, just resting and having fun. At that time I was very interested in swimming, I could do that then.

YT: Russian people would always be associated with nature. Did you rest mostly or work in Ivanovo?

NK: We were just resting. At that time I could allow myself to simply have rest, but not now. When we started to come to Ruza I used to compose there all the time... There is no more real vacation for me. I composed many works in Ruza.

YT: Yes, it's very calm in Ruza – very good atmosphere for work... This whole story about you and Varlamov is so fascinating. I would really like to see that disc that you have at home.

NK: We'll try to find it when you will come next time... if I will still be alive.

YT: Nikolai Grigorievich, you can't talk like that! You have to live long-long life.

NK: I don't think I can do the long one.

YT: But you have to at least try.

NK: Ok, I will try. What is the next question?

Lyudmila Lyadova

Another interesting acquaintance was with Lyudmila Lyadova, whom Kapustin met in the middle of 1970s. Lyudmila Alexeievna Lyadova (born in 1925) is a famous Russian singer and a songwriter.[275] She became known in the late 1940s-early 1950s and is still active today. At the age of ninety two she is still teaching, doing masterclasses, and writing new songs.

Lyudmila Lyadova

---

[275] Lyudmila Lyadova. Accessed November 25, 2017. http://russia-ic.com/people/general/1/508.

YT: Does Lyadova have any connection to the famous Russian composer Anatoly Lyadov?
NK: No, this time there is no connection to the famous composer. She is the one who became famous.
YT: What do you remember about Lyudmila Lyadova?
NK: She was an interesting person to talk with. I remember once, before my trip with Robert Young, I mentioned to her about this tour and she immediately started to talk about Young. It turned out that they knew each other very well.
YT: How did you know each other?
NK: She was a friend of Karamyshev and sometimes attended our rehearsals. I think I knew about her even from the time when I was living in Nikitovka. I was still a »boy« but she was already »blooming«.
YT: Really?
NK: Yes, I heard her voice almost every day on the radio programs. She was a very popular singer.
YT: When did you get acquainted with Lyadova personally?
NK: In the 1970s, when I worked with Karamyshev or maybe even earlier, during my work with Lundstrem.
YT: It was probably very pleasant to hear someone's famous voice every day and then actually meet that person after many years.
NK: Of course! We even became very good friends later.
YT: Did you work with her?
NK: I think I did but not much. She was a very good classical pianist; she could play everything right away.
YT: Did she have good sight-reading skills?
NK: Not only that, overall she had great musicianship. She would play her pieces non-stop for me.
YT: I listened to one of her songs on youtube called »A Miracle Song«.[276] I noticed that the piano part is very developed in spite of the fact that it's still an accompaniment and she was singing at the same time. Her piano texture is quite complicated but I didn't hear even one »dirty« note!
NK: Of course she did have some dirty notes, as we all do, but not many.
YT: Based on what I heard, she has a strong character, feels like she is a very optimistic person. In one of the interviews she said that in her songs even minor keys sound like major.[277]
NK: She was always like that and will be forever.

---

[276] Lyudmila Lyadova »A Miracle Song«. Accessed November 25, 2017. https://www.youtube.com/watch?v=KZs0GKy-xLo.

[277] Lyudmila Lyadova Biography. Accessed February 20, 2018. http://www.biography-life.ru/interview/702-lyudmila-lyadova-u-menya-i-minor-zvuchit-mazhorno.html.

YT: *With fire in her eyes.*

NK (smiling): *That's who she is. She was born to be an artist.*

YT: *Do you know where she lives now?*

NK: *I think she lives somewhere in Moscow.*

YT: *And you never met since then?*

NK: *Never. Time goes by; people change so much…She is probably in her nineties now.*

YT: *Ninety two.*

NK: *See, I just want to keep her in my mind the way I remember her from the 1970s and I want her to think about me in the same way.*

YT: *Young, talented, and charming?*

NK: *If you say so.*

Yuri Silantiev

During the 1970s Kapustin met and worked with another interesting personality, Yuri Silantiev and the Yuri Silantiev Orchestra.

Yuri Silantiev

Yuri Vasilievich Silantiev (1919-1983) was an outstanding conductor, who led the Orchestra of the Russian Central Television and Radio, one of the major Soviet orchestras in the area of popular music, from 1958 to his death in 1983. The orchestra was also known for their appearance in various movies of the Soviet period as well as performing premiers of compositions written specifically for them.[278]

> YT: *I didn't know that the Silantiev Orchestra played the music for such iconic movies as »The Girls« and »Seventeen Moments of Spring«.*
> NK: *And what?*
> YT: *These are landmark movies; everybody watched them a hundred times, and you too probably.*
> NK: *I watched »Seventeen Moments of Spring« once, it was enough.*
> YT: *I still feel that it's a great honor to play in the movies of that category.*
> NK: *Somebody had to do it. It just happened that way – the choice fell on Silantiev.*

---

[278] Yuri Silantiev. Accessed November 25, 2017.
http://www.kino-teatr.ru/kino/acter/m/star/48106/bio/.

YT: *You are just not a big fan of movies.*

NK: *I am not.*

YT: *Do you know approximately when you got to know Silantiev?*

NK: *I knew him from 1970s. I remember we often met at the radio station – he was performing with his orchestra and me with Karamyshev. It was always pleasant to talk to him for a couple of minutes. We had a good relationship. I wouldn't say that we were close friends.*

YT: *But still.*

NK: *Yes. He invited me to play with his orchestra a number of times. I remember I was subbing for Boris Frumkin, his primary pianist, who was actually a good friend of mine.*

YT: *Did you have any other projects together?*

NK: *Yes, the Silantiev Orchestra first performed and recorded my Op. 34»Meridian« and Op. 35 »Closed Curve«.*

YT: *Those two pieces sound so different to me from what you wrote before, I would almost say influenced by the music from movies of that time in Russia.*

NK: *Those two pieces were composed while I was working in the Orchestra of Cinematography, and yes, recording the music for movies was a part of my work there.*

YT: *So, they may have influenced your style of writing.*

NK: *I've never thought about it.*

YT: *The date when these two pieces were written is 1982 and Silantiev passed away in February 1983, at the beginning of the next year; that close in time!*

NK: *Correct.*

YT: *It looks like the performance and recording of two of your opuses, Op. 34 and Op. 35, may be some of his last projects.*

NK: *Looks that way. I have to tell you – nobody expected his death, it happened very suddenly. We were all in shock from this news.*

YT: *For some reason in Silantiev's biography there is an exact time when he passed away – 10 pm on February 8, 1983.*

NK: *It is because he passed away after recording a concert on the Television »Ostankino«, right after they finished shooting.*

YT: *Oh, no… exactly the same situation as with Grover Washington Jr. He passed away in the green room after taping the CBS program in New York City.*[279]

NK: *We never know how long we have left.*

---

[279] Grover Washington Jr. Accessed November 25, 2017. https://www.allmusic.com/artist/grover-washington-jr-mn0000944206/biography.

Disintegration of the Karamyshev Orchestra

In the spring of 1977 a tragic event happened in the life of Nikolai Kapustin – the Karamyshev Orchestra dissolved. As the result of this action all the musicians who played in the band immediately lost their jobs.

YT: Do you know the actual reason for this dissolution?
NK: Nobody knew the reason, we could just guess about it. My vision of it was because he spoiled his relationship with some important people. The thing is – Karamyshev was big, he was famous figure, it was not that simple to put him down.
YT: Did somebody announce the »official« reason?
NK: I think somebody said that at some point there were two leading pop orchestras of the Radio and Television in Russia – Karamyshev and Silantiev Orchestra, and there should only be one. As always, it was a »dark« story so, to answer your question, there was no official reason announced to us.
YT: Were the Karamyshev and Silantiev Orchestras so similar to each other?
NK: Of course not. Karamyshev was more oriented towards jazz music.
YT: In a way you repeated the fate of the Ludvikovsky Orchestra.
NK: Oh yes, similar story, the Ludvikovsky Orchestra was dissolved a few years earlier than the Karamyshev Orchestra.
YT: How did you find out about the dissolution? Did Karamyshev say anything about this?
NK: No, he did not. Somehow it spread within the band.
YT: When did you find out about the dissolution?
NK: I would say a few weeks before if that.
YT: This is such short notice for the dissolution of the band! So many musicians needed to find new jobs in such a limited amount of time.
NK: I don't think anyone was worried about us.
YT: How did you feel about this situation?
NK: We all felt very disappointed. Personally, I didn't have enough time performing with Karamyshev... maybe because it was just five years and I didn't have a chance to get bored with this job.
YT: Maybe you just felt comfortable with this orchestra.
NK: Yes, that too.
YT: What did the members of the Karamyshev Orchestra do after its dissolution?
NK: This I don't know. We all went in different directions.
YT: So, it was impossible to keep the orchestra together.
NK: Definitely not.

YT: The reason I asked this question is that I know that sometimes if serious orchestras go through the dissolution they try to find another job but stay all together, to keep the backbone of the group.
NK: That was not the case, although, the musicians of the Karamyshev Orchestra were very strong. I still feel the big disappointment from that story.
YT: Almost forty years later?
NK: Actually, I think it happened exactly forty years ago.
YT: Ohhh, yes!!! Because now is the spring of 2017… What a strange coincidence. Since this happened in the spring of 1977 – was that the end of the performing season?
NK: I think so. I played with Karamyshev up to his very last concert, the very last note.
YT: What did Karamyshev do after his orchestra disintegrated?
NK: He continued living in Moscow up to his death in 2005.
YT: Did Karamyshev organize any other bands after 1977?
NK: He did not.
YT: What did he do for the last twenty seven years of his life?
NK: I asked him about it. He said he was composing the music for choir for some period of time… but as I see – nothing serious after the dissolution.
YT: I found out that in 1989 Karamyshev composed music for a children's musical called »Colored Snowflake«.
NK: Yes.
YT: It's good that he kept doing something after that painful episode of his life. There are so many examples when people just stop living.
NK: I respect him for that. He was a strong man.
YT: Was Karamyshev an optimistic person?
NK: He was a highly optimistic man. I think this is what helped him to survive after all the difficulties he had to go through.

Russian State Symphony Orchestra of Cinematography/Audition for the Open Position of Pianist

In the spring of 1977, after losing his job with the Karamyshev Orchestra, Kapustin was put into the position of a person who seriously needed to find a new place of work. Being a family man, Kapustin knew how much his wife Alla and their six year old son Anton needed support from him. Luckily enough, at exactly the same time, the State Symphony Orchestra of Cinematography held open auditions for the position of pianist.

The Russian State Symphony Orchestra of Cinematography was one of the oldest Russian orchestras. It started its history from the time of the »silent« movie. In September 1924, in the famous Moscow Cinema Hall »Ars«, the position of pianist who would usually accompany the movies, was replaced by full orchestra. That was the debut of the orchestra which would be known later as the Russian State Symphony Orchestra of Cinematography.[280]

NK: You see, right from the beginning this orchestra was connected to the cinema.
YT: Do you think the audience appreciated that change – replacing the pianist with the orchestra?
NK: I think so.

After experiencing success in the Cinema Hall »Ars«, the orchestra, led by the talented composer and conductor David Semionovich Blok,[281] started to perform in other cinema halls of Moscow, increasing the level of its popularity and demand.

In 1938 the orchestra became a part of the Moscow animation studio »Soyuzmultfilm« (Union of Children's Animation), and later in 1943, received the status of the Russian State Symphony Orchestra of Cinematography.

In 1944 this orchestra became a part of a large project recording the music of Sergei Prokofiev for the movie of Sergei Eisenstein[282] »Ivan The Terrible«. After WWII the orchestra recorded the music for such iconic Russian movies as »Ballad of a Soldier« (1959), »War and Peace« (1966), »The Meeting Place Cannot

---

[280] Russian State Symphony Orchestra of Cinematography. Accessed November 25, 2017. http://www.meloman.ru/performer/rossijskij-gosudarstvennyj-simfonicheskij-orkestr-kinematografii/.
[281] David Semionovich Blok. Accessed November 25, 2017. http://www.kino-teatr.ru/kino/composer/sov/39621/bio/.
[282] Sergei Eisenstein. Accessed November 25, 2017. https://www.culture.ru/persons/680/sergey-eyzenshteyn.

Be Changed« (1979), »Moscow Does Not Believe in Tears« (1980), »Mary Poppins, Goodbye« (1983), and »Burnt by the Sun« (1994). The movies that the Orchestra of Cinematography played for received numerous national and international awards.[283]

During more than ninety years of existence this orchestra had an opportunity to work with such eminent composers as Sergei Prokofiev, Dmitry Schostakovich, Georgy Sviridov, Edison Denisov, Alfred Schnittke, Sofia Gubaidulina, Rodion Shchedrin, Isaak Dunaevsky, Eduard Artemiev, Giya Kancheli, and many more.[284]

As it may be expected, there was serious competition for the position of pianist in the Russian State Symphony Orchestra of Cinematography in the spring of 1977. Going to that audition, Kapustin didn't expect that this might be his last job audition and his last place of work.

> *YT: How did you find out about the open position of pianist in this orchestra?*
> *NK: I remember once, during the last days of my work with Karamyshev, we were talking with a friend of mine, a violinist, also a member of Karamyshev band, about our future. Everybody was worried about it; all kinds of talks were going around. As you know, it is a big deal to find a new place to work, especially for the musician, so he mentioned the Orchestra of Cinematography.*
> *YT: As a good option?*
> *NK: Yes, he said that the salary there is quite high, higher than we had with Karamyshev, and it would be nice if I can get in there.*
> *YT: Is that true about the salary rating in the Orchestra of Cinematography?*
> *NK: Yes, that was true. The only thing that he didn't mention is that you have to work a lot for that kind of money... literally killing yourself. I didn't know about that small detail at that time, so I decided to try. Also, you see, at that moment I didn't think I had any other option. I needed badly to find another job for my family.*
> *YT: Did your friend, the violinist, also try to get into that orchestra?*
> *NK: I don't think so.*
> *YT: Why not? As he said – the salary there was very high.*
> *NK: As well as the level of competition to get in.*
> *YT: I get it. Do you know how many people auditioned for the piano position?*
> *NK: There were many of us.*

---

[283] Among them a Golden Globe Award, an Academy Award (Oscar), prizes on the internationally known film festivals, such as Cannes Film Festival, Moscow International Film Festival, and many others.

[284] State Symphony Orchestra of Cinematography. Accessed November 25, 2017. http://www.meloman.ru/performer/rossijskij-gosudarstvennyj-simfonicheskij-orkestr-kinematografii/.

YT: Since it was an audition, there should be a committee.

NK: Yes, I remember there were a few of them who listened to my playing.

YT: Did you know them?

NK: I knew some of them.

YT: So, everything was serious.

NK: Yes and no.

YT: What do you mean?

NK: I knew that they were going to choose me.

YT: How is that?

NK: I just knew. I was a good fit for them, plus I could improvise.

YT: Did they need a pianist who could improvise?

NK: Of course! That was one of my advantages in comparison with other pianists who also auditioned for this position; most of them came from the classical world.

YT: The State Symphony Orchestra needs an improviser – this doesn't sound right to my ear.

NK: The range of the repertoire, as well as different settings, was quite wide in this orchestra. They could do jazz, pop, classical, whatever... So I consider it as my luck.

YT: The fact that you have so many sides of your piano skills and they needed it?

NK: Yes. After playing for so many years with Lundstrem I felt fairly comfortable with jazz improvisation.

YT: Do you remember what you played for this audition?

NK (smiling): It may sound strange to you but I do remember it.

YT: Really??? How many pieces did you play?

NK: I played two pieces.

YT: Did you play jazz standards?

NK: None of them were in jazz style. The first one was Hindemith, first Interlude from his »Ludus Tonalis« called »Romantic Improvisation«, and the second one was Bartok's Suite Op. 14, third movement »Allegro Molto«.

YT: What an interesting choice of music! I see that both pieces belong to the classical world and both are twentieth century composers.

NK: Yes, I liked it that way.

YT: How did you maintain your technique through all these years? I thought you were playing jazz music since you graduated from conservatory in 1961.

NK: This is true but I also used to compose my own music, which is not that simple and involves serious technique. I used to play my music; and from time to time I played some classical pieces for myself too. So, I kept practicing through all these years to be in good shape as a pianist.

YT: And you did it! These two pieces are quite short but very difficult.

NK: That was my goal – do not take too much time from the committee. Some pianists preferred to play long pieces that made the committee very tired. So, I decided to be short but effective. Both pieces I chose were highly demanding technically.
YT: Did you play your pieces by memory or with the score?
NK: Of course by memory! Who would go to audition like that and play with the score? You would fail the audition before even playing the first note. It was not a problem for me at all, I was a strong pianist.
YT: Why did you choose to play the third movement of the Bartok Suite?
NK: I keep thinking about that myself – why did Bartok change the order of movements for the suite and put the slow movement as a last, fourth movement? I don't understand this.
YT: I see it now, the third movement was an actual Finale for the Suite.
NK: Of course! That's why I decided to play it. It sounds like a last movement – most effective out of all four.
YT: Did you have an interview after you played your program with your committee?
NK: No, I didn't. They talked in between to each other, I was waiting outside.
YT: When did you find out about the result of your audition even though you knew that you would be selected?
NK: Almost right way. After they discussed something very briefly they came out and said that I was in.
YT: Just like that?
NK: I told you – I knew that I would be selected much in advance. It was just an official part I needed to go through, just some regulations, such as an audition.
YT: But you never can be sure by a hundred percent how the audition may go. What if you wouldn't play that well?
NK: Then that would be a different story, but I knew that I would play well – that's the thing.
YT: Alright, it looks like you didn't have a »Plan B« in case you wouldn't be selected for this position, since you were so sure about this one.
NK: You are right, there was no »Plan B«.
YT: Also, it looks like you didn't have any transitional period between the Karamyshev Orchestra and the Orchestra of Cinematography like it happened after you left the Lundstrem Orchestra.
NK: Yes, after Karamyshev stopped I immediately began working in the Orchestra of Cinematography.
YT: Do you know anyone from the Karamyshev Orchestra who also started to work with the Orchestra of Cinematography?
NK: I don't think there were any… I think I was the only one… unfortunately.

Work at the Russian State Symphony Orchestra of Cinematography (1977-1984)

The great news about Kapustin being selected to the position of pianist in the Orchestra of Cinematography pulled all the stress away from his family. However, a new chapter of his life was about to begin, the life of making serious decisions, a life full of moments of happiness and disappointments, and of course the life of composing his own music.

YT: How big was this orchestra?
NK: That was the biggest orchestra I've ever played with. I think there was something like two hundred people all together. It was a completely new experience for me.
YT: That big?
NK: It was a symphony orchestra, let's start with that, and since they also played the music in different styles, they needed different settings, which means involving more musicians.
YT: So, if there were so many people in the orchestra then I suppose there was more than one conductor.
NK: This is exactly right, we had many conductors. I even remember that sometimes we wondered who was going to be the conductor today. Georgy Garanian, a friend of mine from the Lundstrem Orchestra, was one of our conductors for a while, then others too.
YT: That means that the way everything worked inside of this orchestra was quite different from Karamyshev and Lundstrem Orchestras.
NK: Completely different. In the Lundstrem and Karamyshev Big Bands we had only one conductor, he was the leader of the band, and we also knew each member of the band very well. The Orchestra of Cinematography was just the opposite – many conductors and it was impossible to know each member of the orchestra, and there was no actual need for that.
YT: If we would compare your life when you worked with Lundstrem, Karamyshev, and the Orchestra of Cinematography – which would be the most intense?
NK: With no doubts the last one.
AK (joining the conversation): I remember Kolia's job with the Orchestra of Cinematography was so intense that he used to come home in the middle of the day to just rest for forty-five minutes.
YT: Really? Why did you have such a short break?
NK: On a normal day we had a three hour recording session in the morning, another three hour session in the afternoon, and the last three hour session later in the day. The participation in the second recording session was optional, so I was never there.
YT: This sounds like a highly intense schedule to me.

NK: Yes, I didn't like it. That's why I decided to have at least three hours break in between those recordings, and of course preferred to go home to rest a little while instead of just staying there.

AK: And the thing is that the recording studio of the »Mosfilm« is situated an hour away from us, on the other part of Moscow.

YT: And you still decided to go home.

NK: Yes, a little rest helps a lot.

YT: Did you know some of the musicians from this orchestra?

NK: All of them? (smiling) No, I didn't. Of course I knew some of them. Many of them were connected to the college or conservatory, or other musical institutions of Moscow. Some had experience playing jazz, which was also a serious part of my life. So, I had friends there too.

YT: Did you feel scared that you were a part of such a large community and, in a way, you could be lost there?

NK: I wasn't scared, but I did feel uncomfortable. You see, playing with Lundstrem or Karamyshev was a completely different story. You are always on stage, presenting yourself as an artist. Even when we recorded you still feel how much you are related to each member of the band. We were a part of one big family.

YT: I agree. Since it was a huge orchestra I suppose that you may not be the only pianist.

NK: This is true. There were seven of us.

YT: That's a lot!!! Did you know any of these pianists?

NK: I did. Actually, one of the pianists was an old friend of mine, Yulia Gushanskaya.

YT: Was she your age?

NK: She was a little older than me. Actually, Yulia was also a student of Rubbakh. As I remember she immigrated to Israel many years ago.

YT: So, you knew her from the time you studied at the Musical College?

NK: Correct.

YT: Ohhhh, I just realized – you were forty years old when you began working in the Orchestra of Cinematography!

NK: Is this too much or too little?

YT: I think you were just forty years old but you had already achieved so many things – Lundstrem, Karamyshev, and now the Orchestra of Cinematography. Not forgetting the fact that you moved from Ukraine and graduated from the Moscow Conservatory.

NK: This all happened because I started at a very early age, I moved to Moscow when I was just fifteen years old.

The work in the new orchestra dictated the new rules of life. On one hand, there was a big advantage being a part of this orchestra – a settled style of life was one of the things that Kapustin had wanted for more than fifteen years of his touring life with Lundstrem and Karamyshev. On the other hand, the thing that balanced this advantage was the actual job itself, much more intense, stressful, and not as interesting for Kapustin as it was when he worked with Lundstrem or Karamyshev. That was the life of a studio musician.

YT: *Could you talk about your duties in the Orchestra of Cinematography?*
NK: I was one of the pianists.
YT: *Did you compose or arrange music for them?*
NK: No, they didn't need me for that.
YT: *So, this orchestra did not play your compositions.*
NK: No. I worked there only as a pianist, although I was always interested in the orchestras who could perform my music. Even when I came to play with Lundstrem at the beginning of 1960s my main goal was to perform my music with this orchestra. That wasn't the case with the Orchestra of Cinematography.
YT: *So, in a way with the end of the Karamyshev Orchestra you lost a band that could play your music.*
NK: This is exactly what happened. It was very hard for me at that time to find the musicians who could play my music. Some of the pieces from that period are still relatively unknown because nobody performed them even up to the present day.
YT: *In spite of this you still decided to continue composing music for the orchestra – you composed eight orchestral works (Op. 30-35, 37-38) during the time you worked with the Orchestra of Cinematography.*
NK: Yes, composition was always my main priority. Out of those eight opuses that you mentioned only two, Op. 34 and Op. 35, were performed and recorded in the 1980s. They were performed by the Silantiev Orchestra.
YT: *It looks to me that the way your life was going in the late 1970s – beginning 1980s was similar to what we call now life of the studio musician.*
NK: Yes, I agree. That's what was also bothering me – most of the time we didn't have enough time to rehearse the material that we would record.
YT: *How many rehearsals would you have for one piece?*
NK: One or two. I also remember the times when we didn't have rehearsals at all.
YT: *How is that?*
NK: We just played it straight in the studio. There was no time for learning the material. And if you wouldn't play well from your first try it may be your last performance.
YT: *So, people could lose their spot.*
NK: Easily.
YT: *That's a lot of pressure.*
NK: Yes, we were always under pressure. I guess that was one of the reasons why they paid us so well.
YT: *Did you feel comfortable in surroundings like this?*

NK: Not really. I can't say that I was struggling much with this job but it didn't give me pleasure, that's for sure.
YT: I see. So, it was a wide range of material that you had to play and record with the orchestra?
NK: Yes.
YT: The reason I asked this question is that I know that here in the US some »Broadway« musicians, or musicians from any large city, sometimes have to play the same show every day for six-eight years, all depending on how successful the show and how long it would run, and this job would give you very good money as well.
NK: I can't imagine the life like this for myself no matter how much money it would pay.
YT: So, it looks to me that in a way your situation was better - playing different material every day instead of the same?
NK: In a way yes.
YT: What was the most difficult aspect of working with the Orchestra of Cinematography?
NK: First, our work needed to be very fast – everything should be done in a very short period of time, and second, musicians should be very sharp.
YT: The musician should be highly professional.
NK: Yes, one of the main factors of your professional level was your ability to sight-read. You would not survive this work without good preparation in this matter.
YT: But you were already a great sight-reader.
NK: Yes, it was not difficult for me.
YT: How about the other pianists from the orchestra?
NK: This I can't tell. The thing that I know is that this group of musicians was changing periodically; only Yulia and I were kind of permanent pianists.
YT: It was probably hard for them to keep up with this job.
NK: The sad thing about this job is that you have to always be ready for anything… be ready to record, to play… always to be on the alert.
YT: How did the pianists of the orchestra divide the duties between each other?
NK: Pianists were subdivided in two categories – the ones who could improvise and the ones who could not.
YT: That's interesting! Of course you belonged to the first group of pianists, but what about your friend Yulia Gushanskaya? Did she also belong to the first group?
NK: What do you think?
YT: Probably not.
NK: Probably not, but even if you didn't improvise there was still enough work for all of us. Just depending on this factor you would be given this or that project to work on. That's all.
YT: Can you recall something that you enjoyed doing while you worked with the Orchestra of Cinematography?

NK: I felt more comfortable working in combos, smaller groups so to say. It was closer to me.

One of the modern trends of 1960s-1970s in Russia was the idea of playing in combos. More and more musicians were interested in organizing smaller ensembles instead of or in addition to performing in the larger groups. One of the first examples of this movement was a combo called »Golden Eighth« of young jazz musicians organized by pianist Yuri Richkov, rehearsals of which Kapustin used to attend in the late 1950s.[285] By the end of 1970s combo performances had become a predominant form of the jazz experience in Russia.

YT: Could you please tell me about your experience of playing in combos?
NK: Combos would have seven to eight musicians, which I liked more rather than playing in a huge orchestra.
YT: What kind of music did you play in combos?
NK: We played jazz.
YT: Only jazz?
NK: Not only jazz. We played music in different styles, jazz was one of them.
YT: And improvisation would be a part of jazz.
NK: The improvisation was the main part of jazz.
YT: What else did you play in combos?
NK: We played everything from classical music up to the songs of Mirei Matie.[286]
YT: Oh, French chanson – that's pretty far!!!
NK: Yes, these musicians could do this.
YT: And you too! Did you enjoy working with the Orchestra of Cinematography?
NK: I don't know Yana, you ask difficult questions. I am not always ready to answer them in a proper way, so it's hard to tell. For me there were too many people there… Plus, if you want to get good salary then you would have to agree to do all those additional projects they asked you to participate in. It was too much for me, I refused to participate in most of them. I knew that I had to save power for composing my music.
YT: No matter what, you would never stop composing.
NK: That's my life… My music is my destiny.
YT: So, it was getting more and more difficult to live your life like this but you still kept going?
NK: Yes, I tried to do it as long as I could.

---

[285] Saulsky, Chugunov, »A Brief History of Soviet Jazz«. Accessed November 25, 2017. http://www.norma40.ru/articles/sovetskiy-dzhaz-istoriya.htm.
[286] Mirei Matie. Accessed November 25, 2017.
http://www.mireillemathieu.com/biography/?lang=en.

Growing Family of Nikolai Kapustin/Accident in the Summer of 1979

On July 28, 1978 big happiness came upon the family of Nikolai Kapustin – his second son Pavel was born. His first son, Anton, was almost seven years old at that time. The family of Nikolai and Alla was always a subject of big love and adoration for each other.

YT: Do you remember the first days when Pavel was born?
AK (joining the conversation): It was a very hard time for us. It turned out that Pasha (gentle way of saying the name Pavel) was infected in the hospital during the first days of his life. You know how dangerous it may be for the health of the newborn baby. So, Kolia had to contact Andron (Andrei Konchalovsky) to help us.
YT: Did Konchalovsky help you?
AK: Yes, he did. Andron organized the meeting with very good doctors, and we followed their suggestions concerning the treatment for Pasha. I was so relieved when it was over.

Anton, young Pavel, and Nikolai Kapustin

YT: How were you able to raise both of your children? Were your parents able to help?
AK: It was very difficult. Most of the families now and back then had grandparents helping them to raise their children, but our situation was completely different. Unfortunately, our parents were not able to help us. Kolia's parents were living in the Ukraine, and I had only my father, who lived in Novokuznetsk (Siberia). Of course when the

boys grew up a little they were going to the Ukraine every summer to stay with their grandparents. That was a very happy time for them and of course it gave us a little rest.
YT: Did you go to Nikitovka just to bring the children?
AK: Of course we stayed there for a while too if we could. I remember since Nikitovka was a small city the train stop was extremely short, something like two or three minutes, so we had to leave the train very quickly. After Moscow, Nikitovka felt like a very peaceful and restful place. Kolia's house was situated close to the train station, which was very convenient for us.
YT: How many years did you travel to Nikitovka?
AK: I think almost every summer we visited Kolia's parents. Even if we were travelling to the south for vacation – the train would go through Nikitovka, and we used to stop for a week in Nikitovka to see them, and then continue our travel to the south.
YT: Ohhhh, that's so good.
AK: I remember that once Anton was two years old and he lived half a year in Nikitovka with his grandparents.
YT: That long?
AK: Yes, we had to do it. I would have some difficulties at my work if I would stay home with Anton when he was sick, and you know children are often sick. That's why we decided that Anton would stay with his grandparents in the Ukraine for a while. I remember how we packed Anton… It was all his clothes, all the things he needed for life, and even his small bed.
YT: Did Grigory Efimovich (Kapustin's father) and Klavdia Nikolaievna (Kapustin's mother) enjoy Anton's time there?
AK: Oh yes. Grigory Efimovich used to tell Anton interesting stories; also they made toys by hand, I remember all those small soldiers; so they were busy all that time.
YT: So, all the attention went to Anton.
AK: Of course, especially because it was their first grandchild.
YT: Do you recall any memorable moments of your life from that period that made you smile?
AK: I think that's the moment when we moved to a new apartment. Before that we were living in the studio apartment, very lovely but small, and in 1976 we moved to a one bedroom apartment. That was a dream come true moment!
YT: I think all this happened because of your incredible efforts in that direction.
AK: It was clear that Kolia wouldn't do it since he was always busy with his projects, so I had no choice, it should be me.

Alla Kapustina

YT: *Did you teach your children music?*
AK: *Of course we did. The thing is – Kolia was always very busy and I was trying to involve children in the music and I tried to help them as much as I could. Pasha survived two years of the musical school and then I realized that it's probably not for him. Anton learned to play piano without going to the music school, he learned by himself.*
YT: *Could you tell a little bit about each of your sons?*
NK: *Anton got the desire to learn everything on his own from me and I am proud of that. He studied mathematics at the school and later graduated from the Moscow State University in physics.*
YT: *Physics was also your big interest at the time you studied in the secondary school, wasn't it?*
NK: *Not only then. I was always fascinated with science, especially with physics. I am glad that Anton decided to dedicate his life to it.*
YT: *What is Anton doing now?*
NK: *Anton is now living in the United States. He is a Professor of physics at the California Institute of Technology in Pasadena (CA). He is involved in a lot of research in physics and participating in international conferences on physics in the US, Europe, Asia, and in Russia.*
YT: *What about your younger son Pavel?*

NK: Pavel graduated from the Moscow State University of Transport. He lives in Moscow.
YT: So, both of your sons went to different directions in their lives.
NK: Yes, and I feel happy for them.

One of the interests that came across Nikolai and Anton Kapustin at the beginning of 1980s was their common desire to learn foreign languages.

YT: Can you recall how many languages you learned with Anton?
NK: Should I count English?
YT: Of course.
NK: Ok, then it was English, French, Japanese, and Arabic languages.
YT: So, you can talk in five different languages!!!
NK: If you count Russian, then yes. Also, please keep in mind that Alla learned German and was even teaching German for a while in the secondary school here in Moscow.
YT: Oh, no!!! Then there are six languages within one family. This is so impressive! Who initiated the idea to study languages in your family?
NK: That was my idea.
YT: Which languages did you study with Anton?
NK: I remember we were much involved into the Japanese language.
YT: Did you study it with a teacher or on your own?
NK: All the languages we studied with Anton was on our own.
YT: How did you learn the pronunciation?
NK: I bought very good study books with cassettes where the proper way of pronouncing the words was recorded.
YT: And that was enough for you?
NK: Absolutely. We kept talking at the house with Anton in Japanese all the time, I even wrote him letters in Japanese when he spent the summer once at summer camp.
YT: How about Alla Semionovna? Did she learn Japanese with you?
NK: No, she didn't have time.
YT: Then how did she understand your conversations with Anton?
NK: I translated to her.
YT: How far did you go with your study of Japanese?
NK: We finished that study course; it was a big course in three large parts, but we did it.
YT: This is so fascinating! How about Arabic language?
NK: Arabic I decided to study by myself, but the book was not as good as the one for Japanese.
YT: Oh, I hear you. Yes, a good study book is the first step to success in learning anything. I remember all of the different courses and books that I used to study English! Sorry, but it's only one foreign language for myself. How about French and English?

NK: As you already know, I studied French in the secondary school and English in musical college and conservatory.

YT: I still don't understand how you can hold all five languages.

NK: That's the thing – you have to always read or talk in the language. Otherwise it will be gone.

YT: And you kept trying to maintain them all?

NK: Not all at the same time of course, at different times in my life a different language or a couple of languages would go on the front line. I just like reading the literature in different languages; it's in the area of my interests, capito?

In the summer of 1979 a horrible accident happened in the family of Nikolai Kapustin, the consequences of which could have led to a very different scenario in the composer's life.

AK: At that time I was still sitting at home with Pasha (Pavel Kapustin).[287] I received the call from the transport police that my son Anton and Kolia got into a car accident and that Anton was in the emergency room. He was just seven years old, and Kolia was also in the hospital with a broken hand as well as other injuries.

YT: I can't imagine what you felt at that moment....

AK: It was terrifying; I thought I would not be able to survive this. The worst thing is that I had a year old son. I had to leave Pasha with a nanny to visit Anton and Kolia. In addition to that, they put Anton and Kolia in different hospitals – Anton to the hospital for children and Kolia – to the hospital for adults. Anton was discharged from the hospital in a couple of days, basically he had just minor injuries, he was mostly scared, but Kolia was in a hospital for a week.

YT: So, what happened that day?

NK: I was working at that time in the Orchestra of Cinematography and we just got back from our vacation in Ivanovo with Alexander Varlamov. Everything was so comfortable and nice… That day I needed to get my monthly salary at the Cinematography and I decided to go there with Anton. We were walking on the street without violating any pedestrian rules. It was a very narrow one way street. Suddenly, out of nowhere that car appeared driving straight towards me and Anton. I was able to push Anton out of the way. That's all that I remember.

AK: That car knocked them both down but Kolia was hurt much more than Anton.

YT: Did you know who the driver was and did you try to go to the court about this accident?

---

[287] Note by the author: Based on Russian regulations a woman has a right to stay with the child after he's born up to two years receiving a partial salary every month.

AK: There was a trial afterwards; this culprit was also there, a very young man. He gave us his apologies but he didn't go to prison or give any compensation…Nothing happened afterwards, just nothing.

YT: How is it possible that two people were hurt and nothing happened after that?

NK: They said that he was a KGB agent hurrying to his assignment.

AK: I remember somebody during the court said that you still shouldn't hurt people while being on duty as a KGB agent.

YT: Of course!!! Especially that kind of pedestrians – a famous composer with his son! Instead of hurting people the KGB should be protecting them.

AK: The only thing I feel good about is that it all passed with no bad consequences.

YT: How did you overcome your hand injury?

NK: I broke my right hand, it was a double fracture. It was a bad thing on its own but it was even worse because I was preparing for the performance of my Piano Concerto No. 2 (Op. 14).

AK: All the doctors were saying that he needed to do surgery, otherwise he may not be able to play piano anymore, but Kolia didn't listen to them.

NK: I still remember that doctor. She told me to forget about playing piano.

YT: Just like that? What did you answer?

NK: I said that I disagree with her and this is not going to happen.

AK: He didn't do any surgery and kept practicing every day in spite of the fact that doctors were saying that the hand should be without any motion, always in a calm and resting position.

YT: Didn't you have a gypsum bandage on your hand?

AK: He had but he kept practicing even with that bandage.

NK: I think it helped that I didn't stop playing even with my broken hand. I kept training my muscles and it helped me to recover.

YT: It must have been painful.

NK: It was very painful but I had no choice, I needed to play the concerto.

YT: So in other words, it looks like you went against the doctors recommendations?

NK: I never believed in doctors.

YT: That's a big responsibility to take on – all your life was under the big question!

NK: I think intuition helped me. For some reason I knew that I needed to keep practicing.

YT: And you always stood on your own.

NK: Always.

1980: Performance of the Piano Concerto No. 2/ Acceptance to the Union of Moscow Composers

The expected performance happened in 1980 in Moscow, as was originally planned. Nikolai Kapustin himself performed one of his best early works, *Concerto No. 2 for the Piano and Orchestra*, Op. 14, in Tchaikovsky Hall.

YT: *How did the concert go?*
NK: *It went very well, the audience loved it.*
YT: *Did you feel that a year before you had a double fracture in your right hand?*
NK: *No, by then it was completely healed.*
YT: *You are a very lucky man.*
NK: *Yes, I am. Who knows what that double fracture could bring into my life?*
YT: *I know that this concerto was composed for the Karamyshev Orchestra.*
NK: *Yes, and I premiered and recorded it with Karamyshev in the middle of 1970s.*
YT: *With which orchestra did you play this concerto in 1980? By this time the Karamyshev Orchestra was already dissolved.*
NK: *That was a big problem. Some of the musicians were my friends from the Karamyshev Orchestra, some different musicians, but I knew them all.*
YT: *How about the conductor?*
NK: *It was a different person, his name was Alexander Mikhailov. I remember he used to come to our rehearsals with Karamyshev. He attended for the experience I guess.*
YT: *Was there anything special about that premier of your Concerto No. 2?*
NK: *That was my last performance in public as a solo pianist. I haven't gone on stage to play solo piano since then... I did perform chamber music though later on, but not solo.*
YT: *That was thirty seven years ago.*
NK: *Yes.*
YT: *Why did you do that? What happened that day?*
NK: *Nothing happened; I just realized that I am more interested in recording in the studio. I loved recording.*
YT: *Is it because you can do multiple tracks in the studio?*
NK: *That too. You don't feel that stressed in the studio because you can play as many times as you need. As a result of this, the quality of your product is going to be much better rather than performing the same piece live only once.*
YT: *What do you like the most about working in the studio?*
NK: *It's just me and my music....and nothing else.*
YT: *Just the two of us... Still, this is very sad that you stopped performing live as a solo pianist.*
NK: *I do not regret that.*

The year 1980 was also significant in the life of Kapustin because that was the year he was admitted to the »Union of Moscow Composers«.[288]

> YT: *How did it happen that you decided to be a part of the union of composers? I thought you had always been an independent composer with your own mind.*
>
> NK: *Originally, I didn't want to do that, but Muradeli insisted and literally forced me to begin this whole process of being a part of union of composers.*
>
> YT: *Muradeli??? Did you know Vano Muradeli*[289]*???*
>
> NK *(smiling): Of course I did.*
>
> YT: *He is an extremely famous person in the history of Russian musical culture because of the attack from the Russian government on his opera »The Great Friendship« that he composed in 1948.*
>
> NK: *There was nothing like what they said about his opera – »formalist, anti-people music«… Nothing like that at all. He was just »lucky enough« to experience Stalin's disfavor.*
>
> YT: *Was his life ruined after that episode of his life?*
>
> NK: *Not really. Very soon after his »unlucky« opera he wrote the cantata »The Road of Victory« in honor of Stalin. This piece rehabilitated his reputation.*
>
> YT: *What were the requirements for the admission to the Union of Moscow Composers?*
>
> NK: *First, you have to submit a large amount of different material to the committee. I would rather spend that time composing the music. Second, you had to write a serious piece to show your ability as a composer.*
>
> YT: *Which piece did you present?*
>
> NK: *I presented my Piano Concerto No. 2. By then I had already composed that piece.*
>
> YT: *How long does it usually take to get into an organization like this?*
>
> NK: *It varies for each composer. It took me five years to get in.*
>
> YT: *That long?*
>
> NK: *Don't forget that it's a lot of paper work. Actually, five years felt quite reasonable to me, I remember my friend Garanian spent eight years for the same purpose.*
>
> YT: *I see it now; it was a very long process.*
>
> NK: *Very long.*
>
> YT: *You said that you had to rewrite by hand a section of the Concerto No. 2 for the admission so it would look nice on the pages.*
>
> NK: *Not just a section, the whole concerto.*
>
> YT: *Really?*

---

[288] Union of Moscow Composers. Accessed November 25, 2017. http://союзмосковскихкомпозиторов.рф/sect-jazz.htm.

[289] Vano Muradeli. Accessed November 25, 2017. https://www.findagrave.com/memorial/23980719.

NK: Yes. It was painful but I needed it to be done because my original version was written in a very sloppy way.
YT: Ohhh, that is sad.
NK: It was actually a necessary step for me. You can't apply for the union of composers with the piece written that way.
YT: How long did it take you to rewrite the whole concerto by hand?
NK: I think I spent about a month, not longer.
YT: Unfortunately at that time you didn't have a computer program that could write perfect looking scores much faster than you would do it by hand.
NK: Yes, we wrote our music and our letters all by hand.
YT: I guess at the end of the day, that's not such a bad thing.
NK: No, I like looking at those letters once in a while; it brings back memories.
YT: Knowing that it was so hard to get in, what role did the union of composers play in your life?
NK: Honestly, it did nothing for me. I don't think I spend enough time with all their activities; I didn't really care what was happening there.
YT: Why?
NK: I don't know. This organization wasn't important for me at all.
YT: Maybe you didn't really need anyone – you live in the world of your own music, and this world is complete, it functions on its own.
NK: Yes, I exist on my own. I remember they wanted me to compose some kind of songs... absolutely uninteresting project for me.
YT: Did they try to direct you towards what kind of music to compose?
NK: Something like that. And you know – I would never do it.
YT: Did the »Union of Composers« help you in publishing?
NK: Absolutely not.
YT: Really? You would think that this would be one of their main responsibilities.
NK: I thought so too at the beginning but it didn't happen. At the very beginning they organized a lot of meetings that I needed to attend, and then even those meetings stopped.
YT: So, basically the idea of this union was to develop a society of composers, where they could discuss musical questions and share their thoughts on present musical topics.
NK: It was exactly what you were saying – just talking and nothing else.
YT: I remember you showed me the telegram from the »Union of Composers« on your 50th birthday signed by Khrennikov himself.
NK: That's what you would call a formality.
YT: Still, it's a sign of respect I think.
NK: They send this kind of telegrams to all the composers of the union.

First Publishers

Starting from the early 1980s Kapustin began his work with two major Russian publishing companies, both situated in Moscow. The first company was the Publishing House »Muzgiz«,[290] also known as »Muzyka« (Music), and the second one was Publishing House »Sovetsky Kompozitor« (Soviet Composer).[291]

YT: How did your work with the publishers start?
NK: Georgy Garanian gave me this idea. I remember one day he asked me why I do not publish my works. I didn't know what to tell him because I wasn't thinking that somebody would be interested in my works.
YT: But that was not the case.
NK: Yes, publishers became interested in my music and that's how it started.
YT: So, in a way your friend pushed you to begin to publish your music.
NK: Yes, everything always starts with the initial idea, and then the work follows.

In 1983 Kapustin's first piece was published by the Moscow Publishing House »Muzyka«. It was *Toccatina*, Op. 36, written also in 1983.

YT: Do you remember how it happened?
NK: Yes. I remember I had an old friend from my time at the conservatory who worked in the »Muzgiz« for many years. He helped me to publish a lot of my works.
YT: When you work with the publishers do you discuss the length, style, and instrumentation of the piece?
NK: Concerning the instrumentation it's pretty clear – it is solo piano music, at least that's what they were interested in the 1980s. About the style and the length – I think no. They knew what kind of music I was composing.
YT: So, in a way you were free to make all the decisions.
NK: Yes, I was not directed in any way.
YT: Do you remember the second piece that was published?
NK: Yes, it was »Suite in Old Style«, Op. 28.
YT: This is interesting, »Suite in Old Style« was written earlier, in 1977, but published after »Toccatina«, Op. 36.
NK: It happens.
YT: Did you have any other friends who helped you with the promotion of your music in the 1980s?

---

[290] Muzgiz. Accessed November 25, 2017. http://www.music-izdat.ru/About.asp.
[291] Sovetsky Kompozitor. Accessed November 25, 2017. https://www.livelib.ru/publisher/569-sovetskij-kompozitor.

NK: I remember that about the time I published my first piece I met one lady, Lidiya Semionovna Strijakova, who worked at the Ministry of Culture USSR and later in the Ministry of Culture of RSFSR.[292] She claimed that she knew me from the time of musical college where we studied together. She said that she was a year younger than me. However, I do not remember her.
YT: Everybody remembered you because you were a star.
NK: Anyway, she helped me enormously to sell my music to the Ministry of Culture.
YT: What do you mean to sell your works?
NK: Russian Ministry of Culture USSR and RSFSR used to buy music from Soviet composers to keep it as a resource for our culture. It was a big deal to be selected for this purpose.
YT: So, it was like a competition again.
NK: Yes, a big time competition. You can't imagine how many composers applied to present their works for the Ministry of Culture. There was a special committee, a serious number of people, who used to choose the works that deserve it the most.
YT: I guess many composers were rejected.
NK: Yes, they did it very quickly.
YT: That would be a dangerous thing for a young composer — if somebody would reject you a couple of times you may decide to stop composing.
NK: Maybe. I've never received the denial from them.
YT: Good for you! Did they pay a decent amount of money?
NK: Oh yes, the Ministry of Culture always paid very well.
YT: What did you do after they made the decision to buy your music?
NK: You would need to give them the score.
YT: That's all?
NK: Yes.
YT: How about publishing this music? Did the Ministry of Culture publish your music too?
NK: No, that was a completely different story. They needed it only for their collection for the history of music. I had to find other ways to publish those pieces later. And I did, at least some of them.
YT: It looks like the year of 1983 was a happy one for you since your very first piece was published that year and you started to work for the Ministry of Culture.
NK: It was also a very sad year in my life. My father passed away on December 5, 1983.
YT: I didn't know that.

---

[292] RSFSR is an abbreviation for Russian Soviet Federative Socialist Republic.

One of the last pictures of Kapustin visiting his parents in Nikitovka, Ukraine, late 1970s

NK: I remember that year... Strange thing, my mother passed away nine years later, on July 29, 1992, but both of my parents lived exactly the same amount of years, eighty-three.
YT: That is strange.

Russian Jazz Scene in the 1970s-1980s / Music of Nikolai Kapustin

Jazz development in Russia during the 1970s-1980s was literally »blooming«. Jazz orchestras, such as the Ludvikovsky Orchestra, Lundstrem Orchestra, Saulsky Orchestra, Kroll Orchestra, Arbelian Orchestra, Rosenberg Orchestra and many others, were representing the best of the Russian jazz mainstream tradition. In addition to that, jazz gradually became a part of Russian professional musical education:

> *In 1974 to increase the professional level of jazz performance a pop-jazz major was established in the musical colleges of Russia. The first methodic material in the area of jazz, such as »The Basis of Jazz Improvisation« (Igor Bril), »Harmony is Jazz« (Yuri Chugunov), and »Arranging« (Georgy Garanian) appeared around the same time.*[293]

YT: *Can you recall any orchestra or individual jazz musicians that you appreciated from that time?*
NK: *I really enjoyed listening the sound of the Vadim Ludvikovsky Orchestra.*
YT: *Did you like the musicians from his orchestra?*
NK: *They were the best of the best... Of course Zoubov, Bakholdin, Garetkin, Garanian were all there. Their pianist was a good friend of mine — Boris Frumkin. Ludvikovsky was not only the leader and conductor of the band but he also composed music for them.*
YT: *As I remember Ludvikovsky's life was not too easy at the end.*
NK: *Yes, the orchestra dissolved in 1973, very close to the time of dissolution of the Karamyshev Orchestra.*
YT: *Very strange.*
NK: *Yes, what happened to him was a complete mess... Matvey Blanter, one of our leading Soviet composers, tried to help them. He said that the orchestra is famous even abroad and that it was broadcast by BBC.*
YT: *I guess it didn't help.*
NK: *That only made it worse. The answer was — that's why we don't need the Ludvikovsky Orchestra.*
YT: *It looks like any connection to the West culture was highly prohibited at that time in the USSR.*
NK: *Yes, this is true.*

---

[293] Chugunov, Saulsky, »Brief History of Russian Jazz«. Accessed November 25, 2017. http://www.norma40.ru/articles/sovetskiy-dzhaz-istoriya.htm.

YT: *Did you know Ludvikovsky personally?*
NK: *I knew him very well. I met with him once in a while in the »Union of Composers«.*
YT: *Did you work with Ludvikovsky?*
NK: *Actually, yes I did. I wrote numerous arrangements for his band.*
YT: *I didn't know that. Did Ludvikovsky organize another orchestra after the dissolution?*
NK: *No, same as Karamyshev – nothing big after that.*
YT: *Very sad. Can you recall any other musicians that you liked from that time?*
NK: *It is hard to pick one.*
YT: *I remember once, when I was preparing for our conversations, I came across one musician whose name was German Lukianov.[294] Do you know this name?*
NK: *Ohhh yes! I knew Lukianov very well for a long time. I think we go back to 1960s. This is a good example of a jazz musician that I liked very much. He was from Saint-Petersburg, very talented trumpet player and composer too. He actually played in the Ludvikovsky Orchestra at some point for a while.*
YT: *Really?*
NK: *He would play a lot of experimental music; very innovative approach to a jazz composition.*

In the 1970s-1980s in the Russian jazz scene, in addition to traditional jazz, called generally mainstream, a new wave of jazz expression started to appear, the wave of the experiment. Some talented jazz musicians, such as Nikolai Levinovsky,[295] Igor Bril,[296] and Leonid Chizhik,[297] tried to combine elements of jazz with rock, folk, classical, and other styles of music. That's how Russian jazz-rock, folk-jazz, third stream, free jazz, hard-bop, and modal jazz appeared. Chugunov and Saulsky in their book »Brief History of Soviet Jazz« stated:

A new period of jazz development in Russia started in the 1970s; that was the period of the search for new elements of expression, for new styles. As a result of this innovative movement, some of the jazz musicians and composers began working in new stylistic fusions. One of the examples of this fusion could be the ensemble of Alexei Kozlov »Arsenal«, where Kozlov tried to combine the elements of jazz, chamber music, Russian folk music, as well as involving the elements of pantomime in his compositions.[298]

---

[294] German Lukianov. Accessed November 25, 2017. http://www.jazz.ru/pages/lukianov/.
[295] Nikolai Levinovsky. Accessed November 25, 2017. http://www.jazz.ru/pages/levinovsky/.
[296] Igor Bril. Accessed November 25, 2017. http://www.jazz.ru/pages/bril/.
[297] Leonid Chizhik. Accessed November 25, 2017. http://www.leonid-chizhik.de/firma/index.html.
[298] Chugunov, Saulsky, »The Brief History of Soviet Jazz«. Accessed November 25, 2017. http://www.norma40.ru/articles/sovetskiy-dzhaz-istoriya.htm.

The idea of fusion itself was not new in the world of jazz music. This movement came from the United States, when in the middle 1960s jazz musicians tried to experiment with combining jazz with other musical styles. For example, Herbie Hancock in his album »Maiden Voyage« (1965) and Miles Davis in his iconic recording »Bitches Brew« (1970) incorporated the elements of jazz and rock. Miles Davis also became known for his innovations in creating the style of cool jazz in the album »Birth of The Cool« (1957). John Lewis and his »Modern Jazz Quartet« incorporated the elements of jazz and classical music. The example of the Latin-jazz-funk fusion can be seen in the George Duke album »Don't Let Go« (1978).

In order to understand the uniqueness of the music of Nikolai Kapustin it is important to determine the nature of jazz fusion and establish the boundaries of this movement. What is fusion? The definition of jazz-rock fusion in the Grove Music Encyclopedia states that jazz-rock:

A style of music, initiated in the 1960s, which combined the harmonic resources and improvising techniques of modern jazz with the instrumentation, rhythms, and idioms of rock music and funk.[299]

The keystone idea of fusion is that no matter how far jazz would be influenced by other styles, it will still be jazz. The two main components of the style belong to the ideas of the advanced harmonic approach and the improvisatory nature of the music.

The music of Kapustin never had any examples or suggestions towards the improvisation. It may sound like totally improvised music, but it is carefully planned and thoughtfully composed music. The conclusion that appears is that Kapustin does not belong to any of these styles. Kapustin created his own musical style, which is connected to jazz music and its roots, representing the music of modern day classical composer.

YT: Some people call the music of Nikolai Kapustin fusion, some third stream. Do you agree with that placement of your music?
NK: I don't.
YT: Is this true that the music you composed is written out?
NK: Absolutely.
YT: How would you identify yourself – are you a modern day classical composer who uses the style of jazz in his compositions?

---

[299] Gilbert, Mark. »Jazz-rock (jazz)«. Grove Music Online. Accessed March 6, 2018. http://www.oxfordmusiconline.com/grovemusic/view/10.1093/gmo/9781561592630.001.0001/omo-9781561592630-e-2000226300.

NK: *Yes, I am a classical composer who uses jazz idioms in his style, but I don't see myself as a modern day composer.*
YT: *How do you see yourself?*
NK: *My music is different from the modern composers.*
YT: *When I listen to your music, it sounds so fresh; it is the sound of the present.*
NK: *It's all because of jazz.*
YT: *Yes, you took the traditional jazz music from the past and put a new life in it. Your jazz sounds much different from what we call traditional jazz, correct?*
NK: *I agree with that.*
YT: *So, you are a modern day composer!*
NK: *No, I am not.*[300]

---

[300] Note by the author: Here, Kapustin probably set himself aside from the twenty first century composers, who consider being modern today because of their experiments with the new techniques and new sounds.

292

Compositions of 1972-1984 (Ops. 14-39)

Comparing the productivity of Kapustin during the 1960s -1980s it is important to note that the number of pieces he wrote noticeably increased from twelve compositions written in the 1960s, to the seventeen written in the 1970s, and twenty-five written in the 1980s.

> YT: *How would you comment on the fact that your productivity increased from your work with Lundstrem to the work with Karamyshev?*
> NK: *I guess I had a spike of creativity at that point.*
> YT: *That was a long spike which would continue into the 1980s and 1990s later too. Also, looking at your productivity by the decades, during the 1960s you composed twelve pieces (Op.2-Op. 13), but in the 1970s it was already seventeen pieces (Op. 14- Op. 29).*
> NK: *And this is without counting my arrangements!*
> YT: *It looks like you had a little more time when you worked with Karamyshev since you were able to compose more music?*
> NK: *It looks that way… (after a pause) or maybe I just worked harder. The main thing – I started to seriously dedicate myself to composition.*
> YT: *Were all the pieces that you composed during 1972-1977 written for the Karamyshev Orchestra?*
> NK: *All the orchestral works were written for Karamyshev except three opuses, Op. 15- Op. 17, which I wrote as a commission for the radio »Yunost« (Youth) before I joined the band.*

During the twelve years of work with the Karamyshev Orchestra and the Orchestra of Cinematography (1972-1984), including the transitional period of 1972, Kapustin wrote twenty-six compositions, which includes twenty one orchestral works, two chamber pieces, and three pieces for solo piano.

> YT: *It is very interesting that during this period you composed mostly music for the orchestra. Many people think that you compose the music exclusively for the piano.*
> NK: *Yes, you are right. Especially at that time I was composing generally orchestral music.*
> YT: *Did you ever think about the proportion of your piano music to the orchestral and chamber music throughout your career?*
> NK: *Yes, I did. If you would compare my solo piano works with my chamber and orchestral music, percentage wise, you would be surprised… because it's fifty-fifty.*
> YT: *I guess the misunderstanding may come from the question of what we consider as piano music – is it any piece that involves the piano along with other instruments or a piece written specifically for piano?*

NK: Yes, some consider a piano concerto as piano music, but it's orchestral music; same with the piano duet – some think that it's piano music, but it's chamber music.

Joining the Karamyshev Orchestra, Kapustin put himself into the position where he had to compose music for the big band with a string section.

YT: Did you feel obligated to write for the orchestra with strings or was that your own decision?

NK: There were no obligations when I worked with Karamyshev. In theory I could write pieces for the orchestra without strings, but why should I do that? I liked it that way – with strings.

YT: Have you ever done scoring for the big band with strings before you started to work with Karamyshev?

NK: No, I didn't.

YT: Did you feel a little worried about that?

NK: Not really.

YT: Then how did you do that?

NK: I just started to write, that's all. From the very beginning I liked composing for strings very much. As a composer, it gives me more room for the instrumentation. This variety of different colors and new timbres helps to create the modern sound of the orchestra. You know that Lundstrem didn't have strings, so it was a completely new experience for me.

YT: Yes, yes, yes. Did you write any pieces from that period without a string section, just as a contrast?

NK: Yes, as a contrast I did compose a couple pieces without a string group. For example, my Op. 21 »Minuet« for Big-Band and Op. 22 »Pieces for Five Saxophones and Orchestra« are without strings.

YT: If I would ask you to select some pieces from the period of 1972-1984 that deserve more attention from your point of view, which ones would you choose?

NK: From that period I would probably choose my Piano Concerto No. 2 (Op.14), Nocturne for Piano and Orchestra (Op. 20), »Day-Break" for Piano (Op. 26), »Suite in Old Style« (Op. 28), and Piano Sonata No. 1 »Sonata-Fantasy« (Op. 39). But this is only if I would be pushed to answer this question. Personally, all my pieces are special to me.

The *Concerto for Piano and Orchestra No. 2*, Op. 14 (1974) was the first piece that Kapustin composed for the Karamyshev Orchestra after he joined the band in 1972. This concerto signifies the beginning of the new period of Kapustin's life, being a part of the new orchestra, as well as the new period of Kapustin's creativity as a composer. Kapustin himself considers this concerto as one of his the most successful early works. It was recorded by Nikolai Kapustin and the Karamyshev Orchestra in the middle 1970s.

> YT: *In the introductory article for the score of the Piano Concerto No. 2 you mentioned that this work was your »Juvenile Concerto«. Can you explain this?*
> NK: *I consider this concerto being »Juvenile« not because of the age of the composer when it was written, but on the tone and character of the music itself. For example, we call Rachmaninov's Piano Concerto No. 1 a »Juvenile Concerto« because he was eighteen years old when he composed it. This is true, but what I see in this concerto is that it also sounds very young, it expresses the youthful emotions, and I feel the young quality of the music itself.*
> YT: *This is a very interesting point of view.*
> NK: *Of course, based on the age when I composed my second concerto you can't call it »Juvenile«.*
> YT: *The other thing that I just thought about is that we usually call the first concerto of the composer a »Juvenile«, but for you it's the second.*
> NK: *In reality, of course it's my first concerto. I composed it right after I graduated from the conservatory, and was very young.*
> YT: *Unfortunately I didn't hear your first piano concerto and can't say about the music.*
> NK: *Nobody heard it because it was performed in the 1960s but never recorded.*
> YT: *Since the youth quality is so strongly presented in the second concerto can we assume that, because of the emotions of the second concerto, it may also belong to a period of your »Juvenile« music?*
> NK: *You may think so… probably.*
> YT: *Every time I listen to your second concerto I feel the »spring in the air«, young, very bright and fresh emotions.*
> NK: *Yes, this is exactly how I feel listening to this work – it is young in spirit. Also, when I am looking at the score of this concerto I keep thinking to myself – how is it possible that I wrote such a sloppy piano part, with no wonder, with very simple harmonization? I guess my musical style dramatically changed through the years.*
> YT: *Your musical language became more complex.*
> NK: *Yes.*
> YT: *For some reason that concerto doesn't sound simple to my ear at all. I love the sound of it.*
> NK: *Yes, when I listen to that music I like it too, although now I feel that my third concerto is more interesting than the second.*
> YT: *The second concerto is the one which is popular right now.*
> NK: *Yes, but does this matter?*
> YT: *This is a rhetorical question. When did you start to compose your second concerto?*

NK: I composed the main themes for this concerto in the early 1970s, somewhere around 1972 when I was still working with Lundstrem but was getting ready to leave the band. I did a sketch of the second theme of the first movement, the »Andante« theme, and the refrain of the Finale »Rondo«.
YT: Why didn't you compose the concerto at the moment those themes came to you?
NK: I decided to preserve those themes for the future; I felt that something was going to happen with me sometime soon and that I needed to hold it for a while.
YT: This is your intuition working again for you!
NK: I guess.
YT: Every time I listen to your second concerto I keep thinking how organically the piano part exists with the orchestral part. Do you agree with the statement that the genre of concerto can be considered like a competition between the soloist and the orchestra?
NK: Absolutely not. I don't agree with that concept. For me, the soloist and the orchestra are together, they exist on one side, not in opposition to each other. There is no competition in my concertos.
YT: I feel that through your music! It sounds like a united performance, something like how the jazz musicians would play in the band. Is there anything special about this concerto? I can tell you wrote it over some period of time (a couple of years) and carefully selected each and every detail of this work.
NK: This concerto has a special meaning for me. First of all, that was my last solo performance in public, when I performed it in 1980 in the Tchaikovsky Hall. Second, because of that piece, I was accepted to the »Union of Moscow Composers« also in 1980, which was very important for me at that time.
YT: Did you perform this concerto with Karamyshev or just record it?
NK: I did both, I performed and recorded it with Karamyshev.
YT: Did you like that recording of this concerto?
NK: Very much! Sometimes I listen to some of my recordings from the past and I hear something I would change if I would be playing it now, but with this work I wouldn't change anything. It sounds exactly how it should be done. The sad thing is that I keep talking and will continue to that on the youtube recording it is labeled as the Lundstrem Orchestra, but it was performed by Karamyshev Orchestra!!!
YT: Yes, I agree.
NK: The main thing that keeps bothering me all the time is that this is a sign of disrespect to Karamyshev. That's what I am worried about the most.
YT: Since this concerto is very popular, and many pianists are performing it in Russia, Europe, and the United States, do you know any performers that you like?
NK: I like the performance of Elena Los', our Russian pianist, who played this concerto in Switzerland a couple of years ago. When she sent me the recording of it I was pleased to hear it.

YT: Yes, I like this recording too.
NK: Although, they fundamentally changed my instrumentation in this concerto.
YT: How did this happen?
NK: Their conductor wrote me a letter asking my permission to change my original instrumentation. In the beginning, I was against it but then decided to agree because I was interested in hearing what they could do with it.
YT: Did you like what you heard?
NK: I was surprised when I heard it – they did a good job. As you know, my instrumentation is written for the jazz big-band with strings. Their instrumentation is very much different from mine; the only part that they kept from my original instrumentation was drums.
YT: This does not happen very often when the performer decides to change the original instrumentation, correct?
NK: Yes, especially with such a good result.
YT: How about the instrumentation for your other concertos? Did you use the string group again?
NK: Yes, my Concerto No. 3 (Op.48) is also scored for big band with strings. Other concertos are either written for the big band, symphonic orchestra, or chamber orchestra.
YT: You have a whole variety of different orchestrations for your concertos.
NK: Yes, each concerto has its own sound.

The *Nocturne for Piano and Orchestra*, Op. 20 (1974) is one of the pieces that is highly appreciated by the composer himself. The work was composed for, performed, and recorded by the Karamyshev Orchestra.

YT: What can you tell about this Nocturne Op. 20?
NK: Every time I listen to this piece I keep thinking how much I love it. Everything worked so well in there.
YT: I like the theme very much and the way it was presented first at the beginning of the nocturne – just by the piano itself.
NK: Yes, that was the idea, and then the strings appeared.
YT: It is like a conversation between the piano and strings.
NK: I agree.
YT: Is the piece written in F major?
NK: Yes, it's in F.
YT: When I hear that melody, I keep thinking that it's like a song without words; and that words would come on its own if I would just think a little more.
NK (smiling): Maybe.
YT: Did anyone try to compose the lyrics for your nocturne?
NK: I don't think anyone knows about this piece.

YT: *If people would listen to this piece they would see – this is a completely different side of Nikolai Kapustin than the one we already know.*
NK: *This is true.*
YT: *The recording that I listened to on youtube, when you played with Karamyshev, sounds so expressive, emotional, and like we would say – performed with love straight from your heart.*
NK: *If I am not mistaken I may have the vinyl disc somewhere at the house with this recording, where we played with Karamyshev. I feel happy and thankful that this recording still exists – it was a good one.*
YT: *Did you perform this piece with Karamyshev or just record it?*
NK: *I think we played it a couple of times. I even remember once we performed it on the radio.*
YT: *Another thing I noticed – this piece is not very long, just about four minutes in length.*
NK: *Yes, this is my favorite length for pieces like that – around four minutes.*
YT: *Was the score of this piece published?*
NK: *The score of the nocturne was lost.*
YT: *Really?*
NK: *Yes. The only thing that remains is the recording.*
YT: *How did it happen that the score was lost?*
NK: *I left the score in one of the publishing companies and they lost it there somehow. Their attitude towards the scores was always so disrespectful…Many years after I contacted one of my friends who worked there to see if we could find it. He said that there is no chance to find anything now.*
YT: *This is so sad. And you didn't have a duplicate for yourself.*
NK: *Unfortunately, not.*
YT: *Do you think that someone could potentially transcribe this piece?*
NK: *Do you want me to transcribe my own composition that I wrote forty something years ago?*
YT: *Oh no…I didn't mean for you to transcribe it but maybe some other person.*
NK: *I don't know about that.*

The piece »*Day-Break (Sunrise)*« (1976) was composed by Kapustin in two versions: first, there is a solo piano version labeled as Op. 26, and the second, an orchestral version marked as Op. 26A. The first versions of »*Day-Break*« was performed and recorded by Kapustin, and the second version by Kapustin with the Karamyshev Orchestra.

YT: Why did you put two names for this piece – Day-Break and Sunrise?
NK: There is a little difference in the meaning of these two words, at least in Russian language. So, I was thinking that every listener would choose the name which would resonate the most.
YT: How about yourself – which would you prefer?
NK: I like the Sunrise.
YT: Did you compose the piano version of this piece first?
NK: Yes, the orchestral version came later.
YT: When I was listening to this piece for the first time, Oscar Peterson came to my mind immediately.
NK: I wasn't thinking about Oscar Peterson when I composed this piece.
YT: Which version of the piece do you like the most – piano or orchestral?
NK: I like the piano version more.
YT: So, the score of this piano version of Op. 26 also exist?
NK: Of course.
YT: How about the orchestral version?
NK: The only thing that is left for the orchestral version is the recording, the score did not survive.
YT: You have so many scores that were lost.
NK: Too many. I feel thankful that the recording of so many of my pieces can be found on youtube.

The *Suite in Old Style*, Op. 28 (1977) is the first serious work that was specifically composed by Kapustin as a solo piano piece. This suite represents Kapustin's style of solo piano writing up to the present time. It was composed after an almost twenty year break from his early solo piano works written at the musical college and conservatory in the middle of the 1950s.

YT: How did you decide to come back to the solo piano works after such a long break?
NK: I remember I thought to myself – since I didn't write for solo piano from the conservatory time, why don't I write something for a change?
YT: Just like that?
NK: Yes. I guess I felt that I missed it. I don't know…it just happened.
YT: That was a genius idea!
NK: It was a good idea, and then my interest in writing shifted so dramatically that I started to write only for the piano.
YT: When did you compose this suite – while you were working with Karamyshev or already at the Orchestra of Cinematography?
NK: It was kind of both. I started composing this suite while I was working with Karamyshev and finished this piece in the Cinematography.

YT: *Did it affect the music?*

NK: *Not at all. I remember originally I wanted to call it the French Suite.*

YT: *Really? Why didn't you call it that way?*

NK: *Somebody told me that the name French Suite reminds them about the French music… and I didn't want to have that association for my music. If there would be any connection then it's going to be to American jazz.*

YT: *I agree, American jazz or Bach. For some reason, the name French Suite reminds me about Bach but not the French music.*

NK: *For me too. Then I thought – if someone saw it that way there might be others too.*

YT: *And that's how you decided to call the piece »Suite in Old Style«.*

NK: *Correct.*

YT: *You wouldn't mind the connection of your music to Bach?*

NK: *I would not.*

YT: *This suite is a famous piece!*

NK: *Yes, I think this is one of a few of my works that is considered being not as difficult, so it is performed more often.*

YT: *If you can say so about your works –»not as difficult«.*

NK: *Right, all of my music is difficult to play but still this suite is not as hard as for example my other Suite for Piano, which is Op. 92.*

YT: *That may be the reason for the popularity of Op. 28.*

NK: *Plus, the movements are relatively short.*

YT: *Those movements of the suite are still technically demanding. I don't think that pianists with limited technical abilities can perform this piece.*

NK: *Of course not. The pianist must be prepared for my music.*

YT: *Since this is a suite, there should be dances inside.*

NK: *And there are seven Baroque dances – two Gavottes, two Bourees, Allemande, Sarabande, and Gigue. I do not have a Courante though.*

YT: *Since you don't have a Courante I guess you don't follow Froberger's order for the suite – Allemande, Courante, Sarabande, and Gigue?*

NK: *I did not, although, I did start with Allemande and finish with Gigue.*

YT: *I see it now – you followed the standard order for the beginning and ending but not for the middle movements.*

NK: *Same as Bach, the inside movements are varied for his suites.*

YT: *Are your movements written in binary form?*

NK: *Yes, as it is supposed to be.*

YT: *Do you have a repeat sign at the end of each section?*

NK: *Of course, traditionally I do. I even have the first and second ending for those sections.*

YT: *Really? Like in the jazz standard form?*

NK: Yes.
YT: Do you know that some performers do not take the repeats in the Bach suites? Since you have indicated the first and second ending, this will not happen with your music.
NK: It is a horrible thing that pianists do not take repeats. I remember once Richter played a piece of chamber music, also with the repeated parts, and somebody from the ensemble asked him if they want to repeat the parts or not and Richter said – why don't you want to repeat it? Don't you like the music?
YT: That's cool! I do have to admit that if you decided to repeat the parts then it's a serious thing – you can't play it exactly the same way, it should be different somehow.
NK: Sometimes the repeat is just a necessary step; otherwise the parts would be too short.
YT: I agree.
NK: Concerning changing the color on the repeated part, I think everything should depend on the performer – either you want to change something or not.
YT: What would you prefer?
NK: In my opinion both ways will work. It will depend on each piece specifically.
YT: How about your music – would you allow pianists to make some changes for their interpretation, for example changing the dynamics or tempo?
NK: I do. The main factor for me – it should sound good.
YT: I really enjoyed listening to your recording of this suite on youtube.
NK: Yes, I remember I recorded it on my second vinyl disc called »Jazz Pieces for Piano« in 1987.
YT: Do you like any other pianists who recorded the suite?
NK: Yes, I like very much how Yuki Kondo, Japanese pianist, recorded this piece.
YT: Is there any other reason except its popularity that put this piece in a special position? I do feel that this suite has the special meaning for you.
NK: I think everything that I composed before Op. 28 is not that valuable.
YT: Is that supposed to be a joke?
NK: No, I am serious. Starting from this suite that's what should be mostly recognized as my style.
YT: Then let's agree to disagree on this matter.

The *Piano Sonata No. 1* »Sonata-Fantasy«, Op. 39 (1984) appeared between the time Kapustin was working as a pianist at the Orchestra of Cinematography and being a self-employed composer.

YT: When did you compose your first piano sonata?
NK: I started to work on this piece while I was still working at the Cinematography and finished it when I already resigned from that job. So in other words, I left the orchestra while I was composing this sonata.

YT: *This is very interesting – you wrote your Sonata No. 1 (Op. 39) thirty four years after your first piano piece, the Sonata for piano that was composed in Nikitovka in 1950.*

NK: *Yes, it took me a while to get ready for writing my actual first sonata.*

YT: *Is there any reason for this?*

NK: *I guess my life was the main reason – during all these years I was seriously involved in the jazz big-band life as pianist, arranger, and a composer; that's what I was doing in the 1960s and 1970s. Then when it was over, I moved to the solo piano music, back to where I started.*

YT: *So you made a complete circle – coming back to piano music thirty four years after!*

NK: *Yes, but writing for the piano, it doesn't matter in which setting, either for solo, orchestral or chamber music, was always a part of me and will never be gone from me.*

YT: *To the present time you wrote twenty piano sonatas. Is there anything special concerning your Sonata No.1?*

NK: *It is one of my three sonatas that I gave the names to – Sonata-Fantasy; I mostly gave just the numbers to the sonatas.*

YT: *Can we say that this sonata is unusual since it has a characteristic of the sonata as well as the fantasy?*

NK: *Yes, you can say that. The first movement of the sonata is not written in the sonata form.*

YT: *So, the connection to the genre of fantasy affected the form of the piece.*

NK: *Correct. Although, there are a few examples in the Beethoven sonatas where the first movement is also not written in the sonata allegro form.*

YT: *So, the rest of three movements are written in the form that we would expect for the genre of the sonata.*

NK: *Yes. The second is a slow movement and technical finale is in the sonata form.*

YT: *You recorded this work on one of your vinyl discs, correct?*

NK: *Yes, this sonata is on my first vinyl that I recorded in the middle 1980s.*

YT: *You told me earlier that this sonata helped you financially.*

NK: *Yes, since it was one of the pieces that I composed for the Ministry of Culture, it was a big help for us.*

YT: *Do you remember any other works that you composed for the Ministry of Culture?*

NK: *There were so many of them. I remember I composed »Sinfonietta« Op. 49 (1986) and Concerto for Alto-saxophone and Orchestra, Op. 50 (1987) for them, and many other works too.*

A New Turn of Life: Decision to Resign from Orchestra of Cinematography

In 1984 the incredible tension of Kapustin's exhausting job at the Orchestra of the Cinematography was about to come to an end. As people say, our life sometimes leads us to its natural resolution. The major decision of Kapustin's life was about to come – the decision to resign from his official work.

YT: Did anything happen in your life that pushed you towards that decision?
NK: Not really. Just one day I finally got to the point when I realized – that's enough, I can't take it anymore. You see, right from the very beginning of my work with Orchestra of Cinematography I knew that it was not for me.
YT: Why?
NK: I am quite far from the movies, I don't like it. And I always knew about it.
YT: But you still kept working there for seven years!
NK: Yes, that was seven long years of suffering... I don't know where I found the power to keep going. I made it that far.
YT: So, in a way you sacrificed yourself for all that time.
NK: Yes.
YT: Can we say that one of the reasons for resigning from that orchestra was the fact that they didn't play your music?
NK: There were many reasons why I decided to quit my job, and that was one of them. This job started to take away too much time from me. I knew that I would need to compose so much music; I just would not be able to make it all happen because of the time issue if I would continue working there.
YT: So, it was a necessary step.
NK: Definitely. I remember our conductor from the orchestra told me not to leave the orchestra. He said that I would not be able to survive without it, that I would not be able to get back in, and that I would regret it for the rest of my life.
YT: But you still did it.
NK: Yes, I did, and I do not regret it even for a second of my life. What I regret is if I would have quit earlier I would have been able to write more music.
YT: How did Alla Semionovna react to your decision?
NK: You should ask her.
AK (joining the conversation): I thought that we would never be able to survive this situation. I was in shock.
YT: So many things you have to take on yourself during your life!
AK: I thought that I was ready for all the surprises that my life can prepare for me but I guess you never know what can come next.

NK (to Alla Semionovna): Tell her what happened after that.

AK: Soon after Kolia resigned from the work in the Orchestra of Cinematography we received his commission for the Piano Sonata No. 1, right?

NK: Yes, Opus 39.

AK: And at that moment I understood that actually it was not as bad idea as I originally thought. That income lasted half a year at least.

YT: What a happy ending!!!

NK: The main thing is that I proved to Alla and to myself that I am able to exist on my own just being a freelance composer. From that moment, I realized that I don't need to go to the work to get my monthly salary, I don't need to worry about it anymore, and that from now on I can spend all my time on my music. I was happy and relieved.

A new chapter in Kapustin's life as a composer, musician, and simply a family man, started from the moment he left his job at the Orchestra of Cinematography. He left without any regrets or hesitation, with the definite belief in his own power and the support of his family.

YT: Do you have any regrets concerning this period of your life, the years of 1972-1984?

NK: I always felt sorry for Boris Karamyshev… He was a very good man. Those five years that I worked with him was quite a memory. There is one thing I seriously regret – I wish I would have had a chance to play with him more… I miss him a lot.

Chapter Six: Freelancing Composer (1984-1999)

Life in the Soviet Union in the 1980s-1990s

The middle 1980s and 1990s became a turning point in the history of the Soviet Union (USSR). It started in the spring of 1985 when Mikhail Gorbachev[301] came to power bringing serious political and economic changes to the country. This led to the breakdown of the Soviet socialist model of development in Russia. For some people it was a time of big victories, and for some – a time of big disappointments and defeats:

When Mikhail S. Gorbachev (born in 1931) became general secretary of the Communist Party of the Soviet Union in March 1985, he launched his nation on a dramatic new course. His dual program of »Perestroika« (Restructuring) and »Glasnost« (Openness) introduced profound changes in economic practice, internal affairs and international relations. Within five years, Gorbachev's revolutionary program swept communist governments throughout Eastern Europe from power and brought an end to the Cold War (1945-1991), the largely political and economic rivalry between the Soviets and the United States and their respective allies that emerged following World War II.[302]

Surprisingly, the big changes in Kapustin's life and big changes within the USSR occurred at almost the same time - Kapustin resigned from his official job in 1984, and »Perestroika« began in 1985. The »Perestroika« was leading the country to the new ideology – the time of free market and private properties. Kapustin as well decided to exist on his own. The question that follows, is this a coincidence or was Kapustin, being himself a subtle man, anticipating those changes?

YT: I don't think I know any musician or composer who is like you - decided to stop going to the work while just in his forties. This is definitely a bold move!

NK: I told you earlier why I decided to do it.

YT: It is interesting how you advanced your time, getting yourself to a world of competition and free market almost a year ahead of your country!

NK: Yes, I decided to stop working in my official work. I thought I would have enough income to go my own way.

YT: No matter what difficulties that life would give you – that's the sign of a new way of life.

NK: I agree.

---

[301] Mikhail Gorbachev. Accessed December 17, 2017.
https://www.britannica.com/biography/Mikhail-Gorbachev.
[302] Perestroika and Glasnost. Accessed December 17, 2017.
http://www.history.com/topics/cold-war/perestroika-and-glasnost.

YT: Did you feel that those changes in the country were coming up?
NK: I don't know. I lived in my own world and this world was not affected by any political changes in Russia.
YT: So, you are not a political man.
NK: No, I am not.
YT: So, it doesn't really matter for you what happens inside the life of your country.
NK: I didn't say that. I watch political programs and news on TV and listen to the radio.
YT: So it does matter for you what kind of changes we are going through, especially the relationship between Russia and the United States.
NK: All I want is to be informed.
YT: Do you remember the middle 1980s when »Perestroika« started? Was your life different back then?
NK: I don't think.
YT: Do you remember the shortage of goods when the whole country was »standing in lines« with coupons for the grocery products and other necessities of life?
NK: I was not standing in those lines. This is all the bourgeois propaganda.
YT: Well, I remember how my friends and I stood in lines for hours. I also remember that our family used to stock up on cereals, pasta, sugar, canned food, and all those products that can keep long, in case of starvation. My mother used to go to Moscow to buy sausages, mayonnaise, and oranges.
NK: This all sounds strange to me.
AK (joining the conversation): Kolia is right. Luckily, we didn't have to go through what you are talking about with your family. Moscow always lived in better conditions then other cities in Russia.
YT: Yes, actually I agree with that.
AK: Plus, the »Union of Composers« had their own food stores, and after Kolia became a member of the union in 1980, I used to go there to buy some scarce products.
NK: I didn't go there.
AK: Yes, mostly there were wives of the composers who were coming to those stores, but not the composers. Although, I saw sometimes the composers too - the ones that didn't have wives.
YT: I hope you don't mind my next question - what did you buy in those stores?
AK: They had very tasty things – all the food that was difficult to obtain, sausages, chocolate... I remember Pasha, our youngest son, said at that time he tried crabs in cans for the first time.
YT: Crabs in cans? Oh, I see it now – the difference between Moscow and life in other cities was huge. At the time Pasha was tasting crabs in Moscow, Yana was eating pasta with bread in Dzerjinsk.

AK: At my work I remember we used to receive some kind of bag with different kind of goodies in it. I also used to buy some products, meat for example, from the restaurant of the hotel where I was working.

YT: It turned out to be a good thing that you left the position of teacher of German language at the secondary school and began working in the hotel »Pekin« as a German translator, right?

AK: Oh yes. I feel very happy that I made that decision.

YT: I am glad that at that difficult time for the country, you had a chance to maintain the good flow of life.

During the period of Gorbachev as the leader of the Soviet Union, an important event happened in the world that became also a part of Russian history. This event was the deconstruction or »fall« of the Berlin Wall on November 9, 1989. The fall of the Wall led to the reunification of East and West Germany and thereafter the end of the »Cold War«.[303]

YT: There are many different opinions on what happened with East and West Germany in 1989. To me the idea of the end of the Cold War sounds positive and quite promising.

NK: I have visited East and West Germany before the fall of the wall a couple of times.

YT: What did you see?

NK: What do you think – would people who have been separated for forty years still be the same or different?

YT: Probably very different.

NK: Yes. East and West Germany during all these years of separation moved very far from each other. East Germany was a prototype of the Soviet Union and West Germany was the example of the country with free democracy. I think for people from both sides of Germany, the fall of the Berlin Wall was a huge stress.

YT: So, you don't think it was a good idea to tear down the wall.

NK: I don't think so.

Another memorable moment from Russian history happened only six years after the beginning of »Perestroika«. On June 12, 1991 Boris Yeltsin[304] came to power and became the first President of the Russian Federation.[305] Yeltsin carried out economic reforms, resulting in the transfer of state properties to the

---

[303] Fall of the Berlin Wall. Accessed December 17, 2017.
https://www.golos-ameriki.ru/a/berlin-wall/2510614.html.
[304] Boris Yeltsin. Accessed December 17, 2017.
https://www.britannica.com/biography/Boris-Yeltsin.
[305] Boris Yeltsin Biography. Accessed December 17, 2017.
https://yeltsin.ru/news/biografiya-boris-nikolaevich-elcin-prezident-rossii-19911999/.

private sector. As a contrast, this change of the political system was related to the Russian Revolution of October 1917, when private properties became public domain.

The year 1991 was also associated with the collapse of the Soviet Union, and the beginning of the new history – the history of fifteen independent republics. The time of free market, competition, and development of private properties had begun:

> *On December 8, 1991 Russian President Boris Yeltsin, Ukrainian President Leonid Kravchuk, and Speaker of the Belarusian Supreme Soviet Parliament Stanislav Shushkevich, signed an »Agreement on Establishing the Commonwealth of Independent States« during their trilateral summit in Belovezhskaya Pushcha.*[306]

This agreement determined the end of the existence of the Soviet Union as the indisputable power and beginning of the new history of this country as the Russian Federation.

> *YT: What do you think about the rise to a power of Boris Yeltsin - was it a positive or negative process for the history of our country?*
>
> *NK: He destroyed the Soviet Union. The USSR was one of the strongest and most powerful countries in the world, and then this power had disappeared forever in one day.*
>
> *AK (joining the conversation): I remember when Yeltsin was coming to power, me and my friend got so excited about it. I was a big supporter of Yeltsin and believed in everything he said. We were hanging his portraits on the walls and did so many other things to support him.*
>
> *YT: It sounds like in the end you changed your opinion about Yeltsin.*
>
> *AK: Yes, in the end I realized that he was not the person I was thinking about, not to say something more harsh.*
>
> *NK: From the moment I saw Yeltsin on TV taking a ride in the trolleybus in Moscow, I understood everything about him.*
>
> *YT: Yeltsin in the trolleybus?*
>
> *AK: Oh yes, that was a big deal for everybody – Yeltsin, the President of the country, taking public transportation*[307]*!*
>
> *YT: To be closer to ordinary people?*
>
> *AK: I guess.*

---

[306] End of empire plotted in secret forest talks. Accessed December 17, 2017. https://www.rt.com/news/ussr-collapse-agreement-331/, http://tass.ru/politika/3850507.
[307] Leaders and Propaganda: Yeltsin and Putin. Accessed December 17, 2017. http://osvita.mediasapiens.ua/trends/1411978127/vozhdi_i_propaganda_eltsin_i_putin/.

NK: He wanted to be seen as being close to people, but in reality it was nowhere near that. As always, the politics was the dark territory. The only sad thing is that the people are the ones who are going to suffer out of it.

YT: Right, look what happens now, in September 2017 – American Embassy in Moscow stopped awarding the American Visas to the Russian people.[308]

NK: I heard about it.

YT: This was the response of President Trump on Russians who expelled seven hundred and fifty five American diplomats from Russia. From the Russian side this was the reaction on America's sanctions on Russia in July 2017. I am sure there were a number of reasons why the American government decided to put sanctions on Russia, but it looks like it went too far.

AK: And somebody like you and Anton,[309] whose parents live in Russia, are going to suffer.

YT: Exactly, as well as Russian students, artists, scientists, and tourists.

---

[308] Closure of the United States. Accessed December 17, 2017. https://www.novayagazeta.ru/articles/2017/08/24/73577-zakrytie-ameriki.

[309] Note by the author: Here Alla Kapustina refers to their son Anton who is currently living in the United States.

Musical Life of Nikolai Kapustin in the 1980s-1990s/Recording of the Vinyl Records and Compact Discs

The decision to resign from work at the Orchestra of Cinematography was one of the major moves in Kapustin's life. On one hand, this road led him to complete freedom, a comfortable and non-stressful existence as a composer. On the other hand, for Kapustin as a family man, it was a life of the unknown, the life of a person who had to constantly worry about how to support his wife and children. Not many people can find the will to do that, and, even more importantly, not many people can understand and accept that decision for themselves. Only the people with a strong character and deep belief in their abilities are able to do that. With no doubts, Kapustin was one of those people. His wife, Alla Semionovna Kapustina, not only accepted his decision but also helped to overcome all the difficulties of that period of their lives.

> YT: *I can't believe that you were able to decide to take this dramatic step – to leave the job. I don't think many people can do this.*
> NK: *Do you think it was easy for me? Everybody kept saying to me that I have two teenage boys, that I shouldn't do such a foolish thing. Even Alla wasn't on my side at the beginning.*
> YT: *What happened in your life when you left your job at the Orchestra of Cinematography?*
> NK: *Only good things. First, I started to compose very intensively, working on things that I planned to do earlier but never had the time. Second, I didn't want to rush into anything. My life was completely mine, all twenty-four hours a day.*
> YT: *Your productivity as a composer increased dramatically, from twenty seven compositions composed during the years of work with Karamyshev and Orchestra of Cinematography (1972-1984) to sixty compositions composed from the moment you resigned to the end of 1990s (1984-1999).*
> NK: *That's exactly what I am talking about. Composition became my main direction in life; something that I was dreaming about finally came true.*

The new direction of Kapustin's life, being a self-employed composer, didn't move him away from the musical life that he was involved in earlier. Furthermore, having more open time meant he was able to be more active within the musical circles in Moscow.

> YT: *Some may think that once you quit your job, you kind of closed yourself in your flat and decided to dedicate yourself totally to composition. Does this sound right to you?*

> NK: *Of course not. Yes, I quit my job to spend most of my time on composing my music but I didn't move myself away from my musical life. Actually, it's a question – when did I attend the concerts more often– when I was busy working at the Orchestra of Cinematography or when I left it?*
>
> YT: *So, you had a pretty active life after you stopped working at the Cinematography.*
>
> NK: *Of course. I had time now, and I remember we went to many concerts in Moscow with Alla.*
>
> YT: *Was it the concerts of your music or other composers?*
>
> NK: *We did both – sometimes we attended the concerts of my music, but sometimes I was interested in hearing the music of some other composers.*
>
> YT: *That was probably an interesting experience for you, attending the concerts but not performing on them.*
>
> NK: *Yes, to listen and enjoy the concerts but not be a part of it was quite new for me.*
>
> YT: *Probably felt a little strange to you.*
>
> NK: *Maybe just a little.*

One of the things that Kapustin continued doing from the time he left the Orchestra of Cinematography was composing music for commission, which brought additional income to his family.

> NK: *After I left my official job at the Orchestra of Cinematography I kept composing music for commission, especially for the Ministry of Culture. I now had the time to do it.*
>
> AK (joining the conversation): *Yes, that was a big help for us. As you know, Kolia is not the person who stands for himself, but he has friends who know him and who help him through his life. One of them was his friend from the time he studied at the Musical College; she worked at the Ministry of Culture.*
>
> NK: *I told you about her earlier - her name was Strijakova.*
>
> AK: *She knew that Kolia had an exceptional talent and was accepting his works without any problems or complications.*
>
> NK: *And I don't think this happened to all composers who presented their pieces for the Ministry of Culture – they had serious competition there.*

Right around that time, after Kapustin resigned from his work, he began planning to record his own music at the recording studio in Moscow. That project ended up being highly successful and lasted twenty-three years, from 1985 to 2008.

During the 1980s-1990s Kapustin recorded three vinyl discs and six CDs of his compositions. All three vinyl discs were released in the 1980s by the leading record label in Russia – »Melodiya«.[310]

Kapustin's first vinyl disc titled »Nikolai Kapustin« was recorded in 1985 and released in 1986.[311] This disc includes two solo piano works – *Eight Concert Etudes*, Op. 40 and the *Sonata-Fantasia for Piano No. 1*, Op. 39.[312]

Cover of the first vinyl disc »Nikolai Kapustin«, Melodiya, Moscow, 1986

YT: This is so interesting – you composed those two pieces, Sonata-Fantasia No. 1 Op. 39 and Concert Etudes Op. 40 in 1984 and recorded it almost immediately in 1985! This does not happen too often.
NK: It looks that way. I think I started to prepare to record these two pieces right after I finished composing them.
YT: Why did you decide to record first your new pieces but not some of your earlier solo piano works, for example Suite in Old Style, Op. 28?
NK: I thought that etudes and sonata would represent my style of writing better, since it was my newest work.
YT: Do you remember recording that first disc? Was it difficult for you?

---

[310] Note by the author: The record label »Melodiya« at that time was the only company in Russia that was doing sound-recording and production.
[311] Melodiya (C60 23759 008), 1986.
[312] Note by the author: Conversation about Op. 40 will be presented at the latter part of the Chapter VI.

NK: *I don't think it was a difficult process for me. My music was »in my fingers«*[313] *by the time of recording, so I just needed to play it a couple of times. I felt confident about my performances.*

YT: *I am asking because I know that for some musicians recording in the studio is a very stressful process.*

NK: *No, for me it was a pleasant thing to do.*

YT: *What did you feel when your first vinyl disc came to life?*

NK: *To tell you the truth – all that time I wasn't sure that it would come true.*

YT: *But you still kept working on this project.*

NK: *Oh yes, I would not give up.*

YT: *It is fascinating that your very first recording happened in 1985 and the last one, for now, in 2008, so it was a twenty-three year project!*

NK: *Yes, it all ended up as a serious project.*

YT: *When you recorded those discs did you expect that there would be that many?*

NK: *Of course not. I didn't plan anything ahead; I was just centered on the current project at the time.*

The second vinyl disc of Kapustin's music, which was also dedicated to solo piano, was titled »Nikolai Kapustin: Jazz Pieces for Piano«. The disc was recorded in 1987 and released in 1989.[314] This disc included *Suite in Old Style*, Op. 28, *Variations*, Op. 41, and characterpieces such as *Day-Break*, Op. 26, *Toccatina*, Op. 36, *Contemplation*, Op. 47, *Big Band Sounds*, Op. 46, and *Motive Force*, Op. 45.

---

[313] Note by the author: To say a piece is »in my fingers« is an international concept of all pianists, which means that muscle memory completed the work.
[314] Melodiya (C60 28239 000), 1989.

Cover of the second vinyl disc »Nikolai Kapustin: Jazz Pieces for Piano«, Melodiya, Moscow, 1989

YT: *So, during the years of 1985-1987 you were concentrated upon this new project – the recording of your second vinyl disc.*
NK: *I can't say this was my only project – as you know in the 1980s I kept composing music very intensively, but yes, the recording was one of my main directions in life.*
YT: *I noticed that on this disc you recorded some of the pieces that came before your Op. 39 and Op. 40, which was on the first disc, for example »Day-Break«, Op. 26, or »Suite in Old Style«, Op. 28.*
NK: *Yes, I did that, but on the other side I also included the compositions that came after – my »Motive Force«, Op. 45, »Big-Band Sounds«, Op. 46, and »Contemplation«, Op. 47.*
YT: *So, in other words it was a combination of works from the 1970s and 1980s – from the past and from the present time.*
NK: *Correct.*
YT: *It is interesting how the sound of your music from 1970s is different from 1980s.*
NK: *Yes, my musical style changed dramatically through the years.*
YT: *Do you have a piece that you like the most from this recording?*
NK: *This is a difficult question. I told you earlier – all the pieces are equally important to me. Although, on this particular recording I like the latest works more, Op. 45, 46, and Op. 47.*
YT: *So, you like your later works more than the earlier ones.*
NK: *The earlier ones sound old to me. I don't know why people like to play them that much.*

In the introductory article to this vinyl disc Valery Erokhin, Russian musical critic and Kapustin friend from the conservatory years, very imaginatively presented Kapustin as a composer:

> *He doesn't look like the other composers and pianists of our time. His musical style, with all its' unique novelty, originality, and refinement, has something that feels close to us, something that the audience would understand without any difficulties. His piano writing is notable by its perfect pianistic comfortability. His performance manner differs by the precise accuracy of his hand motion that provides the optimal clearness of musical expression.*[315]

YT: I like the words that Erokhin wrote about you in the introductory article to this disc very much. I agree that your music does have something that is so close to us, something that feels like home, and something that you immediately recognize as yours.
NK: I guess it's a good thing.
YT: I can't stop thinking – throughout your life you've always had friends who would understand you, help you, and support you in many different ways.
NK: Yes, I agree. With Valera [Valery Erokhin] we went even further – I moved to Moscow from the Ukraine when I was a teenager, and he, after living many years in Moscow, moved to the Ukraine.
YT: That's sign of true friendship!
NK (laughing): Yes, yes, yes.
YT: There is one thing that I wanted to clarify – in that article Erokhin considers you a composer in a category of the third stream. What do you think?
NK: Yes, this is a good question.
YT: I asked Curtis[316] *about this and he said that the first thing that comes to mind when we are talking about music of the third stream is John Lewis*[317] *and his »Modern Jazz Quartet«.*
NK: Yes, they started this whole thing – combining jazz and classical music.
YT: Yes, but their music is based on the concept of the improvisation as one of the major aspects of the style, and your music is not. So, Curtis suggested that you do not belong to a third stream, but you have your own path combining the classical and jazz music.
NK: Hmmm… I agree. My music may sound like improvisation sometimes but there is no actual improvisation it in.

---

[315] Translated by Yana Tyulkova
[316] Curtis Johnson
[317] John Lewis. Accessed November 25, 2017. https://www.biography.com/people/john-lewis-37484.

YT: And you don't like when musicians take advantage and begin improvising within your compositions.
NK: I don't.

The third and the last vinyl disc of Kapustin solo piano music is called »Nikolai Kapustin: Twenty Four Preludes in Jazz Style«. It was recorded and released in 1989.[318]

Cover of the third vinyl disc »Nikolai Kapustin: Twenty-Four Preludes in Jazz Style«, Melodiya, Moscow, 1989

YT: This disc was recorded exactly two years after your second disc. So, it looks like each of those three vinyl discs took two years to complete – 1985, 1987, and 1989.
NK: I didn't count, but I guess it is right - two years is enough to prepare the new material for the recording.
YT: I think that's an impressive speed. Plus, some of the pieces were newly composed.
NK: I enjoyed working on those recordings.
YT: I noticed one interesting detail concerning your vinyl discs – you didn't put the opus numbers to any of your pieces for all those three vinyl discs, correct?
NK: No, I did not. Then, sometime after, I began to compile a list of my compositions – that's when the opus numbers appeared.
YT: This was a great idea! It keeps music in order, and will also avoid any confusion.
NK: Especially for the composers who have written many works.

---

[318] Melodiya (C60 28999 007), 1989.

YT: Yes, somebody like you! Another thing that I noticed – at the moment of recording of your vinyl discs you were using Russian titles. When did you switch to English names for your works?

NK: Ohhh, that's a difficult question. I remember at some point I was using French titles, like for example my Op. 65 called »Berceuse«, which means »Lullaby«, but I can't recall when exactly I switched the names to English… probably sometime in the 1990s.

YT: So, you recorded three vinyl discs in the 1980s and then in the beginning of 1990s decided to switch to the compact disc, correct?

NK: Actually, this third disc was not the last vinyl disc that I recorded on »Melodiya«.

YT: Really? I didn't know that there was a fourth disc planned.

NK: That's the thing – to record the fourth vinyl disc was our original plan, but it never came true.

In 1990-1991, Kapustin started recording his fourth vinyl disc of solo piano music. He intended to include two of his piano sonatas, *Piano Sonata No. 2*, Op. 54, *Piano Sonata No. 3*, Op. 55, and *Andante*, Op. 58. Unfortunately, this project was not completed until 2001, ten years later. As a result, instead of the vinyl disc the CD disk with the title »Kapustin Plays Kapustin« was released in 2002 in Japan.[319]

YT: What has happened to those recordings?

NK: I still remember the story about the recording of three of my works (Op. 54, Op. 55, and Op. 58). Yeltsin came to power, »Melodiya« ceased to exist and all our musical activities stopped for a while. There is not much you can do during the economic crises in the country. Yelstinism crashed it all.[320]

YT: That was a very difficult time for Russia. Did you at least record those three piano pieces?

NK: Yes, I recorded them in the studio but then they sent the recording back to me and said that they had to »freeze« the project for a while. Of course, I understood everything immediately – it was over. That's why I couldn't move forward with that recording.

YT: Did you get upset because of this sad news?

NK: Not at all. I never get upset because of the trifles.

YT: How did it happen that the CD was finally released in 2002 after eleven years of waiting?

NK: In 2001 two of my friends, the cellist Alexander Zagorinsky and alto-saxophonist Alexei Volkov, recorded my »Scherzino for Cello Solo«, Op. 93 and »Duo for Alto-

---

[319] Triton (DICC-26073), 2002, Octavia Records (OVCT-00026), 2005.

[320] »Melodiya« was a state recording company up to 1989. With the appearance of the free market and development of the private sector in Russia in the 1990s, it was de-monopolized. Accessed November 25, 2017. https://www.culture.ru/institutes/13974/firma-melodiya.

Saxophone and Cello«, Op. 99. I thought that it was time to come back to my earlier recordings and to complete the project that I started at the beginning of 1990s.
YT: That's why this CD includes solo piano and chamber music.
NK: Yes, those pieces were recorded ten years apart.
YT: It's interesting – you don't play on those two pieces of your chamber music – Op. 93 and Op. 99.
NK: How could I possibly do it? There is no piano part there.... but I fixed it for my next recordings of the 1990s.

Starting from 1989, when most of the performers continued using the vinyl discs, Kapustin started to record his music on the compact discs. His first two compact discs compiled the earlier recordings of his three vinyl discs that were recorded by the »Melodiya" in the 1980s.

Accordingly, the disc »Nikolai Kapustin: Jazz Pieces for Piano« (Melodiya, 1989) included *Eight Concert Etudes*, Op. 40, *Sonata-Fantasia No. 1*, Op. 39, *Suite in Old Style*, Op. 28, and *Variations* Op. 41.[321] The disc »Nikolai Kapustin: Twenty Four Preludes in Jazz Style« (Melodiya, 1989) included *Twenty Four Preludes for Piano*, Op. 53 as well as *Day-Break*, Op. 26, *Toccatina*, Op. 36, *Contemplation (Meditation)*, Op. 47, *Sounds of Big Band*, Op. 46, and *Motive Force*, Op. 45.[322]

YT: Why did you decide to re-issue these three vinyl discs on the compact disks? Was it your idea or did someone suggest it to you?
NK: That was the time when compact discs were just coming into use in Russia, and I thought it would be more safe to keep my music in the CD format.
YT: I noticed also that on those two compact discs you were able to include much more music than on the vinyl.
NK: Yes, this is the biggest advantage of recording the music on the CD – you've got much more space. On vinyl it is limited by the size of the vinyl disc. That's why we didn't follow the exact order of my vinyl recordings, but we were able to put the recording of three vinyl discs for two CDs.

In 1991 Kapustin started to work on a new project – recording his third CD disc of solo piano music called »Kapustin plays Kapustin: Jazz Portrait«. The disc was distributed in England by the »Mezhdunarodnaya Kniga« [International

---

[321] Boheme Music (CDBMR 007148), 2000, Triton (DICC-24058), 2000, Octavia Records (OVCT-00021) 2004.
[322] Boheme Music (CDBMR 007149), 2000, Triton (DICC-24059), 2000, Octavia Records (OVCT-00016), 2004.

Book] in 1992.[323] This recording contained all piano works composed and performed by Nikolai Kapustin: *Andante*, Op. 58, *Piano Sonata No. 4*, Op. 60, *Ten Bagatelles*, Op. 59, *Piano Sonata No. 5*, Op. 61, and *Piano Sonata No. 6*, Op. 62.

Cover of disc »Kapustin plays Kapustin: Jazz Portrait«, Moscow, 1991

YT: This is very impressive – you started to record your music in 1985 and just six years after you already had three vinyl discs and three CD discs!
NK: Don't forget that the first two CD discs collected the music of my vinyl discs.
YT: Oh yes, so basically this disc »Kapustin plays Kapustin: Jazz Portrait« was the first CD disc with the new material recorded in the format of the compact disc.
NK: Yes.
YT: But even with that in mind – you recorded three vinyl discs and one compact disc in six years!
NK: Now, this sounds more like truth to me.
YT: This is amazing!
NK: At that point I wasn't thinking about any particular numbers, I was just composing and recording, that's all.
YT: One more detail about this particular recording – those pieces (Op. 58-62) were composed, recorded, and released within two years, 1990-1991. How fascinating is that!
NK: Yes, I got lucky this time.

---

[323] Mezhdunarodnaya Kniga (MK-417051), 1992, Mezhdunarodnaya Kniga Muzyka (MKM-228), 2001, Olympia (MKM-228), 2001, Triton (DICC-26072), 2001, Octavia Records (OVCT-00027), 2005.

In 1998, during their tour in Germany, Nikolai Kapustin and Alexander Zagorinsky recorded a live concert in Hannover. This recording was to be partially used later as the material for their chamber CD disc. Unfortunately, the disc was released ten years later, in 2008.[324] The CD included the works of Beethoven, Chopin, as well as Kapustin's chamber pieces for piano and cello, such as *Sonata for Cello and Piano No. 1*, Op. 63 and *Sonata for Cello and Piano No. 2*, Op. 84. A new version of the solo piano piece *Day-Break*, Op. 26, where he used pizzicato cello accompaniment, was also presented on that disc.[325]

In 1999 Kapustin started to record his sixth CD called »Kapustin Plays Kapustin«, which was entirely dedicated to his chamber music. The disc included *Trio for Flute, Cello, and Piano*, Op. 86, *String Quartet No. 1*, Op. 88, *Divertissement for Two Flutes, Cello, and Piano*, Op. 91, and *Piano Quintet*, Op. 89.[326]

YT: *You started to work on that recording in 1999. When did you finish that project?*
NK: *I think we were done in 2000.*
YT: *Who participated in this recording?*
NK: *There were many people involved in this project. I invited mostly my friends. It was cellist Alexander Zagorinsky, flutists Alexander Korneev and Marina Rubinshteyn, violinists Alexander Chernov and Vladimir Spektor, and violist Svetlana Stepchenko.*
YT: *The disc was released in Japan in 2001.*
NK: *Yes, at that time I was closely working with the Japanese label »Triton«. Japan was recording my discs, videos, and publishing my music.*

---

[324] Classical Records (CR-126), Russia, 2008.
[325] Note by the author: The conversation about the tour in Germany with Alexander Zagorinsky and recording of the CD will be presented in the latter part of the Chapter VI.
[326] Triton (DICC-26067), 2001, Octavia Records (OVCT-00011), 2004.

New and Old Friends of Nikolai Kapustin: Nikolai Petrov, Alexander Zagorinsky, and Hideaki Takaoki

Nikolai Petrov

Nikolai Arnoldovich Petrov (1943-2011) was a Russian pianist, who was known not only within the USSR [Soviet Union] but also widely abroad. He gained popularity from a young age, winning the second place on the International Van Cliburn Competition in 1962 (Texas, USA), the Queen Elizabeth Competition in 1964 (Brussels, Belgium), and becoming the soloist for the Moscow Philharmonic Orchestra in 1965. Petrov had a wide range of piano repertoire, which included more than a hundred pieces. He toured in the USA, Germany, England, Holland, and other European countries.[327]

»*As a pianist he happily combined the highest achievements of the world piano school of playing with the Russian power and range of temperament.*« – Gennady Rozhdestvensky.[328]

Nikolai Petrov

YT: *I remember you mentioned earlier in our conversations that you met Petrov while you studied at the Moscow Conservatory, is this correct?*

---

[327] Nikolai Petrov. Accessed December 17, 2017. https://www.britannica.com/biography/Nikolay-Arnoldovich-Petrov.

[328] Program notes from concert of Moscow Philharmonic Society, season of 2001-2002 (Home archive of Nikolai Kapustin).

NK: Yes, I met Kolia (Nikolai Petrov) in the late 1950s. At that point we were both young – I was in my early twenties and he was in his teens. By the way, he entered the conservatory the year I graduated – in 1961.
YT: Do you remember who his teacher was?
NK: Yes, he studied in the class of Yakov Zak. I think he even did his post-graduate study with Zak.
YT: So, did you stay in contact with Petrov through all these years?
NK: Not really. After I graduated my life changed dramatically, I moved to the world of jazz music, and unfortunately lost the connection with some of my friends from the conservatory.
YT: So, how did it happen that you reconnected with Petrov?
NK: He called me.
YT: Just like that? Were you surprised?
NK: Of course, I was glad to hear his voice after all those years.
YT: When did this happen?
YT: I think it was somewhere at the beginning of 1990s.
YT: Oh, almost thirty years after your graduation!
NK: Yes, we didn't see each other for a long-long time.
YT: What did he say to you during that phone conversation, if it's not a secret?
NK: He said that he played three of my etudes from the »Eight Concert Etudes« Op. 40 all over our country, that he is very interested in my music, and that he was willing to play more, so we decided to meet. That's all.
YT: What happened next?
NK: We met at his house and I played some of my pieces… many different works. I remember I played my Piano Sonatas No. 2 and No. 3, as well as my Piano Concertos No. 5 and No. 6.
YT: How could you do that?
NK: What?
YT: How could you play so many pieces all in one meeting?
NK: First of all, it was my music, and second – I didn't play the complete concertos, I showed him the excerpts.
YT: How about sonatas?
NK: For both sonatas I played the entire piece.
YT: That's a lot. What did Petrov choose?
NK: He decided to play my Sonata No. 2 Op. 54 and Piano Concerto No. 5 Op. 72.
YT: Were you happy with his choice?
NK: Of course I was. He premiered both pieces with standing ovations. By the way, around the same time I recorded my Piano Sonata No. 2.
YT: I remember you told me that.

NK: Yes, I even sent him my recording to listen to.

YT: So, when Petrov played this sonata you knew each and every note of the work.

NK: Basically yes.

YT: Did you have any comments for Petrov?

NK: You should try to critique him – it was almost impossible to do. Although, I do have to admit – the rhythmic side of my works was always a serious thing to work on.

YT: How about Petrov's playing your piece from the jazz perspective?

NK: There was no such perspective in his playing, although he did consider himself a jazz pianist also.

AK (joining the conversation): Petrov always tried to do his best, maybe he understood Kolia's works a little differently, but I think that's ok.

NK: What do you mean – that's ok? He thought that the only possible way that my music should sound is his way. You know, he had a high level of ambition.

AK: And who doesn't have ambition?

YT: Yes, it's very difficult to find the pianist who would play closer to what the composer is thinking.

NK: Although, sometimes it happens... very rarely though.

YT: Do you think that the pianists, who are searching for the interpretation of your music, should look more into your performances?

NK: I don't know this either. One thing I want you to remember Yana – the way I play my music is not the only way it should sound; my performance is not the gauge. Sometimes I listen to something that I recorded earlier and I see that now I would play it differently.

YT: I still see your performances as a guide, as a direction in order to understand your music, and sorry, it does sound to me like a gauge.

NK: It's all about the style of my music, the inside feel.

YT: I noticed that Petrov performed the Piano Sonata No. 2 quite intensively – we have program notes from two of those performances – April 22 and May 18, 1991.

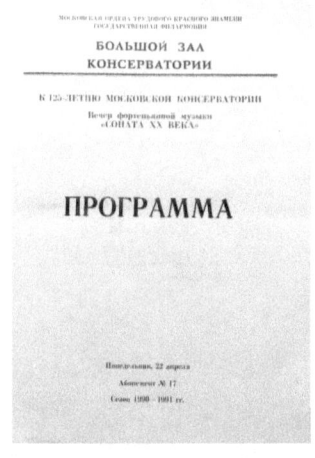
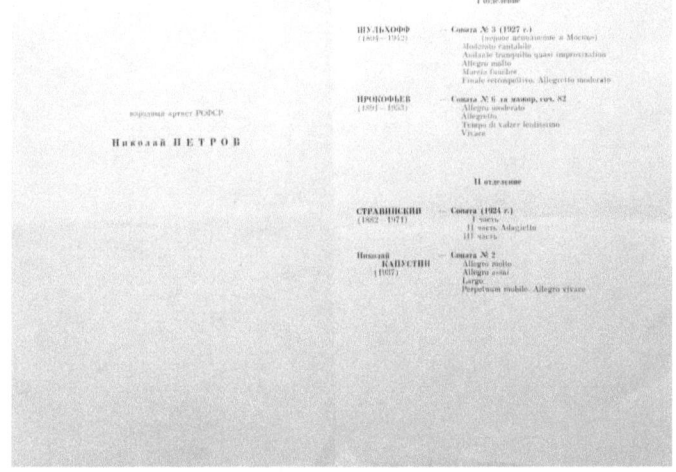

Program notes: Nikolai Petrov performed the premier of Kapustin Piano Sonata No. 2 Op. 54, April 22, 1991, Moscow

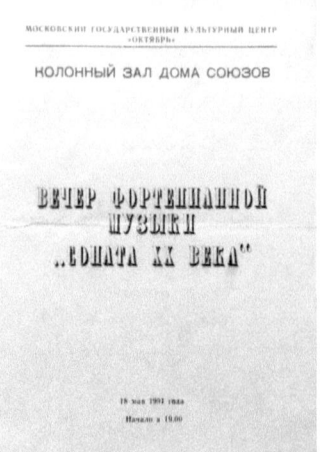

Program notes: Nikolai Petrov performed Sonata No. 2 Op. 54 on the concert »Twentieth Century Piano Sonata« May 18, 1991, Moscow

NK: *Not only that, he also recorded this Sonata No. 2.*[329] *Kolia [Petrov] was the pianist in high demand; I remember he told me that he played up to a hundred concerts a year. You know what that means.*

YT: *Unreal!!!*

NK: *And he didn't repeat his programs from one concert to another, like some pianists do, his range of repertoire was very wide.*

---

[329] Nikolai Petrov, 20th Century Piano Sonatas, Olympia/VIST (OCD 280), 1992.

YT: *Maybe that's why he was interested in your music – because it was different from anything that he played earlier, and it was something new - connected to jazz.*

NK: *You are right, he always wanted to try new things. He was an open-minded pianist, which is very good.*

YT: *Do you know if Petrov actually played jazz?*

NK: *I don't know if you could call it jazz or not, but he played something like boogie-woogie.*

YT: *Really? On the other side, in the 1980s-1990s, there were not that many classical pianists who wanted to play jazz music.*

NK: *I agree. Even more, when I studied it was almost prohibited to play jazz.*

YT: *Yes! Coming back to the premier of the Piano Sonata No.2 – do you remember where it happened?*

NK: *That's the thing I wanted to point out – all Petrov's premiers of my music happened in the big halls, places like Moscow Conservatory or Moscow Philharmonic. It was not just local small places with fewer people in the audience but it always was a serious event. As I remember, he played Piano Sonata No. 2 in the Big Hall of the Moscow Conservatory in April 1991.*

YT: *Do you have the recording of this premier?*

NK: *Yes, there is a video recording on youtube of this performance.*

YT: *Did you attend this premier?*

NK: *Of course I did – we both came, me and Alla.*

YT: *Oh, this is so good! I think Petrov was excited about that.*

NK: *Yes, he was. He played my sonata as the last piece, and at the very end of the concert, while people were presenting the flowers to him, he was searching the audience, trying to find me there.*

YT: *Did he find you?*

NK *(smiling): Yes, he did. He pointed towards me and I stood up and took a bow.*

YT: *Ohhh, I can see clearly now how it all happened!*

NK: *It was nice! After that I saw me and Alla on TV, because this premier was recorded and broadcasted for the TV Channel »Russia: Culture«.*[330]

YT: *This is such a unique recording – you in the beginning of 1990s.*

NK: *Yes, now it's all history.*

YT: *How about the premier of your Piano Concerto No. 5 Op. 72?*

NK: *Unfortunately, there is no recording of this premier, although, it was an extremely successful premier. I actually dedicated my Piano Concerto No. 5 to Kolia [Nikolai Petrov].*

YT: *When did Petrov premiere your Concerto No. 5?*

---

[330] Video of the Nikolai Petrov playing live the premier of Kapustin Sonata No. 2 (Moscow, 1991). Accessed March 4, 2018. https://www.youtube.com/watch?v=o_dzivO5h5o.

NK: It was in the spring of 1995. He played with the Moscow Philharmonic Orchestra in Tchaikovsky Hall, with a very good conductor – Vassily Sinaisky.[331] You know how important the role of conductor is in a performance like that.
YT: How did the audience receive this performance?
NK: The audience went wild, and they couldn't stop clapping.

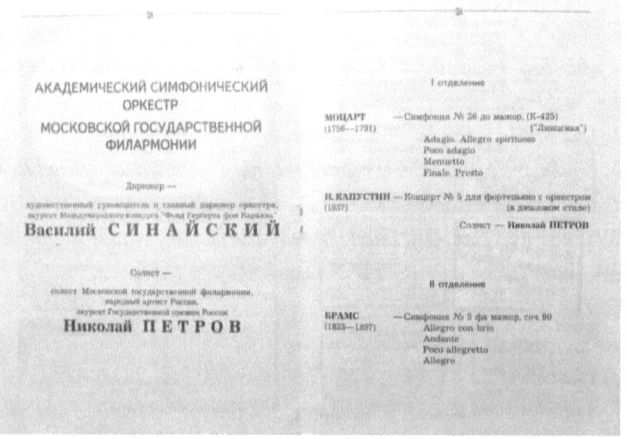

Program notes: Nikolai Petrov performed the premier of Kapustin Piano Concerto No. 5 Op. 72, Moscow, May 27, 1995

---

[331] Vassily Sinaisky. Accessed December 17, 2017.
https://www.intermusica.co.uk/artist/Vassily-Sinaisky

YT: We also have program notes from October 1998 when Petrov played your Concerto No. 5 again. This time he performed Concerto No. 5 on the concert dedicated to the memory of his teacher from the Moscow Conservatory, Professor Yakov Zak.

NK: Yes, this was a different orchestra though, it was the Svetlanov State Symphony Orchestra with Pavel Sorokin as a conductor. This time Petrov played in the Big Hall of the Moscow Conservatory.

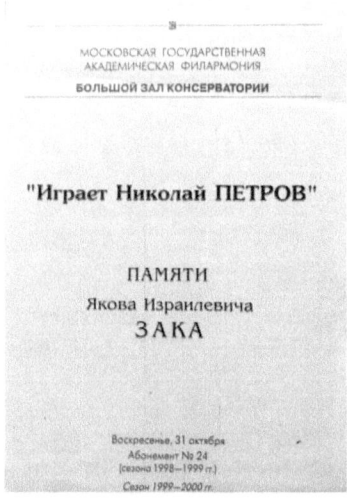

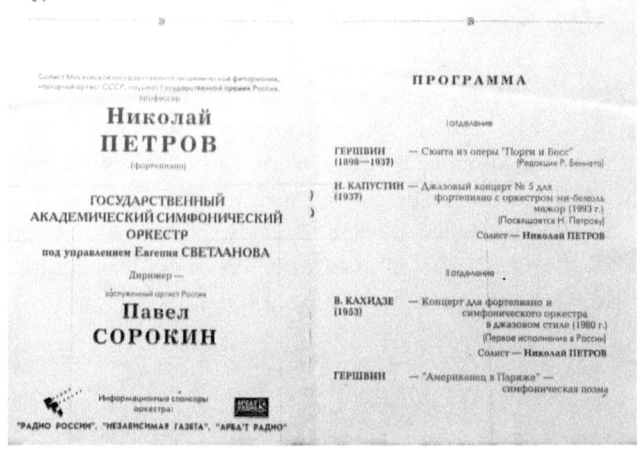

Program notes: Nikolai Petrov performed Kapustin Piano Concerto No. 5 Op. 72, Moscow, October 31, 1998

YT: Did you attend those two performances of your Concerto No. 5?
NK: Of course I did! I attended all the performances of Petrov playing my music.

YT: Which one did you like the most – or maybe they were both equal in value?

NK: For some reason after those two Petrov performances of Concerto No. 5 nobody played it again...in spite of the fact that they were well-done and well-received performances. I really like the music of that concerto. Sometimes I think I wish I would learn this concerto by myself, but it never happened.

YT: Did Petrov play just those two pieces – Piano Sonata No. 2 and Piano Concerto No. 5 or did he play some other works as well?

NK: He played many of my works. The programs that I have now are only the programs that survived. In reality many of the programs just simply dissapeared.

YT: That's what I was thinking.

NK: I remember he also played my chamber works, for example »Trio for Flute, Cello, and Piano«, Op. 86. He also played another premier in the 2000s – my »Quintet«, Op. 89, then of course also my »Etudes«, Op. 40.

YT: You are lucky that there were so many talented musicians from the classical and jazz world around you during all stages of you life.

NK: Yes, I can't complain. Kolia Petrov became a good friend of mine, it was hard to receive the news about his death… Feels like it happened just yesterday.[332]

Alexander Zagorinsky

Alexander Igorevich Zagorinsky (born 1962) is a celebrated Russian cellist. He graduated from the Moscow Conservatory in cello performance in 1986, and completed his post-graduate study in 1988 (class of Professor Natalia Shakhovskaya). Zagorinsky became the laureate of several national and international competitions. Among them were the VIII International Chamber Music Competition in Italy (Trapani, 1988) and the IX International Tchaikovsky Competition in Russia (Moscow, 1990). From 1991 to 2000 he was a member of the Moscow Philharmonic Orchestra. As a performer, Zagorinsky is interested in performing the works of modern composers, such as Edison Denisov, Vyacheslav Dashkevich, Yuri Kasparov, Alexander Rosenblatt, Alexander Shchetynsky, Eugene Galperin, and Nikolai Kapustin.[333]

---

[332] Nikolai Petrov passed away on March 8, 2011 from a massive heart attack, at just sixty-eight years old.

[333] Alexander Zagorinsky. Accessed November 28, 2017. http://www.norge.ru/no/alexander_zagorinsky.html.

Nikolai Kapustin and Alexander Zagorinsky, late 1990s

YT: *When did you get acquainted with Zagorinsky?*
NK: *I met Sasha [Alexander Zagorinsky] in 1995 during the premier of my Piano Concerto No. 5. He was a cello player in the orchestra that performed with Nikolai Petrov.*
YT: *What a productive output of the premier – it was a successful premier, and you got a new friend.*
NK: *I am glad it worked out that way.*
YT: *Do you remember how it happened?*
NK: *I do. His wife, Tatyana Poltorikhina, came to talk to me during that concert. She was also a part of the orchestra. It turned out that we both studied in the Musical College, and she remembered me from that time. So, we decided to meet. They both came to our house, and that was it. Since then I performed with Zagorinsky quite often. That's why I have so much music written for cello.*
YT: *Because you have a friend who is a cellist.*
NK: *Yes. Did you know that Chopin also had a cellist friend and that's why he wrote so much music for cello?*
YT: *No, I didn't. During that meeting with Zagorinsky did you decide to play some pieces or it just started as a friendship.*
NK: *We started to play right away. At that time I had only my first cello sonata (Op. 63). Then I composed the second cello sonata (Op. 84) that I dedicated to Zagorinsky. For some reason this sonata became more popular than the first one.*
YT: *Why do you think this happened?*

NK: I don't know… Maybe when I got acquainted with Zagorinsky I learned the instrument a little better.

YT: Do you mean the cello?

NK: Yes.

YT: Did you perform with Zagorinsky primarily as a duet?

NK: Not always. We played my Flute Trio (Op. 86) with Zagorinsky and Korneev, and in quartet also. We played in different settings.

YT: And in different cities.

NK: Yes, we performed in Russia, and then did two tours in Germany.[334]

YT: So, your friendship with Zagorinsky started in 1995. Do you continue your relationship now?

NK: Yes, he is one of not many who visit me once in a while. Don't read into it – I have many people who are willing to come to my house.

YT: I know that. So, Zagorinsky is your close friend.

NK: Yes, he and his wife Tatyana are our good friends. Zagorinsky is also playing and recording my music quite intensively. He just finished recording my Concerto for Cello No. 2 (Op. 103).

Hideaki Takaoki

One of the new friends that appeared in Kapustin's life in the 1990s was Hideaki Takaoki. The friendship with Takaoki was one of the first steps Kapustin made, which later led to his popularity in the East, particularly in Japan.

Hideaki Takaoki was not a professional musician. His interests were in the area of Television production. However, being a producer and one of the leaders of the Mainichi Broadcasting System,[335] he became one of the biggest supporters of the music of Nikolai Kapustin.

YT: How did your friendship with Takaoki begin?

NK: I remember at some point Hideaki Takaoki used to visit Moscow quite often. As one of the leaders of Osaka Television he probably had many things to do in Moscow.

YT: Did he come to your house?

NK: Yes, same as with you – he found me somehow. Hideaki suggested an idea to compose the paraphrases. That's how I wrote my Paraphrase on »Aquarela do Brazil«, Op. 118, »Blue Bossa«, Op. 123, and »Manteca«, Op. 129.

YT: Really? What a neat idea! I love those pieces so much!

NK: Me too.

---

[334] Note by the author: The conversation about Germany tours and other performances of Kapustin with Zagorinsky will be presented in the latter part of the Chapter VI.
[335] MBS. Accessed December 24, 2017. http://www.mbs.jp/english/.

YT: So, Hideaki Takaoki was also a jazz musician – since he knew Ary Barroso, Kenny Dorham, and Dizzy Gillespie's tunes.
NK: He is a musician in his soul, but not the professional. He can play a little cello and piano, but just for himself. I dedicated my Piano Sonata No. 12, Op. 102 to Takaoki.
YT: Did he visit you often?
NK: He came to our house many times. I remember once I even got acquainted with his wife – a very nice looking lady.
YT: You noticed that.
NK: It's a compliment to Hideaki.

Nikolai Kapustin and Hideaki Takaoki, near the Moscow Conservatory, 1990s

YT: I like very much the picture of you and Takaoki that you took in front of the Moscow Conservatory.
NK: That picture was made as a sign of respect and our Russian-Japanese friendship.
YT: Why did you decide to take it in front of the Moscow Conservatory? Did you have something to do in there?
NK: Oh no, we just thought it's a good idea to have a picture in front of the main musical institution of our country.
YT: That's true.

Beginning of Interest around the Figure of Kapustin/Back to the Life of Performing Artist

In the middle 1990s the world music community was developing an increasing interest in the music of Kapustin. Surprisingly, it didn't come from Russia but from Europe and Japan.

YT: Did you expect that your music, the music of a Russian-Ukrainian composer, would gain its popularity mostly from abroad?
NK: I had no idea that it was going to be that way. This was quite an unusual situation. Even now I am not that famous in Russia.
YT: What do you think was the reason for this phenomenon?
NK: It all happened because of the appearance of the internet, and particularly youtube, where you can upload audio and video recordings. My son Anton was helping me tremendously in this process. He posted many of my recordings, even from the earlier time, from 1960s and 1970s, when I played with Lundstrem and Karamyshev.
YT: I noticed that you have 388,555 views on the youtube for one of your videos – Impromptu No.2, Op. 66!!!
NK: That many?
YT: Yes.
NK: I recorded that video here in Moscow for the Japanese label »Triton«.

At the same time TV channels and newspapers in Russia became interested in the music of Nikolai Kapustin. In addition to that, some eminent Russian musicians, who were also Kapustin's friends, began to collaborate with the composer. Among them were Nikolai Petrov, Igor Boguslavsky, Alexander Korneev, and others.

This is one of the first articles about the music of Nikolai Kapustin, which appeared in the Moscow newspaper »The Morning of Russia« in June of 1995.

Article »Concert in Jazz Style«, Newspaper »The Morning of Russia«, Essue No. 23, June 8-14, 1995

YT: *You are so lucky that this newspaper is preserved at your home archive. Who wrote this article?*
NK: *This was my friend from the conservatory period – Manashir Yakubov. We all lived together in the dormitory of the Moscow Conservatory, so we have some memories to share.*
YT: *I see that some of your friends from the conservatory time still continued being in contact with you through the years. I remember one of your friends from the same period, Valery Erokhin, was working in the Moscow Publishing House »Muzgiz« and was helping to you to publish your works.*

NK: Yes, Valera (Valery Erokhin) also wrote introductory articles for two of my vinyl discs that I recorded in the 1980s.
YT: So, he was also a musical critic.
NK: Yes, he was.
YT: Do you agree with me that the articles like this that appeared in Russia in the 1990s, and the performances of your music by some eminent musicians like Nikolai Petrov, resonated in the Russian musical world?
NK: Of course, the performances of my music by Petrov was an important step for the promotion of my music in Russia, but I guess it was not enough.
YT: What are we missing then?
NK: The environment. It was not the best time for my music to appear I think.
YT: Musically?
NK: Politically.
YT: Oh, you are right - our country was going through big political changes. It was a time of economic crisis, when people were losing their jobs and just trying to survive, so the interest in cultural life was diminished. In other words, it was not the right time for your music to appear.
NK: Plus, I was composing foreign music for the Russian audience - jazz oriented.
YT: Interesting thing, when the same exact scenario happened abroad at the beginning of 2000s, when two eminent performers, Steven Osborne and Marc-André Hamelin, began to play your music, the result was just the opposite. That began the explosion of your popularity in the world.
NK (smiling): Maybe it's because this time it was two of them?
YT: I am serious.
NK: I think the figure of Petrov was not that significant as the figure of Hamelin or Osborne on the world scale.
YT: Oh, do you mean that Petrov was a well-known performer in Russia but not as much as in Europe and the United States?
NK: That's what I think. On the other side, Hamelin and Osborne both were well-known and celebrated pianists abroad. That's why it happened.
YT: Yes, Osborne and Hamelin made an important impact in the promotion of your music abroad. Plus, I think it was the right time at the right place for your music to appear – time when the classical pianists started to be interested in playing jazz.
NK: That could be.

In 1995, after a break of more then ten years, Kapustin decided to return to the concert stage and do live performances.

YT: How did it happen that you changed your mind?

NK: After I left the Orchestra of Cinematography I felt I had enough performing; it was not pleasant anymore.
YT: But then ten years later...
NK: Then, ten years later, I realized that I needed it back.

Kapustin's first live performance after 1980 happened on December 30, 1995 in the Beethoven Concert Hall of the Bolshoi Theatre. Kapustin participated in the premiere of his own work *Piece for Sextet*, Op. 79.

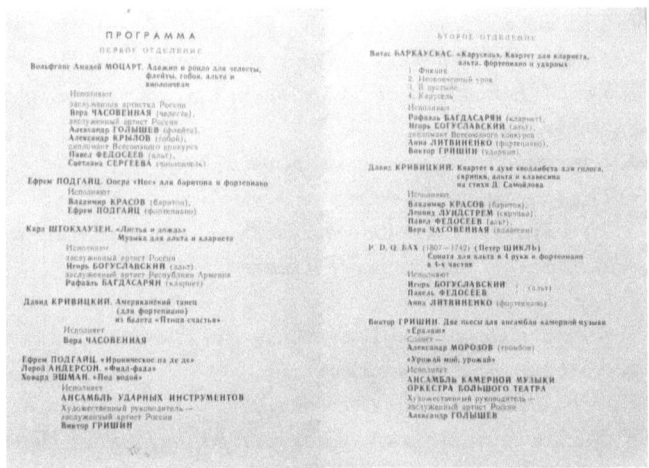

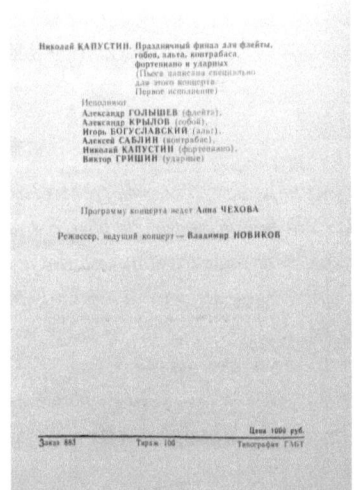

Program notes: New Year Concert, Beethoven Concert Hall, Bolshoi Theatre, Moscow, December 30, 1995

YT: *When was the last time you performed live as a soloist before that concert in 1995?*
NK: *It was in 1980 when I played my Piano Concerto No. 2, Op. 14.*
YT: *These two performances were fifteen years apart! That's a huge break.*
NK: *It felt long to me too.*
YT: *Did you feel comfortable performing on stage after such a long break?*
NK: *It felt different. I used to record my music in the studio during all those years, also I played my pieces for the Ministry of Culture, so I had the technique in my fingers, but this time the situation was quite different.*
YT: *What was so different?*
NK: *Here there was an audience. You know what it means.*
YT: *Yes, I do know. Was it your idea to come back to public performance or did somebody push you towards that?*
NK: *It was violist Igor Boguslavsky who pushed me.*
YT: *This name does sound familiar to me.*
NK: *He is a very well-known Russian violist. By the way, he was a student of the great Vadim Borisovsky.*[336] *Do you know this name?*
YT: *I am sorry…*
NK: *I remember at some point Boguslavsky was even a part of the jury committee for the Tchaikovsky International Competition.*
YT: *So, Boguslavsky asked you to perform together.*
NK: *No, he asked me to compose the piece and to perform it together. He commissioned me to write this piece for the New Year celebration, and gave me very little time to work on it. I was composing it in such a big hurry. I don't like doing that at all.*
YT: *Did Boguslavsky ask you to compose the piece for this particular setting – sextet, correct?*
NK: *Yes, it was his idea.*
YT: *What was the instrumentation of this piece?*
NK: *The piece was written for flute, oboe, viola, double bass, piano, and drums.*
YT: *Since you had so little time to compose the piece, did you have time to rehearse?*
NK: *Yes, that was another question that I was worried about. The good thing is that all the musicians of the sextet, except me, worked together in the Bolshoi Theatre. They knew each other very well and played together for many years.*
YT: *Oh, that means a lot! But still, did you rehearse?*
NK: *Yes, we rehearsed a couple of times. All the musicians were highly professional, so we didn't need to rehearse a lot. It was pleasant to work with them.*
YT: *Did you know those musicians?*

---

[336] Vadim Borisovsky. Accessed December 17, 2017. https://humanities.byu.edu/vadim-borisovsky-and-the-founding-of-the-russian-viola-school/, http://www.mosconsv.ru/ru/disk.aspx?id=22131.

NK: *Of course I did. I feel I knew Boguslavsky for a hundred years.*
YT: *How did the performance go?*
NK: *Surprisingly, it went very well. I remember Alla attended this concert and really enjoyed it.*
YT: *I noticed that on the program this piece is presented as a »Celebratory Finale«, Op. 79.*
NK: *Yes, we performed it right at the end of the concert, it was a finale.*
YT: *And »Celebratory« because of the New Year, correct?*
NK: *Yes.*
YT: *I think only the best pieces are usually scheduled at the very end of the program.*
NK: *I agree, we were the most important performance of the evening, plus it was a premier.*
YT: *This piece has a lucky story – you composed and premiered it the same year, in 1995.*
NK: *Yes, and it was a successful premier.*
YT: *Am I right to say that after this concert you started to have a very active performance life?*
NK: *Yes, December of 1995 was a new beginning of my performing career.*
YT: *Did you perform chamber music only or solo pieces as well?*
NK: *Mostly it was chamber music. You see, at that point I started to collaborate with different musicians, so I was involved in the ensemble performances. Plus, I started to feel that I enjoyed performing more with the other musicians rather than just by myself. It keeps you company.*
YT: *Yes, it's more fun.*
NK: *Exactly.*

On March, 9 1997 Kapustin participated in the Concert of Moscow Philharmonic Seasons, which took place at the Small Hall of the Moscow Conservatory. At that concert Kapustin and Zagorinsky performed the premier of *Cello Sonata No. 1*, Op. 63.

YT: *What do you remember about that premier?*
NK: *This was the beginning of my collaboration with Zagorinsky. I remember we rehearsed a lot before that and I was glad that the premier went very well.*
YT: *The public enjoyed listening to your music?*
NK: *Oh, yes.*
YT: *What was the rest of the program for this concert?*
NK: *I remember there was another pianist at this concert, her name was Marina Evseeva. She performed works by Prokofiev and Rachmaninov with Zagorinsky. They also performed the work written by her father, who was also a composer – Sergei Evseev.*

The concert dedicated to Kapustin's 60th Birthday happened on October 29, 1997 at the »Mirror Hall« of the State Institute of Art Studies in Moscow. The program was centered around chamber music. This time Kapustin invited only one person to participate in his Birthday concert – his friend, cellist Alexander Zaroginsky.

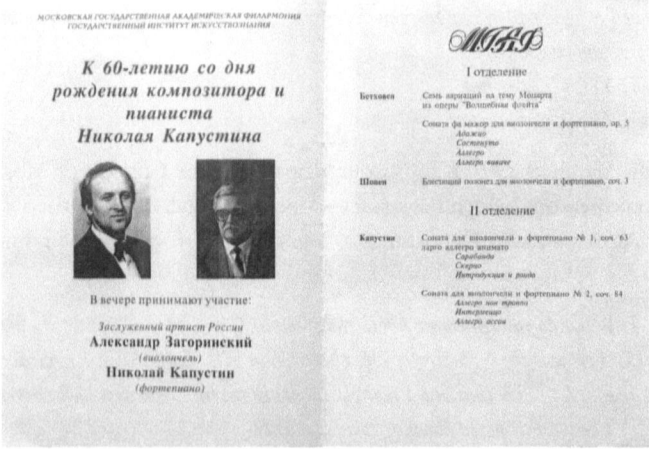

Program notes: Concert dedicated to Kapustin's 60th Birthday, Moscow, October 29, 1997

YT: *I see that the program is entirely dedicated to chamber music.*
NK: *Yes, our program was for cello and piano.*
YT: *Can you tell a little about the pieces that you performed that day?*

NK: In the first part of the concert we played Beethoven's »Seven Variations on Mozart's Magic Flute« (Theme and Seven Variations on »Bei Mannern« from Mozart's The Magic Flute, WoO 46), Beethoven's Cello Sonata No. 1 in F major (Op. 5), and we finished the first part of the concert with Chopin's »Polonaise Brilliante in C major« for Cello and Piano (Op. 3). In the second part of the concert we played two of my sonatas for cello – Cello Sonata No. 1, Op. 63 and Cello Sonata No. 2, Op. 84.

YT: That's an extensive program! How long did it take you to prepare this program?

NK: Quite long, maybe a year or so. At that time we already knew that we were going to do a tour in Germany in 1998, so it was partially in preparation for Germany.

YT: One more thing I wanted to ask you – did you happen to have a Birthday concert for your 50th Birthday in 1987?

NK: I don't think. I remember I just received the telegram from the »Moscow Union of Composers« signed by Khrennikov and that was it. You know, in the middle 1980s I didn't feel the need to perform live because I recorded a lot.

YT: And starting from your 60th Birthday you started to perform your music publicly and at the same time other musicians started to play your music.

NK: Yes, my 70th birthday was celebrated with an extensive concert.

YT: And your 80th birthday…

NK: Let's not talk about what's happening now with my 80th birthday.[337] It's too much…

---

[337] Note by the author: There are many musicians who dedicate their performances in honor of Kapustin's 80th Birthday. The conversation about Kapustin's 80th Birthday will be presented in Chapter VII.

Life Complications: Worries about Alla

A difficult period started in Kapustin's life in the autumn of 1997. His wife, Alla Kapustina, was getting ready to leave Russia for three months for surgery in the United States.

YT: Have you ever been apart from Alla before the autumn of 1997?
NK: No, that was the first time.
AK (joining the conversation): I remember right around that time we finished all the documents for Kolia's pension. I knew that without me it would be difficult for him to do all those things. After it was done I flew to the United States. Believe it or not, it was on his birthday, November 22. This November (2017) it will be twenty years ago.
NK: The time goes so fast.
YT: How did Nikolai Grigorievich live without you all this time?
AK: I asked my sister, Aza, to come from Novokuznetsk to be with Kolia.
YT: And your sister agreed to come?
AK: Of course she agreed. As you know, Kolia has a complex character, but they got along very well.
YT: Because she was your sister!

Aza Pirojkova, Moscow, February 1998

AK: They had a calendar where they marked how many days left until my return, every day for those three months. At that time Pavel, our younger son, still lived with us, he studied at the university, so it was three of them, no four – our cat Boba was still alive too.
YT: Did you write letters to each other?
NK: We had a few phone conversations.
YT: Just a few? I guess you missed each other terribly.
AK: Kolia was deeply involved into composition, plus Aza tried to entertain him. I think she did well.
YT: Where did you stay in the United States?
AK: I stayed with our older son, Anton. He has lived in the United States since 1991.
YT: Did you enjoy staying in the United States?
AK: I have very pleasant memories from that time, with the exception of my worries about the surgery.
YT: How did your surgery go?
AK: It went well.
YT: When did you come back?
AK: I came back on February 23, 1998.
YT: The Military Day?
AK: Yes, as a present to Kolia.[338] I remember they all came to the airport to meet me – Kolia, Aza, and Pasha. Kolia brought flowers for me.
YT: Flowers is your leitmotif of love.
AK: I came back to Russia on February 23rd and the next day went to my work.
YT: That fast? How about overcoming the time difference between Russia and the United States?
AK: I had to go to work.

---

[338] Note by the author: The Military Day in Russia has a special meaning, where all the men are celebrated, those who were a part of the army and those who weren't. It's a celebration of their power.

First Tour in Germany/ Collaboration with Alexander Korneev

At the end of October 1998, Nikolai Kapustin and Alexander Zagorinsky began a new path in their performing career as they travelled to Germany to perform.

YT: *Did you go to Germany with Zagorinsky together or separately?*
NK: *Of course we went together.*
YT: *Did you fly to Germany?*
NK: *No, we travelled by train.*
YT: *It probably took you a very long to get there.*
NK: *Yes, at that time there was no fast speed trains, so it took us around two days to get there, but I always enjoyed traveling on a train…with all those short stops in unknown small cities, or in big ones. It's interesting to observe people and to see how they live.*
YT: *That's true. You probably travelled through many countries to get to Germany.*
NK: *Not that many, it was Belarus, Ukraine, Poland and then Germany. I think that was it. At that time our relationship with Poland and Ukraine was very good, not like now.*
YT: *What was the city of your destination in Germany?*
NK: *We travelled to Hannover, that's where our first performance was. Our tour was organized by the Russian pianist, who lived in Germany for many years. Her name is Natasha Konsistorum. She became a very good friend of our family. I even remember staying at her house with Zagorinsky.*
YT: *That was so nice of her.*

Nikolai Kapustin in the house of Natasha Konsistorum, Hannover, October 1998

NK: We have a very close birthday with her – my birthday on November 22nd, and hers on November 25th.

YT: Do you call each other to congratulate with the birthday?

NK: Believe it or not – every year.

YT: Was Konsistorum also from Moscow?

NK: Yes, she was born in Moscow; I think she graduated from Gnessin Institute. I remember before our first tour to Germany we visited her once in Moscow and she listened to our performance.

YT: Do you mean listened to you – judging your performance?

NK: Yes.

YT: What was the verdict?

NK (smiling): I guess it was ok. We met her approval and started to get ready for the Germany trip.

Nikolai Kapustin and Natasha Konsistorum, Hannover, November 1998

YT: *Did you rehearse a lot before the tour in Germany?*
NK: *Yes, it was very intense. We knew that this tour may lead to our future collaborations and they actually happened.*
YT: *Where did you rehearse?*
NK: *At my house of course.*

The first performance of Kapustin and Zagorinsky in Germany was on November 1, 1998 in Hannover.

YT: *What was your program for this concert?*
NK: *We decided to repeat the same program as from my Jubilee concert.*
YT: *It's a genius idea. You are right – why not repeat the successful performance?*
NK: *Not only that. It takes time to learn the new program.*

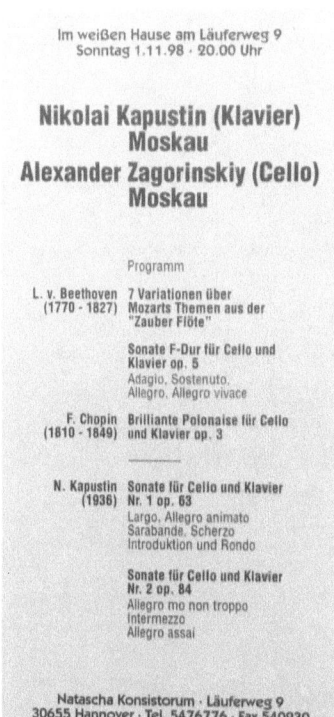

Program notes: Concert of Kapustin and Zagorinsky, Hannover, November 1, 1998

YT: *So, you played works by Beethoven, Chopin, and two of your sonatas for cello and piano (Cello Sonata No. 1, Op. 63 and Cello Sonata No. 2, Op. 84).*
NK: *Yes, that »Polonaise Brilliante« (Op. 3) of Chopin is quite an interesting work, difficult to play... with all those Liszt tricks. Chopin composed this polonaise when he was very young; I think something like nineteen years old.*
YT: *What kind of Liszt tricks?*
NK: *All his difficult technical passages and so on.*
YT: *Is the cello part in this piece as difficult as the piano part?*
NK: *I am not sure, but I think the cello part is easier.*
YT: *How about your two cello sonatas – are they difficult works?*
NK: *Yes, not as much as my solo piano works, but still, there are some places to work on.*

Luckily, this concert of Kapustin and Zagorinsky on November 1, 1998 in Hannover was recorded. Later, in 2008, this performance appeared on the CD.[339]

---

[339] See page 321.

YT: *Did you plan ahead of time for this performance to appear on the CD?*
NK: *Of course not. We just decided to record it for ourselves, but it ended up as a very good quality recording, and we also played well.*
YT: *I think this CD is also unique because you are playing Beethoven and Chopin works. It may be the only recording of you playing these two composers.*
NK: *Yes, we played two Beethoven pieces on that concert – Seven Variations on the Theme from the opera »Magic Flute« by Mozart for Cello and Piano (WoO 46) and Cello Sonata in F major (Op. 5, No. 1). Unfortunately, because of the size of sonata we were not able to put it on the CD, it was too long.*
YT: *Do you still have the recording of it?*
NK: *I am pretty sure that Sasha (Alexander Zagorinsky) has it somewhere.*
YT: *It is fortunate that you have the recording of Chopin's Polonaise on that CD!*
NK: *Actually, you may not know, but there are two Chopin's pieces on that CD – Polonaise (Polonaise Brilliante for Cello and Piano, Op. 3) and Nocturne in Eb major (Op. 9 No. 2, transcription by Pablo de Sarasate).*
YT: *Why was this piece not listed in the program?*
NK: *We performed it as an encore piece.*
YT: *Didn't you play your »Day-Break« Op. 26 as an encore piece on that concert?*
NK: *Yes, we did.*
YT: *So you had two encore pieces?*
NK: *Yes.*
YT: *At the end of each part?*
NK: *Of course not. We played it at the end of the concert, as it was supposed to be. Originally, we planned to play Chopin's »Nocturne« as an encore piece, but after we performed it the audience wanted us to play something else.*
YT: *A second encore?*
NK: *Yes, and we were not ready for that.*
YT: *Did you play your »Day-Break« (Op. 26) by yourself?*
NK: *We needed to finish the concert playing something together with Zagorinsky.*
YT: *But »Day-Break" is a solo piano piece. Did you compose a new version of this piece especially for the Germany tour?*
NK: *I didn't compose any version; we just talked a little about it and then played.*
YT: *Wait a minute, so you didn't do any markings in the score, just talked through it?*
NK: *Yes. I explained to him what I had in mind, we didn't have much time to talk seriously about it – you know how the encores go. Believe me, there was nothing difficult about that piece.*
YT: *So, you talked right before going on stage?*
NK: *Yes, right before the performance.*
YT: *Really? So, was it a surprise for Zagorinsky?*

NK: Probably…but just a little.

YT: Is Zagorinsky a jazz musician?

NK (smiling): He is now.

YT: How did Zagorinsky, being a classically trained musician, agree to do that?

NK: He didn't have a choice; it should be done that way, I knew it.

YT: So you turned Zagorinsky into jazz music and the idea of improvisation on stage.

NK: Yes, I did. That was actually fun to play.

YT: Did you play any other pieces that way – making changes during the actual performance or just a little while before it?

NK: I don't think. It was the only case.

YT: The fact that you played two encore pieces means that the audience loved you in Germany.

NK; Yes, we had successful performances.

YT: I don't think I remember many concerts that I attended where there two encore pieces.

NK: No, this happens quite often, sometimes people play much more than two encores.

YT: But still it's sign of the highest respect from the audience.

NK: That's true.

YT: How long was your trip to Germany in November of 1998?

NK: Something about two weeks I think.

YT: Were you satisfied with your concerts in Germany?

NK: Why did you ask? Of course I was.

After Kapustin's return from Germany his life continued at a high level of intensity. One of the important performances of the late 1990s happened on April 21, 1999 when Nikolai Kapustin collaborated with Alexander Zagorinsky and Alexander Korneev.[340] The trio Korneev-Kapustin-Zagorinsky performed the premier of Kapustin's newly composed piece, *Trio for Flute, Cello, and Piano*, Op. 86.

---

[340] Moscow Conservatory: Alexander Korneev. Accessed December 7, 2017. http://www.mosconsv.ru/ru/person.aspx?id=8766.

Alexander Korneev

Alexander Vasilievich Korneev (1930-2010) was an eminent Soviet Russian flutist and renowned teacher. Korneev won numerous national and international musical competitions. Among them were competitions in Budapest (Hungary, 1949), Berlin (Germany, 1951), Prague (Czech Republic, 1953), and Geneva (Switzerland, 1958). He was very active as a touring artist, performing in Russia, Spain, England, Netherlands, Japan, South Korea, USA, and many other countries. From the middle 1950s he taught at the Moscow Musical College, Moscow Conservatory, Gnessin College, and State Musical Pedagogical Institute named after M.M. Ippolitov-Ivanov.[341]

> YT: I read that Korneev premiered *Shostakovich, Prokofiev, and Khachaturian works.* Also many composers dedicated their works to him.[342]
> NK: Yes, I knew that.
> YT: He also performed with Richter, Gilels, and Nikolaeva...
> NK: And Oborin, and Oistrakh. He was one of them.

---

[341] Internet Resource »My Flute.RU: Alexander Korneev«. Accessed December 7, 2017. http://www.myflute.ru/library/teacher/k/k_177.html.
[342] Ibid.

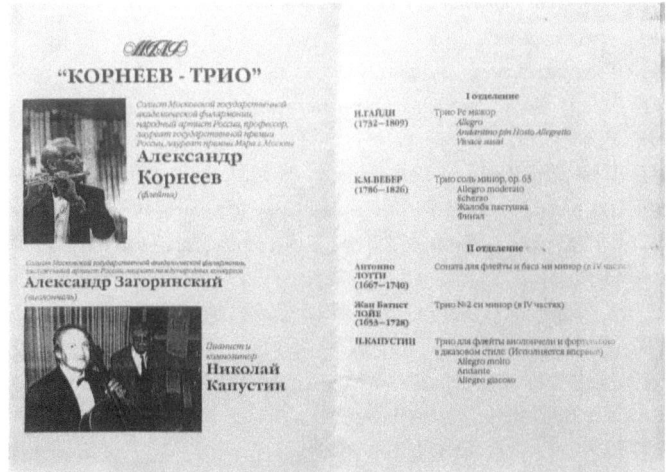

Program notes: Concert of Korneev, Zagorinsky, and Kapustin, Moscow, April 21, 1999

YT: *So, you composed »Flute Trio« (Op. 86) knowing that you are going to perform it?*
NK: *Yes, I wrote that trio very quickly having Korneev and Zagorinsky in mind.*
YT: *How did you get acquainted with Alexander Korneev?*
NK: *I knew him from the time when I studied at the musical college, although, he was much older than me and Zagorinsky.*
YT: *So, you knew each other for a long time.*
NK: *I knew him for a long time but became a friend only at the time when we decided to collaborate together.*

YT: He was one of the famous musicians in Moscow.

NK: Yes, he was well known inside and outside of Moscow musical circles. Korneev won many competitions in Russia and abroad, he was very active as a performer. I remember he was also a well-known pedagogue. He taught at the Moscow Conservatory.

YT: How did he find you after all these years? Or did you find him?

NK: I remember he called in the late 1990s and invited me to participate in one of his performances. He also said that it would be great if we could have something else for that concert.

YT: Was he hinting the idea for you to compose a piece for the concert?

NK: Exactly, and I understood that immediately and began working on a new piece.

YT: And that's how »Flute Trio« Op. 86 came to life?

NK: Pretty much. I knew that Korneev and Zagorinsky were going to play it.

YT: I noticed that you have many pieces that you composed for some specific reason – either some of your friends gave you an idea to compose something, or your reaction to some of the things that happened to you. Is that true that something is always pushing you towards the composition?

NK: There are some pieces like that but not many.

YT: But Op. 86 was one of those »not many«.

NK: Yes.

YT: What did you play on that concert of April 21, 1999?

NK: The program of that concert was quite long. We played Haydn Flute Trio in D major, Weber Trio in G major (Op. 63), then on the second half – Antonio Lotti Sonata for Flute and Basso Continuo in E minor, Jean-Baptiste Loeillet Trio in B minor, and we finished the program with my »Flute Trio« (Op. 86).

YT: So, it was a premier of your trio.

NK: Yes, it was. A little while after we played this piece it became very popular among musicians abroad, and even now many people are playing this work.

YT: How about Russian musicians?

NK: In Russia everything always happens very slowly. Although, I do remember one interesting episode from that concert that proves just the opposite. One lady came to me during intermission and asked to give her the score of my Op. 86. She wanted to copy the score during those fifteen minutes.

YT: What??? Of course you didn't give it to her.

NK (laughing): Of course I did. The funny part was that we played this »Flute Trio« (Op. 86) in the second part of the concert. That was the only piece.

YT: So, she took the score right before your actual performance.

NK: Correct.

YT: What if she wouldn't be back in time or wouldn't bring the score back at all? Did you know this lady?

NK: I had no idea who she was.

YT: I can't believe you did it.

NK: You don't like to live your life dangerously, Yana? I have to tell you – there is some excitement in that.

YT: Did she come back?

NK: Yes, she was perfectly in time.

YT: How did the performance of the trio go?

NK: It was a very successful premier. I was absolutely happy about that.

YT: Did you perform with Korneev and Zagrinsky as a trio somewhere else?

NK: That was the only time we played together with Korneev. Unfortunately, not long after our performance he passed away.

YT: So it was the only collaboration of you and Korneev.

NK: This was the only concert that we played together, but he also recorded this »Flute Trio« Op. 86 on one of my CDs in the late 1990s. I think he also played my »Divertissement for Two Flutes, Cello, and Piano« (Op. 91) on that chamber recording.

YT: This »Flute Trio« Op. 86 has a lucky story – it was composed in 1998 and premiered and recorded right away in 1999.

NK: Yes, that happens sometimes to my works.

YT: So, at the end you became good friends with Korneev.

NK: Yes, very good friends. I remember he was visiting me with Sasha Zagorinsky, and we were sitting in my kitchen, all three of us, discussing our future plans… very good memories.

A Second Trip to Germany

In July 1999 Kapustin took his second trip to Germany. This time he travelled to Europe not only with his friend Alexander Zagorinsky but also with his wife Alla.

YT: *Did you plan that your second tour to Germany would happen so quickly – just a little more than a half a year after your first visit?*
NK: *We didn't. I guess it happened because they liked us the first time and decided not to wait too long and simply invited us the second time.*
YT: *Did you perform a lot during that second trip to Germany?*
NK: *It was also quite an intense time.*
YT: *What did you play during your second tour in Germany?*
NK: *For me the program was the same – I played two of my sonatas for cello and piano. Zagorinsky played also »Bach Suite in G major for Solo Cello«, and together with Natasha Konsistorum they played Brahms »Sonata in E minor«, Op. 38. That was our program.*

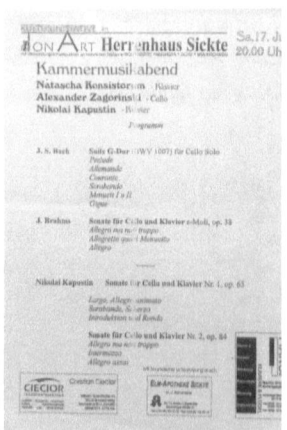

Program notes: Concert of Nikolai Kapustin, Alexander Zagorinsky, and Natasha Konsistorum, Germany, July 17, 1999

YT: *So, you played a little less during that second trip.*
NK: *Yes, it was easier than the first time, but I still played two of my cello sonatas.*
YT: *And you can't relax playing the music of Nikolai Kapustin.*
NK: *Even if I am playing my own music.*
YT: *So, even for you, your music is difficult to play?*

NK: Of course! Do you think that right after I write my last note that I am going to play by memory in the final tempo?

YT: Not that?

NK: Absolutely not. After I finish composing the piece, I also need to learn it, as well as you or anybody else. It may take me a little less time, because I already know the music, but still... it's hard work.

YT: Then why do you compose such difficult music?

NK: Because that's how I hear it, and being difficult doesn't mean bad, it just needs more work.

YT: Alright, back to that concert. So, this time you had a chance to listen to Natasha Konsistorum's playing.

NK: Yes, she played Brahms with Zagorinsky.

YT: What was your impression?

NK: She loves to play the composers I am not a fan of – Medtner and Brahms. In other words, she is playing very well, but her repertoire is confusing.

Coincidently, during the same time in July 1999, Kapustin's son Anton was attending a conference for mathematicians in Potsdam. It was very pleasant news for Nikolai and Alla that they were able to meet Anton in Potsdam and spend some time together.

Nikolai Kapustin and Anton Kapustin, Potsdam, July 1999

YT: If I would ask you – which trip you enjoyed the most, the first or the second one, what would be your answer?

NK: Second one was more fun, because I travelled not just by myself but with Alla, plus we were able to meet with Anton.
YT: I agree – having your family during the tour is a big deal!

Nikolai Kapustin and Alla Kapustina, Potsdam, July 1999

NK: Actually, Alla didn't just accompany me – she was the part of our performances.
YT: Really? What do you mean?
NK: She turned pages for me.
YT: I didn't know that Alla Semionovna...
AK (joining the conversation): Yes, you are right – I've never played a note in my life on any instrument.
YT: Then how did you turn the pages for Nikolai Grigorievich?
AK: Kolia nodded to me at the moment when I needed to turn the page.
YT: Oh no!!! It was probably a huge stress for you just waiting for that sign and not knowing where you are at the piece.
AK: Not really, it was fine.
NK: For me it was not a big deal if she would turn the page in the wrong place – I knew the whole program by memory.
YT: Did this happen?
NK (smiling): Maybe just a couple of times.
AK: I was going on stage like a real artist and turned the pages for Kolia like I knew everything.
NK: And nobody even suspected any trick behind that.
YT: I can say from my own experience – it's a big deal to turn pages for someone.
NK: I agree.

YT: And if in addition to that you don't know what you are doing – I bet I would have a heart attack.

NK: Knowing you – you probably would have.

YT: So, you chose Alla Semionovna to turn the pages for you rather than anybody else?

NK: I would rather see my wife turning pages for me than some unknown stranger.

YT: What a story! Now I see that the second trip to Germany had a little bit of adventure in it. I keep forgetting to ask you – did you have a chance to see the country during those two trips to Germany?

NK: Yes, we did. As you know, some of the tours are organized in such a way that you don't have time for anything except the performance itself, but this was not our case. We had enough time to go to some historical places and to see the country.

YT: Did you like it?

NK: I can't say that I was huge fan of those excursions. If we wouldn't go it wouldn't be a big loss for me, but overall it was nice.

YT: What are you interested in when you travel to the different places?

NK: I am probably more interested in seeing people, how they live, who they are, something like that.

Compositions of 1984-1999 (Ops. 40-99)

The creativity of Kapustin as a composer during the period of 1980s-1990s was set at an incredibly high level. This was his most productive time to date.

YT: *I noticed that during the 1980s you composed twenty-six pieces but during the 1990s the number increased to forty-four pieces! It's almost doubled.*
NK: *This sounds strange to me — forty-four is a big number.*
YT: *Do you think that it may have happened because of the stressful and very tense situation within the country of that time? Was it in a way like a response to the suffering and pain, the way of recovery through the music?*
NK: *I don't think that was my case. My creativity is connected only to me, but not the things that are happening outside my life.*

Looking at Kapustin's output of 1984-1999 it may be noted that in spite of the fact that Kapustin continued writing orchestral works, such as *Sinfonietta for Orchestra*, Op. 48, *Overture for Big Band*, Op. 51, or *Intrada, Piece for Big Band*, Op. 52, the main direction in his writing had switched to solo piano and chamber music. The works for piano included Piano Sonatas (Nos. 2-10), Piano Concertos (Nos. 3-6), *Twenty-Four Preludes and Fugues* (Op. 82), etudes (Ops. 40, 67, and 68), variations (Ops. 41 and 80), and numerous characterpieces. The chamber works included two cello sonatas (Ops. 63 and 84), *Trio for Flute, Cello, and Piano* (Op. 86), *String Quartet No. 1* (Op. 88), *Piano Quintet* (Op. 89), *Piece for Sextet* (Op. 79), *Sonata for Viola and Piano* (Op. 69), and *Sonata for Violin and Piano* (Op. 70). During this time Kapustin also wrote concertos that featured different instruments, for example *Concerto for Alto-Saxophone and Orchestra* (Op. 49), *Concerto for Double-Bass and Symphonic Orchestra* (Op. 76), *Concerto No.1 for Cello and Orchestra* (Op. 85), and *Concerto for Eleven Instruments* (Op. 90).

The major solo piano compositions of that period helped Kapustin gain international popularity. Those pieces were *Eight Concert Etudes*, Op. 40, *Variations for Piano*, Op. 41, *Twenty-Four Preludes*, Op. 53, *Piano Sonata No. 2*, Op. 54, and *Twenty-Four Preludes and Fugues*, Op. 82.

The set of *Eight Concert Etudes*, Op. 40 was composed in 1984. This was the very first work entirely composed by Kapustin after he resigned from his official work at the Orchestra of Cinematography. The etudes represent a continuation of Chopin's concept of the etude genre. They are not just pieces aimed at developing great technique, but also, like a characterpiece, have meaningful characteristics inside of the musical work. Kapustin recorded this set of etudes on his first vinyl disc »Nikolai Kapustin«, which undoubtedly helped promote his music.[343]

> YT: *I think this is a very unique situation – when you not only compose the music but also record your works.*
> NK: *I love doing both of those things, although I do not equally like all my recordings – some of them are good and some not so much.*
> YT: *Do you like how you recorded Op. 40?*
> NK: *That one was good.*
> YT: *Can I ask you about this set of your etudes Op. 40?*
> NK: *Why do you want to talk about them?*
> YT: *These etudes are extremely popular now.*
> NK: *Yes, everybody is playing these etudes now. I don't know if this is a good or bad thing.*
> YT: *I think that's a great thing.*
> NK: *Sometimes it's very painful to see how some untrained pianists are trying to play my works.*
> YT: *I agree with that. For these etudes you write the tonalities right with the name of the etude.*
> NK: *I needed to do that.*
> YT: *It is very interesting that the tonalities of your etudes are based on descending or ascending thirds – C, Ab, E, with only one perfect interval (E to B).*
> NK: *Yes, and generally it's major keys; only two are written in a minor keys.*
> YT: *I remember Beethoven also liked to put his tonalities in thirds, for example in his set of »Bagatelles« Op. 126. Did you plan to do it that way or did it just happen accidently?*
> NK: *Of course I planned it.*
> YT: *Another interesting thing that I noticed was that in Beethoven's Op. 126 the descending tonalities of first four bagatelles form the augmented triad (G-Eb-B) as well as your three etudes (C-Ab-E).*
> NK: *Hmmm... well, I didn't plan that. I do admire Beethoven though. Although, the way my music goes I would see probably more connection to the Russian music, particularly to the music of Sergei Rachmaninov.*
> YT: *This is interesting.*
> NK: *Yes, just play the chord progression itself and you will see where this music is rooted.*

---

[343] See page 313.

Looking more directly at this set of eight etudes, it is important to mention one unusual feature – the characteristic of the cyclic work, as it was pointed out in the introductory article to Kapustin's vinyl disc by Valery Erokhin,

> In the »Eight Concert Etudes«, that contrasted each other in mood and texture, a logically built cyclic concept was also presented. We may indicate the thoughtfulness of the tonal plan of the whole set. In addition, Etudes No. 4 and No.5, as well as No. 7 and No. 8 should be performed without break. In these etudes Kapustin uses various musical-dramatic and compositional tools, for example – the material of the second theme of the Etude No. 8 ties with the material of the middle section of the Etude No. 2.[344]

YT: *I think it is very unique to have cyclic characteristics in the set of etudes.*
NK: *Yes, it's there.*
YT: *What form do you use for those etudes?*
NK: *There are many different compositional decisions concerning the form presented in those etudes, for example etude No. 5 is like a 12-bar blues and etude No. 8 is written in the sonata form.*
YT: *This all sounds very usual and unique to me.*
NK: *I just didn't want to be standard in my approach to form in this set of etudes.*

The piece *Variations for the Piano*, Op. 41 was written the same year as the famous *Eight Concert Etudes*, Op. 40, in 1984, and recorded by Kapustin in his vinyl disc called »Nikolai Kapustin: Jazz Pieces for Piano« in the late 1980s.[345]

YT: *This is a very effective piece. Once you start listening, you can't think about anything else except living through your music. It captivates your attention so strongly.*
NK: *Thank you. That was my intention.*
YT: *Is this the first time you looked at the genre of variations?*
NK: *It was the second time – in the 1960s I wrote »Variations for Piano and Orchestra«, Op. 3.*
YT: *Oh yes, Op. 3 was written in 1962. So, twenty-two years later you are coming back writing variations.*
NK: *Yes, but this time not for the piano and big-band, but just for the solo piano.*
YT: *I just keep thinking – in these »Variations« Op. 41 there are no breaks between variations, although I see the key and the mood changes, and it's not difficult to identify the beginning of the new variation.*
NK: *I think it's ok to be different.*

---

[344] Valery Erokhin, vinyl disc jacket, »Nikolai Kapustin«, Melodiya, 1986.
[345] See page 314.

YT: *Did any other composers write variations with no breaks in between or you are the first one?*
NK: *No, I am not the first one, it was done before.*
YT: *I remember we talked with you earlier about the theme of these variations itself and how some performers see it as a quote.*
NK: *I don't accept the fact that I used Stravinsky's theme from »The Rite of Spring«. I wasn't thinking about him at all while I was composing this piece.*
YT: *It just happened that both of you were looking into the motives that would be rooted in Russian musical culture.*
NK: *Of course, and for me the rhythmic organization of the music is one of the major characteristics of the particular piece. As you see, my rhythm has absolutely no connection to Stravinsky's theme.*
YT: *I agree.*

The *Twenty-Four Preludes*, Op. 53 were composed in 1988. Kapustin recorded this set of preludes on his last vinyl disc called »Twenty Four Preludes in Jazz Style« in 1989.[346]

YT: *It is quite interesting that the original name for this piece in Russian is »Twenty Four Preludes in Jazz Style« but not just the »Twenty Four Preludes« as it exists now.*
NK: *I guess at that time I wanted to point out the connection of my music to jazz, something new that will attract people's attention.*
YT: *Is there anything interesting that we don't yet know about this set of preludes Op. 53?*
NK: *I used the same tonal plan as Chopin in his Preludes Op. 28.*
YT: *Based on the circle of perfect 5ths with the relative key relationships (C-a-G-e)?*
NK: *Yes.*
YT: *Can we say that your preludes are also written in the romanic style or romantically inspired?*
NK: *No, not that. The only thing that relates to the Chopin preludes is the tonal relationships between the preludes.*
YT: *How about the length of the pieces? In Chopin's preludes all the pieces are relatively short.*
NK: *I think mine are longer, although, I do have some short ones too, but not all.*
YT: *It is so good that we can finally see the pieces that are still difficult but relatively short, something around three or four pages in length.*
NK: *I think there are a couple of preludes that are even just one page in length.*
YT: *That short?*

---

[346] See page 317.

NK: *Do you know why this happened?*

YT: *You were writing shorter pieces? I have no idea.*

NK: *Because I needed to put all twenty four preludes on one vinyl disc.*

YT: *Only because of that?*

NK: *That was a serious reason for me. I hope you understand what it means to record music on the vinyl disc. Remember, the timing for vinyl discs was a crucial thing, you needed to think about the length of the pieces that you intend to put on there in advance, otherwise it may be a big problem.*

YT: *And we don't have such a problem now with the CD, correct?*

NK: *Yes, the CD is completely different story.*

YT: *Another question I wanted to ask you concerning this work is about the size of the hand for the pianists who are willing to play this preludes.*

NK: *What about the size of the hand?*

YT: *When I look at some of your preludes, for example the Prelude No. 23 in F major, the stretching of the hands feels surprisingly large for me. I think in order to play this particular piece the pianist should be able to play the 10th without any difficulties in addition to pressing some notes inside of that 10th.*

NK: *Maybe.*

YT: *One of my students is now playing that prelude and I remember one of the chords in the left hand for that piece is Cb -Eb -A and Db, basically enharmonically the B9 chord. My student is doing very well, but his hands are much bigger than mine.*

NK: *You are right, my left hand stretching is better than in the right hand.*

YT: *And you composed your music for yourself being able to play it, correct?*

NK: *Of course.*

YT: *I don't think I can play this piece – no matter how I will stretch I will never be able to play those chords in the left hand. And you can't roll those chords because of the fast tempo. The only possible way for me to play it is, unfortunately, just to omit some of the notes in those chords, which means that your hands are bigger than normal hands.*

NK: *No, they are just normal.*

YT: *Then mine are small.*

NK: *The only thing that is different is that my left hand for some reason has a very good stretching ability. That's why I can play those »difficult« chords, as you say, that's all.*

In 1989 Kapustin composed his *Piano Sonata No. 2*, Op. 54, which is considered to be one of the major works that Kapustin wrote for the solo piano. Kapustin recorded this sonata in one of his CDs at the beginning of 1990s.[347]

---

[347] See page 318.

YT: It is very interesting that two of your major works for the solo piano were composed one right after another – Op. 53 and Op. 54.
NK: Maybe I just had that energy inside, so it would end up being enough for two pieces. For this sonata I even remember the opus number, usually I don't remember those things.
YT: Talking about opus numbers – I know that some composers, for example Debussy, didn't put the opus numbers in their music.
NK: But Shostakovich did.
YT: I remember you said that at the very beginning you didn't put the opus numbers but then decided to use them.
NK: Of course, it's more convenient.
YT: Talking about the numbers – some composers also put the measure numbers.
NK: I do that for my chamber music but not for the solo piano.
YT: Why not to use for the solo piano too?
NK: What for? You are the only person who is playing.
YT: What if I am a teacher and …
NK: I see where are you going. I didn't look that far.
YT: You don't see yourself as a teacher, do you?
NK: Not in my wildest dreams. It wouldn't work for both of us.
YT: Why do you think this Piano Sonata No. 2 became especially famous, and not Piano Sonata No. 3, Op. 55 for example?
NK: I think it's because of the two major pianists who performed it – Nikolai Petrov and Marc-Adre Hamelin, and probably more because of Hamelin.
YT: Why do you think so?
NK: For some reason the Russian premier of Piano Sonata No. 2 performed by Petrov didn't make as big a resonance as the Western premier played by Hamelin in London. My music is more popular in Europe, but not in Russia unfortunately.
YT: Do you see it as one of your most difficult works?
NK: Definitely one of the most difficult ones. Just the last movement itself »Perpetuum Mobile« is very difficult. It goes in a very fast tempo »Allegro Vivace« and the performer has no time to relax at all, the 16th notes go with no stop.
YT: I remember that movement – scarry to play, but fun to listen to.
NK: And this last movement is pretty long. I could potentially write it a little shorter, but no.
YT: So, both Petrov and Hamelin played this piece well.
NK: Yes, technically they are both amazing pianists.
YT: If we would compare the interpretation of Petrov and Hamelin of this sonata what would you say?
NK: It's very different – as day and night.

YT: *Really?*

NK: *Yes, in Petrov's interpretation of the last movement I don't hear that »perpetuum mobile" seed, not that steady in motion, and Hamelin is playing that last movement like a machine – perfect »perpetuum mobile«.*

YT: *So, Hamelin's interpretation was closer to what you had in mind for your piece.*

NK: *That last movement yes. The good thing about that movement is that there is no need to show the jazz inside because the music is more oriented on the technique and fast tempo.*

YT: *How about the other movements of that sonata? Was Petrov's interpretation closer to jazz?*

NK: *I don't know what to tell you. I can't say that Petrov was a jazz pianist.*

YT: *But he played jazz.*

NK: *Do you mean boogie-woogie? For me it's not jazz.*

YT: *In other words, both Petrov and Hamelin were interpreting your music from the classical side.*

NK: *Hamelin even recorded the whole CD of my music, which I really appreciated.*

The cycle *Twenty Four Preludes and Fugues*, Op. 82 was composed in 1997 and is considered by Kapustin to be one of his major works written to date. Kapustin also recorded this milestone work in the autumn of 2000.[348]

YT: *You composed this cycle in 1997, which is forty years since you wrote your first official work – Op. 1 »Concertino for Piano and Orchestra« in 1957.*

NK: *Yes, it took me a while to get ready for the work like that.*

YT: *So, by 1997 you felt that you could do it.*

NK: *I guess. I remember I was thinking about it for a long time, the idea was there, but only in 1997 did the time feel right to me.*

YT: *When you started composing this cycle did you anticipate how hard it would be?*

NK: *I knew that it was going to be a monumental work, that's why it took me so long to get ready for it.*

YT: *Do you remember how you were composing this cycle?*

NK: *It was the summer of 1997... Alla for some reason wasn't at home, maybe she was travelling somewhere, the main thing – she was not around. So I spent all my days alone... going to swim on the river and coming back home, all by myself.*

YT: *This is a great idea to have free time for relaxation in nature after the hard work writing the music at home.*

NK: *Oh no, I was composing music constantly – at home at my desk, at the piano, going to the river, swimming, getting a sunburn on the river shore... composing everywhere.*

---

[348] Note by the author: Conversation about the recording of *Twenty-Four Preludes and Fugues*, Op. 82 will be presented in the Chapter VII.

YT: Did you compose the music non-stop in your head?
NK: Mostly yes.
YT: Did you take at least a pencil with the sheet music to the river?
NK: Of course, I did that.
YT: Still, this sounds a little bit crazy to me.
NK: That's what you do when you have such a difficult task as this.
YT: I agree, it's a lot of pressure – you put yourself into a comparison with other great composers who also wrote the set of »Twenty-Four Preludes and Fugues« – Bach, Shostakovich, Hindemith, Shchedrin…
NK: And Slonimsky too.
YT: What a company!
NK: I think after Bach this is the first real continuation of his idea (long pause)… Because other composers wrote their cycles with some deviations from Bach's »Twenty Four Preludes and Fugues«. For example Hindemith – he wrote just twelve fugues.
YT: How about Shostakovich – he has twenty-four preludes and fugues.
NK: Yes, this is correct, but he has different tonality order than Bach – he goes with the circle of 5ths.
YT: So, Bach's order is the parallel major-minor keys going chromatically up (C-c-C#-c#-D-d and on) and Shostakovich uses cycle of 5th with the relative keys relationship (C-a-G-e-D-b-A-f# and on). How about yourself – what order did you have?
NK: My order is quite interesting – C-g#-F-c#-Bb-f#-Eb-b…
YT: Enharmonically spelling – falling major-minor thirds.
NK: You got it!
YT: Did you use the idea of Bach's fugue when the subject is presented in different voices?
NK: Yes, I did.
YT: So, in your fugue exposition the subject should be presented in all voices, correct?
NK: That's for sure.
YT: Did you have an idea of a minor prelude or fugue ending in a major key?
NK: No, this I decided not to do.
YT: In other words, you decided that something you are going to take from Bach and something left behind.
NK: Correct.
YT: I heard the statement that in Bach's music you can find all the music styles that followed him, for example jazz.
NK: I don't know this saying.
YT: I keep thinking about this idea – for me jazz is not all about which notes to use in a chord but mostly about the style – how to play, the grove of the music.

NK: Of course! And this style didn't appear long after Bach's death. On the other side, Baroque music can be compared to jazz because of the basso continuo...
YT: Which was basically the improvisation.
NK: Yes.
YT: This is true. Did you study Baroque music?
NK: I know what it is all about.
YT: Not to move away from the topic of our conversation – I know that Mozart studied Bach's music very seriously and was in a close relationship with »London Bach«.
NK: This happened because the music of Johann Christian Bach sounded closer to Mozart, but it was not as deep as Mozart's music.
YT: What else should we know about your Op. 82?
NK: This is the most extensive and the most serious work that I wrote for the piano.
YT: How long does the whole set of preludes and fugues last?
NK: Not as long as you might think – it's an hour and twenty minutes... but remember, all of my works for solo piano are not that long.
YT: Of course! An hour is a pretty serious length for one piece. I remember we were talking with you the other day and you said that for the characterpieces the length of your works would be around four minutes and for the length of the piano sonata – around twenty minutes.
NK: Exactly.
YT: On the other hand – if we would compare your cycle of »Twenty-Four Preludes and Fugues« and Twenty Piano Sonatas...
NK: Oh no... of course the piano sonatas would be longer.
YT: How about difficulty – which cycle would be more difficult?
NK: What do you think?
YT: I think »Twenty-Four Preludes and Fugues«.
NK: It just looks that way but in reality there is nothing that difficult in those preludes and fugues. It always happens with my music – it sounds like it's difficult.
YT: But in reality it's not.
NK: No, it's not.
YT: How long did it take you to compose this cycle?
NK: Do you think I remember that?
YT: Something like half a year or so?
NK: Probably something like that. I still can't remember where Alla was when I composed my Op. 82.

YT: *Maybe you were just that much involved in the compositional process that you didn't notice anything around you?*
NK: *No, she was just not around. She was probably travelling somewhere.*

Ruza

A couple of times in this book we've come back to the discussion of the retreat resort for the »Union of Composers« that is situated outside of Moscow, near the small city Ruza. This place has special meaning for Nikolai Kapustin.

There were a few places in the Soviet Union that were organized with the goal of »creating pleasant conditions for the creative work of Soviet composers«.[349] Among those resorts, in addition to Ruza, were Ivanovo (155 miles north-east from Moscow), Repino (near Saint Petersburg), Sartavala (Karelia), Druskininkai (Latvia), Vorozil (Ukraine), and Firiuza (Kirgiz Republic).

The first eight buildings of the resort in Ruza, which is situated just 70 miles west of Moscow, were built before WWII, in 1939. They were later expanded to accommodate more visitors during the 1940s.[350] This is the place where you can feel absolute harmony, comfort and relaxation.[351]

Nikolai Kapustin, Ruza

---

[349] Kiril Tomoff, »Creative Union: The Professional Organization of Soviet Composers, 1939-1953«, Cornell University Press: 2006, p. 55. Accessed December 13, 2017.
https://books.google.com/books?id=tNjPg1HgxZ0C&pg=PA55&lpg=PA55&dq=ivanovo+composers+vacation&source=bl&ots=MI_uCb_jxD&sig=SRGzPp-mIWrrA1MVbdZ1dewxUMns&hl=en&sa=X&ved=0ahUKEwiTt5bF3pDTAhWL2YMKHVOiCZUQ6AEIGjAA#v=onepage&q=ivanovo%20composers%20vacation&f=false.
[350] Tomoff, 55.
[351] Pictures of the resort in Ruza. Accessed December 13, 2017.
http://mskhotels.info/hotel/dom-tvorchestva-kompozitorov-ruza.

NK: I liked going to Ruza very much. Until last year we used to go there every summer with Alla. Now, the condition of this place is close to being completely ruined. No one is talking good care of it. Plus, my health is not allowing me to travel away from Moscow.
YT: I remember this place very well – it's a beautiful and majestic forest.
NK: And the Moscow river.
YT: I didn't know that you have the Moscow river in Ruza.
NK: Of course we have. In the past we used to walk there almost every day for swimming, it was not too far. I composed many of my successful works in Ruza. It was a time of long and pleasant vacations and intense work for me.
YT: Can you name any of these works?
NK: I composed there my »Concerto for Two Pianos and Percussion«, Op. 104 (2002).
YT: Maybe some orchestral works?
NK: I don't think I wrote orchestral works in Ruza.
YT: If we would compare Ruza and your apartments in Moscow – how do you feel?
NK: Ruza was like my second home.
YT: You felt absolute comfort there.
NK: Yes, and no distraction at all. Actually, I tried to find places of nature in Moscow as well.

Nikolai Kapustin, Stroganoff Manor Estate in Brattsevo, Moscow, September 5, 2001

YT: I look at the picture of you in Stroganoff Manor Estate and see the person who is a very happy man, who is completely sutisfed with his life. Is that true?

NK: *He made me to look that way.*
YT: *Who is he?*
NK: *It's a famous Moscow jazz photographer Pavel Korbut.*
YT: *Ohhh, I know this photographer! His picture of Herbie Hankock won on the »Blue Note« the »Jazz Award« for the »Best Photo of the Year« in 2012.*[352]
NK: *Yes, that's him!*
YT: *So, did you say that he asked you to look happy for this picture?*
NK: *Yes, he asked me to look that way.*
YT: *And you did.*
NK: *Yes, and I did well. After that photosession he became a good friend of our family. Alla knows him very well.*
YT: *I just think that in that picture Pavel Kurbut was able to show us the real Kapustin, not just one of the best and highly respected composers of our time, but also a great and absolutely happy man.*
NK: *Nobody used that picture so far.*
YT: *Then this will be the first!*

---

[352] Pavel Korbut. Accessed December 13, 2017. http://www.jazz.ru/pages/korbut/.

Chapter Seven: Years of Increasing Popularity (2000-2018)

The outstanding growth of popularity of the music of Nikolai Kapustin brought him to the point where he is now considered one of the leading modern day composers in the world.

Now that his music is gaining widespread recognition, Kapustin is hailed as a genius of the piano – perhaps the greatest living piano composer.[353]

The explosion of Kapustin's popularity started to appear in May of 2000 when Kapustin and his wife Alla made their trip to England. In a way that moment signified Kapustin introducing himself to the international world scene.

---

[353] Piano Society: Nikolai Kapustin. Accessed January 2, 2018. http://www.pianosociety.com/pages/kapustin/.

Kapustin's Trip to London (May 2000)

The idea of travelling to London didn't happen spontaneously for Kapustin. He was invited to visit Europe and Asia multiple times to attend different events but he was never ready to travel. Only in the spring of 2000 did he decide that the time had come to travel abroad.

YT: *What was the main reason for you to make such a long trip to London?*
NK: *I wanted to attend Hamelin's Western premier of my Piano Sonata No. 2, Op. 54.*
YT: *Is that all?*
NK: *Of course, there were some other things that I planned to do, but you asked me about the main reason – that was the main reason.*
YT: *Do you remember how you travelled to England?*
NK: *We travelled to England by train.*
YT: *By train? That was probably a very long trip.*
NK: *It took us three days to get there.*
YT: *And all of that because you don't like travelling by plane?*
NK: *Do you think that it's not enough reason to switch air transportation to the ground transportation?*
YT: *Absolutely enough. Have you ever taken a flight in your life?*
NK: *Of course I used to fly in the past. We did it quite often with the Lundstrem Orchestra. I just didn't like it anymore – too much stress for me.*
YT: *I didn't know that you used to fly a lot while you were working with Lundstrem.*
NK: *With Lundstrem we mostly travelled by plane. We would not be able to do such intense touring if we would have just travelled by train.*
YT: *I am just curious – do you feel fear while you travelling on the plane?*
NK: *No, I don't.*
YT: *So, in 2000 you thought that it was enough for you and decided to switch your transportation to the train.*
NK: *Yes, absolutely enough.*
YT: *I think going to England by train you travelled through all of Europe probably.*
NK: *Yes, we saw many countries, as well as made a couple of stops to switch trains.*
AK (joining the conversation): *I remember we had to switch trains in Belgium on the way back to Moscow and we had a little time to spare there. We really enjoyed tasting Belgium beer with Kolia.*

NK: I remember we were in that Channel[354] *that goes from France to England, under the La Manche (English Channel). That was an interesting experience for me.*
YT: How long did you travel under the water?
AK: Not very long. The whole trip was around two hours, but in the Channel we were less than an hour I think.
NK: It was interesting to see also who travelled with us on that train.
YT: Who were those passengers?
NK: There were a lot of Arab people on that train. I've never seen them in my life.
YT: I know that you like watching people who are crossing their lives with you for a minute or two.
NK (smiling): Yes, I do.

Nikolai Kapustin and Alla stayed in London in the house of Jan Hoare, who was the secretary of British Liszt Society, and who initiated the idea of organizing the Kapustin Society in London in 2000.

YT: Did you know that Kapustin's Society would be organized in London?
NK: That was one of the goals of my trip – to attend the opening of the society.
YT: Can we talk a little about the Kapustin Society?
NK: There is nothing to say except that it didn't exist long.
YT: In other words, it was organized with good intentions but gradually stopped its' activity.
NK: Yes, I didn't hear from them for a long time now. There was one good thing though that they did for me. They helped me to register my rights as a composer so I would receive the royalty for the performances of my music.
YT: That's an important thing.
NK: Yes, it is.
YT: Did you feel comfortable staying in the house of Jan Hoare?
AK (joining the conversation): We enjoyed staying there very much. Mr. Hoare and his wife Peggy treated us like their dearest friends or family members.

---

[354] Channel Tunnel (or Eurotunnel) is a channel between England and France that was opened on May 6, 1994. The channel is 31 miles long and it takes about 30-35 minutes to go through the tunnel. Accessed January 2, 2018. https://www.britannica.com/topic/Channel-Tunnel.

Kapustin at the house of Jan Hoare (from the right to the left): Jan Hoare, his wife Peggy Hoare, Nikolai Kapustin, Alla Kapustina, a friend of the family of Hoare, and their dog

NK: *Alla became very good friends with Mr. Hoare's wife and they both used to go for walks with their dog, a very smart black labrador.*

YT: *Did you go to those walking promenades?*

NK: *Not really. I generally stayed at the house because I was always busy doing something. I remember at that time I was preparing for the recording of my Twenty Four Preludes and Fugues. They had a wonderful a Bechstein grand piano at the house, so I used to practice my works while I was by myself.*

YT: *So, you didn't lose your time.*

NK: *In the past I've never lost my time, not like now...*

YT: *Am I right that after your return from London you composed your »Piano Sonata No. 11«, Op. 101 called »Twickenham«?*

NK: *Yes, this is true – right after my return.*

YT: *I found out that this is the suburban southwest area of London.*

NK: *That was the area where Hoare's house was situated. I liked that place very much and decided to dedicate this piano sonata to Twickenham. Actually, I remember I was talking one day to Hoare and mentioned that I am planning to dedicate the piece to my London experience. He suggested to use this name and I was absolutely happy with his idea.*

YT: *So, you were inspired by that place.*

NK: Yes, I was. It is sad that a little while after out trip Hoare moved to another place to live and was no longer living in Twickenham.
YT: But your music made that place special.
NK: I hope so.
YT: How long did you stay in London?
NK: About a week or so.
YT: A week is a pretty long time. Were you busy during that visit or did you also have time for relaxation?
NK: It was highly intense trip. Every day something happened – either interviews, meetings, or attendance of some important events.
YT: I remember you said earlier that the main reason why you decided to leave Moscow and to make such a long trip to London was Hamelin's premier of your Piano Sonata No. 2, Op. 54.
NK: Yes, I wanted to hear this sonata, although, originally I didn't want to go to London at all because I don't feel comfortable travelling so far, but they talked me into it.
YT: This trip was an important step in the presentation of you as a composer to international musical circles. I think it was worth it.
NK: Yes, at the end of the day I was glad I did it.

Marc-André Hamelin (born in 1961) is a renowned Canadian pianist and composer. He began his musical study at the Vincent d' Indy School of Music in Montréal (Canada) with Yvonne Hubert. Hamelin graduated from Temple University (Philadelphia, United States) where he studied under Harvey D. Wedeen and Russell Sherman. He won numerous competitions among those were the Canadian Music Competition »Stepping Stone« (Montréal, Canada), the International Piano Competition in Pretoria (South Africa), and Carnegie Hall's International Competition of American Music (New York, United States).[355] The level of craftsmanship and virtuosity of this pianist gained international recognition and gave him the opportunity to perform with major symphonic orchestras around the world. Hamelin is a well-known artist in North America and Europe.[356]

The Western premier of Kapustin's *Piano Sonata No. 2*, Op. 54 by Marc-André Hamelin happened in Blackheath Concert Hall in London on May 14, 2000.[357]

---

[355] Marc-André Hamelin. Accessed January 2, 2018.
http://www.bach-cantatas.com/Bio/Hamelin-Marc-Andre.htm.
[356] Official site of Marc-André Hamelin. Accessed January 2, 2018.
http://www.marcandrehamelin.com/artist.php?view=bio.
[357] From the correspondence with Marc-André Hamelin, March 4, 2018.

YT: *Do you remember your impression from that concert of Hamelin?*
NK: *Of course I remember that day. He played many different pieces by other composers but finished with the premier of my sonata.*
YT: *How did you feel about it?*
NK: *I felt honored.*

Nikolai Kapustin and Marc-André Hamelin, Premier of Piano Sonata No. 2, Op. 54, London, May 14, 2000

YT: *How did you find such an amazing pianist to play your works?*
NK: *I didn't find anyone. I remember while I was touring in Germany in the late 1990s sombody mentioned to me in a conversation that Hamelin was currently performing my works. I was surprised and happy to hear that.*
YT: *And then?*
NK: *And then we ended up writing letters to each other and that's how I received the invitation to attend the premier of my piano sonata.*
YT: *Easy.*
NK: *Exactly, not difficult at all.*
YT: *Do you know why Hamelin chose this particular piece to premier but not any other works, for example Piano Sonata No. 3, Op. 55?*
NK: *I didn't ask him about it.*
YT: *Is it possible that it happened because he heard Petrov's performance of this piece?*
NK: *It is highly possible. Hamelin probably heard it, got interested, and decided to play himself.*
YT: *Sounds like it.*

NK: *Not only did he play the premier of my second sonata, he recorded it the same year,*[358] *but also recorded the whole disc of my music a few years later. There were many of my works on that CD.*

YT: *Do you remember the year this disc was recorded?*

NK: *The disc was recorded in 2004, I guess he wanted to play more of my music, something new.*[359]

YT: *Do you agree that Hamelin's premier your Piano Sonata No. 2 (Op. 54) moved this piece to the level of one of your best works, becoming something like the musical »business card« of Nikolai Kapustin?*

NK: *All I can say is that he made that sonata very famous.*

YT: *Was that CD of Hamelin in 2004 the only disc that was entirely dedicated to your works?*

NK: *Yes, that's what I know. He also recorded my Toccatina, Op. 36 in one of his earlier recordings,*[360] *but that was in 2001, and it was only one work, not the whole disc.*

YT: *Did you stay in contact with Hamelin after the premier?*

NK: *I remember Marc (Hamelin) came to visit us a couple times while we were staying in Hoare's house. Once he even came with his wife.*

YT: *Did this happen after he played the premier?*

NK: *Yes, after the premier.*

YT: *So, you became good friends with Hamelin.*

NK: *Very good friends.*

YT: *Did you talk in English with him?*

NK: *Let's put it this way – I tried my best. As you know, I can read in English very well, I understand it, but my conversational English is not that good.*

YT: *This is interesting – usually people try to develop good skills in communicating in the foreign language, but not many of us use it specifically for reading.*

NK: *I guess I am just different.*

---

[358] Marc-André Hamelin disc »Marc-André Hamelin in a State of Jazz«, Hyperion (CDA67656), London, 2000.

[359] Marc-André Hamelin disc »Nikolai Kapustin: Piano Music«, Hyperion (CDA67433), London, 2004.

[360] Marc-André Hamelin disc »Kaleidoscope«, Hyperion (CDA67275), London, 2001.

Marc-André Hamelin visiting Nikolai Kapustin in the house of Jan Hoare, May 2000

YT: Did you meet with Hamelin after that trip to London?
NK: Yes, I think a few years after our trip he was on tour in Moscow and invited us to come on his concert.[361]
YT: I hope you went to that concert.
NK: Of course we did. We both came – me and Alla. I was glad to see him again after all those years.
AK (joining the conversation): After the concert he invited us to come to the restaurant and spend a little more time together, but it was very late and unfortunately we had to refuse. It was time to go home.
NK: I hope this didn't upset him much.
YT: Was it the only opportunity to see each other?
NK: His visit to Moscow was very short – he came just for one day.
YT: What happened after that?
NK: After that we stayed in contact for a while, but then, as it always happens, it was over. I didn't hear from him for a number of years.
YT: I am sure he remembers you!

---

[361] From the correspondence with Mr. Hamelin (January 30, 2018): This meeting happened on March 2008, when Hamelin performed a concert in the Tchaikovsky Hall in Moscow.

After having this conversation with Kapustin about his friendship with Mr. Marc-André Hamelin I decided to contact Mr. Hamelin. This is what he had to say:

> It is my pleasure to say a few words about Nikolai Kapustin!
>
> I first discovered his music through his second sonata; I was staying at the home of Mike Spring, then working at Hyperion Records, and he put on Nikolai Petrov's recording rightfully thinking I'd be interested. My jaw dropped to the floor, and I immediately wanted to play the piece.
>
> Then I set out to discover as much as I could about him, which wasn't easy, since almost none of the music had been published. I remember getting a lot of music from pianist Steven Osborne, who had been in touch with him, and that's how my collection started. Finding out about Kapustin himself was a lot more difficult; as hard as it is now to believe, a Google search for Kapustin in 1998 produced zero results.
>
> I had the privilege of giving the second sonata's UK première in May of 2000, and for the occasion Kapustin and his wife Alla made the 3-day train journey all the way to London (he refuses to fly). Although my performance at the time was unnecessarily quick overall, I think the occasion was a pleasant one for the composer, whose music so far had only gotten very limited exposure in the West. He seemed pleased with my performance, even if he did say the first movement was too fast (and that was only after I pressed him for an opinion...!)
>
> I later asked him to autograph the only original score of his music I owned at the time (an anthology that included his *Suite in the Old Style*, Op. 28). The score has become a very precious possession!
>
> It's now obvious that Kapustin's time has come – performances of his music have proliferated, and scores are now available through major publishing houses. I am happy to have made a contribution to the dissemination of his wonderful, exhilarating body of work. While being difficult and requiring a high degree of mental discipline and concentration, the music is so well conceived in every single respect pianistically that it's always a joy to play.[362]

This is a copy of the cover of the collection of »Concert Pieces by Soviet Composers«, which includes Kapustin's *Suite in the Old Style*, Op. 28. Hamelin asked the composer to inscribe this score the same day he performed the premier of the *Piano Sonata No. 2*, Op. 54.

---

[362] From the personal correspondence with Mr. Hamelin, January 28, 2018.

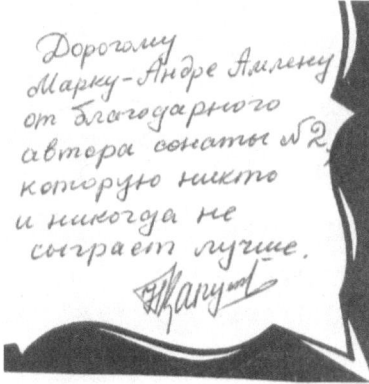

Cover of the collection of »Concert Piece of Soviet Composers« owned by Mr. Hamelin with Kapustin's note

Mr. Hamelin preserved this score for all those eighteen years while wondering what Kapustin had to say to him that day. This is what Kapustin wrote on the cover:

> To dear Marc-André Hamelin from the grateful author of the Sonata No. 2, that nobody will ever perform better.[363]

During the time that Kapustin spent in London he was asked to give a series of interviews to some well-known musical journals and newspapers in England and Japan. Among those were the interviews with the composer for the musical journals *Fanfare* (with Martin Anderson[364]) and *International Piano Quarterly* (with Harriett Smith[365]).

YT: *Do you remember that interview with Martin Anderson?*
NK: *I remember it very well. When I read this interview after it was published I was a little surprised.*
YT: *Why is that?*
NK: *Reading that article I found out that our translator, Ashot Akopian, wasn't that strong in translation from Russian to English, it was too late though. That interview is quite long but some of the statements that I made there do not belong to me – that's not what I said.*

---

[363] From the personal correspondence with Mr. Hamelin, January 30, 2018.
[364] Martin Anderson, »Nikolai Kapustin, Russian Composer of Classical Jazz«, *Fanfare* 24, no. 11 (September/October 2000): 93-97.
[365] Harriet Smith, »Bridging the Divide: The Russian Composer Nikolai Kapustin«, *International Piano Quarterly* 4, no. 13 (Autumn 2000): 54-55.

YT: It looks that Akopian didn't know English well enough to help you with the translation.

NK: No, he knew English well, but he didn't know much about music. For example, I meant to say one thing and he understood it differently.

YT: So, he didn't understand you in Russian then, correct?

NK: Yes, and that upset me very much.

YT: After that trip to London did you receive the invitation to come to some other countries?

NK: Of course I did. I received hundreds of them.

YT: I knew that! That trip to London with all those activities made a serious resonance in the musical world and people became interested in your music and in you.

NK: And all of them received my official »thanks but no«.

AK (joining the conversation): They invited Kolia to go to Japan many times but he didn't want to go.

NK: And Spain too.

Continuation of Recording CDs

After the return from the trip to London Kapustin's life continued to stay at a high level of intensity. One of the reasons for that was a project that had started in 1985, which was the recording of his own music. After the year of 2000 Kapustin recorded four CDs, and all those recordings were released in Japan.

One of the most significant of these recordings was the double disc titled »Kapustin«, which was recorded in September 2000 in Moscow and released in 2001. The disc contained the monumental solo piano work – cycle of *Twenty-Four Preludes and Fugues*, Op. 82, as well as chamber works, such as *Elegy, for Cello and Piano*, Op. 96, *Burlesque for Cello and Piano*, Op. 97, *Nearly Waltz for Cello and Piano*, Op. 98, and *Sonata for Violin and Piano*, Op. 70.[366] Kapustin invited two of his friends to participate in this project – cellist Alexander Zagorinsky and the violinist Alexander Chernov.

Cover of the disc »Kapustin«, Triton, 2001

YT: I am not sure if I know of any composer who wrote a set of twenty-four preludes and fugues, and recorded the whole cycle himself.
NK: Yes, it was a massive volume of work. I know that Shostakovich recorded some of his preludes and fugues but not the whole cycle.
YT: I can't believe it - you had to not only compose it but also learn it from the pianistic side.

---

[366] Triton (DICC-40001-2), 2001, Octavia Records (OVCT-00010), 2004.

NK: *Of course! And that was difficult too. It is very good that I did that recording. Nobody would dare to record the whole cycle.*

YT: *Do you know if anyone tried to record it?*

NK: *Some pianists record a couple of selected preludes and fugues, but nobody did twenty-four preludes and fugues in one recording. To record the whole cycle is a difficult job.*

YT: *Yes, there are not that many pianists who, like Tatiana Nikolaeva and you, can record the entire cycle. She recorded all the Shostakovich Twenty-Four Preludes and Fugues and all Beethoven's Piano Sonatas. I am just curious – when you practiced that set of your preludes and fugues did you work on individual preludes and fugues or played all forty-eight pieces as a whole?*

NK: *I practiced them individually.*

YT: *Since you said that you were practicing even during your trip to London – does that mean that the recording of this disc was close to that date?*

NK: *Yes, the recording was scheduled very soon after my return from England – in September of 2000.*

YT: *Did you record a couple preludes and fugues a day?*

NK: *It was forty-eight pieces all together, so I had subdivided them in groups, there was no other way.*

YT: *Did you record those pieces in a specific order or just follow the order of cycle?*

NK: *I recorded all the pieces in the order that I composed them.*

YT: *This is a very interesting fact because I know that some of the pianists do not follow the order while they record the cycles.*

NK: *I agree, for example Arthur Schnabel didn't follow the order of Beethoven's sonatas when he recorded them, but this was not my case.*

YT: *Remembering Bach's preludes and fugues – some of them are more difficult, and some less. How about the difficulty of your preludes and fugues?*

NK: *Of course, they are all different. The faster ones are usually more difficult. Actually, for me it was easier to record the more difficult ones.*

YT: *Really?*

NK: *Yes, because I practiced them more than the easier ones. In general, in comparison with Bach, I think I have more fugues in a faster tempo. Do you know of any Bach's fugues that go in a fast tempo?*

YT: *I don't remember.*

NK: *Because there are none.*

YT: *This is interesting – I've never thought about Bach's music in the context of the tempo. I think for me if we will be talking about the difficulties in playing Bach' fugues I would probably relate it first to the amount of voices - the fugues that have more voices are usually more difficult. How about your fugues – can we apply this to your fugues?*

NK: I don't think that the amount of voices affects the difficulty of my fugues, it's probably only the tempo.

YT: So, you have something similar to Bach and something just the opposite.

NK: Of course.

YT: Did you play those forty-eight pieces by memory or with the score while you recorded it?

NK: It was not a question, of course by memory.

YT: Did you record something like once a week and then rest and then the next week again, or it was recording every day?

NK: Originally, I planned the recording with a few days in between as a break, but because of the intense studio schedule we blocked four days in a row for that project to be completed. At the end I realized that it was better that way.

YT: I actually agree – once you were centered upon this project - it would be easier to have an intense life for a couple of days and then finish it.

NK: Now, looking back I can't stop thinking – it took me just four days to record twenty-four preludes and fugues.

YT: Yes, you did it very fast. That means that you recorded approximately six preludes and fugues a day!!!

NK: This sounds right to me.

YT: Do you mind me asking – how many tracks in general did it take you to record each piece of that cycle?

NK: In general, I think I recorded each piece twice, but there were some that I kept from the first try, not that many though... but some from the third.

YT: So, you were ready.

NK: Yes, it was in my head and in my fingers. I was ready.

YT: That's very impressive!

NK: You make it sound like it was very difficult work to do.

YT: And it was not?

NK: I was in a good shape as a pianist at that time, so it was not that hard for me to do. I remember we became good friends with the sound engineer who recorded me.

YT: So it was a team effort.

NK: Yes, it was. Big things always happen with a team effort.

The disc that followed, titled »Kapustin Plays Kapustin«, included solo piano works as well as chamber pieces. All the solo piano works, such as *Piano Sonata No. 2*, Op. 54, *Piano Sonata No. 3*, Op. 55, and *Andante*, Op. 58 were recorded in 1991. In 2001 the chamber part of the CD was finished, which included

Introduction and Scherzino for Cello Solo, Op. 93, and *Duet for Alto-Saxophone and Cello*, Op. 99. This disc was released in Japan in 2002.[367]

The disc that came next had special meaning for the composer. It was titled »Nikolai Kapustin: Last Recording«, which was literally meant to be the very last recording of Kapustin playing his original compositions. The CD was entirely dedicated to the solo piano music. It was recorded by Kapustin in 2003 in Moscow and released in 2004 by »Triton«.[368] It included two piano sonatas, *Piano Sonata No. 7*, Op. 64 and *Piano Sonata No. 12*, Op. 102, and numerous characterpieces. The characterpieces included *Berceuse*, Op. 65, *Three Impromptus*, Op. 66, *Three Etudes*, Op. 67, *Impromptu*, Op. 83, and *Paraphrase on the Theme by Paul Dvoirin*, Op. 108.

Cover of the CD »Nikolai Kapustin: Last Recording«, Triton, 2004

YT: I see that around the beginning of 2000s you had a very intense life – you had your trips to Germany and England, then all of your recordings in 2000, 2001, and 2003.
NK: Yes, the end of 1990s and the beginning of 2000s was a very active time for me. I don't complain though.
YT: It feels to me that on this disc you came back to where you started – to the solo piano works.
NK: Yes, I made a complete circle.

---

[367] Note by the author: The beginning of the conversation about this disc was presented in the Chapter VI.
[368] Triton (OVCT-00017), 2004.

YT: Why did you call this disc »Last Recording«? Did you really mean it to be your last one?
NK: At that moment – yes. I have to tell you that at the beginning, in the 1980s, I was recording discs one after another, but after I recorded my Piano Sonata No. 12 in 2003, the very last piece on the disc »Last Recording«, I thought to myself that it might be it – this piece would be my last recorded work, so I stopped recording.
YT: Was there any reason for that decision?
NK: Yes, there was... because I stopped practicing.
YT: Why? Didn't you feel up to it?
NK: Because some other well-known pianists started to record my music. For example, Vadim Rudenko recorded my Piano Sonata No. 8 very well.
YT: I see, but still, it was somebody else, not you.
NK: That »somebody else« was a famous and well-celebrated pianist.
YT: I think that the most interesting performance is the one where composer is playing his own music. Of course, it's a sign of respect when the pianists like Hamelin, Osborn, Petrov, or Rudenko, are playing your music, but for me – your performance would be the most unique and original.
NK: This is your opinion.
YT: Absolutely mine.

The actual last CD of Nikolai Kapustin to this day is called »Kapustin Returns!« The disc was recorded in Moscow and released in 2008 in Japan.[369] As well as the previous disc, it is entirely dedicated to solo piano music. The disc contained twelve compositions, which is the largest number of pieces ever recorded by the composer on one disc. The majority of the pieces are character-pieces: *Paraphrase on »Aquarela Do Brazil« by Ary Barroso*, Op. 118, *Two Etude-like Trinkets*, Op. 122, *The End of the Rainbow*, Op. 112, *Humoresque*, Op. 75, *Fantasia*, Op. 115, *Gingerbread Man*, Op. 111, *Vanity of Vanities*, Op. 121, *Spice Island*, Op. 117, *Paraphrase on »Blue Bossa« by Kenny Dorham*, Op. 123, and *Countermove*, Op. 130. The disc ends with *Piano Sonata No. 16*, Op. 131.

---

[369] Nippon Acoustic Records (NARD-5014), 2008, Octavia Records (OVCT-00094), 2012.

Cover of the CD »Kapustin Returns!« Nippon, 2008

YT: *I really like the name of this disc »Kapustin Returns!« It sounds very affective.*
NK: *It does.*
YT: *Although, I am confused a little bit – how did it happen that after your CD called »Last Recording« another one appeared?*
NK: *It only means that what I originally planned as my last recording was in reality not the last one.*
YT: *If we would relate your life to a musical form – this story of you recording the CD called »Last Recording« and then recording the new CD would go to the false recapitulation section, like Schubert liked to do.*
NK: *Actually, there is a funny story behind that. After I recorded my disc in 2003 »Last Recording«, I seriously thought that I am officially done with recording. However, in five years, in 2008, after thinking for a while, I started to feel that I might be able to record another disc.*
YT: *Yes, during those five years (2003-2008) you composed many pieces.*
NK: *That's the thing, and the majority of them were solo piano works. When I wrote about this idea to my Japanese producer Natsuko Samejima. Of course, she was shocked – how is it possible to record a new disc when we already released the »Last Recording«?*
YT: *What did you do?*
NK: *I did nothing. She said to give her a little time to think about it and that's how she came up with name »Kapustin Returns!«*
YT: *I think this name creates even more attention to your music – sounds to me like a scene from a James Bond movie. What was your reaction?*
NK: *I thought it was a genius idea.*
YT: *Is this disc going to be the last one?*
NK (smiling): *Who knows?*

YT: I keep thinking – on that last disc the very last piece is Piano Sonata No. 16, Op. 131. Do you remember that piece?
NK: I remember this sonata very well. It is sad that out of my twenty sonatas I was able to record only nine.

Concerts of the Music of Nikolai Kapustin in Russia after 2000

After the year 2000 there were number of concerts in Russia that were of great significance to the composer. These concerts were mainly premiers.

The premier of Kapustin's *Quintet in Db major*, Op. 89 happened on January 11, 2001 in Moscow Philharmony Hall. The piece was premiered by Nikolai Petrov and the Shostakovich Quartet.

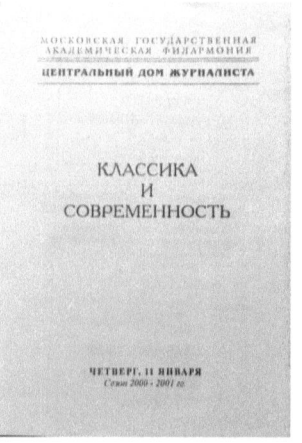

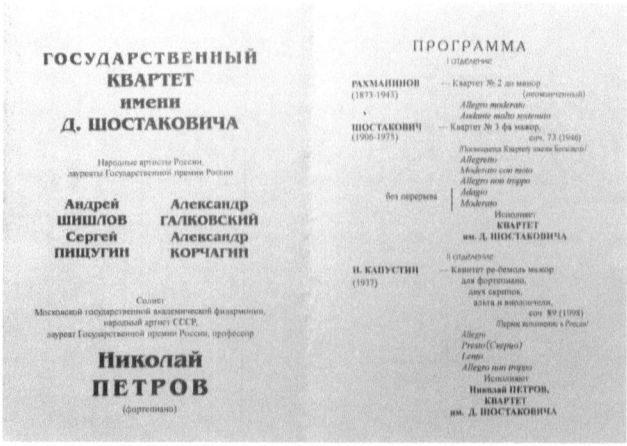

Program notes: Nikolai Petrov and Shostakovich Quartet, Quintet Op. 89, Moscow, January 11, 2001

YT: *I think it was such a serious event that you were able to involve such respectable musicians – the Shostakovich Quartet.*

NK: *It was not me. Kolia (Nikolai Petrov) was able to invite them.*

YT: *Do you remember what they also played that day?*

NK: *In the program was also Rachmaninov Quartet No. 2 in C minor, Shostakovich Quartet No. 3 in F major, and after intermission they played my Quintet, Op. 89. It was a big honor for me that they premiered my piece.*

YT: *How did they play?*

NK: *It was great performance and of course it was very well received.*

YT: *Did you attend this premier?*

NK: *I was on stage turning pages for Petrov.*

YT: *Really?*

NK: *Yes. I am not sure how I did it though.*

The second performance of Kapustin's *Quintet*, Op. 89 by Nikolai Petrov and the Shostakovich Quartet happened on April 8, 2001 in Kremlin Museum Performance Hall within the musical project the Second Musical Festival »Kremlin Musical«.

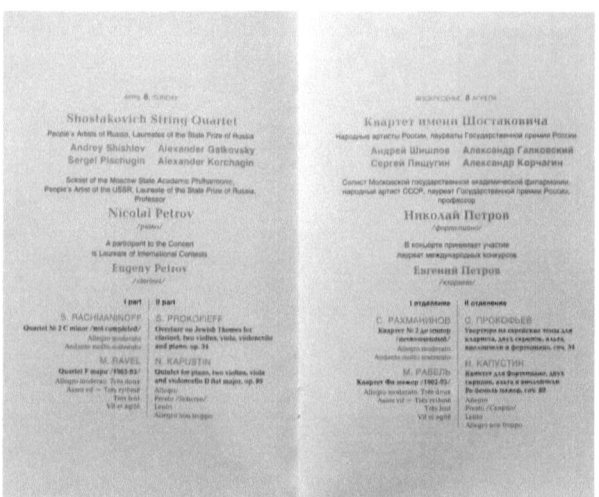

Program notes: II Musical Festival »Kremlin Musical«, Moscow, April 8, 2001

NK: Did you know that Petrov was art-direcor of this festival?
YT: No, I had no idea.
NK: He had many talents – as a performer, teacher, and organizer.
YT: This doesn't happen too often. This is so interesting that the festival took place in the actual museum along with all the exhibits surrounding the performance hall. Did you attend that performance?
NK: Yes, we both came – me and Alla.
YT: I read that the administration of the museum was worried about their exhibits knowing that there is jazz music in the program.[370]
NK (smiling): It wasn't true, they shouldn't worry about it.
YT: Seriously speaking, there is one more thing I wanted to ask you concerning this place – I read that Petrov mentioned that the acoustics in this place were pretty amazing. He said that everything sounded great in that hall.[371]
NK: I agree with that.
YT: How big was that hall?
NK: It was not a very big hall, I would say middle sized. I think it was a perfectly suitable place for chamber music.

Another concert dedicated to the music of Nikolai Kapustin happened on May 10, 2002 in the Great Hall of the Moscow Conservatory. The first part of the concert included *String Quartet No. 1*, Op. 88, performed by Glinka String Quartet and the premier of the *Concerto No. 2 for Cello and String Orchestra*, Op. 103 performed by Alexander Zagorinsky and Moscow Chamber Orchestra under the direction of Constantine Orbelian. The second part of the concert included *Trio for Flute, Cello, and Piano*, Op. 86 performed by pianist Nikolai Petrov, flutist Albert Ratzbaum and cellist Oleg Smirnov and *Quintet for Piano and String Quartet in Db major*, Op. 89 performed by Nikolai Petrov and Glinka String Quartet.

---

[370] Nikolai Petrov opening again »Kremlin Musical«. Accessed January 6, 2018. https://tvkultura.ru/article/show/article_id/30149/.
[371] Ibid.

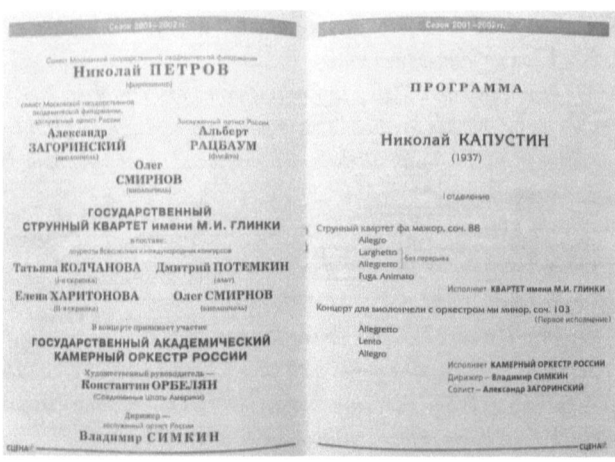

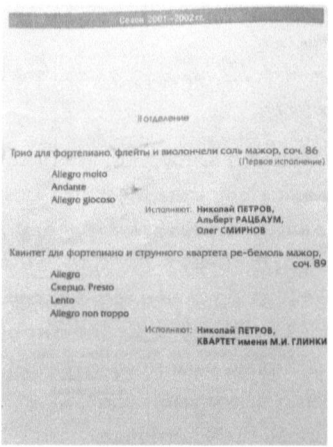

Program notes: Concert of Music of Nikolai Kapustin, Great Hall of Moscow Conservatory, May 10, 2002

YT: *I see that this concert was very extensive – four big works compiled the program.*

NK: *Yes, a lot of people were involved to participate in this concert.*

YT: *Can you tell something that you remember about this concert?*

NK: *The premier of my second cello concerto (Op. 103) didn't go too well that day.*

YT: *Why is that?*

NK: *They stopped in the middle of the piece.*

YT: *Oh, that is not good.*

NK: *Not good at all.*

YT: *Did they continue then or was it over?*

NK: They continued and finished the piece. As you know, my music is difficult to play, especially the pieces that involve many participants.
YT: I can imagine.
NK: Plus, it was the first performance, first time is always harder to play.
YT: Did Zagorisnky play this concerto later?
NK: Yes, he played it many times after this concert. Zagorinsky even recorded the disc of this concerto with Vologda Philharmonic Orchestra this year (2017) and, being respectful, brought it to me.
YT: I see that Petrov played your Trio Op. 86 with flutist Albert Ratzbaum and cellist Oleg Smirnov.
NK: Yes, they did.
YT: It's written on the program that they played a premier of Op. 86. I thought that you played a premier of Op. 86 in 1999 with Zagorinsky and Korneev.
NK: Yes, you are right. They just made a mistake in the program. Things like this happen sometimes.

On September 25, 2002 the Italian pianist Carlo Levi Minzi[372] performed a solo recital in Moscow musical salon »Musical Wednesdays«. The program included the works of Evgeny Poliakov, Frantz Shubert, Robert Shumann, and Nikolai Kapustin.

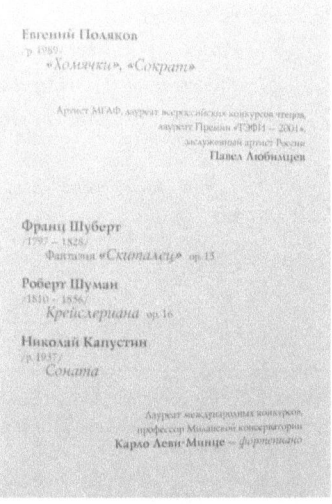

Program notes: Carlo Levi Minzi performed Sonata written by Kapustin, Moscow, September 25, 2001

---

[372] Carlo Levi Minzi. Accessed January 8, 2018. http://www.carloleviminzi.com/.

*NK: As you see from the program note – he played one of my piano sonatas. Unfortunately, they forgot to put the number of the sonata that Minzi performed that day in the program, and I can't recall myself which one it was.*³⁷³

YT: Maybe they thought that this is the only sonata that you composed?

*NK: Maybe. Overall, Minzi played and recorded four of my sonatas – Piano Sonata No. 8, 10, 11, and 12.*³⁷⁴

YT: Did you meet with him?

NK: Yes, he visited me.

*YT: I read in the interview that Minzi gave to the Russian news paper »Moskovskii Komsomolets« that he studied at Moscow Conservatory, class of Vladimir Natanson, for two years*³⁷⁵ *and even tried to talk there in Russian.*³⁷⁶

NK: Yes, he knows a little bit of conversational Russian, and that was enough for us to understand each other.

YT: I like his idea about languages very much – he said that if you go to another country to teach or to give masterclasses the best scenario would be if you would talk in the language of the country that you are going to.

NK: I agree with him, although it would take a lot of effort from you. I just like learning languages for myself, to read in it.

YT: I noticed that Minzi put your sonata as the last piece for the recital program.

NK: This happens pretty often – many musicians put my works as the last number on their recital program.

YT: I think it's a sign of big respect to your music. Usually, the meaning of the last piece is that this is the best work of the recital and it's better this way for the other works that would be played earlier on the program. There is no need to play anything else after this piece.

NK: I agree. That's what I used to do too when I played my recitals.

YT: How do you feel about this – your music now is considered to be the one that musicians put as the finale of their concerts?

NK: This pleases me.

YT: Did you like the Minzi's performance of your sonatas?

---

³⁷³ From the correspondence with Professor Minzi (February 8, 2018): On the solo recital that happened on September 25, 2002 in Moscow Carlo Levi Minzi performed Kapustin's *Piano Sonata No. 12*, Op. 102.

³⁷⁴ CD »Carlo Levi Minzi Plays Kapustin« Etichetta Maestro (M CD 2916), 2012. From the correspondence with Prof. Minzi (February 8, 2018): This disc was later reprinted by CUT Records (CUT 14/04 DG).

³⁷⁵ From the correspondence with Professor Minzi (February 8, 2018): Carlo Levi Minzi studied at the Moscow Conservatory in 1974-1976.

³⁷⁶ MKRU, interview with Carlo Levi Minzi (October 3, 2017). Accessed January 16, 2018. http://www.mk.ru/culture/2017/10/03/pianist-karlo-leviminci-velikoe-chto-italiya-podarila-miru-v-proshlom.html.

NK: He is a Professor of the Milan Conservatory, a very respected person.
YT: And?
NK: Concerning the interpretation of my music – stylistically I feel slightly different. Don't take me wrong, it's a great performance.
YT: So, the question is – are we allowed to be different when interpreting your music?
NK: Of course, yes.

The »Evening of Modern Music« took place on February 7, 2006 in Moscow Philharmonic Hall. The concert included the performances of compositions written by the Russian movie composer Vladimir Dashkevich,[377] American electronic music composer Jon Appleton,[378] and the Russian-Ukrainian composer Nikolai Kapustin, who was combining classical and jazz elements in his music. The performers included cellist Alexander Zagorinsky, and two pianists, Monica Haba and Yulia Turkina.

---

[377] Vladimir Dashkevich. Accessed January 7, 2018. http://propianino.ru/vladimir-dashkevich.
[378] Jon Appleton. Accessed January 7, 2018. http://www.appletonjon.com/biography.htm.

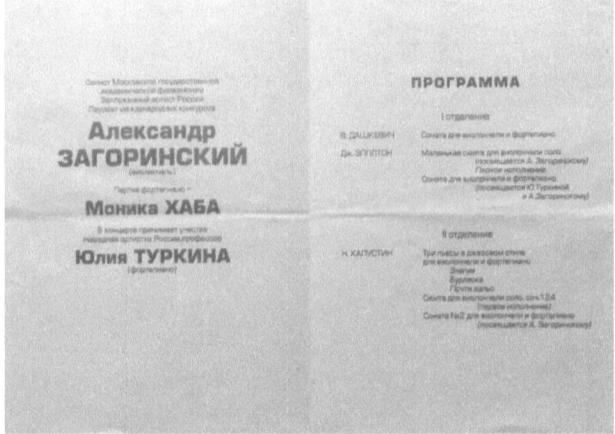

Program notes: Concert of the Modern Music, Moscow, February 7, 2006

YT: Which compositions of yours were performed on that concert?
NK: My music was presented in the second part of the concert. They played my three pieces for cello and piano – Elegy, Op. 96, Burlesque, Op. 97, and Nearly Waltz, Op. 98. Also Zagorinsky premiered Suite for Cello Solo, Op. 124, and the concert closed with Sonata for Cello and Piano No. 2, Op. 84. Funny thing, looking at some of the programs of my music someone may think that I am writing only the pieces deliberately for cello.
YT: But Zagorinsky is a cellist, and he is your friend.
NK: Yes, he is. Chopin also had a cellist friend, for whom he wrote music.
YT: Personally, I like how Zagorinsky is playing.

NK: He plays well when he learns the piece.
YT: Did you listen to the works that were on the first part of the concert – the music of Dashkevich and Appleton?
NK: Yes, I did.
YT: What do you think?
NK: Appleton is definitely not a composer of my taste.
YT: Do you know the composer Vladimir Dashkevich?
NK: Yes, of course I know him.
YT: Do you like his works?
NK: He is a very talented man.
YT: I read that in spite of the fact that Dashkevich was a serious composer, composing symphonies and concertos, he also wrote the music for ninety Russian movies. Some of those movies were highly rated in Russia, for example the legendary movie »Sherlock Holmes and Doctor Watson«.
NK: Each composer decides for himself what to do and what not to do. I decided to refuse writing music for movies because I don't like it. He decided to write, it was his choice.

The Russian Premier of the *Concerto for Violin, Piano, and String Orchestra*, Op. 105 took place on September 30, 2006 in Rachmaninov Hall of the Moscow Conservatory. The piece was premiered by renowned Russian violinist Graf Murja, pianist Alexander Vershinin, and the Kostroma Chamber Orchestra conducted by Pavel Gershtein.

The Honored artist of Russia, Professor of Moscow Conservatory Graf Murja, has a highly impressive list of achievements, including his victories in the international competitions in Russia, Portugal, France, Spain, Italy, South Africa, and other countries. The range of his stylistic interests includes the performance of classical music as well as ethnic music, klezmer music, and jazz.[379]

The pianist Alexander Vershinin is currently a Professor of the Moscow Conservatory and Kurashiki Saku University (Japan). He is active as a performer and teacher, presenting masterclasses in Russia, Japan, South Korea, Spain, France, Italy, Germany, the United States, and other countries. The repertoire of the pianist includes a wide range of musical styles beginning from the works of Classical composers and finishing with the jazz transcriptions and improvisation.[380]

---

[379] Moscow Conservatory: Graf Murja. Accessed January 6, 2018. http://www.mosconsv.ru/ru/person.aspx?id=31398.
[380] Alexander Vershinin. Accessed January 6, 2018. http://www.mosconsv.ru/ru/person.aspx?id=11138.

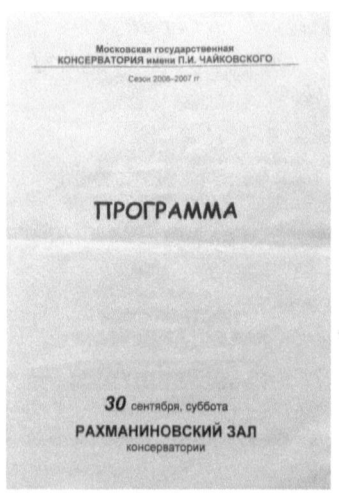
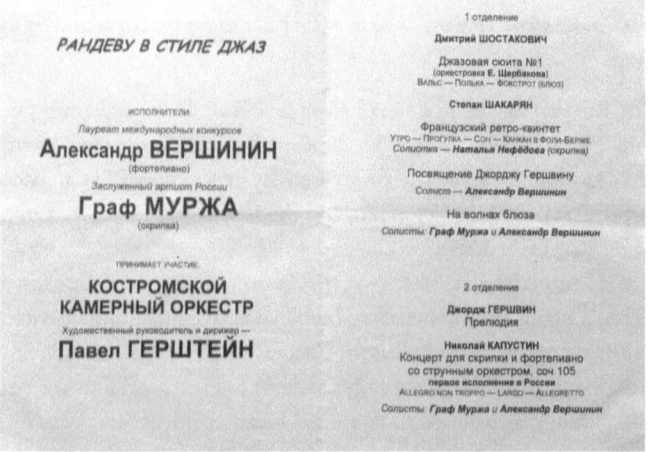

Program notes: Graf Murja, Alexander Vershinin, and Kostroma Chamber Orchestra, Concerto for Violin, Piano, and String Orchestra, Op. 105, Moscow Conservatory, September 30, 2006

YT: *I think it's a very respectable characteristic of the performer when they are interested in playing not only classical music, but also jazz, ethnic, klezmer music, and interested in improvisation as well.*

NK: *Yes, I appreciate musicians who are open minded.*

YT: *The instrumentation of this concerto looks quite interesting to me – for two solo instruments, violin and piano.*

NK: *I like unusual instrumentation, something different from what we already know.*

YT: *Did you attended that premier of Op. 105?*

NK: I don't think.
YT: Why didn't you go? It was at the Moscow Conservatory.
NK: I don't feel obligated to attend each premier of my music even if it happened in Moscow. Plus, Murja has a very interesting characteristic – he has a tendency to disappear for a while.
YT: I read an interview with Graf Mirja about his coming premier of your Violin Concerto, Op. 141 in the internet journal »Classical Music News in Russia«.[381]
NK: Yes, Murja called me a couple days ago about this premier.
YT: Really?
NK: Yes, he said that finally there is a chance to play this concerto, Op. 141, which I actually dedicated to him.
YT: Was he happy about this dedication?
NK: He was happy of course, but he kept postponing the premier for a while now.
AK (joining the conversation): On December 31st (2017) he is going to play it.[382] *Kolia thought that he forgot about this concerto, but all this time Murja remembered about this idea. Today it's hard to find the orchestras to play your music. That's why it took him so many years to organize this performance.*
NK: Murja is very busy performer, and mostly he is playing abroad.
YT: Murja talked about your music in that article. He said that you are the classic who is living among us, the star, who is known in small circles. I think he talks here only about Russia.
NK: Looks that way to me too.
YT: Murja also said that he faced the problem that people don't know your music, your style, so they can't properly perform it. He said: »When you are suggesting to play a concerto written by Kapustin, you got the answer – oh no, let's rather play the concert of Mendelssohn or Brahms instead«.[383]
NK: I agree with him concerning the style – there are not many musicians who really feel my style.
YT: The jazz and classical essence of your music is very unique and this feel does not come overnight to the performer.
NK: And in different countries jazz sounds very different.
YT: Do you see it as an advantage or disadvantage?

---

[381] Ukhanov, Pavel. »Graf Murja: Net nichego legche, chem igrat' na skripke, no…« [There is Nothing Easier than to Play on the Violin, but…]. *Muzikalnii Klondaik*, March 21, 2017. Accessed January 6, 2018. http://www.muzklondike.ru/announc/218

[382] Note by the author: The premier of the *Violin Concerto*, Op. 141 was postponed. It took place on May 25, 2018 at the Moscow Theatre Concert Hall of Pavel Slobodkin. Accessed July 15, 2018. http://www.center-slobodkina.ru/index.php?option=com_jevents&task=day.listevents&year=2018&month=05&day=25&Itemid=1

[383] Ibid.

NK: Do you think being different is considered to be a disadvantage now?
YT: I don't know. What do you think?
NK: Of course not.
YT: How about that part of Murja's article when he speaks about the musicians who want to play Mendelssohn or Brahms music instead of yours?
NK: I don't want to comment on that.
YT: I think some people are just afraid of playing your music because it sounds so different from the music that they are used to hearing – that's what scares them.

The Concert dedicated to the 70th birthday of Nikolai Kapustin took place on December 11, 2007 in the Concert Hall of Gnessin State Musical College. The program included three pieces for cello and piano (*Elegy*, Op. 96, *Burlesque*, Op. 97, and *Nearly Waltz*, Op. 98) as well as *Sonata for Cello and Piano No. 2*, Op. 84 performed by Alexander Zagorinsky and Alexei Muratov. The program continued with *Trio for Flute, Cello, and Piano*, Op. 86 performed by Marina Rubinstein, Alexander Zagorinsky, and Alexei Muratov. The final piece of the night was *Concert for Cello and String Orchestra No. 2*, Op. 103 performed by Zagorinsky and »The Seasons« Chamber Orchestra conducted by Vladislav Bulakhov.

YT: What kind of memories do you have from that concert? Did you feel the celebratory mood?
NK: I don't remember.

Burst of Popularity: Publishers and Performers of the Music of Kapustin after 2000

The wave of enormous popularity came to Nikolai Kapustin at the beginning of 2000s in Europe and the United States. Since the middle 1980s the music of Kapustin has been published by several different publishing companies. First, in Russia by *Muzgiz* (also known as *Muzyka*), *Sovetskii Kompozitor*, and *A-RAM*.[384] Second, starting from 2003 until 2013 Kapustin published his works in Asia by the Japanese publishing company *Prhythm*. Finally, beginning in 2014 Kapustin's works have been published by one of the most celebrated publishing companies in the world, the German publishing company *Schott Music*.

The meeting of Nikolai Kapustin and the director of *Schott Music* Dr. Peter Hanser-Strecker, Moscow, February 2014

NK: I think Schott published something around seventy opuses of my music by now.
YT: This is almost half of your output.
NK: Yes, the other good thing about Schott Music is that they publish not only my solo piano works but my chamber music too.
YT: Yes, many people think that you are like Chopin – generally writing for piano solo.

---

[384] Note by the author: The publishing company *A-RAM* was situated in Moscow but distributed Kapustin's music in England by *MUST*.

NK: That's the thing. Half of my output is orchestral and chamber works. My chamber music is not as famous as piano pieces, but it doesn't mean that it's bad music.
YT: Do you like your chamber music?
NK: Very much.

Since the early 2000s many eminent pianists have performed the music of Kapustin. These pianists, who began to include Kapustin's works in their repertoire and recordings, were a tremendous help in the growing popularity of the composer. Two of the first pioneers in this movement were the Scottish pianist Steven Osborne and the Canadian pianist Marc-André Hamelin.

In 2000 Steven Osborne[385] recorded the CD called »Nikolai Kapustin Piano Music« on the British recording label »Hyperion«.[386] This disc included *Piano Sonata-Fantasia No. 1*, Op. 39, selected preludes from *Twenty Four Preludes*, Op. 53, and the *Piano Sonata No. 2*, Op. 54.

Steven Osborne, CD »Nikolai Kapustin Piano Music«, Hyperion, London, 2000

YT: How did you get acquainted with Steven Osborne?
NK: I've never met Osborne personally, although, it would be a pleasant thing to do, but I can say that I kind of talked to him.
YT: What do you mean – »kind of talked to him«?
NK: One day he called me on the phone.
YT: Really?

---

[385] Steven Osborne. Accessed January 2, 2018. http://www.stevenosborne.co.uk/biography/.
[386] Hyperion (CDA67159), London, 2000.

NK: Yes, he called me, but I can't even call it a conversation. My knowledge of English language goes until the point where I can understand the language but unfortunately I can't speak. Plus, as you know, the pronunciation plays a major role in understanding each other. He tried to talk Russian, but also got the same result as me... So, the conversation was over very quickly. I feel bad about this confusion.
YT: It is sad that Osborne was not able to communicate with you in Russian.
NK: Wouldn't that be nice?
YT: And what happened next?
NK: Nothing happened. I didn't tell you this – Osborne first contacted my good friend Kolia Petrov, who had my number of course. Petrov knew English better than me and was able to communicate with Osborne. Right after the conversation with Osborne Kolia (Petrov) called me and talked in details about his conversation with Osborne.
YT: That conversation was about you.
NK: Yes, about me. He said that Osborne was really enjoying playing my music and he was interested in playing more. He asked me to send him my scores. That's a shorter version of that conversation, like Russians would say »in two words«.
YT: And then he contacted you.
NK: I guess he just wanted to talk to me about the same thing, but... oh well.
YT: Did you send the scores to Osborne?
NK: Of course I did. Why wouldn't I?
YT: Did he play the music that you sent him?
NK: That's how his CD in 2000 came out.
YT: Oh, so that phone conversation through Petrov was in the late 1990s before your trip to London.
NK: Yes.
YT: Talking about this CD – did you like how Osborne played your music?
NK: I not only liked it very much, this was the very first disc of my music recorded by a famous pianist from abroad.
YT: I agree, that's a big deal.

Mr. Osborne was kind enough to share his memories concerning playing the music of Nikolai Kapustin:

Discovering Kapustin's music was a happy accident – I was playing snooker with a friend and he put on Nikolai Petrov's recording of the 2nd sonata. I already loved jazz and so I was very taken with it. I like to think my recording has something to do with the current interest in Kapustin's music, but mine wasn't the first so who knows?
I contacted Petrov first to find a way to contact Kapustin, and indeed, we couldn't understand each other at all! (I learned some Russian as a teenager but it didn't help much.) Petrov brought me many scores from Russia, and I picked from them to make the CD.

The music of Kapustin is one of the most successful fusions of classical and jazz that I know - normally classical/jazz fusions are very lopsided to either the classical or the jazz, but Kapustin manages a rather equal balance of classical form with jazz language. The only composer I can think of who managed something comparable is Bernstein. It's a lot of fun playing Kapustin's music but there's a big challenge for classical players - how do you swing? It's a profoundly different sense of how rhythm works. Even after having listened to years and years of jazz and mucking about with playing jazz a great deal, I still can't properly do it! But that's a big part of the fun - searching for the groove.[387]

A couple of years later, in 2004, Marc-André Hamelin recorded the CD dedicated to the music of Kapustin called »Nikolai Kapustin Piano Music« on the label »Hyperion«.[388]

Marc-André Hamelin, CD »Nikolai Kapustin Piano Music«, London, 2004

The disc contained seven solo piano works of Kapustin including *Variations*, Op. 41, *Eight Concert Etudes*, Op. 40, *Bagatelles*, Op. 59, *Suite in Old Style*, Op. 28, *Piano Sonata No. 6*, Op. 62, *Sonatina*, Op. 100, and *Five Etudes in Different Intervals*, Op. 68. Undoubtedly, the recording of this CD by Marc-André Hamelin helped promote the music of Kapustin to a much greater audience.

---

[387] From correspondence with Steven Osborne, February 28, 2018.
[388] Marc-André Hamelin »Nikolai Kapustin: Piano Music«, Hyperion (CDA67433), London, 2004.

One of the good friends of Kapustin, with whom he became acquainted at the beginning of 2000s, was the Bulgarian pianist Ludmil Angelov.[389] Angelov received international recognition of his talent at the age of fifteen, when he became the winner of the competition in Senigallia (Italy, 1976). Then followed the victories in the major international competitions, such as International Frederic Chopin Piano Competition (Poland, 1985), Palm Beach International Competition (USA, 1990), Piano Masters (Monte Carlo, 1994), World Piano Masters Tour (France, 1997), and others.[390]

Ludmil Angelov

YT: *I didn't know that Angelov was born in Bulgaria.*
NK: *He was born in Bulgaria but for many years he has been living in Spain. Good for him – he moved there with all his family.*
YT: *I read that he won the Chopin competition in 1985.*
NK: *I know that he played a majority of works written by Chopin.*
YT: *Yes, in 1987-1988 he played a cycle of twelve piano recitals that included all solo piano works written by Chopin.*[391]
NK: *I remember he told me that. Angelov is very talented musician.*
YT: *He recorded your Piano Concerto No. 4, Op. 56,*[392] *and I adore it!*

---

[389] Ludmil Angelov. Accessed January 2, 2018.
http://virtuosoartistsmanagement.com/ludmil-angelov-piano/.
[390] Ludmil Angelov: Biography. Accessed January 8, 2018.
http://www.lespritdeladiva.org/ludmilAngelov.
[391] Ibid.
[392] From the correspondence with Ludmil Angelov from January 17, 2018: »The recording which you adore and is up on Youtube, is a live recording of the world premiere performance in Murcia, Spain, with Murcia Symphony Orchestra and José Miguel Rodilla, conductor. Later on, I performed the Concerto No. 4 as premiere in other countries as well: in Turkey (Adana

NK: *Yes, I liked this recording very much as well.*
YT: *How did you get acquainted with Angelov?*
NK: *I wasn't acquainted with Angelov personally, we know each other from our correspondence.*
YT: *And you became good friends.*
NK: *Yes, this is true.*
YT: *Is it possible to become good friends just writing the letters?*
NK: *Of course, it is possible.*
YT: *Do you remember when you started your correspondence with Angelov?*
NK: *I think it was sometime in the beginning of 2000s.*
YT: *Did Angelov perform any of your other pieces?*
NK: *Yes, he played, premiered, and recorded my music, actually he premiered my Piano Sonata No. 14 (Op. 120) with big success. He also recorded an entire disc of my music in 2011 with another pianist from Spain, whose name is Daniel del Pino.*[393]
YT: *It is sad a little that you never met.*
NK: *Actually, there was a chance that we would meet with Angelov.*

In the spring of 2006 Kapustin received an invitation to the XII International Music Festival in Toledo (Spain) to attend the premier of some of his works. The renowned Bulgarian pianist Ludmil Angelov[394] performed the world premiere of *Piano Sonata No. 14*, Op. 120. During the same concert, Mr. Angelov, Spanish pianist Daniel Del Pino,[395] and two percussionists, Juanjo Guillem and Rafael Gálvez, performed the world premiere of *Concerto for Two Pianos and Percussion*, Op. 104.

Symphony, cond. Antonio Pirolli) and Italy (Magna Grecia Symphony Orchestra, cond. Michele Nitti). The Bulgarian premiere of the Concerto, with the Sofia Philharmonic, is planned for November 2018 during my Piano Extravaganza Festival in Sofia«.

[393] Ludmil Angelov and Daniel Del Pino, »Nikolai Kapustin: 2+2 4 Kapustin« (Non Profit Music 1011), 2011.

[394] Ludmil Angelov, participation in the XII Musical Festival in Toledo, June 2006. Accessed January 8, 2018. http://varnasummerfest.org/news_search_results_en.php?page=news_show&newsID=202&nsID=12.

[395] Daniel Del Pino. Accessed January 16, 2018. http://achucarrofoundation.org/legacy-pianists/daniel-del-pino/.

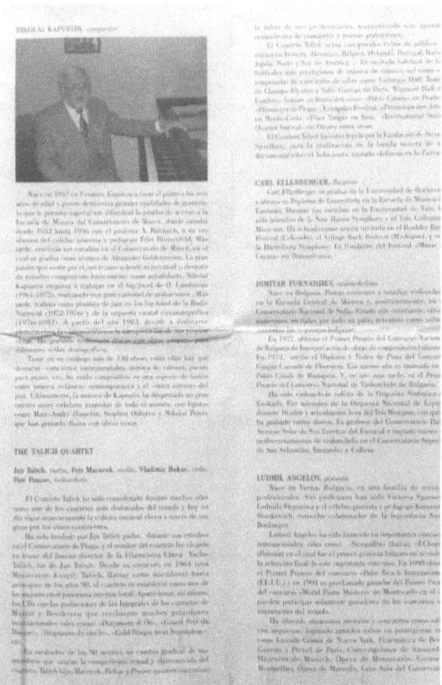

Program notes: Concert dedicated to the Music of Nikolai Kapustin, XII International Music Festival, Toledo, Spain, May 19, 2006

YT: *Did Angelov invite you to come to Spain to listen to the premier of some of your works?*
NK: *Yes, he invited me and Alla. He said he has a house in Barcelona and we would have all the necessary conditions for a good life during our visit.*
YT: *So the main goal was like with Hamelin – to attend the premier of some of your works.*
NK: *Exactly, the only difference was – Hamelin invited me to come to England, and Angelov – to Spain.*
YT: *Did they play just two premiers of your works?*
NK: *There were two recitals dedicated to my music in Toledo at that time.[396] I remember they also performed two of my works for the first time in Spain– Trio for Flute, Cello, and Piano, Op. 86 and String Quartet No. 1, Op. 88.*

---

[396] From the correspondence with Mr. Angelov: During the second concert dedicated to the music of Nikolai Kapustin in Toledo in 2006 the world premiere of the *Double Concerto for Violin, Piano and Strings* (Op. 105) by violinist Alexander Sitkovetsky, pianist Ludmil Angelov, and the chamber string orchestra »Virtuosi Italiani«, was performed and conducted by Marco Boni.

YT: So, we can say that they performed the Western premiers of Op. 86 and Op. 88.
NK: Correct.
YT: With the tone of your voice I can tell that you didn't go to Spain in 2006.
NK: I wanted to go to Spain badly, but unfortunately, we didn't go.
YT: What happened?
AK (joining the conversation): Angelov organized the whole tour for us very carefully, so after all uncertainties we finally decided to go. We already prepared all the documents, visas and everything, but Kolia's sister Fira suddenly got very sick and we had to cancel our trip.
NK: We were ready to go to Spain when we received that sad news about Fira. At that moment I realized that there was no way for me to go to Spain – I needed to take care of my sister.
YT: Probably, Angelov was very disappointed when he found out that you cancelled your trip to Spain.
NK: Yes, he was. From what I remember, I dedicated my Piano Sonata No. 16 (Op. 131) to Angelov.
YT: Did he perform it yet?
NK: Not yet. I recorded the Piano Sonata No. 16 myself on my last CD.
YT: You got ahead of Angelov.

In April 2003 the Japanese pianist from Tokyo Masahiro Kawakami[397] visited Kapustin for the first time in his apartment in Moscow. Since then they started a long time friendship. Now, Kawakami not only performs the works of Kapustin but also organizes the Japan Kapustin Society[398] and the Kapustin Festival. At the present time Kawakami has recorded four CDs of solo and chamber music of Kapustin. His latest project is the recording of »The Complete Piano Works of Nikolai Kapustin«.[399] Undoubtedly, Kawakami helps to promote the music of Kapustin abroad, and particularly in Japan.

---

[397] Masahiro Kawakami. Accessed January 8, 2018.
http://www.cam.hi-ho.ne.jp/pianistas/kawakami_english.html.
[398] Japan Kapustin Society. Accessed February 7, 2018. http://www.kapustin.jp/.
[399] From the correspondence with Masahiro Kawakami, February 5, 2018.

Masahiro Kawakami visiting Nikolai Kapustin and Alla Kapustina, Moscow, 2003

YT: *I just realized that you met with Kawakami almost fifteen years ago.*
NK: *I can't believe it was so long ago.*
YT: *Do you remember that meeting?*
NK: *I remember in 2003 I was recording my Piano Sonata No. 12 (Op. 102) at the studio for my upcoming disc and Masahiro asked to attend that recording session.*
YT: *Did you feel comfortable about that idea?*
NK: *Of course I did. Masahiro visited me many times since 2003. I met his wife and some of his students. I remember they played like a whole recital for me here performing my music.*
YT: *In what language do you communicate with Masahiro?*
NK: *The first time he came with a Russian translator, a Japanese girl, but the other times that he visited us we talked in Russian.*
YT: *In Russian? That's great!*
NK: *It was nice of him.*
YT: *Did you understand him?*
NK: *Of course I did. I think he studied Russian in Japan.*
YT: *I keep thinking — what would happen if I would be a German girl who speaks English and willing to write a book about you?*
NK: *This would never happen. I remember a while ago one German journalist contacted me asking to give him an interview. He said that he speaks Russian fluently.*
YT: *Did you agree?*
NK: *Yes, unfortunately I agreed. That was a big mistake. It ended up that this journalist knows a couple of phrases in Russian, that's all.*
YT: *I guess the interview didn't go well.*

411

NK: It was a disaster. All of this time I kept thinking – why did I agree to do this?
YT: Not to change the subject of our conversation – I know that Masahiro Kawakami premiered many of your works.
NK: Yes, a little while ago he played the premier of My Piano Concerto No. 3, Op. 48 in Tokyo and also my Piano Concert No. 6, Op. 74.
YT: I remember you also mentioned that there were some other musicians from Japan who visited you.
NK: Yes, there is a very good piano duet, both Japanese pianists – Natsuki Nishimoto and Asuka Matsumoto who came to us. Natsuki is also playing my solo piano music.
YT: How do you remember all those japanese names? I feel sorry, but on my ear they might sound very close to each other.
NK: It's all because you don't know the Japanese language. I studied Japanese, so it doesn't sound to me as foreign as it sounds for you.
YT: Can you name some other musicians that you appreciate in how they play your music?
NK: I like violist Christina Rauh, cellinists Eckard Runge and Enrico Dindo, pianists Yuko Kondo, a young Chinese pianist A Bu, Yuja Wang, three Korean girls from the Ahn Trio. The Ahn Trio played my Divertissement in Four Movements for Violin, Cello, and Piano, Op. 126 everywhere – in the United States, Germany, some other countries too. In general, a lot of Asian musicians are playing my music now.
YT: Can we say that the interest to your music started in Asia – countries such as Japan, South Korea, and China?
NK: Yes, you may. My publisher in the past was also from Japan.
YT: Then the interest in your music spread to Europe.
NK: Correct. Now I have a European publisher and many European musicians, from Germany, Spain, Italy… all performing my music.
YT: How about the United States?
NK: I think after Europe the interest to my music spread out to the United States, but that was not a long time ago.
YT: So, we are now living when the interest in your music appears in the United States.
NK: Looks that way to me.
YT: How about Russia?
NK: I will be always known only in very narrow musical circles in Russia, nobody knows me here, which is quite ironic.
YT: I agree.
NK: And also you can't take seriously some of the performances of my music that sounds here in Russia.
YT: What do you mean?
NK: On a big scale it doesn't matter. Those performers from Russia – they are unknown in the world.

YT: Not all I think. Can you give me some names of Russian performers who are playing your music that you like?
NK: I like how Nikolai Rudenko is playing my music, Nikolai Lugansky, Alexei Volodin...
YT: Those are big names.
NK: Yes, they are famous Russian classical pianists. Who else? Elena Los'...By the way, a little while ago Elena Los' visited me with another talented Russian pianist – Dmitry Masleev.
YT: This name does sound familiar to me.
NK: Masleev won the 1st prize on the Tchaikovsky Piano Competition in 2015.
YT: Does Masleev play your music?
NK: Yes, you can find his performances of my music on Youtube. He is a highly virtuoso pianist.

The 80th Birthday of Nikolai Kapustin

A celebration of the 80th birthday of Nikolai Kapustin in 2017 was marked with an extensive series of events dedicated to the music of the eminent composer. First, in Russia on May 31, 2017 Alexander Zagorinsky performed a concert in the Chamber Hall of the Moscow Philharmonic (Moscow, Russia) dedicated to Nikolai Kapustin. The performers included cellist Alexander Zagorinsky, flutist Marina Rubinshteyn, and pianist Ivan Sokolov. The program was dedicated to the cello music of Kapustin, which included *Sonata for Cello and Piano No. 1*, Op. 64, *Sonata for Cello and Piano No. 2*, Op. 84, *Introduction and Scherzino for Cello Solo*, Op. 93, *Suite for Cello Solo*, Op. 124, *Elegy for Cello and Piano*, Op. 96, *Burlesque for Cello and Piano*, Op. 97, *Nearly Waltz for Cello and Piano*, Op. 98, and *Trio for Flute, Cello, and Piano*, Op. 86.

Poster for the concert dedicated to the 80th Birthday of Nikolai Kapustin, Moscow Philharmonic, May 31, 2017

YT: Now I see what you meant when you said that if we would look at some of the programs of your music we may think that you composed deliberately for cello.
NK: I told you.
YT: I have a suspicion that you didn't go to that concert.
NK: I know ahead of time that all those concerts dedicated to my music will go equally well with me or without me. So, there is no need for me to be there.

Another concert occurred in Russia on November 30, 2017 at the Great Hall of the Moscow Conservatory. It was dedicated to the 60th Anniversary of the Russian-Chinese Friendship. The Chinese pianist A Bu and the Igor Butman Moscow Jazz Orchestra performed Kapustin's *Piano Concerto No. 2*, Op. 14 and dedicated this performance for the 80th birthday of the composer.

On January 8, 2018 Kapustin's birthday was celebrated in Japan. A series of three concerts, that all happened in one day, was a part of Japan Kapustin Festival in Tokyo (Japan) organized by Japanese pianist Masahiro Kawakami.[400] The program included twenty-five pieces of numerous excerpts from solo piano music, chamber works, and the orchestral music of Nikolai Kapustin.

Japan Kapustin Festival, Tokyo, January 8, 2018

The 80th birthday of Kapustin was celebrated in Europe as well. On February 10, 2018 the Italian pianist Professor Vito Reibaldi[401] organized a concert at

---

[400] Nikolai Kapustin Official Website. Accessed January 7, 2018. http://nikolai-kapustin.blogspot.ru/.
[401] Vito Reibaldi. Accessed February 5, 2018. http://www.circuitomusica.it/reiglob.

the Conservatory of Music of Niccolo Puccini in Bari (Italy) titled »The 80 years of the Great Nikolai Kapustin«. This concert was a part of the series of events that were dedicated to five leading composers of our time, who incorporated jazz and classical elements in their music: George Gershwin, Earl Wild, Friedrich Gulda, David Brubeck, and Nikolai Kapustin.

The Kapustin concert was entirely dedicated to the solo piano music of the composer. The two professors and the selected students of the Conservatory of Music of Niccolo Puccini[402] performed *Sonatina*, Op. 100, *Andante*, Op. 58, selected pieces from *Twenty-Four Preludes*, Op. 53, *Eight Concert Etudes*, Op. 40, and *Five Etudes in Different Intervals*, Op. 68.

Concert dedicated to the 80th birthday of Nikolai Kapustin, Conservatory of Music of Niccolo Puccini, Bari, Italy, February 10, 2018[403]

YT: How did you get acquainted with Vito Reibaldi?
NK: He found me. I dedicated my Piano Sonata No. 18, Op. 135 to Reibaldi.
YT: Did Reibaldi perform the premire of this sonata?

---

[402] From the correspondence with Vito Reibaldi, February 5, 2018.
[403] From the correspondence with Vito Reibaldi, February 4, 2018: The original date of the concert was December 22, 2017 but it was postponed to February 10, 2018.

NK: *I think so.*[404]
YT: *One interesting detail I wanted to discuss with you – this concert of your music was a part of the series of concerts dedicated to composers of the twenty first century. I know most of the names on that series – you, George Gershwin, Friedrich Gulda, and David Brubeck.*
NK: *For some reason people always compare my music with the music of Gershwin, I am already tired of it.*
YT: *Is that a good or bad thing?*
NK: *It's not a pleasant thing.*
YT: *There is one name on the list of five composers that I am not familiar with – it's Earl Wild. Do you happen to know this pianist-composer?*
NK: *I've never heard this name.*
YT: *I guess this composer is also from the same category as you – the fusion of classical and jazz music. I am going to investigate this name.*

After making a couple easy steps through internet sources I found some interesting information about this American composer Earl Wild. He was a Pittsburgh based composer and performer who became the very first composer to be streamed on the internet. He played music for six American Presidents[405] and his music often sounds close to the music of Nikolai Kapustin.[406]

YT: *I found out that in the 1970s Wild wrote the transcription of Ellington's »I Got Rhythm«.*
NK: *That's the kind of music that we were performing with Lundstrem.*
YT: *I do think there is a difference between you and Wild – you always compose the music and Wild became famous because of his transcriptions of classical and jazz pieces.*
NK: *I agree. I did a lot of arrangements and transcriptions during my life though.*
YT: *Not changing the subject of our conversation – how do you feel about the fact that more and more pianists want to show their adoration to your music dedicating the whole concerts to you?*
NK: *It's good, and I am glad that all those concerts didn't involve my attendance.*
YT: *But I think they probably invited you.*
NK: *Of course they invited me. The recordings of those concerts is enough for me.*

---

[404] From the correspondence with Vito Reibaldi, February 11, 2018: Vito Reibaldi played the world premiere of *Piano Sonata No. 18*, Op. 135 at the »Imperial Castle« in Puglia (Italy) on April 14, 2013.
[405] Earl Wild. Accessed January 6, 2018. http://www.earlwild.com/.
[406] Earl Wild-Gershwin Etude »I got Rhythm«. Accessed January 6, 2018. https://www.youtube.com/watch?v=1MQZ6L1KMOI.

YT: Oh, you have a double advantage – didn't go to the concert and have an opportunity to listen to them at home.
NK: That's what I think.

Presentations and the Beginning of Research on the Music of Nikolai Kapustin

The music of Nikolai Kapustin has gained popularity through performances on international piano competitions and festivals, presentations on national and international conferences, and the beginning of research of his music.

Kapustin's music was performed so far on international piano competitions in the United States,[407] Canada,[408] France,[409] Italy,[410] Austria,[411] and Russia.[412]

YT: I read that in 2013 American pianist Claire Huangci performed your Etude No. 1 »Prelude«, Op. 40 on the 14th Van Cliburn International Piano Competition.[413]

NK: And not only on Van Cliburn Competition pianists are playing my music, on some other highly rated competitions too. For example I remember South Korean pianist Yeol Eum Son played my Variations (Op. 41) on Tchaikovsky Piano Competition.[414]

YT: I think this is a very notable gesture – that your music is performed on the international competitions together with the well-known serious composers.

NK: Yes, that's a good thing. Although, I do remember one of the judges from the Tchaikovsky Competition said that if Yeol Eum Son would play a piece other than Kapustin's then she might be the first one; she won the second place.

YT: I don't think I can comment on that.

NK: There is no need for that.

---

[407] Cleveland International Piano Competition (Cleveland, OH, 2009), Gina Bachauer International Young Artists Piano Competition (Salt Lake City, 2012), Modavi Center Young Artist Competition (California Univercity, CA, 2014), and Ross McKee Piano Competition (San Francisco, CA, 2013).

[408] Knigge Music Competition (UBC School of Music, Vancouver, Canada, 2013).

[409] International Piano Competition »From Bach to Jazz« (Paris, France, 2013).

[410] 5th International Piano Competition Republic of San Marino (San Marino, Italy, 2012).

[411] Eurovision Young Musicians Competition (Vienna, Austria, 2012).

[412] From the correspondence with Wim de Haan, February 6, 2018. For more information on international competition where the music of Kapustin was performed visit http://nikolai-kapustin.blogspot.nl/.

[413] Rorianne Schrade, The Fourteenth Van Cliburn International Piano Competition in Review, *New York Concert Review*, July 8, 2013. Accessed December 18, 2018. http://nyconcertreview.com/articles/the-fourteenth-van-cliburn-international%E2%80%A8-piano-competition-in-review/.

[414] Yeol Eum Son won the 2nd place on the 14th International Tchaikovsky Competition in 2011. On the second round, she performed Kapustin *Variations*, Op. 41. Accessed February 6, 2018. http://www.koreaherald.com/view.php?ud=20130220000893.

One of the first presentations on the music of Nikolai Kapustin happened on July 2, 2011 at the 101st Annual Convention of the Music Teachers' Association of California (MTAC) in Oakland, CA by Evan Chow.[415] One of the latest presentations on Kapustin was the presentation »The Intersection of Classical and Jazz: The Introduction to the Music of Nikolai Kapustin«. The presentation took place in Baltimore, MD (United States) as part of the Music Teacher National Conference (MTNA) on March 21, 2017. The students of Dr. James Miltenberger from West Virginia University (Morgantown, WV) were performing and talking about the music of Nikolai Kapustin.[416]

Before 2000 there had been very little research on the music of Nikolai Kapustin. One of the pioneers of this research was Dr. Jonathan Mann, who wrote the first dissertation on the music of Kapustin, which was called »Red, White, and Blue Notes: The Symbiotic Music of Nikolai Kapustin«.[417] This research document investigated the life and the music of Nikolai Kapustin. It was published in 2006 and became a very influential and helpful source for other doctoral students all other the world in their research on the music and life of the composer. Today, more and more graduate students are dedicating the topics of their dissertation to the music of Kapustin.

In 2005 the Official Kapustin website[418] was established by a friend of Kapustin's from the Netherlands – Wim de Haan. Additionally, in 2007 Wim de Haan began the blog of Nikolai Kapustin,[419] and from December 2017 he created the Facebook page of the composer.[420] Being a webmaster, Wim de Haan[421] is dedicating his efforts to the promotion of the music of Maestro Kapustin.

Needless to say, because of all of these efforts (the musicians who are putting their interest in playing Kapustin's music, researchers and theorists, who write articles and studies on Kapustin, and people who organize concerts) the interest in his music will continue to grow.

---

[415] Evan Chow, presentation on Nikolai Kapustin. Accessed January 12, 2018. https://www.youtube.com/watch?v=sWHX0Pyw_8M.
[416] MTNA National Conference (Baltimore, MD). Accessed February 6, 2018. https://www.mtna.org/MTNA/Engage/Conferences/Handouts/2017/Tuesday.aspx.
[417] Jonathan Mann, »Red, White, and Blue Notes: The Symbiotic Music of Nikolai Kapustin«. Accessed February 6, 2018. https://etd.ohiolink.edu/ap/10?0::NO:10:P10_ACCESSION_NUM:ucin1179852881.
[418] http://www.nikolai-kapustin.info/
[419] Note by the author: This blog was deactivated September 2018.
[420] https://www.facebook.com/kapustincomposer/
[421] From the correspondence with Wim de Haan (February 6, 2018): Wim de Haan is also running websites for such eminent musicians as Tatiana Nikolayeva, Josef Hoffman, and others.

Compositions of 2000-2017 (Ops. 100-161)

The years of 2000 through 2017 were quite an intense period for Kapustin as a composer. During this period, Kapustin composed sixty-two pieces, which included mostly solo piano compositions and chamber works.

The solo piano music of this period included genres of piano sonata, fantasia, sonatina, etude, and paraphrase. Most notably, during this time Kapustin finished composing his cycle of twenty piano sonatas. Thus, he wrote the last ten of his sonatas, starting with *Piano Sonata No. 11*, Op. 101 (2000) and finishing with the *Piano Sonata No. 20*, Op. 144 (2011). The two pieces in the etude genre were *Two Etude-like Trinkets*, Op. 122 and *Etude Courte mais Transcendente pour Piano*, Op. 149. The majority of works written for solo piano during this period are characterpieces – short compositions, approximately four minutes in length with descriptive titles, for example *Gingerbread Man*, Op. 111, *End of the Rainbow*, Op. 112, or *Spice Island*, Op. 117. That group of characterpieces includes three paraphrases, where the composer used themes written by other composers. The paraphrases include *Paraphrase on the Theme of Paul Dvoirin*, Op. 108, *Paraphrase on »Blue Bossa« by Kenny Dorham*, Op. 123, and *Paraphrase on Dizzy Gillespie's »Manteca« for Two Pianos*, Op. 129.

The chamber music of this period includes a variety of different genres, such as concerto, variations, suite, sonata, divertissement, string quartet, piano trio, capriccio, and sonatina. During this time Kapustin composed *Concerto No. 2 for Cello and String Orchestra*, Op. 103, *Sonata for Flute and Piano*, Op. 125, *String Quartet No. 2*, Op. 132, two *Piano Trios for Violin, Cello, and Piano*, Op. 136 and Op. 142, *Piece for String Quartet »Rondo Frivole«*, Op. 150, *Piece for String Quartet »The Last Attempt«*, and *Sonatina for Viola and Piano*, Op. 158.

Very unusual and unique instrumentation for chamber music was presented in the *Concerto for Two Pianos and Percussion*, Op. 104 and *Concerto for Violin, Piano, and String Orchestra*, Op. 105. There is only one piece in Kapustin's chamber music where he used previously composed material. This piece is called *Variations on »Sweet Georgia Brown« for Viola, Alto-Saxophone, Piano, and Bass*, Op. 107, where Kapustin used the famous jazz standard theme written by Ben Bernie and Maceo Pinkard in 1925.

YT: *It looks that you didn't write much orchestral music during that period.*
NK: *Yes, at some point I stopped composing music that involves the big band sound. It all stopped after I finished working with Lundstrem and Karamyshev.*
YT: *So, there was no desire to write orchestral works anymore.*

NK: Yes, although, I wrote a few pieces for the solo instrument and orchestra. For example, I composed three concertos in a row in 2002 – Concerto for Cello and Orchestra No. 2, Op. 103, Concerto for Two Pianos and Percussion, Op. 104, and Concerto for Violin, Piano and String Orchestra, Op. 105.

YT: It is very interesting that you didn't compose the pieces that involved orchestra for some time and then wrote three pieces one after another.

NK: Although, after those three concertos there are only two pieces that involved the orchestra. That was my Violin Concerto, Op. 141 and the second edition of my Piano Concerto No. 1, Op. 147.

YT: I actually wanted to ask you about this second edition of Piano Concerto No. 1 – why did you decide to write it? You kept saying that you don't like your early works that much, and Piano Concerto No. 1 is your Op. 2, written in 1961.

NK: I knew for a long time that it should be done. I knew that but I never had time to change it because I was always busy doing something else.

YT: To change what?

NK: To change the instrumentation.

YT: So, the second edition of the concerto involves the instrumentation.

NK: Of course. I remember I talked with Lundstrem on the phone many years after I stopped working with him and he suggested writing a new version of this concerto, to revise it in other words.

YT: Did you substitute some instruments with the others or make the instrumentation more complex?

NK: No, believe it or not – I simplified the instrumentation. Before that, too many instruments were involved and one musician had to be able to play on a few instruments quickly switching from one instrument to another. Now, I made it the way that one musician is playing only one instrument; it is better that way.

During this period of 2000-2017, Kapustin kept writing the music for commission.

YT: I keep thinking – did you write any music for commission during this period?
NK: Yes, I did. In 2004 I wrote my Sonata for Flute and Piano, Op. 125 and in 2014 – A Little Duo for Flute and Cello, Op. 156 for American flutist Immanuel Davis.[422]
YT: How did Davis find you?
NK: I think he is a friend with three Korean girls from the Ahn Trio, who were playing my music quite intensively at the beginning of 2000s. I think they helped Davis to find me.
YT: Did he come to visit you from the US or just kept in touch through the letters?

---

[422] Immanuel Davis. Accessed January 12, 2018.
https://apps.cla.umn.edu/directory/profiles/davis210.

NK: *We communicated only though the letters.*
YT: *I remember you said that you don't like to compose for the commission anymore.*
NK: *This is true, but it is also known that sometimes some of the best music was composed by the composer for the commission. So, you never know.*
YT: *Did Davis ask you to compose two pieces?*
NK: *No, first he asked me to compose only one piece – Sonata for Flute and Piano, Op. 125.*
YT: *Did he suggest also the genre of sonata and the instrumentation –for flute and piano?*
NK: *Yes, he asked me to write the sonata for flute and piano.*
YT: *How about the second piece?*
NK: *Many years after he asked me to compose another piece, because he liked very much how the first piece turned out. That is how my Op. 156 »A Little Duo for Flute and Cello« came to life.*
YT: *I guess he asked you again for that particular instrumentation – flute and cello.*
NK: *Yes, I remember I was a little surprised with this idea, didn't know what to do with the cello part, but then finally decided to try. I like experimenting with new sounds.*

Some of the most interesting piano works to discuss from the period of 2000-2017 include the *Sonatina*, Op. 100, *Piano Sonata No. 12*, Op. 102, *Nobody is Perfect*, Op. 151, *A Pianist in Jeopardy*, Op. 152, and *Moon Rainbow*, Op. 161.

The piece *Sonatina*, Op. 100 was composed in 2000 and belongs to a group of Kapustin's works that are well-known and extensively performed. This composition is considered to be one of a few pieces written by the composer that, in comparison with his other works, is on the easy side, if we even can apply this term to Kapustin's music.

YT: *Do you like this piece?*
NK: *Not really.*
YT: *Although, many pianists are performing this piece and it seems that they are enjoying your music a lot.*
NK: *They should not do it; it is not the best piece that I wrote.*
YT: *Can you tell a story of how this piece happened to appear?*
NK: *As I told you earlier, the main material of this piece was composed at the time when I studied at the conservatory, in the late 1950s. This was one of my sonatinas for piano solo that I composed at that time. Even knowing that I re-worked the material, you can still see that this is one of my early works.*
YT: *But that could be one of the reasons why it's so popular – since it was written during your years of study at the conservatory it is not that difficult. That's why more pianists can play this piece.*
NK: *This is probably true.*

YT: *If we would compare your Op. 100 with Suite in Old Style, Op. 28, your official first piece written for solo piano, which one would be easier? Or might they be the same in difficulties?*
NK: *Of course Op. 100 is much easier.*
YT: *How did it happen that you decided to come back to your previously composed music?*
NK: *Yes, I usually don't like to come back to previously composed works, but this piece was an exception. A friend of mine from the conservatory time, Grigorenko, ended up working in one of the publishing companies in Moscow. He contacted me in the late 1990s and asked to compose the piece on the easier side so they could publish it.*
YT: *So, the publishing company was interested in publishing the pieces on the easier side?*
NK: *Correct.*
YT: *Why didn't you compose such a piece?*
NK: *I decided I would rather look for something that I composed earlier that might be not that difficult and re-work it rather than forcing myself to compose something that I know I will not like to begin with.*
YT: *This is true. If we would compare your original version of Sonatina and the new version of this piece – what would be the difference? What did you change?*
NK: *I made it more complex.*
YT: *In which way?*
NK: *In the harmonic way. Although, all my changes were not that significant.*
YT: *Do you happen to have the score of that original version of Sonatina from the late 1950s?*
NK: *Unfortunately, the score doesn't exist now. Although, I remember this piece very well, I think I might be able even to play it by memory.*
YT: *After all these years?*
NK: *I used to play it a lot, that's why I remember it.*

The *Piano Sonata No. 12*, Op. 102 was composed in 2001 and is considered by Kapustin to be one of his most successful pieces. He recorded this sonata on his disc »Nikolai Kapustin: Last Recording« in 2003.

YT: *I remember you told me earlier that you liked this sonata a lot.*
NK: *Yes, I do. I was inspired when I composed this work. You know, sometimes it takes you a long time to write a piece, something is not working right, and other times the piece just comes on its own. This was the case with Sonata No. 12; it was not difficult to write at all.*
YT: *I can tell. It flows naturally in a perfect way.*
NK: *That's why I recorded it on one of my last discs.*
YT: *Yes, you even put this sonata as a last composition for the disc that originally was supposed to be the last disc. That means that this piece is special.*

NK: Although, at the end on my actual last disc I finished with Piano Sonata No. 16, Op. 131.
YT: I keep thinking about the form of this sonata – two very contrasting movements. The first movement begins like through composed, almost like an improvisation – free in tempo. From the first listening, you get the sense that all the themes appear on its own very naturally.
NK: But form-wise this piece is clear. For example, it is hard to miss the recapitulation in the first movement.
YT: The second movement begins in the tempo »Allegro Assai« – you like this tempo, don't you?
NK: Yes, the tempo gives you an idea what the piece might be all about.
YT: There is not even one spot in your music where the pianist has rest.
NK: There is none. And for the listener too by the way.
YT: Although, I do have to tell you – every time I hear an extremely difficult technical spot, it follows by the material that is a little bit easy, where the pianist can take a little rest, to breathe so to say. Does this mean that when you compose the piece you also think about the pianists who will perform your music?
NK: I don't know.
AK (joining the conversation): I agree, he does. I remember he told me once that because he is a pianist he is thinking about the other pianists who will play his music too – everything should be comfortable and suitable to play.
YT: I knew that! Because it would literally »kill« the pianists if after one highly difficult spot will come another one.
NK: Yes, Alla is right, that's how it was.
YT: The end of this sonata is expressive, highly technical, moving somewhere to a place where nobody can reach it, an ending that will have the audience shouting »Bravo«!!!!
NK: I like effective endings.
YT: Do you like how other pianists are playing this work?
NK: I like how Yuki Kondo is playing this sonata, and in general, all my music that she performs is well done.

In 2013 there were some unusual circumstances concerning the composition of two of his opuses – *Nobody is Perfect*, Op. 151 and *A Pianist in Jeopardy*, Op. 152.

> YT: *Do you remember the story of how these two opuses, Op. 151 and Op. 152 appeared?*
> NK: *There is a little region of land called Republic of San-Marino, that is situated close to Italy but does not belong to the Italian territory, it's an independent area. Believe it or not - they have an international piano competition on that small piece of land. And I decided to compose the piece for that competition.*
> YT: *Why did you write two?*
> NK: *So they could choose one.*
> YT: *And what happened next?*
> NK: *They wrote me the response that they already chose Chick Corea's piece and they can't afford additional expenses for the second composer.*
> YT: *What was your reaction?*
> NK: *That made me very upset because I didn't want any payment, all I wanted was my music to be performed.*
> AK (joining the conversation): *I remember Kolia used to say – I was trying so hard to compose those two pieces and now the conversation goes just towards the direction of being paid or not. It's music!*
> YT: *Knowing the level of difficulty of your latest works I may assume that they may come to this conclusion because of the difficulties of those two pieces.*
> NK: *I agree with you. Although, the student of Masahiro Kawakami learned »Nobody is Perfect« and played this piece.*
> YT: *How about the Op. 152 »A Pianist in Jeopardy« – has anyone played it yet?*
> NK: *Nobody played it so far.*

The characterpiece *Moon Rainbow*, Op. 161 is the last piano work as well as the last completed piece by Kapustin to the present time.

> YT: *How long is this piece?*
> NK: *As always – no more than four minutes.*
> YT: *I keep thinking how poetic your titles are.*
> NK: *Do you like it too? I asked Antosha (Anton Kapustin) and he suggested this title to me.*
> YT: *I wonder how he comes up with such interesting names.*
> NK: *I think he said that there is a physics term called »moon rainbow« and I keep forgetting to ask him what it means.*
> YT: *I investigated this question about the moon rainbow. It is the unique phenomenon that actually happens very rarely in nature. The main factor of its' appearance is the low*

position of the full moon and the rain. When the raindrops reflect the moonlight, the moon rainbow appears. The first time this miracle was described in the poetry of the nineteenth century. People who saw it were highly impressed.
NK: *I suspected that it existed. I wish I could see it.*

Family Sorrow: Loss of Fira Grigorievna Kapustina

December 10, 2007 was a day of sorrow for the family of Nikolai Kapustin. His beloved only sister, Fira Grigorievna Kapustina, passed away.

YT: Can we talk about your sister's last years of life?
NK: We can.
YT: Was she ill for a long time or did it just happen suddenly?
NK: She was sick for a while. In 2006 we were getting ready for our trip to Spain and received that sad news about her sickness. So, we cancelled the trip and went to Gorlovka (Ukraine) where she lived at that time, to visit her. At that time Gorlovka was a normal city not like now.[423]
YT: Was she at the hospital?
NK: No, she was at her house. I remember we rented an apartment very close to her house and stayed there for a few weeks. After that we came back to Moscow. She lived for a year and a half after that, but on December 10, 2007 she was gone.
YT: Was she sick during all this time?
NK: Yes, she was fighting the illness during all this time.
YT: I feel so sorry for you. Am I mistaken that on December 11, 2007 there was the concert dedicated to your 70th Birthday?
NK: You are absolutely right. Coincidently, these two events happened almost at the same time.
YT: What a horrible coincidence – big celebratory day and a big sorrow day both came one after another.
NK: That was tough– we couldn't cancel the concert that was going to be the very next day, so we had to go through all of that with Alla.
YT: I don't know how you were able to survive it.
NK: I can't say that it happened suddenly, we knew it was coming… but almost on the same day…
YT: Nobody can prepare themselves for something like that.
NK: All my family, my mother, father, Fira, they are all gone now… I am the only one who is left in this world, all by myself.
YT: You have your wife, Alla Semionovna, your children and your grandchildren.
NK: This is true, but I can't compose.
YT: What is stopping you?
NK: I am too old.

---

[423] Note by the author: Here Kapustin refers to the military events that happened in Gorlovka since the summer of 2014.

YT: As one of our Russian classics said – the age is not the amount of the years that you have lived, it is the state of your soul. Did you know that Elliott Carter passed away being ninety-three years old and kept composing his music until the very end?
NK: That wouldn't be my case.
YT: I just remembered another saying on the same subject – it doesn't matter how long you live; what matters is what you leave behind when you're gone.
NK: This is a good one!

Kapustin's Flow of Life

I think it might be of some interest to the readers to learn about the daily life of the composer. The home life of Nikolai Kapustin, as well as his life thirty years ago, is highly organized – his daily routine always begins between five and six in the morning.

YT: Why do you start your day that early?
NK: It's a habit now. I always used to wake up early because of my intense life, and even now, when I am not that busy, it feels right.
YT: So, you have early breakfast.
NK: Yes, it's about 6:00-6:30 am.
YT: What do you do after that?
NK: I used to begin composing right away until the dinner-time, which is always on schedule, at 1 pm.
YT: And after that?
NK: For many years after dinner-time, we would have a nap-time until 5-6 pm.
YT: You have siesta!
NK: You may think that way.
YT: I remember you said that you liked to read before going to sleep.
NK: Yes, reading is a part of my life.
YT: What are you reading now if it's not a secret?
NK: I finished reading that book that we talked about with you the other day – Neuhaus »The Art of Piano Playing«[424] in English.
YT: What do you think?
NK: I like the Russian version better. By the way, I just started to read a new one today – Hindemith's »A Composer's World«.[425]
YT: What is your impression of that book?
NK: This is a very difficult book to read, a lot of philosophical content in there. It feels like you are reading Hegel's book. I remember I tried to read it earlier but decided to postpone it, now I see why I did.
YT: And you also like reading the books on physics and linguistics.
NK: Yes, I remember I read a book on physics a little while ago written by Sean Carroll, an eminent scientist in the US. He is teaching with Anton (Kapustin) in Caltech.[426] Anton actually brought this book for me. Another good book on physics is Paul

---

[424] Heinrich Heuhaus, »The Art of Piano Playing: Teacher's Book«, Moscow, 1958, ISBN-13: 978-0893417567. Accessed January 5, 2018. http://kkart.ru/images/oifi.pdf.
[425] Hindemith, Paul. *A Composer's World*. Cambridge: Harvard University Press, 1952.
[426] California Institute of Technology, Pasadena, CA.

Halpern's »Einstein's Dice and Schrodinger's Cat«. By the way, I already know what is going to be the next book.

YT: What is it?

NK: This is going to be the book on the linguistic. I've already asked Anton to get it for me in Paris.

YT: I don't know anything in physics or mathematics, but can you tell me some other names that you were highly impressed with in this area of science?

NK: James Clerk Maxwell – he was a great physician, wrote books that are so difficult to read. He lived in the second part of the nineteenth century and became famous because of his equations.

YT: Alright, I feel like I am from a different planet in this conversation on physics… Coming back to your daily schedule – how does your day look after 6 pm?

NK: I would have a light dinner with Alla, and then maybe watch TV news or political programs for a while.

YT: Talking about politics – I still remember that New Year of 2000 celebration when five minutes before the New Year in front of all of us on the TV Chanel 1 instead of Boris Yeltsin appeared the unknown person, to congratulate our country with the New Year, whose name was Vladimir Putin.

NK: I knew him.[427]

YT: But still, it was so unexpected – to see instead of Boris Yeltsin somebody else.

NK: That's true.

YT: What is your attitude towards Putin?

NK: This is a provocative question.

YT: Then how about the Ukraine?

NK: What about the Ukraine?

YT: Putin seized Crimea, the part of the country of your motherland.

NK: Please remember that I was born in the Soviet Union, at the time when the Ukraine was a part of the USSR.

AK (joining the conversation): It's so good that he left Nikitovka so many years ago. If he would be living there through his whole life we may never meet and he may not be alive by now because of all the hostilities that happened in the Ukraine lately.

NK: It's sad to say but Ukraine is the hostile country, our enemy… and it has always been that way.

YT: Do you have any distant relatives who are alive now?

---

[427] From August 1999 until the December 31, 1999 Vladimir Putin hold a rank of the Prime Minister of the Russian Government. Accessed February 7, 2018. http://eng.putin.kremlin.ru/bio.

NK: I don't think, everybody passed away... Unfortunately, the politics started to affect the music life lately. Do you know the Ukrainian pianist Valentina Lisitsa[428]?

YT: Of course I know her name but I didn't know she had Ukrainian heritage.

NK: Her performance in Toronto was cancelled because of her negative attitude towards the Kiev government.[429]

YT: Really? I didn't know about that.

NK: And she is a very good pianist, good playing quality-wise.

YT: Coming back to your daily schedule – do you work in the second part of the day?

NK: In the past I used to work on the second part of the day too.

AK (joining the conversation): I remember Kolia used to compose constantly with no breaks at all. Once he came to me to the kitchen and said that he doesn't know what he should do now. I ask him what happened and he said that he just finished one of his pieces, that it's completely done.

YT: And he didn't know what to do after that?

AK: Yes. I said – just sit with me for a while, drink a cup of tea or eat something, but he couldn't find his place... That's how his life looked like in the past.

YT: What time are you going to sleep usually?

NK: Around 10-10:30 pm I am back to my world of reading books.

AK: Sometime when we have visitors, friends or people who come to see Kolia for an interview or because of some concerts, our schedule gets changed a little, which upsets Kolia a lot. He keeps complaining to me that they ruined our day.

YT: You like to set in order all the things around you – perfectly planned as in your music.

NK: Yes, I do.

YT: Do you feel happy with your children?

NK: I feel proud for both of our sons – Anton and Pavel.

YT: How many grandchildren do you have?

AK: We have four grandchildren. The oldest one, Camila, is twenty years old, and the youngest one, Valentina, was born on October 15th 2016, so this October (2017) she will celebrate her first birthday. We adore our grandchildren and always looking forward seeing them.

YT: Do you baby sit them?

AK: I remember you came once to Ruza when Maxim, Pavel's son, who is now six years old, was living with us for a couple of weeks.

YT: Oh, yes, yes, yes! I remember one funny moment of that visit – we were having a tea in the evening on your porch and both, Maxim and Nikolai Grigorievich, kept

---

[428] Valentina Lisitsa. Accessed February 8, 2018. http://www.valentinalisitsa.com/.

[429] In Canada the pianist was forbidden to perform because of her anti-Kiev position. Accessed January 10, 2018. http://www.ntv.ru/novosti/1390018/.

complaining to you about the tea. Maxim was asking you to blow the air on his tea because it was too hot and Nikolai Grigorievich wanted to heat it up again because it was already too cold.

AK: *Yes, this is my world – to find the best comfortable decision for everyone.*

Five-year old Maxim Kapustin, Ruza, June 17, 2015

NK: *I like August in Ruza – it's so warm there… All the trees there needed to be taken good care of, most of them are sick…*
YT: *Do you like watching the nature?*
NK: *I like to listen to the sounds of the forest and feel the evening scents of the trees… I miss it a lot now.*

Epilogue: How I met Nikolai Kapustin

I remember how in the spring of 2013 my teacher at West Virginia University, Dr. James Miltenberger, asked if I happened to know the famous Russian composer, who is writing absolutely unique music, whose name is Nikolai Kapustin. Shame on me, I've never heard this name before! Dr. Miltenberger suggested to investigate this composer and to begin playing his music. That is what I did and that is how it all started. I wrote my first letter to Nikolai Grigorievich and sent it to nowhere, sent it without any hope to receive a response from the composer, but he did answer me!

> NK: *I can't believe it took you so long to find me – you even moved to the United States!*
> YT: *And through the thirty years of my life I was living in Russia, that close to you.*
> AK (joining the conversation): *I remember Kolia didn't want to meet with you at the beginning.*
> YT: *Really? Why not?*
> AK: *Just right before your first visit in 2013 one young lady came to us with the same reason – to take an interview.*
> NK: *That lady was two hours late, that put me into the very upset mood and the interview was completely ruined.*
> AK: *For a while they were sitting in complete silence and then the interview was over. Then Kolia said to me that one lady is enough, and he doesn't want to meet with another young creature of the same kind. But I said that this lady is »another one«. Who knows, maybe she will be better?*

On December 27, 2013 I had a unique opportunity to meet Nikolai Grigorievich Kapustin for the first time. I visited him at his apartment in Moscow. Right after our meeting, in the train going back to Dzerjinsk, the city where my parents live, I wrote my first impression of the meeting with Kapustin. Surprisingly for myself, I wrote it in English! It was a very strong impression; all my three hours in the train passed like one minute:

> *On December 27, 2013, right after Christmas, I met Nikolai Kapustin. The house where he lives in Moscow looks exactly the same as many other buildings in a big city in Russia. Looking at the people passing by I was thinking: »You have no idea who lives in your house, who is your neighbour. You have no idea!« I arrived early, thirty minutes before the set time. So, I decided to wait outside. It was snowing and cold, very cold, and the time was passing by very slowly, with the speed of a walking turtle. Closer I was getting to the precious moment of our meeting, my heart was beating faster and faster. Two minutes before 10:00 am I thought to myself: »Enough waiting!« and I rang the bell.*

YT: Thank you so much Nikolai Grigorievich for the story of your life. I am writing the book but you – you are telling me all about your life and yourself.
NK: What do you think is easier?
YT: I think writing is easier.
NK (smiling): …
YT: To compose the questions for you is not that difficult but for you to remember all the unique information about yourself in such a detail – that's special.
NK: Yes, remembering the past is difficult for me.
YT: It is difficult for everybody. So, Nikolai Grigorievich, today is February 18, 2018 and we are officially done working on our first book »Conversations with Nikolai Kapustin«. I feel so good about it!
NK: What do you mean – our first book?
YT: Because there is going to be another one… sometime soon.
NK: Oh no, what???!!!! Another four years of »suffering«? I will not survive it!

More to come………………………

Nikolai Kapustin and Yana Tyulkova, Ruza, June 17, 2015

Appendix A: Nikolai Kapustin – Chronology

1937   Born on November 22, 1937 in Nikitovka (Ukraine)

1941   Summer: Beginning of WWII.
Kapustin and his family (mother, grandmother, and sister) were evacuated to the south of Russia (city Tokmok, Kyrgyz Republic). His father joined the reserve Soviet Army.

1943   Autumn: Family returns to Nikitovka from the evacuation and lived in the house of neighbors for two years (1943-1945).
Enormous interest in playing piano and appearance of his first piano teacher Piotr Ivanovich Vinnichenko.

1945   Summer: End of WWII and return of Grigory Kapustin to Nikitovka.
The rebuilding of the house.
September 1: The beginning of study at the Secondary School No. 30.

1949   Weekly piano lessons with Lubov' Borisovna Frantsuzova in Artemovsk.

1950   Composes first piece *Piano Sonata*.
Interest in physics.

1952   Trouble with entering exams to the Moscow Musical College and visit of Klavdia Kapustina in order to help Nikolai be accepted to the Musical College as a piano performance student.
September 1: Begins study at the Moscow Musical College.
Serious study of piano with his teacher Avrelian Grigorievich Rubbakh.

1953   Weekly visits to the publishing house *Muzgiz* to purchase new published scores.
Interest in self-education.
Friendship with Evgeniya Pupkova.
Interest in music of Sergei Prokofiev and Sergei Rachmaninov.
March 5: Death of Sergei Prokofiev and Iosif Stalin.
June: Travel back to Nikitovka for the summer break (this happened every year during the study at the college and conservatory).
December: Trip to the city Klin to visit Tchaikovsky's Home-Museum as part of the group of honored students of Moscow Musical College.

1954   Composes *Sonatina* and *Romance in F major* (unpublished early works).
Rubbakh's attempt to publish *Sonatina*.
Close relationship with Andrei Mikhalkov.

	Moving to the house of Sergei Mikhalkov (lived there for two years, 1954-1956).
	Warm relationship with Natalia Konchalovskaya (Andrei's mother).
	First acquaintance with jazz from listening to the jazz programs on the radio-station »The Voice of America« at night.
	Experience with transcribing and playing jazz.

1955   Composes *Polka-Rondo* (unpublished early work).
       Winter: Participates in the concert dedicated to the sixtieth Jubilee of Avrelian Rubbakh (Small Concert Hall of the Moscow Conservatory).
       Visit of Kapustin's parents to Moscow.
       Summer: Travels to Nikolina Gora to the summer house of Mikhalkov's family for vacation.

1956   Composes *Czech Rhapsody* (unpublished early work) and performance of this piece for Aram Khachaturian.
       While living in Mikhalkov's house became acquainted with Ivan Kozlovsky, Oleg Lundstrem, Arno Babajanian, Vladimir Sofronitsky, Yuri Zavadsky, and others.
       June: Successful final exams at the Moscow Musical College.
       Travel to Nikitovka and preparation for the entering exams to the Moscow Conservatory.
       August: Audition to Alexander Goldenweiser and successful entering exams to the Moscow Conservatory.
       Trip to the Russian south with his friends (city of Khosta).
       September 1: Begins study at the Moscow Conservatory at the class of legendary Alexander Goldenweiser.
       Autumn: Experience of accompanying to Tatiana Nikolaeva and Maria Yudina.
       Injury of the right hand and inability to play both hands for half a year.

1957   Composes Piano Sonata for the Left Hand (unpublished work).
       Attends composition lessons with Aram Khachaturian.
       Interest in music of Béla Bartók, Maurice Ravel, late Scriabin, and, for some period of time, interest in atonal music.
       Friendship with Nodar Gabunia, Oxana Yablonskaya, Nikolai Sidelnikov, Viacheslav Ovchinnikov, Vladimir Ashkenazy, and Nikolai Petrov.
       Acquaintance with Sofia Gubaidulina and Alfred Schnittke.
       May: Attends the very first concert of Glenn Gould in Moscow.
       July: Performs the premier of Concertino for Piano and Orchestra (Op. 1) on the Sixth World Festival of Youth and Students in Moscow (with Yuri Saulsky Big Band).

	Autumn: Organizes a Jazz Quintet and plays with the group for a few months in the Moscow hotel »National«.
1958	Recording of Kapustin Quintet was broadcast at the radio-station »The Voice of America«. Travels to Tbilisi (Georgia) to meet with Nodar Gabunia.
Ca. 1957-1958	Composes two Sonatinas (unpublished works)
Ca. 1958-1959	Composes Piano Sonata in C minor [Big Sonata] (unpublished work). Substituting »Methods of Teaching Piano« class with accompanying in the conducting class at the conservatory.
1961	Attends the concert of Karel Krautgartner Big Band; jam-session with the bassist of the Krautgartner's band after the concert in one of the apartments in Moscow. June: Final exams and graduation from the Moscow Conservatory. Summer: Joins the Oleg Lundstrem Big Band as a jazz pianist, arranger, transcriber, and composer. Autumn: Last visit of Grigory Kapustin to Moscow when he attended one of the concerts of Oleg Lundstrem Big Band. Begins touring with Lundstrem in the USSR and abroad, performing with Valery Obodzinsky, Maya Kristalinskaya, Aino Balina, vocal quartets Accord, Lada, and others. Close relationship with the musicians from the Lundstrem Band: Konstantin Bakholdin and Alexei Zoubov. Composes Concerto for Piano and Orchestra, Op. 2. Travels to Tbilisi (Georgia) to meet with Nodar Gabunia.
1962	Composes Variations for Piano and Big Band, Op. 3, Chorale and Fugue for Orchestra, Op. 4, and Piece for Trumpet and Orchestra, Op. 5. Recording of Teddy Wilson's piano part for the movie about the first visit of Benny Goodman Orchestra to the USSR.
1963	Composes Rose-Marie, Fantasia for Orchestra, Op. 6, Fantasia on Three Children's Songs for Orchestra, Op. 7. Collaborates with Leonid Utyosov Big Band. Summer: Trip to Yalta (Russian south) for vacation.
1964	Composes *Toccata* for Piano and Orchestra, Op. 8. Movie *When the Song Does not End* uses the section of *Toccata*, Op. 8 as a video and sound track. Moving to a studio apartment in Maryina Roshcha (Moscow).

1965	June: Performance with Lundstrem on the International Jazz Festival in Prague (Czechoslovakia). September: Touring in Poland (concerts in Warsaw).
Ca. middle 1960s	Tour with Oleg Lundstrem Big Band in Czechoslovakia, where he attends the concert of Karel Vlach Big Band. Acquaintance with Gustav Brom and Kurt Edelhagen. Meeting of Oleg Lundstrem Big Band and Kurt Edelhagen Big Band in Moscow. Performances with Vadim Ludvikovsky Orchestra.
1966	Composes *The Trial*, Piece for Orchestra, Op. 9, *Big Band Sounds (The Sounds of Big-Band)* for Orchestra, Op. 10, and *Estacade* for Big Band, Op. 11. Recording of the vinyl disc »Oleg Lundstrem Orchestra« in recording studio *Melodiya* (Moscow).
1967	Composes *Aquarium Blues* for Big Band, Op. 12. May: Performs with Lundstrem Big Band on the XIV International Jazz Festival »Tallinn-67« (Estonia). November: Touring with Lundstrem in Novokuznetsk (Siberia) where he meets Alla Baranovskaya. December: Celebrating the New Year with Alla Baranovskaya in Moscow.
1968	Composes *Intermezzo* for Piano and Orchestra, Op. 13. July 16: Alla's trip from Novokuznetsk to Moscow to stay forever with Nikolai Kapustin. Summer: Touring with Lundstrem to the Russian south with Alla.
1969	January 3: Wedding of Nikolai Kapustin and Alla Baranovskaya in Moscow.
1970	Recording of the second vinyl disc with Oleg Lundstrem Big Band.
Ca. beginning 1970s	Traveling through Tbilisi, while on tour with Lundstrem, stopping in Tbilisi to meet with Nodar Gabunia.
1971	November 10: Birth of Anton Kapustin. Winter: Attends the masterclass with Duke Ellington in Moscow during the first tour of Duke Ellington Big Band in the USSR.
1972	Leaving the Oleg Lundstrem Big Band. Composes *The Forest Story* for Orchestra, Op. 15, *Nocturne* for Piano and Orchestra, Op. 16, and *Three Pieces* for Orchestra, Op. 17 for the radio »Yunost«.

	Spring: Joins Concert Pop Orchestra of Central Radio and Television »Blue Screen« led by Boris Karamyshev. Work with Karamyshev Orchestra as a composer, pianist, and an arranger
1973	Composes *Four Pieces* for Instrumental Ensemble, Op. 18. October: Touring with Robert Young in the USSR.
Middle 1970s	Friendship and work with Alexander Varlamov, Lyudmila Lyadova, and Yuri Silantiev.
1974	Composes *Concerto for Piano and Orchestra No. 2*, Op. 14, *Etude* for Piano and Orchestra, Op. 19, *Nocturne* for Piano and Orchestra, Op. 20, and *Minuet* for Big Band, Op. 21.
1975	Composes *Piece for Five Saxophones and Orchestra*, Op. 22, *Enigma* for Big Band, Op. 23, and *March* for Orchestra, Op. 24.
1976	Composes *Concert Rhapsody* for Piano and Orchestra, Op. 25, *Day-Break* for Piano, Op. 26, *Day-Break* for Orchestra, Op. 26A, and *Fantasia* for Jazz Quartet, Op. 27. Moving to a one-bedroom apartment.
1977	Composes *Suite in the Old Style* for Piano, Op. 28. Spring: Disintegration of Karamyshev Orchestra Work as a pianist with the Russian State Symphony Orchestra of Cinematography.
1978	Composes *Scherzo* for Piano and Orchestra, Op. 29. July 28: Birth of the second son - Pavel Kapustin.
1979	Summer: Vacation with Alexander Varlamov and Anton Kapustin to Ivanovo. Car accident in Moscow when Nikolai Kapustin and Anton Kapustin were both injured, Nikolai Kapustin had a double fracture of his right hand.
1980	Composes *Two-movement Concerto* for Orchestra, Op. 30 and *Elegy* for Orchestra, Op. 31. Release of vinyl disc of Alexander Varlamov »Compositions in Dance Rhythms« (recordings of 1975-1979) with arrangements of Nikolai Kapustin. Last performance in public as a solo pianist - *Piano Concerto No. 2*, Op. 14 (Tchaikovsky Performance Hall, Moscow). Acceptance to the »Union of Moscow Composers«.

Beginning of 1980s	Interest in learning foreign languages (English, French, Japanese, and Arabic). Work with the first publishers (Muzyka and Sovetsky Kompozitor).
1981	Composes *The Wind from the North* for Orchestra, Op. 32.
1982	Composes *Piece* for Two Pianos and Orchestra, Op. 33, *Meridian* for Orchestra, Op. 34, and *Closed Curve* for Orchestra, Op. 35. Recording of Op. 34 and Op. 35 with Yuri Silantiev Orchestra.
1983	Composes *Toccatina* for Piano, Op. 36, *The Pleasant Meeting* for Orchestra, Op. 37, and *Presentiment* for Orchestra, Op. 38. Publishing of *Toccatina*, Op. 36 in Moscow Publishing House »Muzyka«. December 5: Grigory Kapustin passed away (Nikitovka, Ukraine).
Middle 1980s	Composes the pieces for the Ministry of Culture of USSR and RSFSR.
1984	Composes Piano Sonata No.1 *Quasi una Fantasia* for Piano, Op. 39, *Eight Concert Etudes* for Piano, Op. 40, and *Variations* for Piano, Op. 41. Decision to leave Orchestra of Cinematography.
1985	Composes *Rush Hour* for Ensemble, Op. 42, *An April Day* for Ensemble, Op. 43, *The Morning* for Ensemble, Op. 44, *Motive Force* for Piano, Op. 45, and Concerto for Piano and Orchestra No. 3, Op. 48. Recording of the first vinyl disc »Nikolai Kapustin« in Moscow. March: Mikhail Gorbachev came to a power, »Perestroika« had begun.
1986	Composes *Big Band Sounds (The Sounds of Big-Band)* for Piano, Op. 46. Release of the first vinyl disc »Nikolai Kapustin« in Moscow.
1987	Composes *Contemplation (Meditation)* for Piano, Op. 47, *Sinfonietta* for Orchestra, Op. 49, Concerto for Alto Saxophone and Orchestra, Op. 50, and *Overture* for Big Band, Op. 51. Recording of the second vinyl disc »Nikolai Kapustin: Jazz Pieces for Piano« in Moscow.
1988	Composes *Intrada* for Big Band, Op. 52 and Twenty-Four Preludes for Piano, Op. 53.
1989	Composes Piano Sonata No. 2, Op. 54 and Concerto for Piano and Orchestra No. 4, Op. 56. Release of the second vinyl disc »Nikolai Kapustin: Jazz Pieces for Piano«. Recording and release of the third vinyl disc »Nikolai Kapustin; Twenty-Four Preludes in Jazz Style« in Moscow.

1990	Composes Piano Sonata No. 3, Op. 55, Chamber Symphony for Chamber Orchestra, Op. 57, and *Andante* for Piano, Op. 58.
Beginning of 1990s	Anton Kapustin moves to the United States.
1991	Composes *Ten Bagatelles* for Piano, Op. 59, Piano Sonata No. 4, Op. 60, Piano Sonata No. 5, Op. 61, Piano Sonata No. 6, Op. 62, Sonata for Cello and Piano No. 1, Op. 63, Piano Sonata No.7, Op. 64, *Berceuse* for Piano, Op. 65, and *Three Impromptus* for Piano, Op. 66. May 18: Premier of Piano Sonata No. 2, Op. 54 by Nikolai Petrov in Moscow. Recording of the CD »Kapustin plays Kapustin: Jazz Portrait« in Moscow June 12: Boris Yeltsin comes to power as the first President of the Russian Federation. December 8: The »Agreement on Establishing the Commonwealth of Independent States« was signed between Russia, Ukraine and Belarus' in Belovezhskaya Pushcha which determined the collapse of the Soviet Union.
1992	Composes *Three Etudes* for Piano, Op. 67, *Five Etudes in Different Intervals* for Piano, Op. 68, Sonata for Viola and Piano, Op. 69, Sonata for Violin and Piano, Op. 70, and *Capriccio* for Piano, Op. 71. July 29: Klavdia Kapustina passed away (Nikitovka, Ukraine). Release of the disc »Kapustin plays Kapustin: Jazz Portrait« in England.
1993	Composes Concerto for Piano and Orchestra No. 5, Op. 72, *Ten Inventions* for Piano, Op. 73 and Concerto for Piano and Orchestra No. 6, Op. 74.
1994	Composes *Humoresque* for Piano, Op. 75 and Concerto for Double Bass and Symphony Orchestra, Op. 76.
Middle 1990s	Friendship with Hideaki Takaoki.
1995	Composes Piano Sonata No. 8, Op. 77, Piano Sonata No. 9, Op. 78, and *Piece for Sextet*, Op. 79. May 27: Premier of Piano Concerto No. 5, Op. 72 by Nikolai Petrov and Moscow Philharmonic Orchestra (conductor – Vassily Sinaisky). December 30: First live performance since 1980 - premier of *Piece for Sextet* Op. 79 in Moscow (Beethoven Concert Hall of the Bolshoi Theatre).
1996	Composes *Theme and Variations* for Piano, Op. 80 and Piano Sonata No. 1 Op. 81.

1997	Composes *Twenty-four Preludes and Fugues* for Piano, Op. 82, *Impromptu* for Piano, Op. 83, Sonata for Cello and Piano No. 2, Op. 84, and Concerto No. 1 for Cello and Orchestra, Op. 85. March 9: Performed the premier of Cello Sonata No.1, Op. 63 with Alexander Zagorinsky. October 29: Concert dedicated 60th Birthday at the »Mirror Hall« of the State Institute of Art Studies in Moscow. November 22: Alla Kapustina leaves to the USA for surgery.
1998	Composes Trio for Flute, Cello and Piano, Op. 86, *Seven Polyphonic Pieces* for Piano Left Hand, Op. 87, String Quartet No. 1, Op. 88, Piano Quintet, Op. 89, Concerto for Eleven Instruments, Op. 90, and *Divertissement* for Two Flutes, Cello and Piano, Op. 91. February 23: Alla Kapustina returns from the USA. November: First tour to Germany with Alexander Zagorinsky.
1999	Composes *Suite* for Piano, Op. 92, *Introduction and Scherzino* for Cello Solo, Op. 93, *Ballad* for Piano, Op. 94, *Scherzo* for Piano, Op. 95, *Elegy* for Cello and Piano, Op. 96, *Burlesque* for Cello and Piano, Op. 97, *Nearly Waltz* for Cello and Piano, Op. 98, and *Duet* for Alto Saxophone and Cello, Op. 99. April 21: Kapustin/Zagorisnky/Korneev premier of *Trio for Flute, Cello, and Piano*, Op. 86. July: Second trip to Germany with Alla Kapustina. Meeting with Anton Kapustin in Potsdam. December 31: Vladimir Putin comes to power.
2000	Composes *Sonatina* for Piano, Op. 100, Piano Sonata No. 11 *Twickenham*, Op. 101. Release of the discs »Nikolai Kapustin: Jazz Pieces for Piano« and »Nikolai Kapustin: Twenty Four Preludes in Jazz Style« in Russia and Japan (compiled the music of the three vinyl discs recorded in the 1980s). May: Trip to London with Alla Kapustina. May 14: Western premier of Kapustin's *Piano Sonata No. 2*, Op. 54 by Marc-André Hamelin in Blackheath Concert Hall (London). September: Recording of the *Twenty-Four Preludes and Fugues*, Op. 82 in Moscow for the double disc »Kapustin«.
Beginning of 2000s	Friendship with Ludmil Angelov.
2001	Composes Piano Sonata No. 12, Op. 102.

	January 11: Premier of *Quintet in Db major*, Op. 89 by Nikolai Petrov and the Shostakovich Quartet in Moscow Philharmony Hall. Release of the disc »Kapustin Plays Kapustin« (chamber music) in Japan. Release of the double disc »Kapustin« in Japan.
2002	Composes Concerto No. 2 for Cello and String Orchestra, Op. 103, Concert for Two Pianos and Percussion, Op. 104, Concert for Violin, Piano and String Orchestra, Op. 105, Suite for Viola, Alto Saxophone, Piano and Bass, Op. 106, Variations on *Sweet Georgia Brown* for Viola, Alto Saxophone, Piano and Bass, Op. 107. Release of the disc »Kapustin Plays Kapustin« (piano solo and chamber music) in Japan (solo piano works were recorded by Kapustin in 1991 in Moscow).
2003	Composes *Paraphrase on a Theme by Paul Dvoirin* for Piano, Op. 108, *There is Something Behind That* for Piano, Op. 109, Piano Sonata No. 13, Op. 110, *Gingerbread Man* for Piano, Op. 111, *End of the Rainbow* for Piano, Op. 112, *Wheel of Fortune* for Piano, Op. 113, *No Stop Signs* for Piano, Op. 114, *Fantasia* for Piano, Op. 115, *Rondoletto* for Piano, Op. 116, *Spice Island* for Piano, Op. 117, and *Paraphrase on »Aquarela do Brasil« by Ary Barroso* for Piano, Op. 118. April: Became acquainted with Masahiro Kawakami. Recording solo piano music for the disc »Nikolai Kapustin: Last Recording«.
2004	Composes *Nothing to Lose* for Piano, Op. 119, Piano Sonata No. 14, Op. 120, *Vanity of Vanities* for Piano, Op. 121, *Two Etude-like Trinkets* for Piano, Op. 122, *Paraphrase on »Blue Bossa« by Kenny Dorham* for Piano, Op. 123, Suite for Cello Solo, Op. 124, and Sonata for Flute and Piano, Op. 125. October 20: Release of the disc »Nikolai Kapustin: Last Recording« in Japan.
2005	Composes Divertissement in Four Movements for Violin, Cello and Piano, Op. 126 and Piano Sonata No. 15 *Fantasia quasi Sonata*, Op. 127. The official website of Nikolai Kapustin was organized.
Middle 2000s	Friendship with Ahn Trio.
2006	Composes *Introduction and Rondo* for Piano Solo, Op. 128, *Paraphrase on Dizzy Gillespie's »Manteca«* for Two Pianos, Op. 129, *Countermove* for Piano Solo, Op. 130, and Piano Sonata No. 16, Op. 131.

| | February 7: »Evening of Modern Music« in Moscow Philharmonic Hall where chamber music of Kapustin was performed.
June: Premiere of *Piano Sonata No. 14*, Op. 120 by Ludmil Angelov and *Concerto for Two Pianos and Percussion*, Op. 104 by Ludmil Angelov, Daniel Del Pino, Juanjo Guillem, and Rafael Gálvez at the XII International Music Festival in Toledo (Spain).
September 30: Russian premier of *Concerto for Violin, Piano, and String Orchestra*, Op. 105 by violinist Graf Murja, pianist Alexander Vershinin, and Kostroma Chamber Orchestra (conducted by Pavel Gershtein). |
|------|---|
| 2007 | Composes String Quartet No. 2, Op. 132 and *Six Little Preludes* for Piano Solo, Op. 133.
December 10: Fira Kapustina passed away (Gorlovka, Ukraine).
December 11: Concert dedicated to the 70th birthday of Nikolai Kapustin (Concert Hall of Gnessin State Musical College).
Recording of solo piano music for the disc »Kapustin Returns!« |
| 2008 | Composes Piano Sonata No. 17, Op. 134 and Piano Sonata No. 18, Op. 135.
March: meeting with Marc-André Hamelin during his tour in Moscow.
Release of the disc »Nikolai Kapustin and Alexander Zagorinsky: Live Concert in Hannover (1998)«.
Release of the disc »Kapustin Returns!« in Japan. |
2009	Composes Piano Trio No. 1 for Violin, Cello and Piano, Op. 136, *Good Intention* for Piano Solo, Op. 137, *Sleight of Hand* for Piano Solo, Op. 138, *Holy Cow* for Piano Solo, Op. 139, *Freeway* for Piano Solo, Op. 140, and Violin Concerto, Op. 141.
2010	Composes Piano Trio No. 2 for Violin, Cello and Piano, Op. 142.
2011	Composes Piano Sonata No. 19, Op. 143 and Piano Sonata No. 20, Op. 144.
2012	Composes *Triptych* for Two Pianos, Op. 145, *Capriccio* for Two Pianos, Op. 146 and *Concerto for Piano and Orchestra No. 1* (2nd edition), Op. 147.
2013	Composes *Dialogue* for Solo Piano, Op. 148, *Etude Courte mais Transcendante pour Piano*, Op. 149, Piece for String Quartet *Rondo Frivole* pour quatuor à cordes, Op. 150, *Nobody is Perfect* for Piano Solo, Op. 151, *A Pianist in Jeopardy* for Piano Solo, Op. 152, and *Wandering* for Piano Solo, Op. 153.
December 27: The author's first meeting with Nikolai Kapustin.
2014	Composes Piece for String Quartet *The Last Attempt*, Op. 154, *Allegro* for Piano Trio, Op. 155, and *A Little Duo* for Flute and Cello, Op. 156.

	Japan Kapustin Society was organized in Tokyo.
2015	Composes *Curiosity* for Piano Solo, Op. 157, Sonatina for Viola and Piano Op. 158, *Rainy Weather* for Piano Solo, Op. 159, *Something Else for Piano Solo* Op. 160, *Moon Rainbow* for Piano Solo, Op. 161. Kapustin Festival was organized in Tokyo.
2017	May 31: Concert dedicated to the 80th birthday of Nikolai Kapustin (Chamber Hall of the Moscow Philharmonic). November 30: Concert dedicated to the 80th birthday of Nikolai Kapustin (Great Hall of Moscow Conservatory).
2018	January 8: Concerts dedicated to the 80th birthday of Nikolai Kapustin (Tokyo, Japan). February 10: Concert dedicated to the 80th birthday of Nikolai Kapustin (Conservatory of Music of Niccolo Puccini, Bari, Italy).

Appendix B: Nikolai Kapustin – Discography

Vinyl discs:

1. »Oleg Lundstrem Orchestra«, Melodiya (33C 01333-4), 1966.
Content: Suita v trioh chastiah [Suite in Three Movements] by U. Naissoo, Jaloba [Complaint] by V. Lipand and U. Sutiste, Pesnia bez slov [Song Without Words] by O. Lundstrem, Prazdnichnii ritm [Holiday Rhythm] by B. Gorbulskis and R. Skuchaite, Novoselie [New Dwelling] by B. Trotsuk, Improvizatsia G. Garaniana na temu pesni V. Muradeli »Ne grusti« [G. Garanian's Improvisation on the Theme by Vano Muradeli »Don't Be Sad«], Ekspromt [Impromptu] by O. Lundstrem, Ya vozvrashaus domoi, vokaliz [I'm Coming Back Home, Vocalise] by A. Ostrovsky, Blagodaru [Thank You] by I. Yakushenko, Priznanie [Confession] by A. Kroll, Muzikalnii privet [Musical Greetings] by G. Garanian.

2. »Oleg Lundstrem Orchestra«, Melodiya (D 027931-2), 1970.
Content: Kontsert [Concerto] by I. Yakushenko, Akvarium [Aquarium-Blues, Op. 12] by N. Kapustin, Nebesnie Uzori [Celestial Patterns] by R. Kunsman, Po Novomu Arbatu [On New Arbat Street] by I. Yakushenko, Variatsii dlia f-no [Variations for Piano and Big-Band, Op. 3] by N. Kapustin, Miraj [Mirage] by O. Lundstrem, Kroket [Croquet] by R. Kunsman and V. Gruz, Poiushee more [Singing Sea] by V. Gruz, On Green Dolphin Street by B. Kaper and N. Washington.

3. »Alexander Varlamov: Compositions in Dance Rhythms, Recordings of 1975-1979«, Melodiya (33 C 60-13717-48), 1980.
Content: Nailuchshie pojelaniya [Best Wishes], Proshayas s toboi [Saying Goodbye to You], Den' udach [Lucky Day], Vecher bez zviozd [Evening Without Stars], Parus v more [Sail in the Sea], Nastroenie [Mood], Vsio prohodit [Everything Passes], Malenkii Gorod [Small Town], Uhodiashii za gorizont [Out of the Horizon], Mi eshio vstretimsia s vami [We'll Meet Again].

4. »*Nikolai Kapustin*«, *Melodiya (C60 23759 008), 1986.*
Content: Eight Concert Etudes (Op. 40), Piano Sonata No. 1 »Sonata-Fantasy« (Op. 39).

5. »*Nikolai Kapustin: Jazz Pieces for Piano*«, *Melodiya (C60 28239 000), 1989.*
Content: Suite in the Old Style (Op. 28), Variations (Op. 41), Day-Break (Op. 26), Toccatina (Op. 36), Contemplation (Op. 47), Big-Band Sounds (Op. 46), Motive Force (Op. 45).

6. »*Nikolai Kapustin: Twenty-Four Preludes in Jazz Style*«, *Melodiya (C60 28999 007), 1989.*
Content: Twenty-Four Preludes in Jazz Style (Op. 53)

Compact Discs:

1. »*Nikolai Kapustin: Jazz Pieces for Piano*« *Boheme Music (CDBMR 007148), 2000, Triton (DICC-24058) July 25, 2000, Octavia Records (OVCT-00021), Nov. 17, 2004.*
Content: Eight Concert Etudes (Op. 40), Piano Sonata No. 1 »Sonata-Fantasy« (Op. 39), Suite in the Old Style (Op. 28), Variations (Op. 41).

2. »*Nikolai Kapustin: Twenty-Four Preludes in Jazz Style*« *Boheme Music (CDBMR 007149), 2000, Triton (DICC-24059) July 25, 2000, Octavia Records (OVCT-00016), Nov. 17, 2004.*
Content: Twenty-Four Preludes in Jazz Style (Op. 53), Day-Break (Op. 26), Toccatina (Op. 36), Contemplation (Op. 47), Big-Band Sounds (Op. 46), Motive Force (Op. 45).

3. »*Kapustin plays Kapustin: Jazz Portrait*« *Mezhdunarodnaya Kniga (MK-417051), 1992, Mezhdunarodnaya Kniga Muzyka (MKM-228), 2001, Olympia (MKM-228), 2001, Triton (DICC-26072), October 25, 2001, Octavia Records (OVCT-00027), Aug. 25, 2005.*
Content: Andante (Op. 58), Piano Sonata No. 4 (Op. 60), Ten Bagatelles (Op. 59), Piano Sonata No. 5 (Op. 61), Piano Sonata No. 6 (Op. 62).

4. »*Kapustin Plays Kapustin*« *(chamber music) Triton (DICC-26067), 2001, Octavia Records (OVCT-00011), July 22, 2004.*
Content: Piano Quintet (Op. 89), String Quartet No. 1 (Op. 88), Trio for Flute, Cello, and Piano (Op. 86), Divertissement for Two Flutes, Cello, and Piano (Op. 91).

5. *Double disc »Kapustin« Triton (DICC-40001-2), 2001, Octavia Records (OVCT-00010), July 22, 2004.*
Content: Twenty-Four Preludes and Fugues (Op. 82), Sonata for Violin and Piano (Op. 70), Elegy for Cello and Piano (Op. 96), Burlesque for Cello and Piano (Op. 97), Nearly Waltz for Cello and Piano (Op. 98).

6. *»Kapustin Plays Kapustin« (piano solo and chamber music) Triton (DICC-26073), 2002, Octavia Records (OVCT-00026), Aug. 25, 2005.*
Content: Piano Sonata No. 2 (Op. 54), Piano Sonata No. 3 (Op. 55), Andante (Op. 58), Duet for Alto-Saxophone and Cello (Op. 99), Introduction and Scherzino for Cello Solo (Op. 93).

7. *»Nikolai Kapustin: Last Recording« Triton (OVCT-00017), Oct. 20, 2004.*
Content: Piano Sonata No. 7 (Op. 64), Berceuse (Op. 65), Three Impromptus (Op. 66), Three Etudes (Op. 67), Impromptu (Op. 83), Paraphrase on the Theme by Paul Dvoirin (Op. 108), Piano Sonata No. 12 (Op. 102).

8. *Nikolai Kapustin and Alexander Zagorinsky: Live Concert in Hannover (1998), Classical Records (CR-126), Russia, 2008.*
Content: Beethoven Seven Variations on the Theme from the opera »Magic Flute« by Mozart for Cello and Piano (WoO 46), Chopin Polonaise Brilliante for Cello and Piano (Op. 3), Chopin Nocturne in Eb major (Op. 9 No. 2, transcription by Pablo Sarasate), Kapustin Cello Sonata No. 1 (Op. 63), Kapustin Cello Sonata no. 2 (Op. 84), Kapustin »Day-Break« with cello pizzicato (Op. 26).

9. *»Kapustin Returns!« Nippon Acoustic Records (NARD-5014), 2008, Octavia Records (OVCT-00094) Dec. 19, 2012.*
Content: Paraphrase on »Aquarela do Brasil« by Ary Barros (Op. 118), Two Etude-like Trinkets (Op. 122), End of the Rainbow (Op. 112), Humoresque (Op. 75), Fantasia (Op. 115), Gingerbread Man (Op. 111), Vanity of Vanities (Op. 121), Spice Island (Op. 117), Paraphrase on »Blue Bossa« by Kenny Dorham (Op. 123), Countermove (Op. 130), Piano Sonata No. 16 (Op. 131).

Appendix C: Nikolai Kapustin – Dedications

Name of composition	Opus Number	Year	Dedication
Piano Concerto No. 5	72	1993	Nikolai Petrov
Sonata for Cello and Piano No. 2	84	1997	Alexander Zagorinsky
Piano Sonata No. 11 »Twickenham«	101	2000	Twickenham, area of London
Piano Sonata No. 12	102	2001	Hideaki Takaoki
Countermove	130	2006	Mark-André Hamelin
Piano Sonata No. 16	131	2006	Ludmil Angelov
Piano Sonata No. 18	135	2008	Vito Reibaldi
Good Intention	137	2009	Masahiro Kawakami
Sleight of Hand	138	2009	Masahiro Kawakami
Violin Concerto	141	2009	Graf Murja
Piano Sonata No. 19	143	2011	Alexei Volodin
Triptych for Two Pianos	145	2012	Natsuki Nishimoto/ Asuka Matsumoto
Capriccio for Two Pianos	146	2012	Natsuki Nishimoto/ Asuka Matsumoto
Curiosity	157	2015	Yana Tyulkova

Appendix D: Catalogue of Works by Genre

1. Early Unpublished Piano Works

Piano Sonata (1950)
Romance in F major (1954)
Sonatina (1954)
Polka-Rondo (1955)
Czech Rhapsody for Two Pianos (1956)
Piano Sonata for the Left Hand (1957)
Two Sonatinas (ca. 1957-1958)
Big Piano Sonata in C minor (ca. 1958-1959)

2. Piano Works

A) Piano Solo:
Op. 26: »Sunrise« for Piano (1976)
Op. 28: Suite in the Old Style for Piano (1977)
Op. 36: Toccatina for Piano (1983)
Op. 39: Piano Sonata No.1 »Quasi una Fantasia« for Piano (1984)
Op. 40: Eight Concert Studies for Piano (1984)
Op. 41: Variations for Piano (1984)
Op. 45: »Motive Force« for Piano (1985)
Op. 46: »Big Band Sounds (The Sounds of Big-Band)« for Piano (1986)
Op. 47: »Contemplation (Meditation)« for Piano (1987)
Op. 53: Twenty-Four Preludes for Piano (1988)
Op. 54: Piano Sonata No. 2 (1989)
Op. 55: Piano Sonata No. 3 (1990)
Op. 58: Andante for Piano (1990)
Op. 59: Ten Bagatelles for Piano (1991)
Op. 60: Piano Sonata No. 4 (1991)
Op. 61: Piano Sonata No. 5 (1991)
Op. 62: Piano Sonata No. 6 (1991)
Op. 64: Piano Sonata No.7 (1991)
Op. 65: Berceuse for Piano (1991)
Op. 66: Three Impromptus for Piano (1991)
Op. 67: Three Etudes for Piano (1992)
Op. 68: Five Etudes in Different Intervals for Piano (1992)
Op. 71: Capriccio for Piano (1992)
Op. 73: Ten Inventions for Piano (1993)
Op. 75: Humoresque for Piano (1994)

Op. 77: Piano Sonata No. 8 (1995)
Op. 78: Piano Sonata No. 9 (1995)
Op. 80: Theme and Variations for Piano (1996)
Op. 81: Piano Sonata No. 10 (1996)
Op. 82: Twenty-four Preludes and Fugues for Piano (1997)
Op. 83: Impromptu for piano (1997)
Op. 87: Seven Polyphonic Pieces for Piano Left Hand (1998)
Op. 92: Suite for Piano (1999)
Op. 94: Ballad for Piano (1999)
Op. 95: Scherzo for Piano (1999)
Op. 100: Sonatina for Piano (2000)
Op. 101: Piano Sonata No. 11 »Twickenham« (2000)
Op. 102: Piano Sonata No. 12 (2001)
Op. 108: Paraphrase on a Theme of Paul Dvoirin for Piano (2003)
Op. 109: »There is Something Behind That« for Piano (2003)
Op. 110: Piano Sonata No. 13 (2003)
Op. 111: »Gingerbread Man« for Piano (2003)
Op. 112: »End of the Rainbow« for Piano (2003)
Op. 113: »Wheel of Fortune« for Piano (2003)
Op. 114: »No Stop Signs« for Piano (2003)
Op. 115: Fantasia for Piano (2003)
Op. 116: Rondoletto for Piano (2003)
Op. 117: »Spice Island« for Piano (2003)
Op. 118: Paraphrase on »Aquarela do Brasil« by Ary Barroso for Piano (2003)
Op. 119: »Nothing to Lose« for Piano (2004)
Op. 120: Piano Sonata No. 14 (2004)
Op. 121: »Vanity of Vanities« for Piano (2004)
Op. 122: Two Etude-like Trinkets for Piano (2004)
Op. 123: Paraphrase on »Blue Bossa« by Kenny Dorham for Piano (2004)
Op. 127: Piano Sonata No. 15 (Fantasia quasi Sonata) (2005)
Op. 128: Introduction and Rondo for Piano Solo (2006)
Op. 130: Countermove for Piano Solo (2006)
Op. 131: Piano Sonata No. 16 (2006)
Op. 133: Six Little Preludes for Piano Solo (2007)
Op. 134: Piano Sonata No. 17 (2008)
Op. 135: Piano Sonata No. 18 (2008)
Op. 137: Good Intention for Piano Solo (2009)
Op. 138: Sleight of Hand for Piano Solo (2009)
Op. 139: Holy Cow for Piano Solo (2009)
Op. 140: Freeway for Piano Solo (2009)

Op. 143: Piano Sonata No. 19 (2011)
Op. 144: Piano Sonata No. 20 (2011)
Op. 148: Dialogue for Solo Piano (2013)
Op. 149: Etude Courte mais Transcendante pour Piano (2013)
Op. 151: Nobody is Perfect for Piano Solo (2013)
Op. 152: A Pianist in Jeopardy for Piano Solo (2013)
Op. 153: Wandering for Piano Solo (2013)
Op. 157: Curiosity for Piano Solo (2015)
Op. 159: Rainy Weather for Piano Solo (2015)
Op. 160: Something Else for Piano Solo (2015)
Op. 161: Moon Rainbow for Piano Solo (2015)

B) Piano and Orchestra:
Op. 1: Concertino for Piano and Orchestra (1957)
Op. 2: Concerto for Piano and Orchestra No. 1 (1961)
Op. 3: Variations for Piano and Big Band (1962)
Op. 8: Toccata for Piano and Orchestra (1964)
Op. 13: Intermezzo for Piano and Orchestra (1968)
Op. 14: Concerto for Piano and Orchestra No. 2 (1974)
Op. 16: Nocturne in G major for Piano and Orchestra (1972)
Op. 19: Etude for Piano and Orchestra (1974)
Op. 20: Nocturne for Piano and Orchestra (1974)
Op. 25: Concert Rhapsody for Piano and Orchestra (1976)
Op. 29: Scherzo for Piano and Orchestra (1978)
Op. 33: Piece for Two Pianos and Orchestra (1982)
Op. 48: Concerto for Piano and Orchestra No. 3 (1985)
Op. 56: Concerto for Piano and Orchestra No. 4 (1989)
Op. 72: Concerto for Piano and Orchestra No. 5 (1993)
Op. 74: Concerto for Piano and Orchestra No. 6 (1993)
Op. 147: Concerto for Piano and Orchestra No. 1 (2nd edition) (2012)

3. Works for Other Solo Instruments

A) Cello Solo:
  Op. 93: Introduction and Scherzino for Cello Solo (1999)
  Op. 124: Suite for Cello Solo (2004)

B) Solo Instrument and Orchestra:
  Op. 5: Piece for Trumpet and Orchestra (1962)
  Op. 50: Concerto for Alto-Saxophone and Orchestra (1987)
  Op. 76: Concerto for Double-Bass and Symphony Orchestra (1994)
  Op. 85: Concerto No. 1 for Cello and Orchestra (1997)
  Op. 103: Concerto No. 2 for Cello and String Orchestra (2002)
  Op. 105: Double Concerto for Violin, Piano and String Orchestra (2002)
  Op. 141: Violin Concerto (2009)

4. Chamber Music

  Op. 18: Four Pieces for Instrumental Ensemble (1973)
  Op. 27: Fantasia for Jazz Quartet (1976)
  Op. 42: »Rush Hour« for Ensemble (1985)
  Op. 43: »An April Day« for Ensemble (1985)
  Op. 44: »The Morning« for Ensemble (1985)
  Op. 57: Chamber Symphony for Chamber Orchestra (1990)
  Op. 63: Sonata for Cello and Piano No. 1 (1991)
  Op. 69: Sonata for Viola and Piano (1992)
  Op. 70: Sonata for Violin and Piano (1992)
  Op. 79: Piece for Sextet (1995)
  Op. 84: Sonata for Cello and Piano No. 2 (1997)
  Op. 86: Trio for Flute, Cello and Piano (1998)
  Op. 88: String Quartet No. 1 (1998)
  Op. 89: Piano Quintet (1998)
  Op. 90: Concerto for Eleven Instruments (1998)
  Op. 91: Divertissement for Two Flutes, Cello and Piano (1998)
  Op. 96: Elegy for Cello and Piano (1999)
  Op. 97: Burlesque for Cello and Piano (1999)
  Op. 98: »Nearly Waltz« for Cello and Piano (1999)
  Op. 99: Duet for Alto-Saxophone and Cello (1999)
  Op. 104: Concerto for Two Pianos and Two Percussions (2002)
  Op. 106: Suite for Viola, Alto-Saxophone, Piano and Bass (2002)
  Op. 107: Variations on »Sweet Georgia Brown« for Viola, Alto-Saxophone, Piano and Bass (2002)
  Op. 125: Sonata for Flute and Piano (2004)

Op. 126: Divertissement in Four Movements for Violin, Cello and Piano (2005)
Op. 129: Paraphrase on Dizzy Gillespie's »Manteca« for Two Pianos (2006)
Op. 132: String Quartet No. 2 (2007)
Op. 136: Piano Trio No. 1 for Violin, Cello and Piano (2009)
Op. 142: Piano Trio No. 2 for Violin, Cello and Piano (2010)
Op. 145: Triptych for Two Pianos (2012)
Op. 146: Capriccio for Two Pianos (2012)
Op. 150: Piece for String Quartet »Rondo Frivole« pour quatuor à cordes (2013)
Op. 154: Piece for String Quartet »The Last Attempt« (2014)
Op. 155: Allegro for Piano Trio (2014)
Op. 156: A Little Duo for Flute & Cello (2014)
Op. 158: Sonatina for Viola and Piano (2015)

5. Orchestral Music

A) Big Band:
Op. 4: Chorale and Fugue for Orchestra (1962)
Op. 7: Fantasia on Three Children's Songs for Orchestra (1963)
Op. 9: »The Trial« for Orchestra (1966)
Op. 11: »Estacade« for Big Band (1966)
Op. 12: »Aquarium Blues« for Big Band (1967)
Op. 15: »The Forest Story« for Orchestra (1972)
Op. 17: Three Pieces for Orchestra (1972)
Op. 21: Minuet for Big Band (1974)

B) Big Band with Strings:
Op. 6: »Rose-Marie« Fantasia for Orchestra (1963)
Op. 10: »Big Band Sounds (The Sounds of Big-Band)« for Orchestra (1966)
Op. 22: Piece for Five Saxophones and Orchestra (1975)
Op. 23: »Enigma« for Big Band (1975)
Op. 24: March for Orchestra (1975)
Op. 26A: »Sunrise« for Orchestra (1976)
Op. 31: Elegy for Orchestra (1980)
Op. 32: »The Wind from the North« for Orchestra (1981)

C) Little Big Band:
　　Op. 51: Overture for Big Band (1987)
　　Op. 52: »Intrada« for Big Band (1988)

D) Symphonic Orchestra:
　　Op. 30: Two-movement Concerto for Orchestra (1980)
　　Op. 34: »Meridian« for Orchestra (1982)
　　Op. 35: »Closed Curve« for Orchestra (1982)
　　Op. 37: »The Pleasant Meeting« for Orchestra (1983)
　　Op. 38: »Presentiment« for Orchestra (1983)
　　Op. 49: Sinfonietta for Orchestra (1987)

Appendix E: Letters about Kapustin

1. Letter of Nikolai Kapustin to his parents (ca. 1953-1954):

   Good Day! How long should I wait for my mother, Klavdia Nikolayevna[430], to visit? I think I will get to the point when I will have no money by the time of my birthday, because the stipend is coming only on the 23rd. Father, do me a favor – can you force mother to come here as soon as possible? Please, don't forget I am living here without any clothes, and it's snowing here already. A few days ago I played »Pictures at an Exhibition« of Mussorgsky. It was a successful performance, I got an »A.« Until I see you again, Mikola (Ukranian way of saying Nikolai).[431]

2. Letter of Nikolai Kapustin to his parents (winter 1955):

   Hello to all! During this past month I had enough adventure. I finished the story with the recruitment office just now on February 20th. So everything is alright – I am going to the army in autumn (it's a joke). ....
   Not long ago there was an evening dedicated to Feodor Shaliapin. There was Kozlovsky and now I am very well acquainted with him. A week ago I had a chance to drink a wine with Khachaturian. I even played for him my compositions. After that Khachaturian said that I should enter the Conservatory as a composer.
   On the 16th (of March) Sergei Vladimirovich [father of Andrei Mikhalkov] came back from his trip to Italy. He presented me with many different things: Italian mouthpiece cigarette holder to which you can insert glass cylinders with the anti-nicotine (filters), two packages of the anti-nicotine (not cotton but salt – higher quality),[432] Italian and American cigarettes, matches that light up from any object, a badge from the Olympic games, and chewing gum.
   I did not buy the new suit yet. Yesterday I played in the Small Hall of the Conservatory wearing the old suit. The concert was dedicated to Rubbakh's sixtieth Jubilee and the forty years of his pedagogical career. The first part of the concert involved his current students' performance. The second part was his former students. I was supposed to finish the first part of the concert, but it ended up that Jenia (Evgeniya Pupkova) came late on purpose so she could end the first half. What a pig!
   I played Ravel's Play of Water [Jeux d'eau] for a half hour and, of course, Don Juan [Liszt's Reminiscences de Don Juan]. It turned out to be okay. They asked me to come on

---

[430] Note by the author: Kapustin referred to his mother with her middle name (Klavdia Nikolayevna), which was considered to be a sign of the biggest respect and adoration to his parents.
[431] The letter translated by the author.
[432] Note by the author: In Russia in the 1950s people smoked Russian cigarettes with no filter. The cigarette holder and filters represented a new generation of cigarettes that were not available in Russia at that time.

stage to bow five times. In addition, I accompanied Andrei [Mikhalkov] in Khachaturian's Piano Concerto, so I was on stage for forty-five minutes! Soon, maybe, I will send you the pictures. The thing is - they were taking pictures from the hall and from the stage. Usually, only the »big« masters get pictures from the stage. So, it was a little comical. If Fira will find mistakes in this letter, then it will be the last one. All the best. Main typewriter, Nikolai Kapustin.[433]

3. Letter of Nikolai Kapustin to Alla Kapustina (April 11, 1970):

Hello my dear Allochka!
You probably know from Moolya[434] *that we are going to finish not on the 18th but on the 17th. That means that I am going to be home on Saturday which makes me very happy – the first two days we will spend completely together.*
I don't have anything to write about myself; we are performing two concerts a day. I don't have any more power at all, and I am not the only one who feels this way. I don't want to talk about this.
We are now in the city called Rubtsovka. The name of the city, especially its ending »ka« tells you a lot already. In other words, Nikitovka looks more attractive.
Today at 6 pm is the first concert and the second at 9 pm, tomorrow is the same thing. The next day, thank you, just one. We are then going to Ust-Kaminogorsk for four days. All together we have six days left. One more thing – the letter may not reach you, I don't have any more envelopes with the air mail stamp on it.
I am in a hurry; now is a quarter to five and we are leaving at 5 pm. I have to run. So, in a week I will be home. We are flying to Alma-Ata on May 7th. I will have twenty days to rest, I thought it would be less.
My pen is going to finish soon (already diluted by the water), that's why I am calling it a day. Wait for me. I miss you like I've never missed you before, more than ever. Kisses, your Kolia.
P.S.: What kind of a joke happened with our house?

4. Letter of Nikolai Kapustin to Alla Kapustina (December 20, 1970):

Hello Allochka!
This night we arrived to Murom.[435] *Now is December 20th, 1 pm, and I just woke up. I have to go to the concert at 5 pm. We played eighteen concerts already. If there will be two concerts a day until the end of the tour it will be thirty six altogether. Two of them we will play without any payment, so it is thirty four concerts, and this is already 400 rubles if not*

---

[433] The letter translated by the author.
[434] Note from the author: Moolya Lundstrem was the wife of Igor Lundstrem, the brother of Oleg Lundstrem. Both couples lived in the same apartment building and shared all the news between each other concerning the touring of the Lundstrem Orchestra.
[435] Murom is the city in Vladimir region of Russia.

more. About our trip in January – it probably will not happen because Dima doesn't want to work again with those people; he suggested we work again in Moscow, but the conditions are very questionable. I need to think about it.

We will stay in Murom for four days, then one day in Arzamas, and one day somewhere close to Gorky. From Gorky we are going to Moscow. If there will be a chance to leave right after the concert, me, Gravis, Igor, and Dima will be taking the taxi and going to Marina Roscha.[436]

How are you doing there without money my poor dear? You probably sent money to your parents, this is in vain. By the way, for a week already we are travelling without Vadim; he is always going ahead of us organizing the places for our concerts in the next cities. Therefore, we can't get paid until we see him. I keep living on a daily allowance. In other words, see you in five days, maybe only on the railway train station as we pass by. In this case I will send you the telegram. Kisses, your Kolia.

5. Memories of Oxana Yablonskaya:

It is easy to talk about the music of Nikolai Kapustin, and it is not as easy to talk about Kolia as a person.

When we studied at the conservatory, Kolia seemed a little strange to me – everybody was talking all the time, laughing loudly, missing classes (of course not often and not the private piano) but he was different. Goldenweiser himself never missed classes and was never late. I remember Nikolai's performance of Beethoven's Variations, Op. 35 very clearly. He never came to the lessons with Goldenweiser unprepared. His performances were always well planned, and all the technical difficulties of the pieces were worked out.

In between the classes he played jazz… I remember very often he played one of his compositions, I think it's now called Sonatina, Op. 100. It was written in the style of Mozart, and we all tried to play it by ear. It's starts as an easy piece, but it changes quickly.

I remember his performance with Nodar Gabunia of Bartok's Concerto for Two Pianos and Percussion very well – it was a sensation at that time… In general, he reminded me Goldenweiser himself – always prim, seasoned, and never any kind of sloppiness that students often allow themselves.

Once I found the phone number of Kapustin and called him from the United States. We didn't talk probably for fifty years (!!!). I invited him to Italy. Unfortunately, he refused to come, he said that he is no longer travelling long distances. He was surprised that I was talking about his music. He said: »How do you know about my music?« I answered that the whole world knows his music, that he made a revolution in classical music, and that everybody admires his music, including me. To tell you the truth, he was surprised to hear that… sincerely surprised.

The music of Kapustin made a revolution – his music is easy to recognize, performed everywhere, and very popular. It is difficult though to perform Kapustin's music the way he

---

[436] Marina Roscha – place where Kapustin lived in Moscow.

plays himself. I remember I was listening somebody else's performance of Kapustin and was delighted by them until the point when I heard Nikolai playing his compositions... No one can even get close to his interpretation. He is a brilliant pianist, who can play with the real jazz rhythm that is necessary for the performance of his music. I adore his music, play it myself, and assign it to my students. In the whole world you can constantly hear his solo piano compositions on international competitions, festivals... everywhere.[437]

6. Memories of Alexei Zoubov:

I don't remember how I first heard about Kapustin – it was so long ago, probably somewhere in the middle 1950s. The rumors started to flow by then that there is a piano student at the conservatory that has enormous technique and talent and was quite a novelty. He writes and plays real jazz compositions. For us, who just started to play jazz, the music that wasn't much appreciated and even considered dangerous by the Soviet regime, every new musician appearing in this field, especially of Kapustin's caliber, was a source of excitement.

Pretty soon I, Bakholdin, and some others hooked up with Nikolai, and the idea was born to create a quintet, where Kapustin was deservingly accepted as a leader.
We had a problem finding a place to rehearse and Kolya Samoilenko, a violinist with the State Symphony Orchestra and jazz aficionado, invited us to his place. It was a rather small room, a typical Soviet »communal« apartment where a bed, a grand piano, and a large semi-professional tape recorder took most of the space. This did not leave much room for five musicians with their instruments including upright bass and a drum set. Our enthusiasm overcame all these small inconveniences and we started to work. We started mostly with American standards, that's what the new audience demanded. We had to transcribe the tunes from bad quality recordings and later from the albums that came from the west. Kapustin's amazing ability to transcribe in minutes what would take about ten times more for me or Bakholdin astonished us and, yes, made us envious! Unlike us, Kapustin was a real professional, and we were still amateurs striving to grow into professionals, and compensating with our abundant enthusiasm.
We got a gig at the restaurant »National« which turned into a favorite place for musicians, composers and jazz fans. The restaurant was always packed, the administration and waiters loved us, but the music was supposed to be approved by the Moscow special office, and when some inspector finally came and listened to our music from outside the hall, the next day we lost the gig.
Some Americans visiting the restaurant brought the news about our group and rebirth of jazz in Soviet Union to the United State. Kapustin's quintet ended up featured in a special section on Soviet jazz in Encyclopedia of Jazz by a famous American jazz critic Leonard Feather.

---

[437] From the correspondence with Oxana Yablonskaya, February 27, 2018.

The quintet, as I said, was playing mostly American standards, the public was hungry for American music. All this time Kapustin never stopped writing more and more, unfortunately there wasn't that much exposure of his music to wider audience.

Oleg Lundstrem's band was born in the thirties in Shanghai. It consisted of Russian musicians, mostly children of Russian engineers and workers for the Siberian railroad living in Harbin. Just like us, they got »infected« by the jazz »virus« and moved to Shanghai. At that time Shanghai was a pretty cosmopolitan center with a solid demand for Jazz music. In 1947 they decided to immigrate to Russia - the country that they still considered their homeland. But it was still the Soviet Union, nobody knew what to do with them, and they were sent to settle in Kazan' to keep them from spreading the decease of jazz.

After the death of Stalin in 1953 the atmosphere for jazz very slowly started to change for the better and the Lundstrem band was activated again. We heard them when they came to Moscow about 1957 - we couldn't even imagine a big band of that class existing in the Soviet Union. Many musicians in the band were getting old, retiring, or even dying. Oleg Lundstrem started to look for the new blood, so to speak, young, improvising in the contemporary style musicians. That's how we were hired by Lundstrem around the beginning of the sixties, and I, Bakholdin and Kapustin enjoyed getting together again. The Lundstrem band became the place were Kapustin started to use the new side of his musical abilities, he started to write and compose for the big band. We loved to listen to and play his music enormously.

When The Orchestra of State Radio and Television with Vadim Ludvikovsky as a leader was formed in 1966, Kapustin continued writing, mostly arranging for the band, showing the ability to write brilliant arrangements. I still have the recording of his arrangement of Alexander Varlamov – I was happy to play solo there.[438]

7. Memories of Mark-André Hamelin:

It's my pleasure to say a few words about Nikolai Kapustin!

I first discovered his music through his second sonata; I was staying at the home of Mike Spring, then working at Hyperion Records, and he put on Nikolai Petrov's recording rightfully thinking I'd be interested. My jaw dropped to the floor, and I immediately wanted to play the piece.

Then I set out to discover as much as I could about him, which wasn't easy, since almost none of the music had been published. I remember getting a lot of music from pianist Steven Osborne, who had been in touch with him, and that's how my collection started. Finding out about Kapustin himself was a lot more difficult; as hard as it is now to believe, a Google search for Kapustin in 1998 produced zero results.

I had the privilege of giving the second sonata's UK première in May of 2000, and for the occasion Kapustin and his wife Alla made the 3-day train journey all the way to London (he refuses to fly). Although my performance at the time was unnecessarily quick overall, I

---

[438] From correspondence with Mark-André Hamelin, March 6, 2018.

think the occasion was a pleasant one for the composer, whose music so far had only gotten very limited exposure in the West. He seemed pleased with my performance, even if he did say the first movement was too fast (and that was only after I pressed him for an opinion...!)

I later asked him to autograph the only original score of his music I owned at the time (an anthology that included his Suite in the Old Style, Op. 28). The score has become a very precious possession!

It's now obvious that Kapustin's time has come – performances of his music have proliferated, and scores are now available through major publishing houses. I am happy to have made a contribution to the dissemination of his wonderful, exhilarating body of work. While being difficult and requiring a high degree of mental discipline and concentration, the music is so well conceived in every single respect pianistically that it's always a joy to play.[439]

8. Memories of Steven Osborne:

Discovering Kapustin's music was a happy accident - I was playing snooker with a friend and he put on Nikolai Petrov's recording of the 2nd sonata. I already loved jazz and so I was very taken with it. I like to think my recording has something to do with the current interest in Kapustin's music, but mine wasn't the first so who knows?

I contacted Petrov first to find a way to contact Kapustin, and indeed, we couldn't understand each other at all! (I learned some Russian as a teenager but it didn't help much.) Petrov brought me many scores from Russia, and I picked from them to make the CD.

The music of Kapustin is one of the most successful fusions of classical and jazz that I know - normally classical/jazz fusions are very lopsided to either the classical or the jazz, but Kapustin manages a rather equal balance of classical form with jazz language. The only composer I can think of who managed something comparable is Bernstein. It's a lot of fun playing Kapustin's music but there's a big challenge for classical players - how do you swing? It's a profoundly different sense of how rhythm works. Even after having listened to years and years of jazz and mucking about with playing jazz a great deal, I still can't properly do it! But that's a big part of the fun - searching for the groove.[440]

---

[439] From the personal correspondence with Mr. Hamelin, January 28, 2018.
[440] From correspondence with Steven Osborne, February 28, 2018.

Appendix F: Personalities

I. Sources in Russian Language

Adzhemov, Konstantin Khristoforovich (1911-1985)
http://www.mosconsv.ru/ru/person.aspx?id=9038

Alexandrov, Anatoly Nikolayevich (1988-1982)
https://dic.academic.ru/dic.nsf/enc_biography/2047/Александров

Babajanian, Arno (1921-1983)
http://babajanyan.ru/biography_arno_babadzhanyana.html

Bashkirov, Dmitry (born 1931)
http://www.mosconsv.ru/ru/person.aspx?id=8936

Blok, David Semionovich (1888-1948)
http://www.kino-teatr.ru/kino/composer/sov/39621/bio/

Blumenfeld, Felix (1863-1931)
http://www.krugosvet.ru/enc/kultura_i_obrazovanie/muzyka/BLU-MENFELD_FELIKS_MIHALOVICH.html

Borisovsky, Vadim (1900-1972)
http://www.mosconsv.ru/ru/disk.aspx?id=22131

Bril, Igor (born 1944)
http://www.jazz.ru/pages/bril/

Dashkevich, Vladimir (born 1934)
http://propianino.ru/vladimir-dashkevich

Dolgov, Vitaly (1937-2007)
http://info-jazz.ru/community/jazzmen?action=show&id=53
http://www.km.ru/muzyka/encyclopedia/dolgov-vitalii

Ellington, Edward Kennedy »Duke« (1899-1974)
http://sevjazz.info/index.php?option=com_content&view=article&id=444:2012-04-28-12-40-04&catid=48:jazz-stars&Itemid=50

Eisenstein, Sergei (1898-1948)
https://www.culture.ru/persons/680/sergey-eyzenshteyn

Eshpai, Andrei (1925-2015)
http://www.mosconsv.ru/ru/person.aspx?id=9012

Gabunia, Nodar (1933-2000)
https://dic.academic.ru/dic.nsf/enc_music/1801/Габуния

Garanian, Georgy (1934-2010)
http://garanian.ru/
http://www.jazz.ru/pages/garanian/

Gilels, Emil (1916-1985)
http://www.mosconsv.ru/ru/disk.aspx?id=22188

Goldenweiser, Alexander (1875-1961)
https://dic.academic.ru/dic.nsf/enc_music/2110/Гольденвейзер
http://www.mosconsv.ru/ru/person.aspx?id=121142
http://progulkipomoskve.ru/publ/muzei_moskvy/muzej_kvartira_pianista_a_b_goldenvejzera_v_moskve/27-1-0-1766

Golubev, Evgeny (1910-1988)
http://www.music-dic.ru/html-music-keld/g/1855.html

Gagarin, Yuri (1934-1968)
https://ria.ru/spravka/20140309/998590852.html

Glière, Reinhold (1875-1956)
http://www.mosconsv.ru/ru/person.aspx?id=34741

Gnessin, Mikhail (1883-1957)
http://eleven.co.il/article/11216

Grinberg, Maria (1908-1978)
http://magazines.russ.ru/znamia/1999/5/inger.html
http://www.alefmagazine.com/pub1630.html

Gubaidulina, Sofia (born 1931)
http://www.biografija.ru/biography/gubajdulina-sofya-sofiya-azgatovna.htm

Igumnov, Konstantin (1873-1948)
http://www.mosconsv.ru/ru/person.aspx?id=121136

Kabalevsky, Dmitry (1904-1987)
http://www.mosconsv.ru/ru/person.aspx?id=37115

Karamyshev, Boris (1915-2003)
http://kkre-4.narod.ru/karamishev.htm
http://www.kino-teatr.ru/kino/composer/sov/31415/works/

Katz, Isaac (1922-2009)
http://nnovcons.ru/obrazovanie/fakultety/fortepiannyy-fakultet/
http://famous-birthdays.ru/data/22_sentyabrya/katz_isaak_iosifovich.html

Khachaturian, Aram (1903-1978)
http://www.mosconsv.ru/ru/person.aspx?id=45795

Konchalovskaya, Natalia (1903-1988)
https://www.pravda.ru/culture/culturalhistory/personality/24-01-2003/35059-konchalovskaja-0/

Konchalovsky, Andrei (born 1937)
http://konchalovsky.ru/life/biography

Konchalovsky, Piotr (1876-1956)
http://www.artcyclopedia.ru/konchalovskij_petr_petrovich.htm

Korbut, Pavel (born 1946)
http://www.jazz.ru/pages/korbut/

Korneev, Alexander (1930-2010)
http://www.mosconsv.ru/ru/person.aspx?id=8766
http://www.myflute.ru/library/teacher/k/k_177.html

Kozlovsky, Ivan (1900-1993)
http://www.belcanto.ru/kozlovsky.html

Krautgartner, Karel (1922-1982)
http://www.jazz.ru/mag/171/krautgartner.htm

Kroll, Anatoly (born 1943)
http://www.jazzmap.ru/rus/bands/Anatolij-Kroll-kompozitor-dirizhur-dzhazovyj-pianist.php

Leschetizky, Teodor (1830-1915)
http://w.histrf.ru/articles/article/show/lieshietitskii_leszetycki_leschetizky_tieodor_teodor_theodor_fiodor_osipovich

Levinovsky, Nikolai (born 1944)
http://www.jazz.ru/pages/levinovsky/

Lhevinne, Rosina (1880-1976)
http://enc-dic.com/enc_music/Levina-R-4072.html

Liadova, Lyudmila (born 1925)
http://www.biography-life.ru/interview/702-lyudmila-lyadova-u-menya-i-minor-zvuchit-mazhorno.html

Ludvikovsky, Vadim (1925-1995)
http://nashenasledie.livejournal.com/121134.html

Lukianov, German (1936-2007)
http://www.jazz.ru/pages/lukianov/

Miansarova, Tamara (1931-2017)
http://miansarova.narod.ru/bio.htm

Mikhalkov, Nikita (born 1945)
https://24smi.org/celebrity/287-nikita-mikhalkov.html

Mikhalkov, Sergei Vladimirovich (1913-2009)
https://bigenc.ru/literature/text/2219210

Minzi, Carlo Levi (born 1954)
http://www.mk.ru/culture/2017/10/03/pianist-karlo-leviminci-velikoe-chto-italiya-podarila-miru-v-proshlom.html

Murja, Graf (born 1973)
http://www.mosconsv.ru/ru/person.aspx?id=31398

Myaskovsky, Nikolai (1881-1950)
http://filarmonia.kh.ua/nikolaj-myaskovskij/

Nemenova-Lunts, Maria Solomonovna (1874-1954)
https://dic.academic.ru/dic.nsf/enc_music/5438/Неменова
http://aquarius-classic.ru/person?sid=129

Neuhaus, Heinrich (1888-1964)
http://www.mosconsv.ru/ru/person.aspx?id=121143

Nikolaev, Alexander Alexandrovich (1903-1980)
http://dic.academic.ru/dic.nsf/enc_biography/91502/Николаев
http://www.musenc.ru/html/n/nikolaev.html

Nikolaeva, Tatyana (1924-1993)
http://www.mosconsv.ru/ru/person.aspx?id=41223
http://musicseasons.org/tatyana-petrovna-nikolaeva/

Oistrakh, David (1908-1974)
http://www.mosconsv.ru/ru/person.aspx?id=126114

Ovchinnikov, Viacheslav (born 1936)
http://vyacheslavovchinnikov.ru/ru/content/?id=26

Ovchinnikov, Vladimir (born 1958)
http://www.mosconsv.ru/ru/person.aspx?id=31514

Rosner, Eddie (1910-1976)
http://www.jazz.ru/mag/78/reading.htm

Rubbakh, Avrelian (1895-1975)
https://search.rsl.ru/en/search#q=руббах аврелиан григорьевич

Saulsky, Yuri (1928-2003)
http://www.amumgk.ru/pages/people/people_10693.html

Schulzhenko, Klavdia (1906-1984)
http://telegrafua.com/country/13888/
http://www.peoples.ru/art/music/stage/shulzhenko/

Schwartz, Egil (born 1935)
http://www.kino-teatr.ru/kino/acter/m/ros/380891/bio/

Shaliapin, Fiodor (1873-1938)
http://www.aif.ru/culture/person/fedor_shalyapin_maloizvestnye_fakty_i_vehi_tvorchestva

Sidelnikov, Nikolai (1930-1992)
https://dic.academic.ru/dic.nsf/enc_biography/112490/Сидельников

Silantiev, Yuri (1919-1983)
http://www.kino-teatr.ru/kino/acter/m/star/48106/bio/

Sofronitsky, Vladimir (1901-1961)
http://www.mosconsv.ru/ru/person.aspx?id=130953

Surikov, Vasily (1848-1916)
http://artsurikov.ru/

Tolkunova, Valentina (1946-2010)
http://www.kino-teatr.ru/kino/acter/w/star/4322/bio/

Tolstoy, Lev (1828-1910)
http://enc-dic.com/colier/Tolsto-lev-nikolaevich-6464.html
Goldenweiser, Alexander. Vblizi Tolstogo: Zapisi za piatnadtsat' let [Close to Tolstoy: Notes for Fifteen Years]. Vol. 1-2, Moscow: Goslitizdat, 1922-1923, 1959.

Tretiakov, Viktor (born 1946)
http://web.archive.org/web/20110910195253/http://www.biograph.ru/bank/tretyakov_vv.htm

Tsfasman, Alexander (1906-1971)
http://www.jazz.ru/mag/372/tsfasman.htm

Varlamov, Alexander Egorovich (1801-1848)
http://files.school-collection.edu.ru/dlrstore/fce0a0ac-d965-0f7e-bc0b-a5c5faa33405/Varlamov bio.htm

Velikanova, Gelena (1922-1998)
http://www.kino-teatr.ru/kino/acter/w/star/283859/bio/

Vershinin, Alexander (born 1965)
http://www.mosconsv.ru/ru/person.aspx?id=11138

Weinshtein, Iosif (1918-2001)
http://jazzquad.ru/index.pl?act=PRODUCT&id=296

Yakushenko, Igor (1932-1999)
http://kkre-17.narod.ru/jakushenko.htm

Yeltsin, Boris (1931-2007)
http://yeltsin.ru/news/biografiya-boris-nikolaevich-elcin-prezident-rossii-19911999/

II. Sources in English, French, Italian, Latvian, and Polish Languages

Angelov, Lyudmil (born 1961)
http://virtuosoartistsmanagement.com/ludmil-angelov-piano/
http://www.lespritdeladiva.org/ludmilAngelov
http://varnasummerfest.org/news_search_results_en.php?page=news_show&newsID=202&nsID=12

Ashkenazy, Vladimir (born 1937)
https://www.britannica.com/biography/Vladimir-Ashkenazy
http://www.vladimirashkenazy.com/biography.php

Appleton, Jon (born 1939)
http://www.appletonjon.com/biography.htm

Bakholdin, Konstantin (1936-1987)
https://www.findagrave.com/memorial/108410686

Balina, Aino (born 1935)
http://lr2.lsm.lv/lv/raksts/muzikju-jubilejas/dziedatajai-aino-balinai-80.a51573/

Berman, Lazar (1930-2005)
https://www.allmusic.com/artist/lazar-berman-mn0002041344

Borisovsky, Vadim (1900-1972)
https://humanities.byu.edu/vadim-borisovsky-and-the-founding-of-the-russian-viola-school/

Brom, Gustav (1921-1995)
http://www.radio.cz/es/rubrica/musica-clasica-jazz/gustav-brom-de-cometa-del-swing-a-rey-del-jazz

Chizhik, Leonid (born 1947)
http://www.leonid-chizhik.de/firma/index.html

Cliburn, Harvey Lavan »Van« (1934-2013)
https://www.britannica.com/biography/Van-Cliburn

Davis, Immanuel (born 1969)
https://apps.cla.umn.edu/directory/profiles/davis210

Del Pino, Daniel (born 1972)
http://achucarrofoundation.org/legacy-pianists/daniel-del-pino/

Denisov, Edison (1929-1996)
http://www.musicologie.org/Biographies/d/denissov.html

Duet Mitchell Dwike (1930-2013) and Willie Ruff (born 1931)
https://www.allmusic.com/artist/dwike-mitchell-mn0000132649/biography

Edelhagen, Kurt (1920-1982)
http://jazzprofiles.blogspot.com/2013/07/orchester-kurt-edelhagen.html

Ellington, Edward Kennedy »Duke« (1899-1974)
https://www.britannica.com/biography/Duke-Ellington

Gabunia, Nodar (1933-2000)
http://www.nodargabunia.com/start.html

Gershwin, George (1898-1937)
https://www.britannica.com/biography/George-Gershwin
http://gershwin.com/

Gilels, Emil (1916-1985)
http://www.emilgilels.com/

Glazunov, Alexander (1865-1936)
https://www.britannica.com/biography/Aleksandr-Glazunov

Goodman, Benny (1909-1986)
https://www.britannica.com/biography/Benny-Goodman

Gorbachev, Mikhail (born 1931)
https://www.britannica.com/biography/Mikhail-Gorbachev

Gould, Glenn (1932-1982)
https://www.britannica.com/biography/Glenn-Gould
https://glenngould.com/

Gubaidulina, Sofia (born 1931)
https://www.britannica.com/biography/Sofia-Gubaidulina

Hamelin, Marc-André (born 1961)
http://www.bach-cantatas.com/Bio/Hamelin-Marc-Andre.htm
http://www.marcandrehamelin.com/artist.php?view=bio

Jarrett, Keith (born 1945)
https://www.keithjarrett.org/

Kawakami, Masahiro (born 1965)
http://www.cam.hi-ho.ne.jp/pianistas/kawakami_english.html
http://japanpianoopen.eu/jury/masahiro-kawakami.html

Leonov, Alexey (born 1934)
https://www.theguardian.com/science/2015/may/09/alexei-leonov-first-man-to-walk-in-space-soviet-cosmonaut

Leschetizky, Teodor (1830-1915)
http://www.britannica.com/biography/Theodor-Leschetizky
https://www.gutenberg.org/files/43915/43915-h/43915-h.htm

Lewis, John (1920-2001)
https://www.biography.com/people/john-lewis-37484

Liadova, Lyudmila (born 1925)
http://russia-ic.com/people/general/l/508
https://www.youtube.com/watch?v=KZs0GKy-xLo

Lisitsa, Valentina (born 1973)
http://www.valentinalisitsa.com/

Lloyd, Charles (born 1938)
https://www.charleslloyd.com/

Matie, Mirei (born in 1946)
http://www.mireillemathieu.com/biography/?lang=en

Minzi, Carlo Levi (born 1954)
http://www.carloleviminzi.com/

Muradeli, Vano (1908-1970)
https://www.findagrave.com/memorial/23980719

Naissoo, Uno (1928-1980)
http://www.emic.ee/uno-naissoo

Namyslowski, Zbigniew (born 1939)
http://culture.pl/pl/tworca/zbigniew-namyslowski

Osborne, Steven (born 1971)
http://www.stevenosborne.co.uk/biography/

Panov, Nikolai (born 1945)
http://www.persona.rin.ru/eng/view/f//20907/nikolai-panov

Petrov, Nikolai (1943-2011)
https://www.britannica.com/biography/Nikolay-Arnoldovich-Petrov

Putin, Vladimir (born 1952)
http://eng.putin.kremlin.ru/bio

Reibaldi, Vito (born 1959)
http://www.circuitomusica.it/reiglob

Richter, Sviatoslav (1915-1997)
https://www.britannica.com/biography/Sviatoslav-Richter

Schoenberg, Arnold (1874-1951)
https://www.britannica.com/biography/Arnold-Schoenberg

Schnittke, Alfred (1934-1998)
https://www.britannica.com/biography/Alfred-Schnittke
http://americansymphony.org/alfred-schnittke-nagasaki/
http://intoclassics.net/news/2009-09-15-2454

Scott, Cyril (1879-1970)
http://www.cyrilscott.net/

Shearing, George (1919-2011)
http://www.georgeshearing.net/

Sinaisky, Vassily (born 1947)
https://www.intermusica.co.uk/artist/Vassily-Sinaisky

Tarkovsky, Andrei (1932-1986)
https://www.britannica.com/biography/Andrey-Arsenyevich-Tarkovsky

Washington, Grover Jr. (1943-1999)
https://www.allmusic.com/artist/grover-washington-jr-mn0000944206/biography

Young, Robert (1935-2011)
https://www.thestage.co.uk/features/obituaries/2011/robert-young/

Ulyanov [Lenin], Vladimir (1870-1924)
https://www.biography.com/people/vladimir-lenin-9379007

Utyosov, Leonid (1895-1982)
http://russiapedia.rt.com/prominent-russians/music/leonid-utyosov/

Vlach, Karel (1911-1986)
http://jazz-jazz.ru/?category=download&altname=karel_vlach__vte345iny_v_lloydu_i._19391942_1994

Wild, Earl (1915-2010)
http://www.earlwild.com/
https://www.youtube.com/watch?v=1MQZ6L1KMOI

Yablonskaya, Oxana (born 1938)
https://www.puigcerdamusic.com/oxana-yablonskaya

Yeltsin, Boris (1931-2007)
https://www.britannica.com/biography/Boris-Yeltsin

Yudina, Maria (1899-1970)
http://www.bach-cantatas.com/Bio/Yudina-Maria.htm
http://www.classicfm.com/discover-music/latest/maria-yudina-stalin/

Zagorinsky, Alexander (born 1962)
http://www.norge.ru/no/alexander_zagorinsky.htm

Zavadsky, Yuri (1894-1977)
https://www.britannica.com/biography/Yury-Alexandrovich-Zavadsky

Zoubov, Alexei (born 1936)
http://alexeiz.com/bio.php

Appendix G: Miscellaneous

I. Sources in Russian

Central Music School for Gifted Children
https://cmsmoscow.ru/

Fall of the Berlin Wall
https://www.golos-ameriki.ru/a/berlin-wall/2510614.html

Leaders and Propaganda: Yeltsin and Putin
http://osvita.mediasapiens.ua/trends/1411978127/vozhdi_i_propaganda_eltsin_i_putin/

Lucerna Concert Hall (Prague, Czech Republic)
https://goout.net/en/concert-halls/great-hall-lucerna/ckf/

Mainichi Broadcasting System (Japan)
http://www.mbs.jp/english/

Melodiya - recording company in Moscow (Russia)
https://www.culture.ru/institutes/13974/firma-melodiya

Mosconcert
http://www.mosconcert.com/aboutus/

Moscow Musical College
http://www.amumgk.ru/

Muzgiz – publishing house in Moscow (Russia)
http://www.music-izdat.ru/About.asp

Nikolina Gora (Russia)
http://www.utro.ru/articles/2004/03/31/293600.shtml

Rosconcert
https://dic.academic.ru/dic.nsf/enc_music/6580/Росконцерт

Ruza Resort (Russia)
http://mskhotels.info/hotel/dom-tvorchestva-kompozitorov-ruza

Sovetsky Kompozitor – publishing house in Moscow (Russia)
https://www.livelib.ru/publisher/569-sovetskij-kompozitor

Union of Moscow Composers
http://союзмосковскихкомпозиторов.рф/sect-jazz.htm

II. Sources in English

Channel Tunnel (England – France)
https://www.britannica.com/topic/Channel-Tunnel

Ivanovo Resort (Russia)
https://books.google.com/books?id=tNjPg1HgxZ0C&pg=PA55&lpg=PA55&dq=ivanovo+composers+vacation&source=bl&ots=MI_uCb_jxD&sig=SRGzPp-mIWrrA1MVbdZ1dewxUMns&hl=en&sa=X&ved=0ahUKEwiTt5bF3pDTAhWL2YMKHVOiCZUQ6AEIGjAA#v=onepage&q=ivanovo%20composers%20vacation&f=false

Perestroika: Gorbachev Era
http://www.history.com/topics/cold-war/perestroika-and-glasnost

Perestroika in the USSR
http://russiapedia.rt.com/of-russian-origin/perestroika/
https://www.britannica.com/topic/perestroika-Soviet-government-policy

Soviet Security Service KGB
https://www.britannica.com/topic/KGB

Bibliography

I. Printed Sources

1. Sources in Russian Language

A) Primary sources:

Feiertag, Vladimir. »Alexander Varlamov«. In *Dzhaz. Entsikopedicheskii spravochnik* [*Jazz. Encyclopedic Guide*], Saint Petersburg: Skifia, 2008, 104.

Goldenweiser, Alexander. »Ob ispolnitel'stve« [About the Performance]. In *Voprosi fortepiannogo ispolnitel'stva: Ocherki, statii, vospominaniya*, edited by Sokolova M. G., Moscow: Muzyka, 1965.

»O postanovke ruk i borbe s napriajeniem« [About the Hand Position and the Struggle with Tension]. In *Uroki Goldenweizera*, compiled by S. V. Grokhotov. Moscow: Classica XXI, 2009. 248 pp.
http://blagaya.ru/skripka/violin_azbuka/ruki/gold-o-postanovke/

Neuhaus, Heinrich. »Ob iskusstve fortepiannoi igri: Zapiski pedagoga« [The Art of Piano Playing: Teacher's Book], Moscow: Gosudarstvennoe Muzikalnoe Izdatelstvo, 1958, 200 pp.
http://kkart.ru/images/oifi.pdf

Stravinskaya, Ksenia. »Priezd I. F. Stravinskogo v SSSR (sentyabr'-oktiabr'1962)« [The Visit of I. F. Stravinsky to the USSR, September-October 1962], *Muzika*, Saint-Petersburg, 1978, pp. 84-164.
http://www.opentextnn.ru/music/personalia/stravinsry/?id=3566

Tsentral'noe statisticheskoe upravlenie gosplana SSSR. Chislennost' naseleniya SSSR na 17 yanvaria 1939 [All-Union Population Census on January 17, 1939]. Moskva: Gosplanizdat, 1941. 268 pp.
http://istmat.info/files/uploads/46314/rgae_7971.16.54_naselenie_po_perepisi_1939.pdf

Voennaya literatura: Pervoistochniki [Military Literature: Primary Sources]. *The Battle for Berlin*. Russian Archive: World War II, Vol. 15 (4-5). Moscow, 1995.
http://militera.lib.ru/docs/da/berlin_45/12.html

B) Secondary sources:

Erokhin, Valery. Vinyl disc jacket, »Nikolai Kapustin«, Melodiya (C60 23759 008), 1986.

Evgeniya Grigorievna Pupkova: Pereigravshaya vsego Baha. Biografiya [One Who Played all Bach's Works: Biography of Evgeniya Grigorievna Pupkova]. http://pupkova.ru/biography/

Feiertag, Vladimir. »Big-bendi 60x godov« [Big-Bands of 1960s]. In *Istoriya dzajovogo ispolnitelstva v Rossii*, Saint-Petersburg: Skifia, 2010.

Gafarov, Iskander. »Nikolai Kapustin. Shtrihi k portretu« [Nikolai Kapustin: Strokes to the Portrait]. Molodoi *uchionii*, no. 2 (2013): 445-446. https://moluch.ru/archive/49/6252/

Minkh, Nikolai. »Zametki muzikanta« [Notes of the Musician]. In *Sovetskii dzhaz: Problemi, Sobitiya, Mastera* [Soviet Jazz: Problems, Events, Masters], ed. Alexander Medvedev and Olga Medvedeva. Moscow: Soviet Composer, 1987, 401.
http://www.belousenko.com/books/art/SU_jazz_1987.pdf

Moshkow, Cyril. »Bendlider Oleg Lundstrem (1916-2005): 100 let so dnia rozjdeniya" [Bandleader Oleg Lundstrem (1916-2005): Celebrating 100th Year of His Birth]. *Dzhaz RU*, 04.01.2016.
http://journal.jazz.ru/2016/04/01/oleg-lundstrem-centennial/

———. »95-letie otechestvennogo dzhaza. Chast' II: Khronologiya dzhaza v Rossii« [95th Jubilee of Native Jazz. Part II: Chronology of Jazz in Russia]. *Dzhaz RU*, October 1, 2017.
http://journal.jazz.ru/2017/10/01/russian-jazz-timeline/

Nemenova-Lunts, Maria. »Otrivki iz vospominanii ob Aleksandre Skriabine« [Excerpts from the Memories of Alexander Scriabin]. *Muzikalnii sovremennik*, no. 4/5 (1916): 97-110.

Nikolaiev, Alexei. »Alexander Varlamov." In *Sovetskii dzhaz: Problemi. Sobitiya. Mastera* [*Soviet Jazz: Problems. Events. Masters*], ed. Alexander Medvedev and Olga Medvedeva, Moscow: Soviet Composer, 1987, 346-49.

Sarukhanov, Piotr. »Zakritie Ameriki« [Closure of the United States], *Novaya Gazeta*, no. 93, Moscow, August 25, 2017.
https://www.novayagazeta.ru/articles/2017/08/24/73577-zakrytie-ameriki

Saulsky, Yuri and Chugunov, Yuri. »Sovetskii jazz: 1950e godi« [Soviet Jazz: 1950s]. In *The Brief History of Soviet Jazz*.
http://www.norma40.ru/articles/sovetskiy-dzhaz-istoriya.htm

Ukhanov, Pavel. »Graf Murja: Net nichego legche, chem igrat' na skripke, no…« [There is Nothing Easier than to Play the Violin, but…]. *Muzikalnii Klondaik*, March 21, 2017.
http://www.muzklondike.ru/announc/218

Yankovsky, Valentin. »Alexander Varlamov – Standing at the Roots of Soviet Jazz«, *Muzikalnii Ogoniok*, January 29, 2014.
http://shanson-e.tk/forum/showthread.php?p=506261

Yakubov, Manashir. »Kontsert v djazovom stile« [Concert in Jazz Style]. *Utro Rossii*, no. 23 (June 8-14, 1995): 9.

2. Sources in English Language

A) Primary sources:

The Central Committee's decree of 10 February 1948, »On Muradeli's opera The Great Friendship«, translated by Nicolas Slominsky, *Music Since 1900*, 5th ed., New York: Schirmer Books, 1994, pp. 1055-1057.

B) Secondary sources:

Anderson, Martin. »Nikolai Kapustin, Russian Composer of Classical Jazz«, *Fanfare* 24, no. 11 (September/October 2000): 93-97.

Gilbert, Mark. »Jazz-Rock«, Grove Music Online. March 6, 2018.
http://www.oxfordmusiconline.com/grovemusic/view/10.1093/gmo/9781561592630.001.0001/omo-9781561592630-e-2000226300

Myung, Kim. »Son Yeol-Eum's Life much More than the Piano«, *The Korea Herald*, February 20, 2013.
http://www.koreaherald.com/view.php?ud=20130220000893

Smith, Harriet. »Bridging the Divide: The Russian Composer Nikolai Kapustin«, *International Piano Quarterly* 4, no. 13 (Autumn 2000): 54-55.

Tomoff, Kiril. »Creative Union: The Professional Organization of Soviet Composers, 1939-1953«, New York: Cornell University Press, 2006, p. 55.
https://books.google.com/books?id=tNjPg1HgxZ0C&pg=PA55&lpg=PA55&dq=ivanovo+composers+vacation&source=bl&ots=MI_uCb_jxD&sig=SRGzPpmIWrrA1MVbdZ1dewxUMns&hl=en&sa=X&ved=0ahUKEwiTt5bF3pDTAhWL2YMKHVOiCZUQ6AEIGjAA#v=onepage&q=ivanovo%20composers%20vacation&f=false

II. Internet Sources

1. Sources in Russian Language

A) Primary sources:

Vsesouznaya perepis' naseleniya na 19 yanvaria 1989 [All-Union Population Census on January 19, 1989]. Vol. 1. Part 1. Graph 3. Demoskop Weekly.
http://www.demoscope.ru/weekly/ssp/sng89_reg2.php

Nikolai Petrov playing the premier of Piano Sonata No. 2 (Op. 54), TV channel »Rossiya: Kultura«, Moscow, 1991.
https://www.youtube.com/watch?v=o_dzivO5h5o

B) Secondary sources:

Benny Goodman in the USSR (documentary movie, 1962), TV channel Retro, March 30, 2014.
https://www.youtube.com/watch?v=BLUZFVY7_uk

Istoriya goroda Gorlovka [History of the City Gorlovka]. Historical-Patriotic Site of the City Gorlovka, ed. Sergei Borodin, 2012.
http://gorlovca.ru/index/istorija_gorlovki/0-8

Istoriya sozdaniya fil'ma »Mi iz dzhaza« [History of the Creation of the Movie »We are from Jazz«]
https://www.vokrug.tv/product/show/my_iz_dzhaza/

Kapituliatsia Germanii [Surrender of Germany]. International United Biographical Center.
http://geroiros.narod.ru/wwsoldat/OPER/ARTICLES/041-kapitul.htm

Khrushchev Thaw, New World Encyclopedia.
http://www.newworldencyclopedia.org/entry/Khrushchev_Thaw

Krizis na Ukraine: V Kanade zapretili vitupat' pianistke iz-za eio anti-Kievskoi pozitsii [Crisis in the Ukraine: In Canada the Pianist was Prohibited to Perform Concerts Because of Her Anti-Kiev Position], NTV News, 04.07.2015,
http://www.ntv.ru/novosti/1390018/

Moscow Tchaikovsky Conservatory
http://www.mosconsv.ru/ru/book.aspx?id=131310&page=131311

Moscow Tchaikovsky Conservatory - Student Research and Creative Society
http://www.mosconsv.ru/ru/groups.aspx?id=139436

»Nikolai Petrov snova otkrivaet Kreml' Muzikalnii« [Nikolai Petrov is Opening again Kremlin Musical], TV channel »Kultura«, Moscow, 04.13.2009.
https://tvkultura.ru/article/show/article_id/30149/

Russian State Symphony Orchestra of Cinematography
http://www.meloman.ru/performer/rossijskij-gosudarstvennyj-simfonicheskij-orkestr-kinematografii/

Saint-Petersburg Rimsky-Korsakov Conservatory
http://www.conservatory.ru/

The Year of 1962 in Russia (visit of Benny Goodman Orchestra)
http://www.gorzvuk.com/enciclopedia/history/1962/

Titov, Kirill. »Kak raspalsia SSSR: 25 let nazad bilo podpisano Belovejskoe soglashenie« [Disintegration of the USSR: Twenty Five Years Ago the Belavezha Agreement was Signed], TASS, December 8, 2016.
http://tass.ru/politika/3850507

Zanuda, Anastasia. *Vtoraya mirovaya voina dlia Ukraini: Pereosmislenie* [WWII for the Ukraine: Rethinking]. BBC News: Ukraine. May 6, 2015.
http://www.bbc.com/ukrainian/ukraine_in_russian/2015/05/150506_ru_s_ukraine_ww2

Ziser, Igor. »Sinkopi djazovoi sudbi. Ocherk tvorcheskogo puti Olega Lundstrema i ego orchestra (k 100-letiu), chast 2« [Syncopations of the Jazz Fate. Essay on Creative Life of Oleg Lundstrem and His Orchestra]. *Polnii Dzhaz* 2.0, September 30, 2016.
http://journal.jazz.ru/2016/09/30/oleg-lundstrem-orchestra-02/

2. Sources in English Language

A) Secondary sources:

Ankeny, Jason. *Oleg Lundstrem: Artist Biography*. All Music.
http://www.allmusic.com/artist/oleg-lundstrem-mn0001230706/biography

Chow, Evan. Presentation »The Music of Nikolai Kapustin: Virtuosic Jazz in Classical Form«, Music teachers' Association of California (Oakland CA, July 2, 2011).
https://www.youtube.com/watch?v=sWHX0Pyw_8M

Cox, Savannah. *Moscow, The 1957 Host of The World Festival of Youth and Students*. ATI, August 12, 2014.
http://all-that-is-interesting.com/moscow-1957-host-world-festival-youth-students

End of Empire Plotted in Secret Forest Talks (Beloveshskaya Pusha), *RT Question More*, December 28, 2011.
https://www.rt.com/news/ussr-collapse-agreement-331/

Fordham, John. *Oleg Lundstrem*. The Guardian, October 28, 2005.
https://www.theguardian.com/culture/2005/oct/28/russia.jazz
Ishvina, Olga. *Ukraine Crisis: Pro-Russian Attack in Ukraine's Horlivka*. BBC News, April 14, 2014.
http://www.bbc.com/news/world-europe-27018199

Oleg Lundstrem. Russia-InfoCentre.
http://www.russia-ic.com/people/general/l/381/

Koda, Cub. Review on Charlie Parker CD »Charlie Parker with Strings: The Master Takes« (recorded November 30, 1949 - May 22, 1953). AllMusic.
http://www.allmusic.com/album/charlie-parker-with-strings-the-master-takes-mw0000313067

James Miltenberger, Lillian Green, and Yana Tyulkova. Presentation »The Intersection of Jazz and Classical Music: An Introduction to the Music of Nikolai Kapustin«, MTNA National Conference (Baltimore, MD, March 21, 2017).
https://www.mtna.org/MTNA/Engage/Conferences/Handouts/2017/Tuesday.aspx

Schwarm, Betsy. Bartok Sonata for two Pianos and Percussion, Encyclopedia Britannica,
https://www.britannica.com/topic/Sonata-for-Two-Pianos-and-Percussion

III. Nikolai Kapustin Websites

http://www.nikolai-kapustin.info/

https://www.facebook.com/kapustincomposer/

https://en.schott-music.com/shop/autoren/nikolai-kapustin

Kapustin Society (Japan)
http://www.kapustin.jp/

Kapustin Piano Society (England)
http://www.pianosociety.com/pages/kapustin/

www.ingramcontent.com/pod-product-compliance
Lightning Source LLC
Chambersburg PA
CBHW020603300426
44113CB00007B/495